Maitreya, the Future Buddha

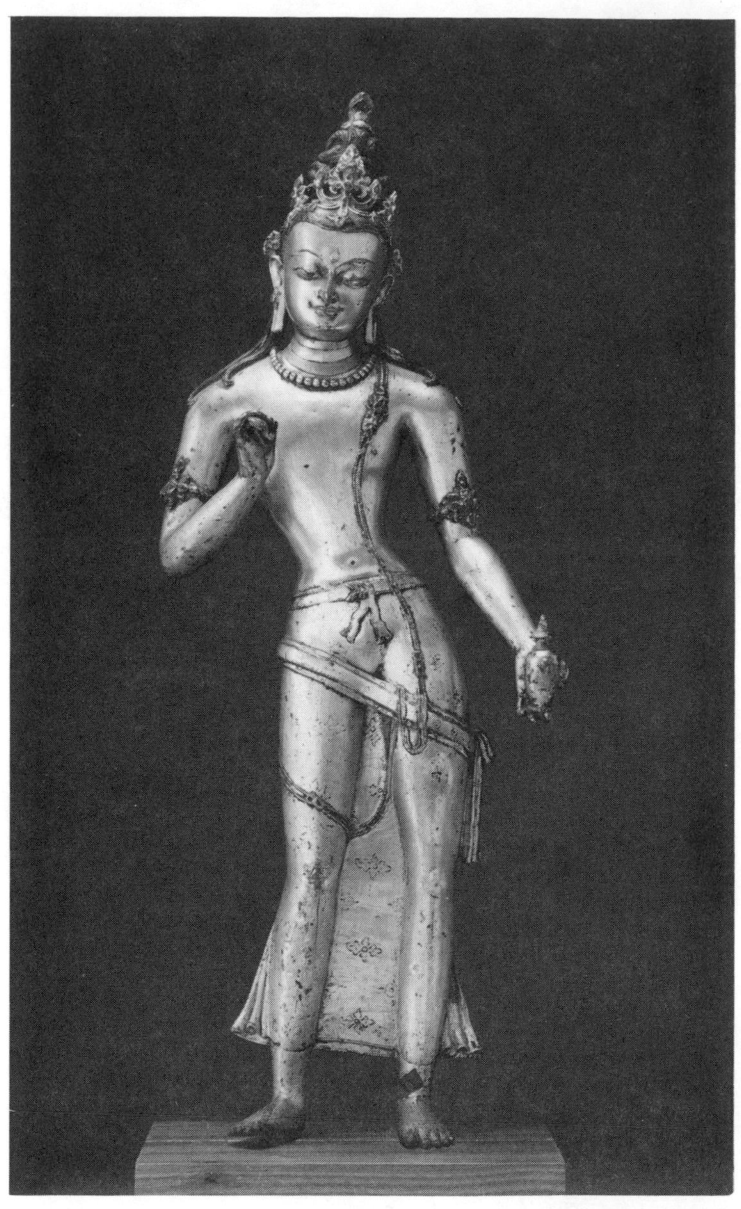

Standing Maitreya. Nepali, ninth to tenth centuries. Gilt copper with polychrome. Height, 66 cm. Photo courtesy of the Metropolitan Museum of Art. 1982.220.12.

Maitreya, the Future Buddha

Edited by

ALAN SPONBERG
Princeton University

HELEN HARDACRE
Princeton University

CAMBRIDGE UNIVERSITY PRESS
Cambridge
New York New Rochelle Melbourne Sydney

Published by the Press Syndicate of the University of Cambridge
The Pitt Building, Trumpington Street, Cambridge CB2 1RP
32 East 57th Street, New York, NY 10022, USA
10 Stamford Road, Oakleigh, Melbourne 3166, Australia

First published 1988

Printed in the United States of America

Library of Congress Cataloging-in-Publication Data

Maitreya, the future Buddha.

Papers presented at a conference at Princeton University.

Includes index.

1. Maitreya (Buddhist deity) – Congresses.
I. Sponberg, Alan. II. Hardacre, Helen, 1949–
III. Princeton University.
BQ4690.M3M34 1988 294.3'421 87–10857
ISBN 0 521 34344 5

British Library Cataloguing-in-Publication applied for.

Contents

Contributors

Karen L. Brock is Assistant Professor of Japanese Art at Washington University in Saint Louis. She coauthored *Autumn Grasses and Water Motifs in Japanese Art* and has translated catalogues on Japanese painting for exhibitions in Japan and the United States. She is currently writing *Editor, Artist, and Audience in Japanese Picture Scrolls.*

Martin Collcutt is Professor in the Departments of East Asian Studies and History at Princeton University. He is the author of *Five Mountains: The Rinzai Zen Monastic Institution in Medieval Japan* and is currently working on a history of Japanese religion in the late sixteenth and early seventeenth centuries.

Christine M. E. Guth has taught Japanese art at Princeton University, the University of Pennsylvania, and the Institute of Fine Arts of New York University. She is the author of *Shinzō: Hachiman Imagery and Its Development.*

Helen Hardacre is a member of the Department of Religion at Princeton University and the author of *Lay Buddhism in Contemporary Japan: Reiyūkai Kyōdan, Kurozumikyō and the New Religions of Japan* and *The Religion of Japan's Korean Minority.*

Padmanabh S. Jaini is Professor of Buddhist Studies in the Department of South and Southeast Asian Studies at the University of California, Berkeley. He is the author of *The Jaina Path of Purification,* and his critical editions include *Abhidharmadīpa with Vibhāṣāprabhā-vṛtti, Laghutattvasphoṭa, Sāratamā: Ratnākaraśānti's Pañjikā on the Aṣṭasāhasrikā-Prañāpāramitā-sūtra, Paññāsa-Jātaka,* and *Lokaneyyappakaraṇaṃ.*

Joseph M. Kitagawa is Professor Emeritus of the History of Religions in the Divinity School of the University of Chicago, as well as former Dean of the

Divinity School and Professor in the Department of Far Eastern Languages and Civilizations, also of the University of Chicago. His publications include *Religion in Japanese History* and *Religions of the East*. He has recently edited *The History of Religions: Retrospect and Prospect* and two volumes of writings by Joachim Wach. Forthcoming are two collections of Professor Kitagawa's own essays, *On Understanding Japanese Religion* and *Religious Understanding of Human Experience*.

Lewis Lancaster is Professor of East Asian Buddhism in the Department of Oriental Languages and a member of the Group in Buddhist Studies at the University of California at Berkeley. In addition to his publications on Chinese Buddhism, Professor Lancaster has compiled *The Korean Buddhist Canon: A Descriptive Catalogue*, and he is editing a new series entitled Studies in Korean Religion and Culture.

Miyata Noboru is Professor of Folklore at Tsukuba University in Ibaragi, Japan. Professor Miyata has published a number of works on Maitreya in Japan and other aspects of popular religion, including *Miroku shinkō no kenkyū, Minzoku shūkyōron no kadai, Toshi minzokuron no kadai, Tsuchi no shisō, Ikigami shinkō, Edo no saijiki*, and *Onna no reiryoku to ie no kami*. He is also a senior editor of a major collection of folklore studies: *Nihon minzoku bunka taikei*.

Jan Nattier is a specialist in Central Asian languages who did graduate work in Central Asian Languages and Buddhism first at Indiana University and later at Harvard University, where she is currently writing her doctoral dissertation on the decline of the Dharma, based on Tibetan and Mongolian sources. She is also working on a documentary and bibliographic survey of resources for the study of Buddhism in Soviet Central Asia and Chinese Turkestan (Xinjiang).

Daniel L. Overmyer is Professor and Head of the Department of Asian Studies at the University of British Columbia. In addition to several articles on the history of Chinese religions, he has published *Folk Buddhist Religion: Dissenting Sects in Late Traditional China, Religions of China: The World as a Living System*, and with coauthor David K. Jordan, *The Flying Phoenix: Aspects of Chinese Sectarianism in Taiwan*. His current research is on Chinese popular religious texts from the sixteenth to the twentieth centuries.

Alan Sponberg teaches in the Department of Religious Studies at Stanford University. He has published on Buddhism in South Asia and East Asia, with special interest in the early transmission of Buddhism into China. He is currently completing a two-volume study of Yogācāra Buddhism in India and China.

Hue-Tam Ho Tai is Associate Professor of Sino-Vietnamese History at Harvard University. She is the author of *Millenarianism and Peasant Politics in Vietnam* and has just completed a study of the social and intellectual origins of the Vietnamese Revolution.

Preface

The Princeton Maitreya Project grew out of a casual conversation I had with Jan Nattier at the American Academy of Religion meeting in 1979. In discussing possible topics for a future AAR panel, we discovered a mutual interest in Maitreya, stemming from work each of us was doing in quite different areas. Jan's research on Central Asian Buddhism had led her to work on the *Kšanti nom*, a lay confessional text in Uighur that presents a distinctively Central Asian variation of the Maitreya cult. That in turn had led her to raise the broader question of the place of Maitreya in South Asian Buddhism. By a comparably indirect route, I had begun to wonder about the nature of Maitreyan devotionalism in the fourth through seventh centuries. My research on the transmission of Yogācāra Buddhism from India to China had made it clear that the Maitreya cult was a central feature of the religious life of the Chinese philosopher monks Hsüan-tsang and K'uei-chi. I believed that any understanding of their philosophical thought required more insight into the place of Maitreya in their practice of Buddhism. As Jan and I began to explore the range of Maitreya-related topics, it quickly became apparent how central the Maitreya cult, in one form or another, has been throughout the history of Buddhism. Although many developments of the Buddhist tradition have been more prominent than the Maitreya legend at any given time or place, there is perhaps no other, save the cult of Śākyamuni, that has been as universal and as pervasive.

In the fall of 1980, Helen Hardacre joined the project, bringing another important perspective on the Maitreya cult. Her research on Reiyūkai and other "new religious" movements in Japan had made her curious about the power of the Maitreya theme even among popular religious groups that often explicitly reject the Buddhist establishment and its concerns for orthodoxy. Adding the Maitreya-related interests of three of our previous teachers, Masatoshi Nagatomi, Joseph Kitagawa, and Daniel Overmyer, we realized that we had the core of something more than a conference panel, and we began to plan a year of activities at Princeton during 1981–2 that would culminate in a conference exploring the Maitreya theme from as many different perspectives as possible.

With the enthusiastic support of the Department of Religion and the East Asian Studies Program along with the assistance of the university administration, Professors Kitagawa and Overmyer were invited to spend part of the year in residence at Princeton, the former as a short-term Stewart Lecturer and the latter as a long-term Stewart Lecturer and Humanities Council Fellow. With the assistance of the Council for the International Exchange of Scholars, we were also able to invite for part of the year Miyata Noboru, a prominent Japanese scholar with a special interest in Maitreya in Japanese popular religion. In addition to lectures by these visiting scholars, we scheduled a graduate seminar on Maitreya in Japan and an undergraduate seminar to explore the theme of messianic and millenarian movements in a variety of cultural and historical settings.

Finally, with the assistance of the National Endowment for the Humanities we brought the year of activities to a close with a conference of scholars invited from a number of universities across North America. The meeting was designed to be a working conference, and we sought to bring together scholars doing research on aspects of the Maitreya myth from a variety of disciplinary perspectives. The realm of Maitreya-related research is so diverse that we could not hope for any systematic coverage, especially geographically. We chose rather to make the best use of Princeton's resources by focusing primarily on Maitreya in East Asia. This volume includes all of the presentations discussed at that conference with the exception of the papers by Stanley Tambiah on Maitreya in Thailand, by Masatoshi Nagatomi on the *Maitreya-vyakarana,* and by Michael Strickmann and Robert Thorp on Maitreya in early Chinese Buddhism; the first of these is forthcoming elsewhere, and the latter three were not available for publication. The papers that are included in this volume were revised as much as possible to reflect the broader understanding that emerged as the conference proceeded.

The uniqueness of the conference, and also its significance, lay in the fact that it brought together a diverse group of scholars working from a variety of perspectives on a common theme expressed in a number of very different cultural settings. This diversity of approach and interests proved, even more than we had expected, to be what gave the conference its vitality and its value for all of us. It was only by confronting Maitreya in so many different guises that we were able to discern the centrality and complexity of his role in the cultural history of Asia, and only by realizing the applicability of such a range of disciplinary approaches that we were able to recognize how broad our efforts to understand such a figure must be. Each of us began with a relatively narrow picture of Maitreya's role, one defined by our own interests and method of study. But through the composite picture that emerged during the conference, we came to see how rich and how complex a figure Maitreya has in fact been, and from that we were able to see much more even in the material we thought we already knew. That broadening of our view of Maitreya's place in Buddhism was something that could have come only from the interaction of so many different perspectives.

Our objective with this volume has been to preserve and convey the diversity of opinion and approach that characterized the conference, along with the interaction it stimulated. All of us who attended the conference were struck by the continuities present in the Maitreya myth throughout its developments. Even so, we did not always agree on the interpretation of the common elements identified. Does the Maitreya myth, for example, represent an eschatological world view already present in the origins of South Asian Buddhism? On this and some other topics discussed in the chapters that follow, important differences of opinion remain. In order to stimulate future research on Maitreya, we believe that it is as important to report the range of differing interpretations as it is to record the points on which consensus was reached. If there was one thing, however, on which all participants agreed without reservation, it is the need for further work, especially on the South and Central Asian expressions of the Maitreya tradition.

There is much that has not been reported in this record of the conference proceedings, much that came from the spontaneous interaction of the participants. If, as I would submit, the greatest value of the conference lay in that interaction and the discussions it stimulated, the ultimate fruit of the conference will be seen not just in the chapters of this volume, but even more in the work that will follow, in the future research it is hoped that our efforts will inspire.

A project of this nature involves the efforts of a number of people and institutions. It would not have been possible without the support of Princeton University, especially the Department of Religion, the East Asian Studies Project, and the Office of Research and Project Administration. The conference itself was funded in large part by a grant from the National Endowment for the Humanities.

Special thanks go to the three scholars who served as moderators at the conference: Yü Chün-fang of Rutgers, Miriam Levering of the University of Tennessee, and John Holt of Bowdoin College, and also to three graduate students, Norman Havens, Bob Wakabayashi, and Stephen Teiser, who made a record of the conference discussion. Finally, we thank our departmental administrator, Lorraine Fuhrmann, the person who took care of the thousand details so crucial to the success of the conference.

ALAN SPONBERG
Princeton, New Jersey

Abbreviations

T Takakusu Junjirō 高楠順次郎 and Watanabe Kaigyoku 渡邊海旭 (eds.), *Taishō shinshu daizōkyō* 大正新修大藏經 (Tokyo: Daizō Shuppan, 1924–32).

ZZ Maeda Eun 前田慧雲 and Nakano Tatsue 中野達慧 (eds.), *Dainihon zokuzōkyō* 大日本續藏經 (Kyoto: Zōkyō Shoin, 1905–12).

Japanese names are cited in the standard form, that is, with surname first.

Introduction

ALAN SPONBERG

Nearly 2,500 years ago Siddhārtha Gautama, scion of a noble family in a minor republic located north of the Ganges River, renounced the householder's life and, after a period of spiritual practice, declared himself to be a Buddha, an "awakened one," one who has realized the truth about the nature of human existence, the truth about suffering and liberation. Teaching a "middle path" between asceticism and sensory indulgence, this mendicant gathered about himself a group of devoted followers over the next forty years, founding what was eventually to become one of the great world religions. According to the earliest texts, Gautama taught that his pragmatic method for spiritual cultivation was open to anyone and that there were others who had realized the same truths about human suffering and liberation before him. He was, we are told by the tradition, only the most recent of a long line of previous Buddhas stretching back into the beginningless past.

In some early canonical scriptures, this idea of previous Buddhas is elaborated to include the idea of yet more Buddhas to come, the idea that there will be other Buddhas in the future. Most prominently, we find the story of Maitreya, a "being of enlightenment" (*bodhisattva*), who is presently cultivating the final stages of the path to liberation that will lead him to become the next Buddha for this world system. The prospect of a future Buddha, yet another in the long line of Buddhas, offers an attractive possibility. Although liberation from suffering is possible for anyone at any time according to Buddhists, those beings fortunate enough to live at a time when a Buddha is active in the world are far more likely to realize the arduous goal of bringing all craving to cessation. Given the notion of individual human existence as a series of lives stretching over eons of time, it is not surprising that the ideal of gaining rebirth at one of those rare times when a Buddha is active in the world came to be seen as an attractive prospect in its own right. Though perhaps initially a minor figure in the early Buddhist tradition, Maitreya thus came to represent a hope for the future, a time when all human beings could once again enjoy the spiritual and physical environment most favorable to enlightenment and the release from worldly suffering.

The story of Maitreya, the future Buddha, became a tradition that has played some role, often a central one, in the cultural history of virtually every period and every area of Buddhist Asia. Indeed, one finds a variety of quite distinctive expressions of that tradition, a variety that often obscures the underlying motifs that have tended to persist throughout Maitreya's variegated development and transformation. The Maitreya legend has provided a symbol rich in possibility for culturally specific, local elaboration, yet it has also continued throughout to draw on a group of core themes and aspirations deeply rooted in the Buddhist culture common to most of Asia. Every Buddhist culture has appropriated this appealing figure, each in its own way, and it is because of this historical development of cultural variations on a set of common themes that a study of Maitreya's many guises provides a superb opportunity to observe the fascinating process by which Buddhism shaped, and was shaped by, a series of cultural encounters reaching across Asia from the Deccan to the islands of Japan.

The idea unifying the apparently diverse studies collected in this volume is twofold. We seek first of all to establish the continuity that characterizes Maitreya's role throughout the 2,500-year history of Buddhism in South, Southeast, and East Asia. At the same time, however, we want to illustrate the manifold variation with which the continuity of those core themes has been expressed and modulated. This twofold focus will illustrate the inherent flexibility and multivalence of the Maitreya figure within the tradition, as well as the remarkable capacity of Buddhism to adapt its symbols to the needs of different Asian cultures. No understanding of Buddhism could be complete without an awareness of Maitreya's role within the tradition, and no understanding of Maitreya would be complete unless commensurate attention were given to both aspects of his character, the continuity and the variation, each equally necessary for understanding the attraction he has held for so many Buddhists over the ages.

Along with the figure of Gautama himself, Maitreya is one of the few truly universal symbols occurring throughout the Buddhist tradition, one holding a role of importance in Theravāda as well as Mahāyāna cultures. Unlike that of the historical Buddha, however, Maitreya's role, though pivotal, remained relatively underdefined and open-ended. In every Buddhist culture Maitreya is a symbol of hope, of the human aspiration for a better life in the future when the glories of the golden past will be regained. That much remains constant in all the varied instances of the Maitreya cult we shall examine here; it represents what we have called the core of the tradition.

Equally striking, however, are the elaborations of that core theme, the variety seen in the different guises in which we find Maitreya playing out his role as guarantor of the future. We find him portrayed at times as a diligent bodhisattva cultivating the path to enlightenment on earth and later as a celestial bodhisattva resplendent in his heavenly abode in Tuṣita. At times he appears as an otherworldly object of individual devotion and contemplation, at others as the militant leader of political extremists seeking to establish a new order here and now. We see him at times as a confessor of sins and at times as the muse of scholiasts.

Perhaps no other figure in the Buddhist pantheon combines both universality and adaptability in the way that Maitreya does. Modern scholarship has just begun to appreciate the complexity of this figure. It will require much more work to assess fully both aspects of Maitreya's place in Buddhism, and a complete picture of Maitreya remains well beyond our resources here. One of the aims of this volume is to establish that both aspects of the Maitreya tradition are necessary for any comprehensive understanding and, moreover, that neither aspect can be understood independent of the other.

To make the diverse material presented here accessible to both specialist and nonspecialist, we have divided the book into two parts: The first comprises two essays that consider the place of Maitreya in the broader study of the history of religions, and the second presents a variety of more specialized studies focusing on various expressions of the Maitreya legend in South and East Asia. Part I thus serves as a general introduction to the study of Maitreya, with Joseph M. Kitagawa's essay surveying the picture of Maitreya that prevailed in modern scholarship before the new research presented in subsequent chapters and Jan Nattier's study suggesting new approaches for evaluating the diversity of conceptions found in different expressions of the Maitreya myth. These two studies establish a framework for relating the diversity of the more specialized studies that follow. Both essays provide an invaluable service in suggesting alternative interpretative models for assimilating various Maitreya developments and in underscoring the importance of a more comprehensive perspective on the place of Maitreya, not just in Buddhism, but in the more general history of religions as well.

The culturally specific and more specialized studies making up Part II are divided into three geographic areas: Maitreya in South Asia, in continental East Asia, and in Japan; each of the sections is preceded by a brief introduction. Unfortunately, no single volume can cover the full range of Maitreya's development. There is nothing here, for example, on the crucial developments that took place in Central Asia, and far too little attention has been given to the unique role of Maitreya in Southeast Asian Buddhism. Even so, the essays included are sufficient to demonstrate our twofold theme, and they also provide, of course, a variety of new data and interpretation for those interested in Maitreya in various area-specific contexts.

Finally, in the epilogue I return to the general theme stated above, attempting to summarize the issues raised in this volume while also presenting a prospectus for future research on Maitreya-related subjects, one that outlines a three-pronged approach suggested by the types of research presented in these essays.

I

Maitreya and the History of Religions

1

The Many Faces of Maitreya

A Historian of Religions' Reflections

JOSEPH M. KITAGAWA

Introduction

To a historian of religions who is concerned with both the universal and the particular meanings of religion, the phenomenon of Maitreya presents a fascinating case study. As a future Buddha, he symbolizes the consummation of the rich legacy of Buddhist religious experience derived from the enlightenment of Gautama Buddha. Although some texts speculate on later Buddhas who will come after him, as other chapters in this volume indicate, from the point of view of most Buddhist lay people, as well as many ordained clerics, Maitreya's arrival would represent essentially a final dispensation. Accordingly, this figure's consummation of Buddhist heritage sometimes casts him in the role of an eschatological cosmic savior who, at the end of the empirical world order, will establish a utopian state of justice, peace, and truth. This face of Maitreya demands special consideration – a treatment in terms of eschatology.

Here Maitreya exemplifies a universal yearning of *homo religiosus*. Thus the question to me is, How "universalizable" is this motif of Maitreya, that is, how can the perennial human vision of the end of the world and the eschatological hopes of *homo religiosus* throughout history be illumined through a consideration of the eschatological side of Maitreya? The following reflections are an attempt to consider this question from the viewpoint of a historian of religions.

The Religious Vision of the End of the World

My understanding of the religious vision of the end of the world is based on a simple premise: Every religion, every culture, and every civilization has a characteristic view of the future as well as a characteristic way of recollecting the past, which together influence its understanding of the meaning of present existence. This is what Augustine had in mind when he stated, "There are three times: [first] a present of things past, [second] a present of things present, and [third] a present of things future." According to him, the "present of things past" is associated with memory, the "present of things present" with sight, and the "present of things future" with expectation.[1] These three foci – the expectation of the future, the recollection of the past, and the understanding of the present – are intricately interwoven in a kind of "mental prism" that sorts out significant items from a mass of data and relates historical realities to the realm of fantasy, hope, and imagination. This prism has the built-in features of forgetfulness and optical illusion. And more often than not, one's mental prism is colored by one's religious notions and perceptions.

Take, for example, the notion of progress, a word derived from *gressus*, or "step," implying an act of stepping forward to a situation more desirable than one's current situation. In this regard, we must recognize the difference, as pointed out by Paul Tillich, between the "concept" of progress, which is just an abstraction, and the "idea" of progress, which is an interpretation of a historical situation in terms of the "concept" of progress, with or without a verifiable basis. As such, the "idea" of progress involves our mental decision or affirmation; and it often becomes a symbol as well as a way of life, a "doctrine" about the law of history, or even an unconscious "dogma" of progressivism.[2]

Clearly, the notion that the future promises to be better than the present, leading to the triumph of the good at the end of the world, is based not on empirical observation, but on speculation and affirmation. Such speculation and affirmation are often associated with a religious vision of the coming of the cosmic ruler, universal king, or world savior at the end, as we find in various religious traditions, East and West. There are as well *negative* forms of progressivism, which view the future in terms of a successive erosion of values, though this is still often associated with a belief in the coming of a supramundane figure who redresses all evils at the end of the world.

Of the cosmic saviors or rulers known in the history of religions, I shall depict two prominent figures who have inspired a series of messianic ideologies and who have thus influenced people's view of the future in many parts of the world. The first is Saošyant of Iranian Zoroastrianism; the second is the *cakravartin* of India, whose image became closely intertwined with that of the future Buddha.

Saošyant

According to the ancient Iranian religion of Zoroastrianism, history consists of the cosmic conflict between the just god Ahura Mazdāh and the forces of evil. Human beings are destined to choose sides and to participate in this conflict. Zoroastrianism articulated in a characteristic way the notion of the end of the world, *eschaton,* and the doctrine about the end, *eschatology.* According to Zoroastrian eschatology, at the end of the cosmic cycle of twelve thousand years, the savior and judge, Saošyant, born miraculously from a maiden and the seed of Zoroaster, will appear and revivify creation, casting the devil into hell and purging the human race of the stain of sin. Then the entire human race will enter a paradise where all will enjoy eternal bliss and happiness, and "the material world will become immortal for ever and ever."[3]

"The significance of Zoroastrianism," writes R. C. Zaehner, "lies not in the number of those who profess it, but rather in the influence it has exercised on other religions [e.g., all Gnostic religions – Hermetism, Gnosticism, Manichaeism], and particularly on Christianity, through the medium of the Jewish exiles in Babylon who seem to have been thoroughly impregnated with Zoroastrian ideas."[4]

Zoroastrianism influenced Judaism most heavily in its eschatology, including the notions of the messianic era of national restoration, the coming of the new eon of God's kingdom, and the celestial hereafter for the deceased, as well as in its understanding of sacred history. According to Jewish *Heilsgeschichte,* Jahweh, who chose the nation of Israel to be his own, will one day fulfill his promise by establishing his rule on earth. Understandably, Christianity, which was born as a messianic movement within the Jewish fold, inherited the Iranian-inspired Jewish eschatological outlook. But when early Christians realized that the expected return of Christ (*parousia,* "arrival" or "presence") would not be realized as soon as they had anticipated, or perhaps already had been partially realized at the Pentecost, they were compelled to come to terms with the social realities of their contemporary situation. Such a scenario is a familiar one in the history of religion, repeated again and again in many religious traditions.

Cakravartin

Turning to India, we find an ancient mythical ideal of a just and virtuous world monarch, the *cakravartin* – a divinely ordained superman (*mahāpuruṣa*) – who, owing to his moral supremacy and military power, has a special place in the cosmic scheme as the final unifier of the earthly realm. Heinrich Zimmer speculates that the conception of the *cakravartin* can be traced "not only to the earliest Vedic, but also to the pre-Vedic, pre-Aryan traditions of India, being reflected in various Buddhist and Jain writings as well as in the Hindu *Purāṇas.*"[5] We learn from E. J. Thomas:

> The original meaning of this term [*cakravartin*], as even Kern admitted, was probably "one who controls (*vartayati*) or rules over the sphere of his power (*cakra*)," but it came to be understood as "one who turns a *cakra*." With this change of interpretation *cakra* became a blank term to be given a meaning according to the ideas of fitness of the commentators. It is usually understood as "wheel," but how the wheel was conceived never clearly appears in the legend.[6]

Significantly, the figure of the *cakravartin* came to be accepted as the monarchical ideal in the later Vedic imperial ideology; in addition, it provided a paradigm for Buddhist speculations regarding the person and mission of the Buddha.

It is interesting that the career of this humble mendicant came to be seen as a spiritual counterpart of the universal monarch, sharing the same physical marks and appropriating many of the symbols of the *cakravartin*, including the *cakra*.[7] Meanwhile, in the third century B.C., King Aśoka proclaimed Buddhism the religion of the vast Indian empire. Aśoka came to be regarded as a model of the Buddhist monarch, foreshadowing the Buddhist image of the universal monarch (*cakravartin*) who is yet to come.

Maitreya

Buddhist speculations on the nature of a Buddha not only equated him with the *cakravartin* but also developed such notions as the existence of previous Buddhas, multiple Buddhas, three bodies of Buddha, and bodhisattvas. The stream of foreign religious and art forms that flowed into India from Bactria and Iran shortly before and after the common era greatly influenced the piety, imagination, and artistic sensitivities of both Hindus and Buddhists. It was this religious and cultural milieu that made a decisive impact on Buddhist views of the future, as exemplified by the emergence of the figure of Maitreya, whose coming would mark the fulfillment of Buddha's law as well as the establishment of universal peace and concord. Many scholars speculate that it was the Iranian notion of the cosmic savior, Saošyant, that inspired the Buddhist belief in Maitreya. For example, A. L. Basham states: "Under the invading rulers of Northwest India Zoroastrianism and Buddhism came in contact, and it was probably through this that the idea of the future Buddha became part of orthodox [Buddhist] belief. . . . And by the beginning of the Christian era, the cult of future Buddha, Maitreya, was widespread among all Buddhist sects."[8]

It is a matter of some importance that the three famous Chinese pilgrims who visited India in search of the Dharma made references to

Maitreya. Fa-hsien, who left China in 399, seemed to assume that the image of Maitreya in Udyāna was an ancient statue. Two centuries later, Hsüan-tsang (ca. 596–664), who left China in 629, gave a dramatic personal account concerning Maitreya. As he was sailing on the Ganges toward Prayaga (the modern Allahabad), his boat was attacked by pirates, who attempted to kill him as a sacrificial offering to the ferocious Sivaite goddess Durga. Hsüan-tsang asked for a few moments' respite so that he could prepare to enter *nirvāṇa* peacefully. Then, to follow his account as told by René Grousset, Hsüan-tsang

> meditated lovingly upon the Bodhisattva Maitreya and turned all his thoughts to the Heaven of the Blessed Ones, praying ardently that he might be reborn there in order to offer his respects and pay homage to the Bodhisattva; that he might hear the most excellent Law expounded and reach perfect enlightenment (Buddha-hood); that he might then redescend and be born again on earth to teach and convert these men and bring them to perform the acts of higher virtue, to abandon their infamous beliefs; and finally that he might spread far and wide all the benefits of the Law and bring peace and happiness to all creatures. He then . . . sat down in a posture of contemplation and eagerly bent his thoughts upon the Bodhisattva Maitreya. . . .
>
> All of a sudden . . . he felt himself raised up to Mount Sumeru, and after having passed through one, two and then three heavens he saw the true Maitreya seated upon a glittering throne . . . surrounded by a multitude of gods. . . . Suddenly a furious wind sprang up all around them . . . beating up the waves of the river and swamping all the boats.[9]

As might be expected, the terrified brigands repented and threw themselves at Hsüan-tsang's feet. Grousset also describes the stūpa situated near the Deer Park, which is believed to be the place where the Buddha prophesied the messianic role of Maitreya.[10]

A little after Hsüang-tsang's time, I-tsing (I-ching), who in 671 left China for India via the Southeast Asian maritime route, expressed his passionate devotion to Maitreya "in language like that which Christian piety uses of the second coming of Christ," to quote Eliot's characterization.[11] "Deep as the depth of a lake be my pure and calm meditation. Let me look for the first meeting under the Tree of the Dragon Flower when I hear the deep rippling voice of the Buddha Maitreya."[12] By the time I-tsing returned to China in 695 A.D., he had seen signs of the general decline of Buddhism, including devotion to Maitreya, in India.

Dimensions of Buddhism and Maitreya

When we consider the status and place of Maitreya, it might be helpful to locate him in each of the three levels of meaning that we usually attach to Buddhism, that is, (1) Buddhism as religion, (2) Buddhism as culture, and (3) the Buddhist-oriented sociopolitical order.

Maitreya in Buddhist Religion

Buddhism, like other religions, is concerned with the perennial problems of human existence. According to its claim, human beings, in order to be really human, must see all of existence in relation to Ultimate Reality (*nirvāṇa*), however positively or negatively it is understood. Buddhism is unique among all soteriological religions in that it acknowledges no revealer behind Gautama Buddha's enlightenment experience. However, as in the case of other soteriological religions, the religious experience of the Buddha and Buddhists has been expressed in three forms: (1) theoretical, (2) practical, and (3) sociological. Here again we can see the importance of Maitreya in reference to these three forms of the expression of Buddhist experience.

1. The framework for the theoretical expression of Buddhist experience is the affirmation of the Three Treasures (Tri-ratna): Buddha, Dharma (doctrine), and Saṃgha (religious community). Although these Three Treasures are an interrelated and mutually dependent triad, each of them is also the focus of both religious and philosophical theories, that is, Buddhology (the nature of the Buddha and Buddhaness), concepts of reality, and ecclesiology (the soteriological nature of the Buddhist community), all integrally related to a beatific vision or image of *nirvāṇa*. It should be noted that the affirmation of the Three Treasures is common to the soteriologies of all schools of the Hīnayāna, Mahāyāna, and Esoteric (Tantric) traditions.

As mentioned earlier, Buddhological speculation developed a wide variety of notions and interpretations of the nature of the Buddha, previous Buddhas, multiple Buddhas, and bodhisattvas. The Hīnayāna tradition acknowledges Metteyya (Maitreya) together with Gautama as a bodhisattva, or "a being destined for enlightenment of Buddhahood." In the Mahāyāna and Esoteric and traditions, Maitreya is a savior side by side with other "celestial" bodhisattvas, Buddhas, and savior figures. In all these traditions, Maitreya holds a special place as the future (final) Buddha, even though his futureness has been understood in various ways.

Buddhist speculation on the nature of reality and Ultimate Reality, which is a cornerstone of soteriology, was incorporated into various theories of cosmology, anthropology, and eschatology. In this regard, we might recall the four focal points in Śākyamuni Buddha's life: (1) the prediction of

Dīpaṅkara, (2) the stage when he became irreversible, (3) the sojourn in the Tuṣita Heaven (the fourth of the six heavens in the *kāmadhātu,* or "world of desire"), and (4) the attainment of Buddhahood.[13] Following Śākyamuni's footsteps, and in accordance with his prediction, the bodhisattva Maitreya is believed to be in the Tuṣita Heaven, waiting for the time of his messianic mission. With the rise of the Mahāyāna tradition, Buddhist cosmology developed a number of pure lands, or Buddha fields, each with a celestial bodhisattva residing in it. In the course of time, the popularity of the Tuṣita Heaven was superseded by the glamorous Sukyāvatī, the abode of Buddha Amitābha.

2. In principle, the practical expressions of Buddhist experience are more important than other forms of expression because the central question of Buddhism is not "*What* is *nirvāṇa*?" but rather "*How* does one attain *nirvāṇa*?" In the main, the practical expressions of Buddhism have two related dimensions: cultus (both corporate and individual) and service to fellow beings. Elsewhere I have touched on the two modes of the Maitreya cult based on the "ascent" and "descent" motifs, both of which have greatly enriched the Buddhist cultic life.[14] Maitreya was venerated not only as the lord of the Tuṣita Heaven, where many Buddhists aspired to be reborn after their death, and as the future Buddha, whose coming was eagerly awaited by the faithful; he was also regarded as the paradigm of the ideal follower of Buddha's path. For example, in the *Sūtra on the Original Vow Asked by the Bodhisattva Maitreya,*[15] the Buddha explains the virtuous power with which Maitreya reaches Buddhahood:

> The bodhisattva Maitreya three times daily and three times every night put his clothes in order, restrained his body, folded his hands, bowed his knees upon the ground, and, turning towards the ten quarters, pronounced the following stanza (*gāthā*):
>
> "I repent all my sins,
> I encourage and assist all the virtues of the Road,
> I take refuge in and pay reverence to the Buddhas,
> That they may cause me to obtain the unsurpassable
> Wisdom."[16]

This example fostered various forms of penitential service as a part of the worship of Maitreya.

The devotees of Maitreya were also expected to perform "Dharma actions," not only for themselves to avoid the wicked path and false knowledge, but also to help others follow the path of Maitreya. Undoubtedly, Maitreya had many qualities that were attractive to many people. "Maitreya," say Robinson and Johnson, "unlike the Buddhas before him, is alive, so he can respond to the prayers of worshippers. Being compassionate . . . he willingly grants help; and being a high god in his present birth, he has the power to do so. His cult thus offers its devotees the advantages of theism and Buddhism combined."[17] It should be noted that, for the adherents of Maitreya, devotion and service are two complementary features of the "practical" expression of their Buddhist experience.

3. The "sociological expression" of Buddhism is also essential for its soteriology. As E. J. Thomas rightly stressed, the Buddhist movement began "not with a body of doctrine, but with the formation of a society bound by certain rules."[18] According to the conviction of the early Buddhists, the Buddhist community (Saṃgha), consisting of monastics and laity, was the only vehicle to actualize the Dharma that had been disclosed through Buddha's enlightenment experience. To be sure, from the beginning the monastic life was accepted as the core of the Buddhist path. But the monastic components (*Śrāvaka-saṃgha,* consisting of *bhikṣu* and *bhiksuṇī*) and the lay components (later called *bodhisattva-ana,* referring to *upāsaka* and *upāsikā*) were seen in relation to each other as inner and outer circles of the same group. Soon, however, the monastics began to consider themselves spiritual elites and the guardians of the Dharma. This tendency became accentuated after the recognition of Buddhism as the religion of the empire under King Aśoka in the third century. Since then, the relationship between the monastics and the laity has been understood to be vertical, with the monastics as the elites on top and the laity at the bottom; this has been especially true in the Theravāda and other Hīnayāna schools, which have been established in South and Southeast Asia. In the Mahāyāna tradition, however, the excessive "monastification" of the ethos of the Buddhist community has been avoided.

It is worth noting that in the process of the institutionalization of the Buddhist community, Maitreya, recognized by every group as the future Buddha, did not serve as the object of any independent sectarian movement, as did Amitābha. Rather, most followers of Maitreya were content to have their devotional confraternities (which might be characterized as a "collegium pietatis") within the Buddhist community ("Ecclesiola in Ecclesia").[19] This was not true, however, in China, where the figure of Maitreya has inspired many protest and revolutionary groups outside the Buddhist community, as I shall discuss presently.

Maitreya and the Buddhist Culture

Historically, Buddhism, which we have portrayed as a soteriological religion, has shaped and influenced culture, which is a domain of values, ideologies, arts, and imagination. In this respect, the figure of Maitreya – seen either as a prince or a bodhisattva or as the future Buddha – has aroused the imagination of artists from the early days of the Gandharan sculptures in India to later paintings and sculptures in China, Korea, and Japan.[20]

Equally significant is the impact Maitreya had on the cultural values and orientations of people in various Buddhist nations in terms of encouraging "merit making" and providing hope for the future. Just as wealth, health, longevity, power, and status in this life were believed to be the results of good karma, many lay people were eager to accumulate merit and thereby ensure a good rebirth. In this respect, the belief in Maitreya, the future Buddha, provided a pointed focus and strong incentive for the merit-making laity. According to Rahula, "Some laymen seem to have had a note book called Puññapotthaka, 'Merit-Book,' in which their meritorious deeds were recorded. This was usually intended to be read at the death-bed, so that the dying man might gladden his heart and purify his thoughts to ensure a good birth."[21] For example, the famous Singhalese king Duṭṭha-Gāmaṇī (r. 101–77 B.C.), a devotee of Metteyya who was noted for his generous welfare activities, kept a "merit book," which was read at his deathbed. Such an orientation in cultural values also influenced many Buddhists' sense of status. As Margaret Mead discovered in modern Burma, "All status, except that of the king, was achieved, and achievement was open to anyone through accumulation of merits."[22]

It has often been observed by outsiders that the Buddhist culture takes the suffering and transitoriness of life very seriously. For example, Saichō, or Dengyō-daishi (767–822), the patriarch of the Japanese Tendai school, wrote the following statement when he was about twenty years of age:

> The phenomenal world, from remote past to distant future, is full of sufferings, and there is not room for peacefulness. The lives of all beings, tangled as they are with difficulties and complications, present only sorrows and no happiness. The sunlight of the Buddha Śākyamuni has been hidden in the distant cloud, and we have not as yet seen the glimpse of the moonlight of the merciful future Buddha [Maitreya].[23]

Likewise, many other Buddhists lamented the fact that they were destined to live during the period between the two Buddhas, yet their outlook on life was not so firmly negative. I might add that to the modern mind the Buddhist notion of karmic retribution resembles Josiah Royce's idea of the "hell of the irrevocable," which implies that "I can do good deeds in the future, but I cannot revoke my past deed." In the Buddhist context, however, the order is reversed: "I cannot revoke my past deed, but I can do good deeds now for the future." Such an understanding of karma offered a plausible resolution of a cluster of existential questions and problems for those who sensed the misfortune of living during the time between the two Buddhas. Moreover, the anticipation of the coming of the future Buddha Maitreya gave them grounds for optimism and hope.

Maitreya and the Buddhist-Oriented Sociopolitical Order

It is safe to conjecture that, in its early days, Buddhism was not concerned with the social or the political order. Monks and nuns left the world at the time of their admission to monastic life. Lay Buddhists always stressed the desirability of peace, order, and harmonious interhuman relationships, as evidenced by the scattered references in the canonical writings to the Buddha's attitude toward monarchs and principalities. But Buddhism as such did not articulate what might be termed Buddhist social or political theories or philosophies. Moreover, the early Buddhist notion of the "world" (*lokadhātu*) was that of a religious, not a geographical, universe and referred to "the area on which the light of the sun and moon shines, i.e., the four Continents around Mt. Sumeru."[24] Accordingly, as Rahula succinctly points out, "the idea of the 'establishment' of Buddhism in a given geographical unit with its implications is quite foreign to the teaching of the Buddha."[25]

The "spacialization" of the Buddhist notion of the world took place under Aśoka, who established the *śāsana* (Buddhism) as an institution in his country. "Like a conqueror and a ruler who would establish governments in countries politically conquered by him, so Aśoka probably thought of establishing the *śāsana* in countries spiritually conquered (*dharma-vijita*) by him. . . . [And following Aśoka's example], the *śāsana* was established in [Ceylon] with the establishment of the boundaries or the *sīmā*."[26] It is worth noting that although Aśoka was devoted to the Three Treasures (Buddha, Dharma, Saṃgha), he created a new triad – the Buddhist kingship, Buddhist-inspired general morality called *dharma* (but actually once-removed from the Buddha's Dharma itself),[27] and the Buddhist state – as the second order of the Three Treasures, as it were. In addition, in post-Aśokan Buddhism, these two levels of the Three Treasures often coalesced, especially in the South and Southeast Asian Buddhist traditions. I might add that, historically, Aśoka's formula has been the only tangible norm for the relation of Buddhism to the sociopolitical order that was acceptable to many Buddhists until the modern period.

Undoubtedly, the center of the second level of the Three Treasures was the notion of the Buddhist king, a notion that combined the assimilated features of the *cakravartin*, the royal Buddhahood, and Metteyya (Maitreya). The most conspicuous example of this type of Buddhist king is the aforementioned Singhalese king Duṭṭha-Gāmanī, who was believed to be connected with the Buddha both as his disciple and as his kinsman:

> According to the Great Chronicle tradition he was a direct descendant of Gautama's paternal uncle, Amitodana. Moreover, it is foretold that from the Tuṣita Heaven into which Duṭṭha-Gāmanī entered at his death, as the proper reward for his piety, he will eventually be reborn on earth in the days of the next Buddha, Metteyya. The two will, in fact, be sons of the same mother and father: "The great king Duṭṭha-Gāmanī, he who is worthy of the name of king, will be the first disciple of the sublime Metteyya; the king's father will be his [Metteyya's] father, and the king's mother his [Metteyya's] mother.[28]

There were other Buddhist kings in South and Southeast Asia who, without claiming such a close kinship relation with Metteyya as did Duṭṭha-Gāmanī, nevertheless aspired to ascend to Metteyya's heaven upon death or to be reborn when Metteyya descends to earth. In addition, the symbols of Metteyya/*cakravartin* were often domesticated by the Buddhist kings to legitimate their reigns. Such domestication occurred at the expense of the other side of the Metteyyan motif, however; that is, any attempt to criticize the ills of the empirical social and political order was abandoned. Only in the modern period has the Metteyyan ideal become associated with anticolonial revolutionary movements. We have yet to see whether the eschatological Metteyyan vision will remain alive as a necessary corrective to the status quo in the postcolonial Buddhist nations in Asia.

In the Mahāyāna tradition, which had spread to Central Asia, China, Korea, and Japan, Maitreya found a formidable rival in the Buddha Amitābha, who also had emerged from the cross-cultural and cross-religious northwestern Indian milieu near the beginning of the common era. The figures of Maitreya and Amitābha were closely intertwined in those countries.

In China, as in the Hīnayāna countries, the combined image of Maitreya and the universal monarch, *cakravartin,* was appropriated and distorted by rulers eager to enhance their kingship with Buddhist symbols. It was in China that the two modes of the Maitreya cult developed, based on the "ascent" and "descent" motifs, respectively. Gradually, however, the "ascent" type of the Maitreya cult, which stressed one's rebirth in the Tuṣita Heaven, was eclipsed by the popularity of the cult of Amitābha, who was believed to have vowed to bring all sentient beings to his blissful Pure Land. The
mitābha devotees were greatly influenced by a negative progressivism,
held that the period of the true Dharma was destined to be succeeded by
of the counterfeit Dharma and by the period of the decline and
harma and that the dreaded "last period" was fast approach-
of urgency that intensified the popular devotion to the
bha. Meanwhile, the "descent" motif of the Maitreya
s of rebel and revolutionary movements outside the

Buddhist community. Many of these movements failed, however, because they lacked leadership and coherent programs for social and political reconstruction.

As in China, the Maitreya cult in Korea and Japan, which attracted many devotees, was never an eschatological and prophetic religious force, due largely to Buddhism's all too eager effort to be assimilated into the cultural and political fabric of both countries. In the twelfth and thirteenth centuries, Japan suffered a series of natural calamities, social unrest, and political instability, as though to confirm the arrival of the period of the Latter End of the Dharma (*mappō* 末法). It was in Japan that the Pure Land and the Nichiren 日蓮 groups (and not the Maitreya cult) developed intense pietistic movements. It should be noted, however, that during the nineteenth century, when the foundation of the feudal society was shaken by both external and internal factors, the "descent" motif of Maitreya inspired the notion of the rectification of social order (*yonaoshi* 世直し), as exemplified by a series of messianic cults.

In retrospect, it is evident that the potentialities of Maitreya as the symbol of eschatological vision as well as the religious and ethical critique of empirical sociopolitical order have rarely been actualized in the history of Buddhism.

The Buddhological and Religious Meaning of Maitreya

In dealing with such a multidimensional figure as Maitreya, historians of religions face an almost insurmountable task of familiarizing themselves with the scholarly research of specialists in various areas and disciplines. To keep up with the ever-growing Buddhological scholarship – with the historical, philosophical, ethical, textual, iconographical, cultural, institutional studies in different branches of Buddhism, to say nothing of studies of its practical aspects – is an enormous task. Moreover, the study of Maitreya requires some knowledge of the historic interaction between Buddhism and Zoroastrian, Manichean, and other religions in Central Asia, between Buddhism and Hinduism in India, and between Buddhism and other religious traditions of Southeast Asia, Tibet, Mongolia, China, Korea, and Japan.

Historians of religions must also be concerned with theoretical, thematic, and methodological issues pertaining to the general history of religions, such as religious cosmology, spiritual geography, sacred biography, sacred history, religious anthropology, narratology, symbols, myth, and ritual. The most demanding task is, of course, systematizing and organizing these rich and often contradictory data into a discernible pattern of meanin[illegible] which requires constant checking of *religionswissenschaftliche* procedures, d[illegible] and generalizations in terms of Buddhological data and vice versa. [illegible] regard to Maitreya, the sort of checking I have in mind raises the following questions:

1. In what manner does the study of Maitreya illuminate our understanding of the nature of the Buddha and bodhisattvas? Are they saviors (Conze), "Docetic" phenomena (Anesaki), or the "hypostasization" of Dharmic principles? Are we to understand that "heavenly" bodhisattvas, for example, are personalizations of the Buddha's qualities (e.g., compassion and wisdom)? Quite apart from their "historicity," what is their "ontological" status? Are we to assume that they have been preordained in the cosmological schema? Or do they come into being by means of the devotee's "visualization" or the adept's magical power? (Maitreya in the Esoteric, or Tantric, Buddhist tradition opens a series of other questions.)

2. Related to the first question is one regarding the relationship between the Buddha and Maitreya. Are they two figures, or are they essentially one figure (T. W. Rhys Davids)? Assuming that Maitreya is an eschatological figure, how crucial is eschatology to Buddhist soteriology? What is the relationship between eschatology and Buddhist ethics?

3. What is the relationship between the figure of Maitreya and millenarianism (Suzuki Chūsei, Sarkisyanz, Mendelson, Overmyer, Naquin, etc.)? Did the "prophecy" about Maitreya have millenarian connotations? Or did millenarian movements "discover" Maitreya as an appropriate symbol?

4. What is the range of attitudes that the Buddhist community holds towards Maitreya? Is he one of many interchangeable objects of adoration and/or adherence? What features of Maitreya are venerated by monks? By the laity? In this respect, Tambiah's observation is interesting: "The *bodhisattva* who stirs the imagination and holds the greatest promises for the Thai village is Maitreya, the next Buddha who will arrive to bring salvation to the world."[29] He also reports, however, that "in Ceylon the protective guardian god Natha has been identified with Maitreya."[30]

Although many more questions could be asked, I will now suggest a few ways of relating Buddhological and *religionswissenschaftliche* inquiries regarding the phenomenon of Maitreya. As a historian of religions, I assume that, as in the case of other religious traditions, the Buddhist community sees three levels of meaning – *theos, mythos,* and *logos* – in a phenomenon such as Maitreya. The level of *theos* refers to the dimension of the corporate and individual experience of sacral reality (Ultimate Reality or Nonreality), which cannot be explicated but only experienced. This level of meaning, however, has often been narrated in *mythos,* which is the religious language par excellence. (In our time, some hermeneuts have been engaged in the task of "demythologization" in order to return to the level of *theos*, but I will not discuss the subject here.) In many religious traditions, including the Buddhist tradition, philosophers and theologians have attempted to develop coherent sets of theoretical statements (*logos*) derived from and based on *mythos*.

For the most part, the historian of religions is interested in the *mythos* rather than the *logos* and the *theos*, because he or she is looking for the "horizon of religious meaning" derived from myths, symbols, and cults, and not philosophical or theological meaning and truth. The historian of religions is also concerned with (1) what has happened (history), (2) what the religious community believes has happened (sacred history), and (3) the relation of these two kinds of historical meanings.

It is the task of the historian of religions to look for universal meaning in various religious traditions. For example, the Buddhist formula of the Three Treasures is based on a universal affirmation that Dharma can be "experienced" (although not explicated by discursive language) by the human being (of which the Buddha is the prototype) and that this religious experience can be shared by others in the corporate fellowship of men and women (the community of faith). In such a community, the nature of levels of reality, including Ultimate Reality (Dharma), can be disclosed through the life and teaching of the one who had the paradigmatic religious experience, and the life and teaching of that person can in turn be "experienced" in terms of his soteriological qualities (e.g., the compassion and wisdom of the Buddha).

Of course, such a religious meaning does not exist in abstraction. Each religious tradition, which exists in particular histories, develops its own pattern of meaning-structure as manifested in the threefold expressions (i.e., theoretical, practical, and sociological). For example, the Buddhist pattern has produced not only canonical writings, but also rich narrative traditions, including sacred biographies, genealogies, chronicles, and a variety of stories. And as in other religious traditions, the Buddhist community has cemented its sense of identity by the repetition of rituals as well as by constant retelling of these narrative accounts. In this setting, the notion of Maitreya was accepted because of the inner logic of the "Buddhist pattern," which affirms that the "sacred time" must be seen in its three dimensions (the past and the future in reference to the present) and that the anticipation of the end of the world impinges on one's religious path (*marga*) here and now.

To the historian of religions, concerned as he or she is with both the universal and the particular dimensions of religion, the Buddhist tradition, especially the phenomenon of Maitreya, is an alluring subject. Following the principle of the "priority of the whole," the historian of religions regards the Buddhist experience, as much as the Hindu, Islamic, Jewish, or Christian experience, not as someone else's experience but as an essential part of our whole religious experience. It is the exciting task of the historian of religions to re-cognize what has been cognized as soteriological meaning by others as "our own." Only then – only when that which has been foreign has been assimilated as our own – can the historian of religions move a step forward and appraise that which has become his or her own as an objective something to be studied academically.

NOTES

1 Augustine, "The Confessions," trans. E. B. Pusey, in *Great Books of the Western World* (Chicago, 1952), 18:95.
2 Paul Tillich, *The Future of Religions,* ed. J. C. Brauer (New York, 1966), 64–5.
3 R. C. Zaehner, *The Teachings of the Magi* (London, 1956), 150.
4 R. C. Zaehner, "Zoroastrianism," in *The Concise Encyclopedia of Living Faiths,* ed. R. C. Zaehner (New York, 1959), 209. He also comments, "Christianity claims to be the heir of the prophets of Israel. If there is any truth in this claim, it is no less heir to the Prophet of ancient Iran, little though most Christians are aware of this fact."
5 Heinrich Zimmer, *Philosophies of India,* ed. Joseph Campbell (New York, 1951), 129.
6 E. J. Thomas, *The Life of Buddha as Legend and History,* 3d ed. (London, 1949), 219.
7 Ibid., 219–26; Zimmer, *Philosophies,* 130–1.
8 A. L. Basham, *The Wonder That Was India* (New York, 1954), 274.
9 René Grousset, *In the Footsteps of the Buddha,* trans. J. A. Underwood (New York, 1971), 127–8.
10 Ibid., 148–9.
11 Sir Charles Eliot, *Hinduism and Buddhism,* 3 vols. (New York, 1954), 2:22.
12 I-tsing, *A Record of the Buddhist Religion as Practiced in India and the Malay Archipelago (A.D. 671–95),* trans. J. Takakusu (Oxford, 1986), 213.
13 Edward Conze, *Buddhist Thought in India* (Ann Arbor, Mich., 1967), 235.
14 See my "The Career of Maitreya, with Special Reference to Japan," *History of Religions* 21, no. 2 (November 1981): 115. For the importance of Maitreya in Tibetan Buddhism, see Stephen Beyer, *The Cult of Tara: Magic and Ritual in Tibet* (Berkeley & Los Angeles, 1978).
15 Translated into Chinese by Dharmarakṣa I in A.D. 266–317; *Nanjio Catalogue,* no. 55.
16 Cited in M. W. de Visser, *Ancient Buddhism in Japan,* 2 vols. (Paris, 1928), 1:260–1.
17 Richard H. Robinson and Willard L. Johnson, *The Buddhist Religion: A Historical Introduction,* 2d ed. (Encino, Calif., 1977), 103.
18 E. J. Thomas, *The History of Buddhist Thought,* 2d. ed. (New York, 1951), 14.
19 For a characterization of the "collegium pietatis" and so on, see Joachim Wach, *Sociology of Religion* (Chicago, 1944), 174–81.
20 Even after a casual and amateurish perusal of the following books, I have been impressed by the rich variety of artistic representations of Maitreya: Alice Getty, *The Gods of Northern Buddhism* (Rutland, Vt., 1962), plates 15-a, 31-l, 60-d, and 66; H. F. E. Visser, *Asiatic Art in Private Collections of Holland and Belgium* (New York, 1952), plates 76, no. 149; 80, no. 156; and 83, no. 159. See also Choi Sunu, *5000*

Years of Korean Art (Seoul, 1979), plates 211, 216, 217, 218, 219, 220, 221, and 232. The half-seated Maitreya statue was very popular in China, Korea, and Japan before the seventh century.

21 Walpola Rahula, *History of Buddhism in Ceylon: The Anurādhapura Period, Third Century BC–Tenth Century AD* (Colombo, 1956), 254.

22 Margaret Mead, ed., *Cultural Patterns and Technical Change* (New York, 1955), 26.

23 Cited in W.-T. Chan, I. R. al Faruqi, J. M. Kitagawa, and P. T. Raju, eds., *The Great Asian Religions: An Anthology* (New York, 1969), 266.

24 See Hajime Nakamura, *Ways of Thinking of Eastern Peoples: India–China–Tibet–Japan,* ed. Philip P. Wiener (Honolulu, 1964), 434.

25 Rahula, *History of Buddhism,* 54.

26 Ibid., 55.

27 On Aśoka's understanding of Dharma, see Amulyachandra Sen, *Aśoka's Edicts* (Calcutta, 1956), 34.

28 Trevor Ling, *The Buddha: Buddhist Civilization in India and Ceylon* (New York, 1973), 186–7.

29 S. J. Tambiah, *Buddhism and the Spirit Cults in North-East Thailand* (Cambridge, Eng., 1970), 46–7.

30 Ibid., 48.

2

The Meanings of the Maitreya Myth

A Typological Analysis

JAN NATTIER

Introduction

Any typology, including the one presented in this chapter, is in some sense an artificial creation. In the real world we do not meet "types"; we meet real people, with infinitely varied experiences of the world and with equally varied means of expressing them. Yet if we are to say anything at all about our fellow human beings, we must categorize them to a certain degree – whether as Hindus, Buddhists, optimists, pessimists, or millenarians.

The typology developed in this chapter is based on a set of variables that can be considered central to the Maitreya myth in all its forms. By combining these variables in every possible way, we derive a total of four logically possible "types," or versions, of the Maitreya myth. Though these categories are morphological types, not "ideal types" like those employed by Max Weber, much of what Weber said about the uses and limitations of his conceptual categories is applicable here as well.[1] I will not try to recapitulate his discussion; suffice it to say that an ideal type (or typological category) is *not* the phenomenon itself, but is rather a conceptual yardstick against which a variety of phenomena can be measured. If we allow our typology to remain transparent – that is, if we allow the phenomena themselves to remain our primary focus, using the typology merely as a framework to illuminate their relative positions – then it can serve to amplify our vision of the people and ideas we wish to undertand. If we do not, such categorization can actually detract from our understanding by leading to a premature pigeonholing of the subject matter.

In the discussion that follows, each of the four basic forms of the Maitreya myth is analyzed and, where possible, illustrated with examples of its occurrence in history. It is by no means a foregone conclusion, however, that representatives of each type should actually occur. As we shall see below, some types are far more common than others, and the relative fullness or emptiness of a given category is in itself a valuable piece of information. This typology, then, is not designed to force the living forms of the Maitreya myth into a neat geometrical structure; much less does it suggest that the four categories are in some sense symmetrical, with each form carrying equal weight in the history of the Buddhist tradition. Rather, the objective of this enterprise is to provide a set of analytical "latitude and longitude" lines, which can then serve to highlight – not to mask – the irregular contours of the many ways in which Maitreya has been understood by his devotees.

As the chapters in this volume clearly demonstrate, the Maitreya myth occurs in Buddhist literature in a wide variety of forms. There are stories from China in which Maitreya is described in messianic terms and is expected to usher in a "golden age" for his followers;[2] in texts from the Turfan region of Central Asia, by contrast, Maitreya appears as a most conservative figure, guaranteeing the continuity of the Dharma established by Śākyamuni (and, incidentally, the stability of the local government) into the distant future.[3] We read of Tibetan mystics aspiring to rebirth in Maitreya's heavenly realm[4] and of Japanese peasants hoping to be reborn during Maitreya's tenure on earth.[5] Finally, although the majority of traditions place Maitreya's coming in some unimaginably distant age,[6] in a few cases the myth has been rewritten to foretell his appearance in the immediate future.[7]

It is clear that an important priority in the field of Maitreya studies is the continuing translation and analysis of the individual sources at our disposal. Yet the richness of even the relatively small number of Maitreya traditions available to date suggests that it is not too early to begin an analysis of these materials as a group – to examine some of the basic elements of the Maitreya myth, to analyze the important differences among its versions, and ultimately to compare these versions with myths from other religious traditions (particularly those coming under the heading of "messianic" or "apocalyptic") that may or may not be analogous to them.

As a preliminary means of fulfilling these three objectives, we outline in this chapter a working typology of Maitreya traditions. In order to do this, it is necessary first to select the key variables in the Maitreya myth – that is, to decide which variations in the myth are of fundamental religious significance and which are merely peripheral. We begin from the standpoint that as a myth (rather than a mere legend or heroic tale)[8] the story of Maitreya conveys something of fundamental significance to the life of the believer. Specifically, the myth opens up the possibility of a personal encounter between the believer and Maitreya, and it is this possibility that I have taken to be the pivotal element of the myth.[9]

It is important to state at the outset of our analysis that not every appearance of Maitreya in Buddhist literature consitutes, ipso facto, an instance of the Maitreya myth. Like countless other Buddhas and bodhisattvas in the Buddhist (particularly Mahāyāna) pantheon, Maitreya often appears in Buddhist literature merely as a member of the supporting cast – to second a statement made by someone else, to ask a question (and thus provide an opportunity for the Buddha to expound on a given topic), or merely to join in the chorus of those who "praise the words of the Lord" in the closing passages of so many Mahāyāna sūtras. Such appearances clearly do not constitute a Maitreya myth as such (any more than the similar appearances of Mañjuśrī, for example, could be said to represent a Mañjuśrī myth). Rather, these familiar figures are simply called into service to enhance or to validate a teaching that focuses elsewhere. Such appearances of Maitreya in Buddhist (and even in non-Buddhist)[10] literature are legion, and to analyze them all would be a formidable undertaking. We have chosen, therefore, to include in our analysis only those texts in which Maitreya plays a central role – those works in which Maitreya is the main focus and in which the concept of a Buddha of the future is a central and organizing principle.

Having restricted our analysis to accounts of this type and having chosen the motif of the eventual encounter between the believer and Maitreya as the focus of our analysis, it becomes clear that not all versions of the Maitreya myth describe or look forward to this encounter in the same way. Indeed, there are two major areas of disagreement: (a) *where* the encounter between Maitreya and the believer will take place (i.e., whether they will meet on earth or in the Tuṣita Heaven)[11] and (b) *when* the encounter will occur (in the broadest terms, whether the believer expects to see Maitreya during his or her present lifetime or at some time after death). Combining these two variables in all possible ways, we come up with four logically possible versions of the Maitreya myth:

1. *Here/now:* In this version of the myth, the believer expects to meet Maitreya on earth, during his or her present lifetime.
2. *Here/later:* The believer expects the meeting to take place on earth, but at some time after the believer's death (i.e., in a future rebirth).
3. *There/now:* In this "visionary" recension of the Maitreya myth, the believer strives for an immediate encounter with Maitreya, who is (according to the basic structure of the myth in all its versions) currently residing in the Tuṣita Heaven.
4. *There/later:* The believer may aspire to a rebirth in Maitreya's otherworldly paradise, the Tuṣita Heaven, after this present lifetime.

In the following discussion we examine each type in detail; we note which types occur most frequently and which should rather be described as exceptional cases. Once we have analyzed the mythology of Maitreya from this perspective, it will then be possible – though this is beyond the scope of the present analysis – to apply the same typology to similar figures in other religious traditions, a procedure that should highlight both the similarities and the differences between them.

Here/Later: A Deferred Golden Age

Though the sequence of categories just outlined might suggest that we take the here/now version of the Maitreya myth as our point of departure, we will begin instead with the version that is by far the most common in the canonical literature: the here/later interpretation. Indeed, this might well be described as the "standard" recension, for – as we shall see below – this category contains not only the greatest number of versions of the Maitreya myth, but the oldest ones as well.[12]

In essence, the here/later version runs as follows. Although Maitreya's advent is not expected for many millions of years, the Buddhist concept of rebirth allows ordinary believers – provided that by virtue of their good karma they are worthy of such a reward – to look forward to being reborn on earth during Maitreya's time, to hear him preach the Dharma, and ultimately to attain the final goal of *nirvāṇa*. Scriptures containing the here/later version usually devote considerable attention to the details of the paradise-like conditions that will obtain on earth during Maitreya's Golden Age, which are clearly an incentive for ordinary Buddhists to strive for rebirth during Maitreya's time. It is not the details of those decriptions, however, that are most important for our purposes. More useful for understanding the religious impulse behind such works are the concluding sections, which offer various exhortations to the reader or listener. In virtually all cases, believers are exhorted to practice faithfully the Buddhism taught by Śākyamuni; in some, they are urged to support the existing order (i.e., the government and in particular the monastic system) as well.[13]

Given the obvious allure of the Maitreyan Golden Age described in these scriptures, it is striking that not a single canonical Maitreya text turns to "active apocalypticism" – that is, to exhortations to help bring about Maitreya's age in the immediate future. The absence of this impulse is certainly not due simply to fatalism; the date of Maitreya's advent, though distant, is never definitively stated in these texts, and the idea of a future golden age is hardly evidence of a purely pessimistic view of life. Rather, what may have restrained the authors of these scriptures from indulging in the urge to "speed the millennium" was their awareness of the context in which the Maitreya myth evolved – that is, the Buddhist theory of an oscillating universe.

It is difficult to say with certainty that a given idea was ever shared by all Buddhist sects; yet it is clear that the idea that the Dharma would undergo a decline after the time of Śākyamuni was part of a relatively early layer of the Buddhist tradition.[14] A systematic form of this theory, incorporating alternating periods of rise and decline, is given by the *Abhidharmakośa* in its chapter on cosmology (3, vv. 89d–98), where the periods of manifestation of the universe (alternating with periods of "nothingness," or nonmanifestation) are said to consist of twenty "phases," or *kalpas,* all but the first and last of which contain equal periods of evolution and devolution. In simplified form, the concept of the decline and rise of history is the following. At the beginning of each manifestation cycle, the world is at its peak. The life span of human beings is eighty thousand years; there is neither warfare nor poverty, and all the requisites of life are easily attained. Then an imperceptible decline sets in; the human life span gradually diminishes, until it reaches a nadir of only ten years. Likewise, conditions of life decline. People begin to quarrel with one another, sickness and famine spread, and survival itself becomes more and more difficult. Then, following a brief period of warfare among the remaining human beings, the cycle reverses itself. Each succeeding generation lives longer, until at last the peak life span of eighty thousand years is reached once again. According to the common mythology, human history is now in the lower ranges of a decline cycle. During the time of Śākyamuni, it is said, the human life span was one hundred years, but now it has fallen below that figure. This decline is expected to continue until the nadir of ten years is reached and the cycle reverses itself. It is after this low point has been traversed, when the world gradually evolves toward another "peak," that Maitreya will descend to earth. Although the details of the system recorded in this text may not have been shared by all Buddhist schools, we do have evidence that the idea that the present age forms part of a devolutionary (or decline) cycle was part of the world view in which the Maitreya traditions were elaborated.[15]

Within this cosmological perspective, it becomes clear that one would not want to speed up the pale of history in order to bring about Maitreya's advent; inevitably, the *decline must come first.* Given this scenario, there is no incentive to accelerate the pace of events, for – at least in the short term – things can only get worse.[16]

According to the here/later version of the Maitreya myth, then, the only means of access to Maitreya's Golden Age is to die and be reborn at the time of Maitreya's appearance on earth, which this tradition (in common with all versions except those of the here/now type) assigns to the distant future. The religious impact of this message is obvious: The highest good is to be obtained not in this life, but in a future one; and the goal of this life should be to act in such a way that this good (i.e., the meeting with Maitreya and the subsequent attainment of *nirvāṇa*) will eventually be obtained.

Maitreya texts of the here/later type are quite explicit in their descriptions of the kinds of activity that will bring the desired meeting about.

A key feature is the making of the merit: In addition to the observance of the ordinary moral precepts for lay Buddhists, here/later texts advocate the support of the Sangha (the monastic community), the veneration of texts dealing with Maitreya, and even the practice of the confession of sins.[17] In sum, it is not extraordinary measures of any kind, but rather the patient accumulation of the moral and spiritual prerequisites that will eventually lead to an encounter with Maitreya.

There/Later: A Maitreyist "Pure Land"[18]

Like the here/later interpretation of the Maitreya myth, the there/later version lies well within the confines of the orthodox tradition. We have seen that Maitreya (according to all the canonical versions of the myth) is currently residing in the Tuṣita Heaven, awaiting the right time for his appearance on earth. For those who found Maitreya's predicted advent too distant to offer immediate religious solace, this framework offered an obvious solution: By the accumulation of merit, ordinary Buddhists could cause their next birth to take place in the Tuṣita Heaven, where they could encounter Maitreya (still in his bodhisattva form) in person.

There is speculation that this interpretation of the Maitreya myth, which so strongly resembles traditions urging believers to strive for rebirth in Amitābha's Western Paradise, may initially have been stimulated by Amidist thinking;[19] it is certain that in China and Japan this "Pure Land" Maitreyism was ultimately absorbed by the Amidist myth.[20] Whatever the historical relations between the two traditions, the religious similarities between them are obvious. Both offer the believer a rebirth in a reasonably accessible paradise, from which the final step to *nirvāṇa* can be taken much more easily than is possible on earth.

It is clear that the there/later form of the Maitreya myth has been severely dehistoricized: It no longer matters to the believer when, or even whether, Maitreya will appear on earth. Of course, the two perspectives can be (and sometimes were) combined; we have records of lay Buddhists wishing for an immediate rebirth in the Tuṣita Heaven, to be followed by a meeting with Maitreya on earth in a subsequent lifetime.[21] Nevertheless, in the there/later versions of the myth the focus has clearly shifted from the future evolution of the earth as we know it to a life in an otherworldly paradise.

Despite the change of scene to the Tuṣita Heaven, the there/later version shares one important feature with the here/later account. In both, the emphasis on a future life results in a certain degree of devaluation of the present. Aside from the importance of making merit in this existence, there is little concern with the realities of this world, which pales in comparison with Maitreya's paradise. The two versions of the myth, in fact, are to a large degree functional equivalents of one another. In both, the focus is on the rewards to be gained in the afterlife, and the means to their attainment are virtually identical.[22]

There is, however, one important difference between the two. Whereas the here/later version of the myth retains a degree of historical awareness – particularly when the intervening "Age of Fighting" is stressed as the predecessor of Maitreya's age – in the there/later version even this marginal historical grounding disappears. There is now little difference between the Maitreyist scenario in its there/later form and the life-after-death promises of any other heaven-oriented religion.

There/Now: The Mystical Alternative

Not everyone, of course, was willing to wait so long for a vision of Maitreya's paradise. There have also been gifted "religious virtuosi" (to use Max Weber's term) who, unwilling to delay the attainment of the highest good until another incarnation, sought the vision of Maitreya in this very life.

The notion of a mystical encounter with Maitreya as bodhisattva has been closely linked with the tradition of scriptural commentary, particularly that of the Yogācāra school (where Maitreya – whether or not the name originally referred to a historical person – is considered to be the author of a number of important philosophical texts). His role as "patron saint of commentators" was not, however, restricted to dictating Yogācāra literature of Asaṅga. Tao-an (d. 385) turned to Maitreya for help with difficult scriptural passages,[23] and Saṅgharakṣa, the author of an earlier (non-Mahāyāna) *Yogācārabhūmi* text, is also known to have been one of Maitreya's devotees.[24] As the next Buddha, Maitreya was regarded by these doctors of the law as an unparalleled source of information on difficult doctrinal issues.

In traditional accounts of mystical encounters with the heavenly bodhisattva, there is sometimes a fine line between the ascent of the believer to the Tuṣita Heaven and the descent of Maitreya to earth. To the recipient of such a vision, the difference between the two may be of little importance; nevertheless, for typological completeness we should note that both "ascent" and "descent" encounters are recorded.[25] The later version bears a superficial resemblance to the traditions of the here/now type discussed below, but the two should not be confounded. Though both involve appearances of Maitreya on earth, the "descent" variation of the there/now myth is distinguished by the fact that Maitreya does not take on any ongoing earthly form capable of intervening directly in history.[26]

Though there are accounts of spontaneous visions of Maitreya by unsuspecting persons,[27] the ascent to the Tuṣita is generally accomplished by cultivating the practice of *samādhi*.[28] We might note in passing that such a method is essentially restricted to the "professional" religious, since it requires a considerable amount of leisure time as well as the firm conviction of the value of visionary experience.

It is not surprising, therefore, that the there/now form of the Maitreya myth never became the predominant form of the tradition in any Buddhist country. Moreover, it is worth noting that those who took this visionary approach to the meeting with Maitreya frequently combined it with at least one other approach (most commonly, the aspiration for rebirth in the Tuṣita Heaven).[29] There is, of course, no difficulty in harmonizing this visionary interpretation with what we might call the "mainstream myth": It requires no rewriting of the canonical accounts (all of which agree that Maitreya is in the Tuṣita Heaven at present), and it in no way alters the time frame within which Maitreya's eventual appearance on earth will take place. In sum, it was an ideal form of the myth for those whose religious aspirations exceeded the bounds of merely acquiring merit and waiting for a rebirth in Maitreya's presence.

Here/Now: Visions of a New Earth

With this version of the Maitreya myth we come to a form that diverges radically from those we have discussed so far. Whereas there are numerous examples of the three types of the myth outlined above, those that can be classified as here/now traditions – that is, versions in which the believer can expect to meet Maitreya on earth during his or her present lifetime – are few and far between. We have no examples at all of Maitreya traditions of this type from India or Central Asia, and even in Chinese and Southeast Asian sources, where such interpretations are attested, the here/now versions of the myth constitute a distinct minority.[30]

We have already seen that in the mainstream version of the Maitreya myth the advent of the future Buddha is placed in the distant future (5,670,000,000 years from now, according to some scholastic traditions).[31] To create a here/now form of the Maitreya myth, then, it was necessary to rewrite this common tradition, shortening the time frame of Maitreya's advent dramatically to allow believers to anticipate his coming in the near future. It is not a foregone conclusion, then, that there should be *any* versions of the myth that fit into this category; what requires explanation is not why there are not more examples of the here/now form of the myth, but how and why it should have appeared at all.

With its prediction of the imminent appearance of a messianic figure, the here/now version of the Maitreya myth has sometimes taken a revolutionary (or "apocalyptic") turn. The earliest documented form of the myth, however, was used for quite the opposite purpose. A "proestablishment" interpretation of the here/now version seems to have evolved during the Northern Wei dynasty (386–534), when these proto-Mongol rulers of northern China made use of the Maitreya myth to bolster their own authority. Following in the footsteps of Fa-kuo, a late fourth-century monastic leader who had proclaimed that "the emperor is himself the *tathāgata,*"[32] later Northern Wei rulers seem to have encouraged the identification of themselves with the bodhisattva Maitreya.[33]

Such "realized eschatology" (i.e., the notion that the radical transformation of the world expected to occur at the end of time has already taken place) may initially have served to shore up the questionable authority of a non-Chinese dynasty; yet once this here/now version had become current, there was little to prevent opponents of the existing regime from reinterpreting the myth for their own purposes. In fact, aside from rather sporadic appropriations of the myth by those actually in power,[34] the here/now version of the Maitreya myth has been used predominantly by antiestablishment groups.

A number of incidences of genuinely revolutionary here/now versions of the Maitreya myth are recorded in Chinese sources. As early as the middle of the sixth century, an apocryphal sūtra (i.e., a sūtra composed in China, not translated from an Indian original) predicted an apocalyptic battle between the forces of good and evil, the descent of Maitreya, and the renewal of the world in an ideal form.[35] Such apocalyptic speculations evidently stimulated a number of antiestablishment movements; during the brief period from 610 to 613 C.E., three different people proclaimed themselves to be incarnations of Maitreya, led insurrections aimed at overthrowing the existing (Sui) dynasty, and ultimately were put down by the authorities.[36] Such Maitreyist uprisings, which continued to occur sporadically over the next several centuries, provide clear evidence of the continuing power of this here/now interpretation in the Chinese context.

It is noteworthy that these Chinese believers, despite the fervency of their messianic expectations, had no Buddhist canonical text on which to base their hopes.[37] Indeed, there is no Buddhist text known to this writer in *any* canonical collection (whether Chinese, Tibetan, Pali, or fragmentary Sanskrit) that describes Maitreya's appearance on earth as imminent. Rather, the canonical texts are unanimous in asserting that Maitreya will remain in the Tuṣita Heaven for many millions (if not billions) of years, until the time is right for his appearance on earth, generally in an already actualized golden age.

How, then, were these Chinese Buddhists able to reinterpret the Maitreya myth so drastically? It is certainly beyond the realm of a nonsinologist to attempt to answer this question; yet studies of the Chinese materials published to date have suggested at least two contributing factors:

1. The preexistence of a tradition of an imminent messianic appearance in Taoism made it easy for Chinese hearing of

Maitreya for the first time to assimilate the Buddhist myth into the Taoist context, thus converting it from a here/later version to a here/now account.[38]

2. The close link between church and state in pre-Buddhist Chinese thought (and, in particular, the concept of the "mandate of heaven") made political matters an important part of religious doctrine and supplied, under certain circumstances, a clear justification for revolutionary activity.[39]

The presence of these two factors suggests that the Maitreya myth was transformed into an ideology of rebellion in China *not* because Chinese Buddhists were simply more prone to revolution, or perhaps more oppressed, than the people who had transmitted the mythology of Maitreya to them; rather, the myth was reinterpreted in China (and in certain other settings)[40] because the ideological background was conducive to such a change.[41]

Whatever the relative weight of these factors (and perhaps of others not considered here), the religious impact of this reinterpretation of the Maitreya myth is clear: It allowed ordinary people to hope for the imminent appearance of a messianic figure and, with his appearance, for the inauguration of a new and brighter age. At the same time, this interpretation gave the members of the ruling class a potential tool for the legitimation of their own power. In sum, the here/now version (in both its revolutionary and its legitimizing forms) offered a decidedly this-worldly interpretation of the Maitreya myth.

Applications of the Typology: A Cautionary Note

Having described the four versions of the Maitreya myth, we have exhausted the logically possible combinations of the here/there and now/later variables outlined above. This does not imply, however, that we have dealt with all the possible forms in which Maitreya can appear or that we have done full justice to the ways in which he has been perceived over the centuries by his devotees. First, as already noted, we have included in our analysis only those world views in which Maitreya plays a central role. Thus we have excluded a wide variety of sources in which he makes only a cameo appearance – sources that, although legitimately omitted (we believe) from the present study, might well prove an interesting subject of analysis in another context. Second, our separation of the Maitreya myth into four distinct categories does not imply that these four versions are mutually exclusive. On the contrary, we have already noted that in certain instances two versions of the myth can easily be combined; particularly common are the conjunction of the there/now version with the there/later interpretation,[42] and the there/later with what we might call the "here/even-later" version (i.e., the expectation of an immediate meeting with Maitreya after death, to be followed by a subsequent rebirth during Maitreya's tenure on earth at a much later date).[43] It is important to note, however, that such combinations are not merely random. There is no logical (or mythological) difficulty, for instance, in combining the present experience of a meditative vision of Maitreya with the expectation of a future rebirth in his Tuṣita Heaven; nor is there any incongruity (given the Buddhist assumption of multiple rebirths) in envisioning a heavenly rebirth in Maitreya's paradise, to be followed by an earthly one under similar circumstances.

In addition to such simultaneous combinations (in which more than one interpretation of the myth can be held by a single individual at a given time), we might note that instances of sequential combinations are also known to occur. A nonactualized or failed messianic appearance, for instance, can result in the reinterpretation of a here/now version of the myth in here/later (or, more commonly, there/later) terms. Likewise the appeal of the here/later account may be gradually overtaken – due to the more immediate appeal of an imminent rebirth in the Tuṣita Heaven – by the there/later version.

In dividing the Maitreya myth into these four categories, then, our primary objective has been to point out the *differences* among various interpretations of the myth. We have tried to show, for example, that the "ascent" and "descent" (i.e., heavenly and earthly) scenarios frequently used as analytical categories in studies of Maitreya in East Asia, though perhaps representing a legitimate distinction, are not in themselves adequate categories for analysis, and that not all the "descent" versions of the myth are necessarily revolutionary in import. In so doing we have attempted to expand the number of perspectives from which the Maitreya myth can be viewed and thus to make the mythology of the future Buddha more available to interpretation both within the Buddhist context and in comparison with other religious traditions.

Maitreya in Comparative Perspective: A Buddhist "Messiah"?

An issue of particular interest to the historian of religions is the extent to which Maitreya can be described as a messianic figure. A related issue, with a slight difference in emphasis, is the degree to which the Maitreya myth can be considered apocalyptic. To deal with these questions in depth would require a considerably more extended format than that of the present chapter; nonetheless, the typology we have developed here provides a framework within which a few general remarks can be made.

We have seen that the Maitreya myth appears in four distinct versions (or better, is told with four distinct types of emphasis). Of these, three can easily be harmonized with the canonical texts. The fourth – the here/now version, in which the time frame has been radically altered to allow for Maitreya's imminent appearance – cannot. It is only this fourth version that can properly be called apocalyptic.[44] Although the other three versions may also anticipate a radical change in the conditions of life in this world, they place it so far in the future and attribute it to so gradual a process of change that this is not in any sense an apocalyptic event.

Moreover, the materials we have explored here raise some question as to whether Maitreya can properly be described as a messianic figure. If we restrict ourselves to the etymology of the word (Hebrew *māshîaḥ,* "anointed")[45] we encounter little difficulty, for Maitreya is certainly the "designated heir" of Śākyamuni in all the versions of the myth. The problem lies in our tendency, as Westerners, to assimilate the Maitreya tradition to those messianic myths we know best – those of Judaism and Christianity. Whatever the original meanings of the term "messiah" in those traditions, the word has come to signify a religious figure who not only is designated as the successor of earlier prophets, but comes to inaugurate a wholly new era as well. This, in the vast majority of cases, Maitreya *does not do.* The canonical texts are unanimous in stating that Maitreya will not personally bring about the Golden Age; rather, he will appear when that era has already (and gradually) come into being.[46] Moreover, a key attribute of the messiah in most Jewish and Christian literature – his role as ruler – is utterly alien to the canonical versions of the Maitreya myth, although it does appear in certain apocryphal texts composed in China.[47] Indeed, it is striking that most of the canonical Maitreya texts (especially the earliest ones) show a clear subordination of the political realm to the "spiritual" one. In the Sanskrit *Maitreyāvadāna,* for example, there is both explicit criticism of kings in general ("O Śakra, kings are those who do filthy things")[48] and a deliberate subordination of kingship to Buddhahood: When Maitreya attains enlightenment, the seven jewels symbolic of the unequaled power of the world-ruling emperor (*cakravartin*) will disappear, and the emperor himself will renounce his throne after hearing Maitreya preach.[49]

We must be cautious, then, in drawing analogies between Maitreya and the messianic figures of other religious traditions. Although the here/now versions of the myth may well offer material for such comparisons, not all of the other versions do,[50] and it is vital to specify what form of the myth we have in mind when doing comparative work.

Concluding Remarks: A Note on the Origins of the Myth

Earlier in this century the issue of whether Maitreya might be a foreign import into the Buddhist tradition – specifically, the question of his possible affinities with the Iranian deity Mithra – was hotly debated by

Buddhist scholars. After an initial flurry of articles, in which each extreme – that Maitreya was simply "Mithra in Buddhist garb," on the one hand, or that the two were totally unrelated, on the other – was argued,[51] the debate subsided without having been resolved. Several decades later, the issue has still not been decided. This may be attributed in part to the fact that data on the growth and evolution of Buddhism in the Iranian-speaking world are still quite limited (though Soviet archaeology is making significant progress in this regard).[52] Alternatively, the original question may have been put too simply: The religious crosscurrents in western Central Asia may have interacted in a manner far more subtle than the wholesale borrowing of prefabricated motifs, and the figure of Maitreya would be an excellent candidate for such complex influences and reactions.

Though it is still not possible to offer a decisive verdict on the question of Maitreya's alleged Iranian ancestry, we have enough data to offer some general indications as to the Buddhist milieu in which the mythology of Maitreya first arose. One point that bears directly on this question (though it has not been developed in detail in this chapter) is that only a minority of Maitreya texts exhibit any essentially Mahāyāna elements. Though a few canonical works certainly represent Mahāyāna recensions of the tradition,[53] the main lines of the story contain no such features: Those who attend Maitreya's "three assemblies" become arhats, for example, and not bodhisattvas, and there is nothing in Maitreya's teachings to mark him as the preacher of a "new vehicle." Even in the "Mahāyānized" versions of the myth, it is usually possible to remove the specifically Mahāyāna elements of the tale without altering the main thread of the story.[54] It is worth noting that the non-Mahāyāna recensions of the Maitreya myth generally provide more details of Maitreya's career (and especially of his future life on earth) than do the Mahāyāna ones, strongly suggesting that this mythology was elaborated, in the main, outside the Mahāyāna fold.

Moreover, in those Mahāyāna texts where Maitreya appears as a secondary figure, we sometimes find him in a position of clear subordination to other members of the Buddhist pantheon. In the *Lotus Sūtra,* for example, Maitreya is portrayed as asking rather unintelligent questions (which are dealt with handily by his colleague Mañjuśrī),[55] and Maitreya's slowness in perceiving the Buddha's intention to preach the *Lotus Sūtra* is linked to his previous desire for personal aggrandizement – a weakness that earned him the title "Bodhisattva Fame Seeker" in a former incarnation.[56]

Even in those Mahāyāna texts that are ostensibly devoted to Maitreya, we can sometimes detect a seemingly deliberate attempt to undercut his importance. In a few such works Maitreya is associated not with the usual Golden Age, but rather with the highly undesirable "final five hundred years of the Law" – without, however, any prediction that he will somehow overcome this "evil age." In the *Maitreya-siṃhanāda-sūtra* (The lion's roar of Maitreya), we are even told explicitly that the "desire to see the Buddha[s] of the future" is one of the faults or defilements of the Hīnayānists.[57]

The available evidence, then, strongly suggests that Maitreya's origins are to be sought in a non-Mahāyāna milieu. In this regard it may be significant that two of the most important Maitreya texts from Central Asia carry the specific sectarian label of Vaibhāṣika, that is, Sarvāstivāda, one of the most important of the non-Mahāyāna Buddhist schools.[58]

Maitreya is thus in many respects not what we might expect him to be. Though he is a bodhisattva, he is not the product of a Mahāyāna environment; though he is a future Buddha, he rarely takes the form of a world-changing messianic figure. Unlike Amitābha Buddha or any of the distinctively Mahāyāna celestial bodhisattvas,[59] Maitreya appears simply as a traditional Buddha, whose preaching reaches only those whose own karma has prepared them to hear his message. His actions are "intransitive," as it were, in contrast to the "transitive" efforts of those Buddhas and bodhisattvas who intervene directly in the cosmic process in order to save their followers.

We find ourselves, then, in the presence of a Buddha figure who resembles his predecessors in virtually every respect[60] and whose primary function is to guarantee the continuity of the Buddhist tradition by preaching the same Dharma as those who have gone before.

NOTES

My thanks are due to a number of people, in particular to Professor Masatoshi Nagatomi, who served as a sounding board for many of the ideas presented here and as a guide through the Japanese secondary literature; to the staff of the Harvard-Yenching Library, for help with Chinese romanization systems old and new; and to Dr. Larry V. Clark, who introduced me to the pleasures and pitfalls of studying Buddhist texts from Chinese Turkestan. I also thank Professor Alan Sponberg and Professor David Eckel for helpful comments on an earlier draft of this chapter.

1 See Weber's discussion of the uses and limitations of ideal types in "Religious Rejections of the World and Their Directions" (1915), reprinted in H. H. Gerth and C. Wright Mills, eds., *From Max Weber: Essays in Sociology* (New York: Oxford University Press, 1946), 323–4.

2 On Maitreya as a messianic figure in China, see Daniel L. Overmyer, *Folk Buddhist Religion: Dissenting Sects in Late Traditional China* (Cambridge, Mass.: Harvard University Press, 1976), especially chaps. 5 and 8; and Susan Naquin, *Millenarian Rebellion in China: The Eight Trigrams Uprising of 1813* (New Haven, Conn.: Yale University Press, 1976), especially pt. 1. The examples cited in this paragraph are not intended to represent the unique (or even the most common) versions of the Maitreya myth in the geographical area listed. Rather, they illustrate the variety of the Maitreya traditions and the extent of their geographical diffusion.

3 These include the Uighur (Old Turkic) *Maitrisimit,* a text translated from the dramatic work in *toχrï* (= Tokharian A?) dealing with Maitreya's life and works; the Tokharian A fragments of the same text; and the *Kšanti nom,* an Uighur confession text for Buddhist laity in which Maitreya plays a key role. Both Uighur works date from around the tenth century, whereas the Tokharian A fragments are at least two centuries older.

4 The Tibetan scholar Bu-ston (1290–1364) expressed his hopes for rebirth in Maitreya's Tuṣita Heaven at the close of book 1 of his *History of Buddhism* (Tib. *Chos-'byung*); see E. Obermiller, trans., *The Jewelry of Scripture by Bu-ston*, 2 vols. (Heidelberg: Harrasowitz, 1939), 1:89–90.

5 See Janet R. D. Goodwin, "The Worship of Miroku in Japan" (Ph.D. diss., University of California, Berkeley, 1977; University Microfilms Order no. 7812579), especially chap. 3.

6 This is true of all known canonical versions of the Maitreya myth and of most extracanonical versions as well.

7 See the section on the "here/now" version of the myth.

8 Though "myth" is often defined (e.g., by Mircea Eliade) as a "story of [divine] origins," such a definition is problematic in the Buddhist context, where the concern is less with beginnings (*saṃsāra* being regularly referred to as "beginningless") than with endings – i.e., with bringing an end to the painful round of rebirth. To avoid this difficulty, we have chosen a more general definition of myth as "a story that conveys to the believer something of fundamental significance to his or her own life." Admittedly, this is a minimalist definition (cf. Paul Tillich's definition of religion as "ultimate concern"), but it seems to work well in the present context, and we use it here for pragmatic reasons.

9 Any choice of "pivotal elements" in a myth is, of course, to some degree arbitrary. The validity of a given choice should be demonstrated by the degree to which the resulting typology clarifies the subject matter. A third polarity (suggested by David Eckel and Alan Sponberg), that of "communal" vs. "individual" orientation, is a useful analytic category, but we have not included it as a separate variable in this study because it generally overlaps (rather than expands) the categories already derived. Briefly, in considering the effects of this variable it would be important to distinguish between communal vs. individual *salvation,* on the one hand, and *practice,* on the other. All four varieties of the Maitreya myth have been expressed in communal practices; even the cultivation of *samādhi* (designed to bring about an immediate vision of Maitreya) can be practiced by a group. The concept of communal *salvation,* however, is far less common. In fact, it is essentially coterminous with a subgroup of the here/now category: the apocalyptic interpretation (in the sense used below, note 44) of the myth. The emphasis on the redemption of believers as a group is, of course, not limited to Buddhist apocalyptic thinking, but is found in a variety of millenarian movements.

10 Of particular interest are the numerous appearances of Maitreya in the Central Asian Manichaean literature. See, for example, the references to Maitreya (whose name appears variously as *mytrq, mytrg, mytr'gr,* and *mytr*) in W. Henning, *Ein manichäisches Bet- und Beichtbuch* (= *Abhandlungen der Preussischen Akademie der*

Wissenschaften, Phil.-Hist. Klasse, no. 10 [1936]), p. 19, lines 44–5, 57; p. 20, l. 90; p. 21, l. 98; and p. 45, l. 20.

11 On the Tuṣita Heaven and its role in Maitreyist mythology see Paul Demiéville, "Le *Yogācārabhūmi* de Saṅgharakṣa," *Bulletin de l'Ecole Française d'Extrême-Orient,* 44 (1954): 376–7.

12 The earliest texts in which Maitreya appears are often difficult to classify within the framework we have chosen, since Maitreya has not yet become a central object of concern. Such works include the Pali *Cakkavattisīhanāda-sutta,* in which the story of Maitreya is given in capsule form; the Sanskrit *Maitreyāvadāna,* in which the story is developed in more detail but still stops short of offering the reader or listener the hope of a personal encounter with Maitreya; and according to some writers (e.g., Etienne Lamotte, *Histoire du bouddhisme indien* [Louvain: Institut Orientaliste, 1958; rpt. 1967], 775–6), the Pali *Suttanipāta* (chap. 5, vv. 976–1149), in which two disciples of the Buddha named Ajita and Metteyya are mentioned. In the latter text there is, however, no mention of Metteyya's status as future Buddha, and Ajita (subsequently used as an epithet of Maitreya) is simply the name of one of his fellow disciples.

13 See, for example, the Tibetan *Maitreya-vyākaraṇa* (Lhasa no. 350), which closes with the words "Donc ayez un esprit de piété pour Cākyamuni, ce Vainqueur! et alors vous verrez Maitreya le parfait Bouddha, le meilleur de bipèdes" (v. 100; translated in S. Lévi, "Maitreya le consolateur," in *Mélanges R. Linnossier* [Paris: Leroux, 1932], 2:397). Similarly, Kumārajīva's translation of the *Mi le hsia sheng ching* (Taisho no. 453) closes with the following exhortation: "Ihr sollt fliessig sein, reinen Geist bewahren und alle *kuśala-mūla's* pflanzen, dann werdet ihr ohne Zweifel (dereinst) die Leuchte der Welt, den Buddha Maitreya, zu Gesichte bekommen" (l. 76; from the German paraphrase by Watanabe, in E. Leumann, *Das Zukunftsideal der Buddhisten* [Strasbourg: Trubner, 1919], 236). Both the Pali *Anāgatavaṃsa* and the Maitreya chapter of the Khotanese *Book of Zambasta* stress the importance of maintaining the existing monastic order. The former states that all beings will see Maitreya when he appears on earth *except* those who "create a schism in the sangha, perform the five crimes constituting 'proximate karma' [*anantariya*], cherish wholly heretical views, and slander the noble disciples" (English translation by H. C. Warren, *Buddhism in Translations* [New York, Atheneum, 1968], 485–6). The *Book of Zambasta* goes into greater detail, quoting Śākyamuni as follows: "There will be no deliverance only for those who have committed an *anantariya:* [who] have treated as unauthoritative the Buddha-Law, the Mahāyāna; [who] have spoken of faults of the Āryas: that he has been born for the sake of non-birth; have taken away, removed, plundered that given to the Bhikṣusaṅgha; have caused obstruction to *pravrajyā;* who have accepted one holding a false view; have struck, destroyed those wearing red robes on account of me; have harmed the *śramaṇya* of the nuns; who has as domestic woman harmed the *śramaṇya* of the monks, which was not harmed before. These will not see the Buddha Maitreya" (chap. 22, vv. 306–11; English translation in R. E. Emmerick, *The Book of Zambasta* [New York: Oxford University Press, 1968], 337). Finally, the concern with maintaining the existing order is explicitly extended to the

government in the Uighur confession text *Kšanti nom,* where those making the confession are made to say, "If we have disturbed the realm and [its] law, if we have joined in national disturbances, if I [*sic*] have thought wrong thoughts toward the holy, blessed nobles; further, if we have aroused the cities and countries and made them into two factions, if we have gone from city to city, from country to country, [and] from realm to realm as a spy and messenger; now we repent and acknowledge all [our sins]" [text E, ll. 17–22; English translation in Jan Nattier, "The *Kšanti nom:* An Uighur Buddhist Confession Text for Laity," *Journal of Turkish Studies* (forthcoming)]. In the concluding section of the text, in which the merit accrued from having the confession copied can be transferred to others, the rulers are frequently included in the list of recipients (Nattier, *Kšanti nom,* 44).

14 Lamotte (*Histoire,* 210–22) cites decline-of-the-Dharma traditions from a number of sources, representing the Sarvāstivāda, Theravāda, Mahīśāsaka, Dharmaguptaka, and Haimavata schools as well as Mahāyāna traditions. Not all of these include decline *and* rise components; indeed, it is a peculiar feature of Buddhist apocalyptic literature that it includes texts that speak *only* of decline, with no promise of subsequent redemption (see, for example, the quotations from the *Candragarbhaparipṛcchā* in Bu-ston's *Chos-'byung* in Obermiller, trans., *Bu-ston,* 2:170–7).

15 Several Maitreya texts refer explicitly to a period of decline that must precede Maitreya's advent. The *Anāgatavaṃsa* (Warren, *Buddhism in Translations,* 482–5) and its Tibetan translations (Lhasa nos. 36, 349) describe in detail the decline of the world that culminates in the "Age of Fighting." The Maitreya chapter in the Khotanese *Book of Zambasta* refers in passing to a period of decline (see Emmerick, *Zambasta,* 305), as does I-ching's *Mi le hsia sheng cheng fo ching* (Taishō no. 455; see Watanabe's German paraphrase in Leumann, *Das Zukunftsideal,* 271).

It is interesting that there is an apparent conflict between the decline-and-rise theory and the tradition of the *bhadrakalpa* (good eon), according to which Maitreya is the fifth of five (or in later, more developed traditions, the fifth of one thousand) Buddhas who are to appear in this unusually fortunate age. It is, of course, theoretically possible to locate a comparatively brief "evil age" within an overarching "good eon"; yet the two traditions do not occur together in any text examined by this writer. The fact that the thrust of the *bhadrakalpa* motif is generally positive and optimistic, whereas the decline-and-rise scenario (in which a period of warfare and disease must precede the arrival of the Golden Age) serves quite the opposite purpose, suggests that the two motifs may have evolved in different contexts, embodying quite distinct senses of history.

16 The standard Hindu theory of history is even more pessimistic: The universe oscillates in the sense that it is periodically created (or, better, manifested) and destroyed, but there is no longer an evolutionary phase. Rather, the world is at its peak when it comes into existence and goes through a devolutionary process until, when history has reached its nadir, it is finally destroyed.

17 In Central Asian texts (particularly those Uighur texts from the Turfan region cited in note 3) Maitreya is explicitly involved in the process of the confession and expiation of sins. The influence of the Manichaean confession formulas on the

development of the Buddhist confession of sins in Central Asia is the subject of a work in progress by this writer; see also the discussion by Jes P. Asmussen (who, however, takes the opposite view, arguing that it was the Buddhist confessions that led to the development of the Manichaean ones) in his *X^u āstvānīft: Studies in Manichaeism* (Copenhagen: Prostant Apud Munksgaard, 1965), 234.

18 Though the description of Maitreya's Tuṣita Heaven as a "pure land" has become commonplace in East Asian (particularly Japanese) scholarship, this label is actually a misnomer. As part of the *kāmadhātu*, the lowest of the three spheres of this world system, Tuṣita is still subject to many of the impurities that have been removed from Amitābha's Sukhāvatī. Thus Tuṣita is technically not a "pure land," while unlike Sukhāvatī it *is* part of this world system – a point used for polemical purposes by both sides in the medieval Chinese debates on the relative merits of the two heavens (see Chapter 4, this volume).

19 On the influence of Amidist beliefs on the development of the there/later form of the Maitreyist myth see N. Péri, review of Matsumoto Bunzaburō's *Miroku jōdo ron*, in *Bulletin de l'Ecole Française d'Extrême-Orient*, 11 (1911): 447. This theory has been contested, however, by P. Demiéville; see his "Le *Yogācārabhūmi*" (cited in note 11).

20 On the eventual absorption of there/later Maitreyism by Amidist (Pure Land) beliefs, see Joseph M. Kitagawa, "The Career of Maitreya, With Special Reference to Japan," *History of Religions*, 21, no. 2 (1981): 121, and Kenneth Ch'en, *Buddhism in China: A Historical Survey* (Princeton, N. J.: Princeton Univerity Press, 1964), 405.

21 On rebirth in the Tuṣita Heaven followed by a later rebirth in Maitreya's presence on earth, see Goodwin, "The Worship of Miroku," 31.

22 Goodwin (ibid., 11) has noted that the importance of merit making was never lost in Maitreya-centered Buddhism in Japan, in contrast to the emphasis on "other-power" that eventually developed in the Pure Land cult of Amitābha.

23 Demiéville, "Le *Yogācārabhūmi*," 377 and n. 1.

24 Ibid., 382.

25 There have been differences of opinion in Buddhist historical sources themselves as to whether a given encounter with Maitreya constituted an "ascent" by the believer or a "descent" by Maitreya. Demiéville ("Le *Yogācārabhūmi*," 381) notes, for example, that Chinese sources sometimes describe Asaṅga's receipt of the *Yogācārabhūmi* in the former terms and sometimes in the latter.

26 Specifically, Maitreya in his earthly appearances of the there/now variety seems to restrict his activities to conveying doctrinal information to his devotee. To the extent that he has any effect at all on human history, he does so only through the intermediary of the human recipient of this vision.

27 Among those granted a vision of the Tuṣita Heaven without, apparently, having made any effort to receive it are a king of Ceylon who attained a vision of the Tuṣita on his deathbed (Demiéville, "Le *Yogācārabhūmi*," 383), a king of Khotan transported to the Tuṣita to see Maitreya via an arhat's magical powers (R. E. Emmerick, *Tibetan Texts Concerning Khotan* [New York: Oxford University Press, 1967], 53–5), and a sculptor taken up to the Tuṣita for a firsthand look at the

subject of his art (see James Legge, trans., *A Record of Buddhistic Kingdoms* [Oxford: Clarendon Press, 1886], 24–5).

28 Demiéville, "Le *Yogācārabhūmi*," 379–80.

29 Those "religious virtuosi" who pursued an immediate vision of Maitreya sometimes combined this there/now version of the myth with another (canonically sanctioned) version. See, for example, the cases of Tao-an (E. Zürcher, *The Buddhist Conquest of China,* Leiden: Brill, 1959, 194–5) and Hsüan-tsang (N. Péri, review of Matsumoto, p. 447 and n. 2), both of whom combined their visionary experiences with aspirations to be reborn in the Tuṣita Heaven.

30 See Chapter 5, this volume. Though the Japanese inherited their Buddhism (via a Korean intermediary) from the Chinese, the here/now interpretation seems to have occurred only sporadically – and even then, more implicitly than explicitly – in Japan. See Goodwin, "Worship of Miroku," 198–201.

31 See William E. Soothill, *A Dictionary of Chinese Buddhist Terms* (London, 1937; rpt. Delhi: Motilal Banarsidass, 1977), 456b.

32 Ch'en, *Buddhism in China,* 146.

33 Evidence for this interpretation is presented in Satō Chisui, "The Character of Yün-kang Buddhism," *Tōyō Bunkō: Memoirs of the Research Department,* 6 (1978): 39–83.

34 Other examples of the use of the here/now Maitreya myth for the legitimation of existing political structures include the claim of Empress Wu (r. 683–705) to be the bodhisattva Maitreya (see Antonino Forte, *Political Propaganda and Ideology in China at the End of the Seventh Century* [Naples: Istituto Universitario Orientale, 1976], especially chap. 3), the similar (but soon abandoned) claims of the founder of the Ming dynasty (Ch'en, *Buddhism in China,* 434–5), and the tradition that Maitreya repeatedly took on incarnations among the kings of Khotan (see Emmerick, *Tibetan Texts,* 25, 29). Finally, there is a tradition that Maitreya was considered to be the "patron saint" of Agni, one of the cities along the northern Silk Route through Chinese Turkestan (and, incidentally, the home of "Tokharian A," the language of the Maitreyist fragments cited in note 3); see Heinrich Lüders, "Weitere Beiträge zur Geschichte und Geographie von Ostturkestan," in *Sitzungsberichte des Preussischen Akademie der Wissenschaften* (Phil.-Hist. Klasse), 1930, pt. 1, 28–31. On the predominance of the revolutionary interpretation of the here/now Maitreya myth in China, see the works by Overmyer and Naquin cited in note 2.

35 See E. Zürcher, "Prince Moonlight: Messianism and Eschatology in Early Medieval Chinese Buddhism," *T'oung Pao,* 68 (1982): 35 and n. 64.

36 See Overmyer, *Folk Buddhist Religion,* 82–3.

37 Overmyer (*Folk Buddhist Religion,* 150) notes that there is no evidence that any folk Buddhist group used canonical Maitreya scriptures as an authority.

38 On pre-Buddhist messianic traditions in China see Anna K. Seidel, "The Image of the Perfect Ruler in Early Taoist Messianism: Lao-tzu and Li Hung," *History of Religions,* 9, nos. 2 and 3 (1969/1970): 216–47. The links between these motifs and later Chinese Buddhist apocalyptic literature are discussed in Zürcher, "Prince Moonlight."

39 On the concept of "mandate of heaven" see Charles O. Hucker, *China's Imperial Past: An Introduction to Chinese History and Culture* (Stanford, Calif.: Stanford University Press, 1975), 54–5; and Herrlee G. Creel, *The Origins of Statecraft in China,* vol. 1: *The Western Chou Empire* (University of Chicago Press, 1970).

40 The here/now form of the Maitreya myth has also appeared in Burma (E. Sarkisyanz, *Buddhist Backgrounds of the Burmese Revolution* [The Hague: Nijhoff, 1965]), in Vietnam (Hue-Tam Ho Tai, *Millenarianism and Peasant Politics in Vietnam* [Harvard East Asian Series 99] [Cambridge, Mass.: Harvard University Press, 1983]), and in Thailand (Stanley Tambiah, *The Buddhist Saints of the Forest and the Cult of Amulets: A Study in Charisma* [Cambridge University Press, 1984]). In the Vietnamese case Chinese influence was certainly a contributing factor; in Burma, protomessianic ideas may have been derived from Chinese, Hindu, or pre-Buddhist traditions. A comparative study of Chinese and Southeast Asian apocalyptic movements would make a substantial contribution to our understanding of the dynamics of Maitreyist messianism.

41 A problem that has plagued scholars attempting the sociological analysis of millenarian movements is that oppression or deprivation is not, in itself, sufficient to bring about popular revolt. Far less is it enough to lead to a religious rebellion – that is, to the creation of apocalyptic myths predicting the downfall of the oppressor or to the actualization of such mythology via revolutionary activity. For these to happen, other contributing factors seem to be required: (1) For the creation of apocalyptic mythology to take place, the political system must be invested with religious significance; that is, it must be seen as a key element in the cosmic structure, not as a trifling creation of mere humans. When the political structure is thus sacralized, its overthrow or perversion by those not adhering to the proper religiopolitical traditions will then be seen not merely as an injustice or a breach of tradition, but as an affront to the cosmic order, calling for a religious response. When concrete action (i.e., the removal of the usurper or other offender) is impossible, one response is the creation of apocalyptic mythology. (2) For a millenarian rebellion to take place, an additional factor must be present: The would-be rebels must believe that their enterprise is divinely sanctioned, and this may (but need not) include the notion that a messianic figure has already appeared, or is about to appear, to act as leader. These ideas are generally supplied by a preexisting apocalyptic mythology; if such a tradition is present, the experience of oppression or deprivation may then be sufficient to lead to millenarian revolt.

It is interesting that the creation of apocalyptic mythology and its actualization through popular rebellion are often entirely separate phenomena, occurring at different times and supported by different social strata. Apocalyptic mythology is often generated by those recently expelled from power in a religiously based political system; examples can be found in ancient Israel (Paul D. Hanson, *The Dawn of Apocalyptic* [Philadelphia: Fortress Press, 1975]), Iran (Samuel K. Eddy, *The King is Dead* [Lincoln: University of Nebraska Press, 1961]), and pre-Buddhist China (Seidel, "Image of the Perfect Ruler"). Under these circumstances, such mythology serves to reinforce the threatened identity of those recently ousted from power, while at the same time justifying their reluctance to take concrete (and probably suicidal) political action. The result is the development of what might be called "passive apocalyptic" – an outlook that anticipates the overthrow of the illegitimate religiopolitical order but expects the initiative for such action to come from divine power(s) without any human assistance. It is this outlook that is described by Paul Hanson in his well-known observation that "[Hebrew] prophetic eschatology is transformed into apocalyptic at the point where the task of translating the cosmic vision into the categories of mundane reality is abdicated" (*Interpretation,* 25 [1971]: 454).

There is, however, another type of apocalyptic thinking that is not at all passive. According to this outlook, what is called for is not the patient anticipation of divine intervention, but rather an active partnership with these cosmic forces, that is, direct intervention in the process of history on the part of the believers to help bring about the millennium. It is this type of apocalyptic that can serve as the stimulus for concrete political action, often of a revolutionary, antiestablishment type. Such "active apocalyptic" is most frequently the result of the interaction between millenarian expectations, originally engendered by an ousted elite, and severe oppression or deprivation suffered by the lower strata of society. Once created, apocalyptic mythology thus takes on a life of its own, and under certain circumstances can stimulate revolutionary activity that its originators would have considered foolhardy.

"Active" and "passive" apocalyptic, thus seen, represent two distinct phenomena that are best understood if we treat them separately (and in addition trace their periodic interactions with one another). In the present context, we can sharpen our insight into both the creation of Maitreyist mythology and its subsequent impact by incorporating this distinction into our analysis.

42 For examples see note 29.

43 See Chapter 4, this volume. For an example of this combination of interpretations in Japan see Goodwin, "The Worship of Miroku," 31.

44 By "apocalyptic" we mean a world view that anticipates the radical overturning of the present religiopolitical order as a result of action by forces operating on a cosmic (i.e., transhuman) level. The term "apocalypse" comes from the Greek title of the New Testament book of Revelation (ἀποκάλυψις), but it has been applied by extension to any system of thought resembling the one found in that book. A variety of definitions of "apocalyptic" are in current use; see, for example, those of D. S. Russell, according to whom apocalyptic thought (or, more precisely, apocalyptic literature) includes such features as pessimism, dualistic thinking, use of numerological calculations, pseudonymity of authorship, "pseudo-ecstasy" as source of inspiration, and esoteric forms of expression (*Method and Message of Jewish Apocalyptic* [Philadelphia: Westminster Press, 1964], 105), and of Paul Hanson, who defines "apocalypticism" (*Interpreter's Dictionary of the Bible,* suppl. vol. [Nashville, Tenn.: Abingdon Press, 1976], 28) as "a system of thought produced by visionary movements; builds upon a specific eschatological perspective in generating a symbolic universe opposed to that of the dominant society."

45 For a discussion of the origins and development of messianic terminology in the Hebrew scriptures, see Raphael Patai, *The Messiah Texts* (New York: Avon,

1979), xxi–xxiv. A useful interpretive essay is Gershom Scholem's "Toward an Understanding of the Messianic Idea in Judaism," in his *The Messianic Idea in Judaism and Other Essays on Jewish Spirituality* (New York: Schocken, 1971; rpt. 1978). A challenge to Scholem's approach and a plea for recognition of the diversity of messianic thinking within the Jewish tradition are made by Jacob Neusner in "Messianic Themes in Formative Judaism," *Journal of the American Academy of Religion,* 52, no. 2 (1984): 357–74.

46 Compare the distinction in Christian beliefs between "premillennial" and "postmillennial" views. The former refers to the idea that Christ will return before the establishment of the millennium (the Christian equivalent of the Buddhist Golden Age) and will personally help to establish it, while the latter view anticipates the return of Christ only *after* the millennium has come into being. The premillennial view is generally the more radical of the two, anticipating a sharp break between the present and future to be initiated by the messiah figure himself; the postmillennial view, by contrast, lends itself to a gradualist (evolutionary) interpretation. The observation of George Shepperson that "pre- and post-millennialism correspond, in the secular sphere, to the revolutionary and reformist attitudes to social change" (in Sylvia Thrupp, ed., *Millennial Dreams in Action* [New York: Schocken, 1970], 45) is in general valid; yet two qualifications should be mentioned.

First, the postmillennial view will express itself in an activist and relatively optimistic outlook (Shepperson's "reformist attitude") only if its ideological context includes the idea that human actions can contribute to the approach of the millennium and if this idea is accompanied by the assumption that history is evolving in an "upward" direction. If (as in the canonical Maitreya texts discussed above) an intervening decline cycle is expected to precede the millennium, a reformist attitude will hardly be encouraged, since during the decline phase of the cycle any change must necessarily constitute "regress" rather than progress. The Maitreyist case would suggest that a postmillennial view accompanied by the expectation of such an intervening decline is likely to lead to an internalization of the reformist spirit, that is, to an emphasis on personal ethics and morality, as we have seen in the Maitreyist stress on "good works."

Second, although the premillennial view may indeed be revolutionary under certain circumstances, this is by no means always the case (if by "revolutionary" we mean an active attempt to bring down the existing power structure). Indeed, the premillennial view appears in two quite distinct forms: (1) an "anticipatory" version, in which the focus is on the future advent of a messianic figure, and (2) an "actualized" version, in which the messiah is thought already to have appeared. It is the latter case that is typically revolutionary, with its believers working to replace the existing order by a totally new one under the leadership of a messianic figure. In the anticipatory version, by contrast, a genuinely revolutionary impulse is less likely to arise; in many cases, its believers respond to the messianic hope by taking a passive stance, emphasizing a withdrawal of allegiance from the established order in expectation of its eventual overthrow or transcendence by a messianic figure.

47 Maitreya is described as becoming "king of the territory of Han" in the apocryphal *Cheng ming ching*; see Zürcher, "Prince Moonlight," 38–9.

48 "Maitreyāvadāna" in P. L. Vaidya, ed., *Divyāvadāna* (Darbhanga: Mithila Institute, 1959) 35, l. 11.

49 Ibid., 37, ll. 13–14.

50 The here/later version of the Maitreyist myth, though the most common in the early canonical sources, is the most difficult to find parallels to in non-Indian traditions because its internal logic requires the concept of rebirth. (No doubt some religious traditions that do not assume rebirth as a matter of course have evolved similar traditions by making the advent of the messianic figure an "exceptional case" that will allow his or her followers to appear on earth even though they have already died.) The there/now version is, of course, common to all mystical traditions (though the visionary communion takes place more frequently with a deity than with a messianic figure who has not yet appeared on earth), and the there/later version can exist in any tradition that stresses a heavenly afterlife.

51 Maitreya's Iranian origins were advocated by J. Przyluski, "La croyance au Messie dans l'Inde et dans l'Iran," *Revue de l'Histoire des Religions,* 100 (1929): 1–12, and "Un dieu iranien dans l'Inde," *Rocznik Orientalistyczny,* 7 (1931): 1–9. This view is supported by S. Lévi, "Maitreya le Consolateur," in *Mélanges R. Linossier,* 2 (Paris, 1932): 360, whereas E. Abegg opposes it in his *Der Messiasglaube in Indien und Iran* (Berlin, 1928).

52 Useful summaries of this research are given in Grégoire Frumkin, *Archaeology in Soviet Central Asia* (*Handbuch der Orientalistik,* 7 Abt., 3 Bd., 1 Abschn.; Leiden: Brill, 1970), and B. A. Litvinsky, "Outline History of Buddhism in Central Asia," in B. Gafurov et al., eds. *Kushan Studies in U.S.S.R.* (Calcutta: R. D. Press, 1970), 53–132. Updates of ongoing work can be found in *Sovetskaya arkheologiya* and in the more specialized journals published by the individual Soviet republics in this region.

53 Examples of Mahāyānist recensions include the *Kuan mi le pu sa shang sheng dou shuai t'ian jing* (Taishō no. 452) and its Tibetan translation (Lhasa no. 200), the Maitreya chapter of the Khotanese *Book of Zambasta,* and the Chinese and Tibetan *Nandimitrāvadāna* (see note 54). Of these only the first has been rewritten in such a way that it is now an *essentially* Mahāyānist work. The non-Mahāyāna character of another Maitreya text, the Sanskrit (and Tibetan) *Maitreya-vyākaraṇa,* has been pointed out by Gregory Schopen in "Hīnayāna Texts in a 14th Century Persian Chronicle," *Central Asiatic Journal,* 26 (1982): 225–35.

54 The *Nandimitrāvadāna* (Taishō no. 2030; Peking no. 5647) provides an especially interesting example of the Mahāyānization of an essentially non-Mahāyāna text. Though this work was first examined by Western scholars (S. Lévi and F. Chavannes, *Journal Asiatique,* 2 [1916]: 139–77) for its listing of the divisions of a Mahāyāna canon, it is clear that this portion was a late addition to an essentially non-Mahāyāna text. The main lines of the narrative (focused on the role of the "16 Arhats" in protecting the Buddhist Dharma and on the eventual appearance of Maitreya) contain no Mahāyāna features whatsoever, and those that are found in

subplots (e.g., the listing of the Mahāyāna canon) are clearly secondary and could easily be removed without disturbing the flow of the story.

55 Leon Hurvitz, *Scripture of the Lotus Blossom of the Fine Dharma* (New York: Columbia University Press, 1976), chap. 1, pp. 4–21. Again Maitreya appears as the doubtful and confused questioner in chap. 25, pp. 228–36.

56 Ibid., 15, 20.

57 See the *Ārya-maitreya-mahāsiṃhanāda-nāma-mahāyāna-sūtra* (Tib. *'Phags-pa byams-pa'i seng-ge'i sgra chen-po zhes-bya-ba theg-pa chen-po'i mdo*), Lhasa no. 67 (vol. 39 [ca]), 160B:3–5, 160B:7–161A:2.

58 Texts with this attribution include the Agnean ("Tokharian A") *Maitreyasamiti* and its Uighur counterpart, the *Maitrisimit*. It is perhaps significant that the branch of the Mahāyāna with which Maitreya is most closely associated – the Yogācāra school – is closely linked to the Vaibhāṣika tradition of scriptural commentary.

59 On the distinction between earthly and celestial bodhisattvas see the article by D. Snellgrove, "Celestial Buddhas and Bodhisattvas," in Mercea Eliade, ed., *The Encyclopedia of Religion*, vol. 3 (New York: Macmillan, 1987), 133–44.

60 The primary features that distinguish Maitreya from earlier historical Buddhas (i.e., Buddhas who form part of a continuous earthly lineage, in contrast to primarily celestial Buddhas such as Amitābha) are the following: (1) Maitreya is to appear during the time of a world-ruling king (*cakravartin*), unlike Śākyamuni, who taught during a period of many petty kingdoms in northern India. (2) Maitreya is to be welcomed by a disciple from Śākyamuni's time, Kāśyapa, who either will remain in a state of suspended animation (according to most Maitreya texts) or will actually die but be revived when Maitreya appears (according to the *Divyāvadāna*) and will convey to Maitreya the robe that is the symbol of the lineage of his predecessors. Kāśyapa's remains (or, alternatively, his hibernating body) remain hidden in Mt. Kukkuṭapāda until the time of Maitreya's advent. (3) Unlike Śākyamuni, who was born and lived during an age of petty warfare among competing kings, Maitreya will teach during a golden age in which human life will have reached its highest peak of perfection. (4) Whereas Śākyamuni (and his predecessors) came from a *kṣatriya* (warrior) lineage, Maitreya will be born to a *brahman* (priestly) class.

It is intriguing that all of these features (except perhaps the last) have analogies in Iranian apocalyptic literature. The idea that the prophet's pathway is paved by the king (the so-called patron-priest motif) dates back to Zoroaster himself, and the idea of a future golden age is likewise a common feature of his literature (though certainly not its exclusive possession). Most striking, however, is the concept of the "hidden disciple" who awaits, in a state of apparent death, the advent of the savior. In Zoroastrian literature the figure is *Kərəšaspa* (the resemblance of this name to that of Kāśyapa was already noted by Przyluski in *La légende de l'empereur Açoka* [Paris: Geuthner, 1923], 178–9), who awaits the advent of the Iranian savior figure Saošyant in a state of suspended animation (see Geo Widengren, *Les religions de l'Iran* [Paris: Payot, 1968], 68 and n. 1). Again, these features make sense in an Iranian religious context but are difficult to account for in the Buddhist one.

Finally, it is worth noting that a prototype of Maitreya's "three assemblies" (at which 96, 94, and 92 *koṭis* of listeners, respectively, are said to attain arhatship) can be found in the Pali literature. According to the *Mahāpadāna-sutta* (sutta no. 14 of the *Dīgha-nikāya;* English translation in T. W. Rhys Davids and C. A. F. Rhys Davids, trans. *Dialogues of the Buddha,* pt. 2 [New York: Oxford University Press, 1910], 4–41; = *Sacred Books of the Buddhists,* vol. 3), the first three of the "seven Buddhas of the past" (Vipassi, Sikhi, Vessabhu) – though not, interestingly, the four previous Buddhas of this *bhaddakappa* (Kakusandha, Koṇāgamana, Kassapa, and Gotama) – each held "three assemblies" at which successively decreasing numbers of listeners attained arhatship (for details see Rhys Davids and Rhys Davids, ibid., 6–7).

II

The Core Tradition and Its Subsequent Variation

Maitreya in South Asia

Introduction

ALAN SPONBERG

When did the legend of Maitreya emerge in early Buddhism, and what were the iconographic and mythic motifs originally associated with this figure? Although most of the chapters in this volume deal with later developments of the Maitreya myth, especially those that occurred in East Asia, we must first look at the South Asian origins of the legend, at the core tradition that provided the basic themes so richly elaborated in the subsequent appropriation of Buddhism in Central, East, and Southeast Asia. The origins of the Maitreya legend remain frustratingly obscure, however. Was the idea of a future Buddha an independent innovation of the early Buddhists, one going perhaps as far back as Gautama himself? Or was it a later Buddhist incorporation of the messianic aspirations so prominent among the peoples of India's northwestern frontier? At what point was Maitreya identified as the successor to Gautama, the next Buddha for this world? And why was some figure more prominent in the Buddha's discourses or among his immediate followers not designated to play this important role? The names and epithets of Maitreya and the Persian cult figure Mithra (Mitra) certainly appear to be closely related, a fact that has long suggested some derivative influence. But in which direction did the influence flow: from Iran to India, or vice versa, or in both directions interactively?

Such questions regarding Maitreya's origins have been the subject of much speculation and controversy, especially in the European scholarship of the first half of this century. Although most of the early modern scholarship sought to derive the Maitreya legend from sources outside the Gangetic homeland of Buddhism, the question of external influence versus indigenous origins was never conclusively resolved, and more recent studies have continued to push the development of the Maitreya legend farther back into the earliest periods of Buddhism in India. Certainly the pioneering work of Matsumoto Bunzaburō, Sylvain Lévi, Jean Przyluski, Jean Filliozat, and others did a great deal to identify the important textual sources and religious themes associated with the multivalent figure of Maitreya, drawing attention at the same time to the pervasive influence his legend has had on various Asian cultures. Even so, as valuable as that early work remains, there remains much to be done before a clear picture of Maitreya in early Indian Buddhism will begin to emerge.

Addressing this need for a more detailed picture of Maitreya in the early sources, Padmanabh Jaini provides in Chapter 3 a survey of the principal references to Maitreya in the surviving South and Southeast Asian Buddhist literature. While noting a significant, though passing reference to Maitreya as a future Buddha in the *Dīgha-nikāya*, Jaini focuses his inquiry on the *Mahāvastu*, a canonical work of the Mahāsāṅghikas compiled over a period stretching from the second century B.C.E. through the third or fourth century C.E., arguing that here is formulated for the first time a list of future Buddhas with Maitreya at the head as the immediate successor to Śākyamuni. For Maitreya to have attained this preeminent position, however, he must have already had a well-developed hagiography, one that would have allowed him to be easily integrated into the bodhisattva path of four stages that plays such a prominent role in the *Mahāvastu*. Jaini's strategy is to use that influential four-stage model as a framework for analyzing the scattered references to Maitreya's bodhisattva career found in a number of Sanskrit, Pali, and Khotanese sources.

Based as it is on such a variety of sources, the reconstruction of Maitreya's career that Jaini assembles is purely heuristic, of course, and could never have been fully elaborated in any one line of the tradition. Even so, this strategy proves to be highly effective in that it provides a useful device for analyzing variation in the available accounts in light of an influential model current within Buddhist circles of the time. One example of the effectiveness of this device can be seen in the manner in which it draws our attention to significant omissions in the Maitreya legend, elements that would have been expected by Buddhists of the time, elements that would have been expected of one attaining the role of Gautama's successor. The absence of any canonical account of the occasion when Maitreya receives anointment (*abhiṣeka*) from Gautama as the next Buddha is one prominent example. Jaini's highly original approach thus helps us understand how the early Buddhists would have incorporated the emerging interest in Maitreya into their broader picture of Buddhist cosmology and practice, and it also helps us note anomalies in the tradition that might not be immediately apparent to our modern eyes.

After carefully surveying a number of scriptural sources, Jaini concludes that Maitreya must already have been well established as the future Buddha in the pre-Mahāyāna schools. But that raises an important question: Which group of Buddhists was most responsible for this significant development? Considering the early Theravādins as unlikely candidates despite the reference to Maitreya in the *Dīgha-nikāya*, Jaini feels that the elaboration of a Maitreya cult was most likely an innovation of the Mahāsāṅghikas, the school responsible for a number of proto-Mahāyāna ideas. Jaini does point out, however, that the depiction of Maitreya in the *Mahāvastu* is notably free of the supernatural (*lokottara*) qualities that otherwise characterize the distinctive Mahāsāṅghika notion of Buddhahood, a fact that, taken along with the *Dīghanikāya* reference (and its parallel occurrence in the Chinese translation of the *Dīrghāgama*), strongly suggests that the Mahāsāṅghikas had earlier sources for their Maitreya cult, sources that one would think must predate the first great schism of the Buddhist Sangha at the Council of Pāṭaliputra in the fourth century B.C.E. Whatever the original source of the notion of Maitreya as the next Buddha, the idea was adopted by both the most conservative Theravādins and the authors of the Mahāyāna Sūtras, a fact that Jaini believes further increases the likelihood that it was the Mahāsāṅghikas who served as the primary conduit for introducing and developing the Maitreya cult. Although the specific origins of the Maitreya legend remain obscure, it is certain, Jaini feels, that the core idea of a future Buddha need not be attributed to foreign influence. This final conclusion he draws after noting parallel notions among the early Jains and Ājīvakas in order to show that the anticipation of future Jinas or Tīrthaṅkaras appears to have been a long-standing tradition in India, one already popular at the time of Gautama himself.

The picture that emerges from this chapter, then, is one of an ancient and fully indigenous Buddhist tradition of a future Buddha, or rather of future Buddhas, one of whom was identified quite early as Maitreya, a figure who gained increasing importance and veneration in all schools of Indian Buddhism. The Mahāsāṅghikas appear to have been most responsible for developing this tradition, their innovations being subsequently fed back into the archaic tradition present in all the schools. While asserting the South Asian Buddhist origins of the future Buddha concept, we still must not overlook the possibility that the early Buddhists developed their Maitreya tradition in response to the growing interest in Middle Eastern messianic cults on the northwestern frontier. Thus the case for seeing the future Buddha theme as an independent Indian Buddhist innovation still leaves open the possibility of an interactive influence in the subsequent development of the tradition.

3

Stages in the Bodhisattva Career of the Tathāgata Maitreya

PADMANABH S. JAINI

Introduction

Although considerable differences exist in Buddhist thought concerning the nature of a Buddha and the number of bodhisattvas for whom a prophecy has been made concerning future Buddhahood, Buddhists are unanimous in declaring the bodhisattva Maitreya to be the next Tathāgata,[1] the immediate successor to the Buddha Śākyamuni. One would expect such an heir apparent to have been a historical person closely associated with the Buddha, someone like the elder (*thera*) Ānanda (before he disqualified himself by becoming an arhat!), the chief attendant of the Teacher during his lifetime and transmitter of his sermons after his *parinirvāṇa*. Or one would suppose him to have been a contemporary king emulating the noble example of the bodhisattva Prince Vessantara, who could be singled out by Gautama publicly for such an honor. Maitreya, at least in the Theravāda canon, is neither, and hence there has lingered the suspicion that this legendary figure was added to the earlier genealogy of the Buddhas under the influence of a foreign cult of the Messiah (e.g., the Zoroastrian Saošyant or the Persian-Greek Mithras Invictus).[2] Whatever the source of the cult of Maitreya, it is certain that his unanimous elevation to the position of successor to Śākyamuni, over the heads of other equally legendary but more powerful bodhisattvas (e.g., Mañjuśrī and Avalokiteśvara), could not have been possible unless he was fully integrated into the traditional structure of the bodhisattva path.[3] The aim of this chapter is to trace the stages, as depicted in the Pali and Sanskrit literature, in the bodhisattva career of Maitreya, culminating in the prophecy of his future Buddhahood.

The only surviving South Asian texts that deal exclusively with Maitreya, the Pali *Anāgatavaṃsa* and the Sanskrit *Maitreya-vyākaraṇa*, are both noncanonical, and their date and authorship are uncertain. In the canonical literature of the Theravādins, Maitreya is mentioned only once, and rather casually, in the *Cakkavattisīhanāda-sutta* of the *Dīghanikāya*. Among the Mūla-Sarvāstivādins, Maitreya receives a less casual, yet not complete treatment in the *Maitreyāvadāna* of the *Divyāvadāna*. The *Mahāvastu*, the canonical text of the Lokottaravādi-Mahāsāṅghikas, which developed the concept of bodhisattvas as supernatural beings, was apparently responsible for initiating a list of future Buddhas with Maitreya at its head. It therefore serves as an excellent starting point for the study of Maitreya's career as a bodhisattva.

Turning to the Mahāyāna Sūtras, one finds Maitreya mentioned in almost all the Vaipulyasūtras, and in some of these he is active either as an interlocutor or as a preacher, enjoying a status similar to that of the bodhisattva Mañjuśrī. In the postcanonical period, the Theravādins appear to have lavished greater attention on Maitreya. The *Anāgatavaṃsa* draws exclusively upon the *Dīgha-nikāya* passage found in the *Cakkavattisīhanāda-sutta*, as does its complementary *Maitreya-vyākaraṇa* (together with a Khotanese recension of it called *Maitreya-samiti*) upon the *Divyāvadāna*. At a still later date, around the fourteenth century, the Theravādins too found it necessary to establish a line of future Buddhas, as evidenced by the *Dasabodhisattuppattikathā*, in which nine other persons known to the Pali canon (including King Pasenadi of Kosala) were selected to follow Maitreya in succession as Buddhas. There is also a small Southeast Asian Pali text called the *Pañcabuddhabyākaraṇa* that narrates an unusual story about Maitreya's birth as a lion in the company of four other bodhisattvas of our eon. Finally, mention should be made of two popular works, one in Sinhalese called *Śrī Saddhammāvavāda-saṅgrahaya* and the other in Thai called the *Phra Pathomsomphōthikathā*, which contain new episodes leading to the prophecy of Maitreya's future Buddhahood. This, then, is the textual material available to us in the South and Southeast Asian traditions, which can be studied to identify the stages of Maitreya's bodhisattva career.

The *Mahāvastu* itself talks of four stages in the career of a bodhisattva.[4] The first is called *prakṛti-caryā*, or "natural career," during which a future bodhisattva leads a righteous life, worships the Buddhas, and cultivates the roots of merit (*kuśala-mūla*). The second stage is called *praṇidhāna-caryā*, "the resolving stage," during which he vows to attain enlightenment (*bodhi*). This is always done in the presence of a Buddha, who prophecies (*vyākaraṇa*) the aspirant's future Buddhahood, whereupon he comes to be designated as a bodhisattva. The third stage is called *anuloma-caryā*, "the conforming stage," during which the bodhisattva progressively approaches the goal through various *bhūmi*s by fulfilling the ten *pāramitā*s. The final stage is called *anivartana-caryā*, "the preserving career," or the point at which it becomes impossible for the bodhisattva to turn away from the path; he then becomes destined (*niyata*) for Buddhahood. Once he attains this stage, he will be anointed (*abhiṣeka*) by a Buddha as his immediate successor and will be reborn in the

Tuṣita Heaven. The bodhisattva's final incarnation from Tuṣita will be his last birth, when he will become a Tathāgata and will attain *parinirvāṇa* at the end of his life.

Prakṛti-caryā of Maitreya

The literary material available to us on Maitreya is varied, and there is no unanimity among Buddhists concerning the events of his bodhisattva career. Only the *Mahāvastu* provides a glimpse into the prebodhisattva stage of Maitreya. As a matter of fact, this stage in the career of a bodhisattva is of little consequence, and there are no canonical narratives dealing with it even for Siddhārtha Gautama. Only a pair of Southeast Asian "extracanonical" Pali texts narrate an event concerning a female incarnation of Siddhārtha in which she offered oil to a monk so that he would worship a Buddha named Porāṇa-Dīpaṅkara on her behalf.[5] This meritorious act is believed to have led to her eventual rebirth as the brahman Sumedha, during the time of the Buddha Dīpaṅkara as described in the *Buddhavaṃsa*.[6] One would have expected to meet with a similar story about Maitreya, but no such account has come down to us.[7] The *Mahāvastu* account referred to above appears in the first book when Śākyamuni narrates to Mahā-Maudgalyāyana his countless previous births during which he served thousands of Buddhas. In the middle of this narration, there is a reference to Maitreya, which, being out of context, seems likely to be a later addition. While speaking about a Buddha called Suprabhāsa, Śākyamuni says:

> "Suprabhāsa was the name of the Tathāgata when bodhisattva Maitreya, as the universal king (*cakravartin*), Vairocana, was aiming at the perfection of enlightenment in the future, and thus first acquired the roots of goodness. And when Suprabhāsa was the Tathāgata, the measure of man's life was four times 84,000 crores of years, and men lived more or less to this age. . . .
>
> "Then Mahā-Maudgalyāyana, when the *cakravartin* King Vairocana had seen the exalted Suprabhāsa, he experienced a supreme thrill, ecstasy, joy and gladness. For ten thousand years he honored. . . . Then he conceived the thought: 'May I become in some future time a Tathāgata . . . as this Exalted Suprabhāsa now is. Thus may I preach the dharma . . . as the Exalted Suprabhāsa now does.' "[8]

Normally, such a resolution made in the presence of a Buddha brings forth a prophecy (*vyākaraṇa*) such as the one that the brahman Sumedha obtained from the Buddha Dīpaṅkara regarding his future Buddhahood. In this case, however, the Buddha Suprabhāsa did not respond to the wish of the *cakravartin* Vairocana. As if he were explaining this strange phenomenon, Śākyamuni adds, "Even so, Mahā-Maudgalyāyana, there is something to add to this, for it was after forty-four *kalpa*s that Maitreya conceived the thought of enlightenment."[9]

Whatever the reason for the long delay, it is clear from this statement that Maitreya's *prakṛti-caryā* lasted at least from the time of his meeting with the Buddha Suprabhāsa until his *bodhicitta praṇidhāna*. The *Mahāvastu* does not specifically mention the name of the Buddha who accepted his *praṇidhāna* and confirmed it by a prophecy (*vyākaraṇa*) concerning its fulfillment. This event probably occurred at a much later time, under the Buddha Ratnaśikhi, as described in the *Divyāvadāna*.

Praṇidhāna-caryā of Maitreya

In the *Divyāvadāna* account, the would-be Buddha Maitreya is not a *cakravartin* but an ordinary king named Dhanasammata who lived during the time when the Buddha Ratnaśikhi was born in Jambudvīpa. The father of this Buddha was a king named Vāsava, who was waging war against King Dhanasammata. Perceiving his imminent defeat, King Vāsava approached his son, the Buddha Ratnaśikhi, and asked him, "O Lord, at whose feet do all kings prostrate themselves?" The Buddha replied, "At the foot of a *cakravartin*." Hearing this, King Vāsava made a resolution: "May I become in a future life a *cakravartin*." He then received a prophecy from the Buddha that he would become a *cakravartin* by the name of Śaṅkha. Later, his opponent, King Dhanasammata, the victorious king, asked the Buddha, "At whose feet do the *cakravartin*s prostrate themselves, Sir?" And when told that they prostrate themselves at the feet of a Tathāgata, King Dhanasammata made a solemn resolution that he would himself become a Tathāgata. The Buddha Ratnaśikhi then prophesied, "O King, you will become a Tathāgata by the name of Maitreya, when the life span of men would have reached 80,000 years."[10] Thus according to the *Divyāvadāna*, Maitreya entered his bodhisattva career under the Buddha Ratnaśikhi.

Anuloma-caryā of Maitreya

Having made a *praṇidhāna* to become a Buddha, Maitreya must have performed heroic deeds similar to those of Gautama in his past lives. During this period, Maitreya may have been born as an animal and practiced the perfection of keeping the precepts or giving away his life. Unfortunately, no such story is known, nor does Maitreya play any part in the 547 birth stories of Gautama as described in the *Jātakatthavaṇṇanā*. There is, however, a single story, called the *Pañcabuddhabyākaraṇa*, originating in Chieng Mai/Laos (ca. the fifteenth century), which commemorates a holy place called Duṅ Yaṅ, sacred to the memory of the bodhisattva Maitreya. According to this extracanonical *jātaka*, Maitreya was born in Duṅ Yaṅ as a lion in the company of four other bodhisattvas, namely, Kakusandha, Koṇāgamana, Kassapa, and Gotama, who were born, respectively, as a rooster, snake, tortoise, and bull.[11] They kept the precepts (*śīla*) together at Duṅ Yaṅ and resolved that whoever among them attained Buddhahood should revisit that spot and leave behind a strand of hair as a relic. The story does not give details of the *pāramitā*s fulfilled by Maitreya in this rebirth as a lion, but the *jātaka* is indicative of the Southeast Asian belief that all five bodhisattvas of the present eon, called the *bhaddakappa* (Skt. *bhadrakalpa*), had been playmates and that Gautama himself acted more as a colleague than as a teacher of Maitreya in his past life.

The next story referring to Maitreya's fulfillment of the *pāramitā*s (or failure to do so) occurs in the *Divyāvadāna*, no. 22. In this story a bodhisattva called Candraprabha wishes to cut off his head and offer it to a brahman named Raudrākṣa, but the guardian deity of the royal park prevents the brahman from approaching the bodhisattva. When Candraprabha learns of this, he orders the deity not to hinder his fulfillment of the *dāna-pāramitā* and cites the example of Maitreya, who suffered a great setback because of a similar obstruction:

> "This is [the spot], O guardian deity, where Maitreya had turned away. [How?] Maitreya the bodhisattva, who had [once] abandoned himself to a tigress and had proceeded [on the bodhisattva course] for forty *kalpa*s, had been compelled to turn his back upon [his career because of a similar obstruction] in once giving away his head."[12]

This story of Maitreya is not attested to elsewhere, but the Pali *Dasabodhisattuppattikathā* continues the theme with a similar motif. According to this text, Maitreya was born in the past in the kingdom of Kurus, in the city of Indapatta, as a *cakravartin* king named Saṅkha. He was the first *cakravartin* to appear in that eon, and the Buddha of that *kalpa* had not yet appeared. The *cakravartin* proclaimed that he would give away is kingdom to anyone who would bring him the good news of the appearance of a Buddha in the world. In the course of time, there appeared the Buddha Sirimata, and he arrived within the kingdom of Saṅkha. A poor man informed the *cakravartin* of the arrival of the Buddha in his kingdom, and after relinquishing his throne to him, the *cakravartin* started out on foot to meet the Buddha. Lord Sirimata, knowing the aspirations of the *cakravartin,* decided to appear before him. He took on the guise of a young man riding a chariot, drove to where Saṅkha was walking, and asked him to mount the chariot. When they arrived at the assembly, the Buddha miraculously appeared before Saṅkha, seated in full glory. The Buddha then gave a sermon on *nirvāṇa*, and Saṅkha, wanting to worship the Buddha with the best gift that he could give, cut his head off at the neck with his bare nails and presented it to the Buddha with the words, "May this gift of mine result in omniscience." With this heroic deed he fulfilled the perfection of giving and was born in the Tuṣita Heaven, where he was known as Saṅkha Devaputta.[13]

These are the only references that one finds in non-Mahāyāna works pertaining to Maitreya's *anuloma-caryā*. The *Anāgatavaṃsa*, the Theravāda text on the lineage of the future Buddha, only casually mentions that Maitreya had served under four Buddhas, namely, Sumitta, (a former) Maitreya, Muhutta, and Gotama.[14] The names of the first three Buddhas are not attested to elsewhere, and the text furnishes no details concerning Maitreya's service under Gautama.

Maitreya, Mañjuśrī, and Gautama

The Mahāyānists, of course, were not lax in compiling their own biographies of the Buddhas. The entire *Lalitavistara* is devoted to the life of Siddhārtha Gautama, and the *Sukhāvatīvyūha* describes how a monk named Dharmākara, practicing under the direction of the Buddha Lokeśvararāja, became the Buddha Amitābha by the sheer power of his ardent aspiration. One would expect that, in view of the extraordinary position held by Maitreya, the Mahāyānists would have produced a similar work to demonstrate the reasons for his anointment as the next Buddha. Surprisingly, however, no biography devoted exclusively to Maitreya has come down to us. There are nevertheless a number of references, in texts as early as the *Saddharmapuṇḍarīka-sūtra* and as late as the *Suvarṇaprabhāsa-sūtra*, to incidents that bring Maitreya and Mañjuśrī together and relate them to Gautama in some incarnation. The "Vyāghrī-parivarta" of the *Suvarṇaprabhāsa-sūtra* seems to allude to a period long before either Mañjuśrī or Maitreya had entered the bodhisattva path. The story narrates how Gautama, as a bodhisattva, gave away his life to a hungry tigress. The bodhisattva was once born as the youngest son of King Mahāratha and was known as Mahāsattva. His two elder brothers were Mahāpraṇāda and Mahādeva, identified, respectively, with Maitreya and Mañjuśrī. One day the three brothers went to a forest and saw a tigress who had recently given birth to five cubs and was extremely hungry. Mahādeva (Mañjuśrī) saw her and wondered how she would ever be able to search for food. Mahāpraṇāda (Maitreya) lamented, saying, "Alas! It is extremely difficult to sacrifice oneself!"[15] Mahāsattva (Gautama), however, went fearlessly into the forest and offered his body to the tigress. This story is not contained in the *Jātakatthavaṇṇanā*, but found its way, via the *Jātakamālā* of Āryaśūra,[16] into the *Jinakālamālī* in a greatly revised form. In both the *Jātakamālā* and the *Jinakālamālī* Mañjuśrī is omitted from the story altogether and Maitreya is made the chief disciple of the brahman mendicant Gautama. When the latter sees the hungry tigress, he orders Maitreya to scavenge some meat from a lion's kill to feed her. But before Maitreya can return, the bodhisattva, overcome by compassion, gives his life to the tigress and saves the cubs from being eaten by her.[17]

The connection between Mañjuśrī and Maitreya persists in their *anuloma-caryā*, as is illustrated in the "Nidāna-parivarta" of the *Saddharmapuṇḍarīka-sūtra.* It is said that Maitreya saw a great miracle of a ray emanating from the forehead of the Buddha Śākyamuni and was overwhelmed by it. He wanted to know the reason for the display of such a miraculous power. He decided that Mañjuśrī must have witnessed similar signs from earlier Tathāgatas and should therefore be able to explain it to him. Responding to his request, Mañjuśrī addressed Maitreya by his first name Ajita and said:

> "I remember that, in the days of yore, . . . more than a countless eons ago, there was born a Tathāgata called Candrasūryapradīpa. Training under the aforesaid Lord there was a bodhisattva named Varaprabha, who had 800 pupils. It was to this bodhisattva that the Lord . . . taught the sermon called the *Saddharmapuṇḍarīka*, which was also preceded by a similar display of a ray issuing from his *ūrṇā-kośa*. . . . Eventually the Lord Candrasūryapradīpa entered into *parinirvāṇa*. . . .
>
> "The monk who then was the preacher of the law and the keeper of the law, Varaprabha, expounded it for fully eighty intermediate *kalpas*. . . .
>
> "Among the pupils of Varaprabha . . . was one who was slothful, covetous, greedy for gain and clever.
>
> "He was also excessively desirous of glory, but very fickle, so that the lessons dictated to him and the reciting done by him faded from his memory as soon as they were learned.
>
> "His name was Yaśaskāma. . . . He propitiated a thousand *koṭi*s of Buddhas, to whom he rendered ample honor. He went through the regular course (*anuloma-caryā*) of duties and saw the present Buddha Śākyasiṃha.
>
> "He shall be the last [i.e., the next] to reach supreme enlightenment and become a Lord known by the family name of Maitreya, who will educate thousands of *koṭi*s of creatures."[18]

After narrating this story, Mañjuśrī revealed the identity of the characters involved to Maitreya:

> "He who then, . . . was so slothful, was thyself, and it was I who then was the preacher of the law.

"As on seeing a foretoken of this kind, I recognize a sign such as I have seen manifested before. Therefore, for that reason I know,

"That decidedly the chief of the Jinas . . . is about to pronounce the excellent sūtra which I have heard before."[19]

That Mañjuśrī was a teacher of Maitreya eons ago and that the latter was his slothful pupil need not be a revelation. What is astonishing is that the author (or the compiler) of the *Saddharmapuṇḍarīka-sūtra* should not have noticed any anomaly in presenting Mañjuśrī as more knowledgeable about the Buddha rays than Maitreya, who was acknowledged as the "anointed" one and should therefore have been far more advanced toward Buddhahood than the former!

Bodhisattva Maitreya's *Anivartana-caryā*

The apprenticeship of Maitreya under different Buddhas must have come to an end by the time Gautama himself had achieved Buddhahood. We have seen how Gautama and Maitreya met in their past lives, as in the "Vyāghrī-parivarta" of the *Suvarṇaprabhāsa-sūtra*. We now move forward to the time when Maitreya encountered Gautama after the latter's attainment of Buddhahood. The encounter is alluded to in a passage of the *Mahākarmavibhaṅga* in which Gautama praises Maitreya for undertaking noble actions that befit a bodhisattva. While illustrating a category of actions called *maheśākhya-saṃvartanīya-karmas* (actions resulting in exalted births as a *cakravartin* or a Buddha) the text quotes from the *Purvāparāntaka-sūtra* (The sūtra of the past and future), in which the Buddha is said to have uttered the following words of inspiration on behalf of the bodhisattva Ajita: "Truthfully, O Ajita, this [act] prepares your mind for the noble aspiration, to leave the Sangha [and seek solitude]."[20] The passage is rather enigmatic, since quitting the community of monks should not be considered an appropriate action for a bodhisattva. But if we recall Mañjuśrī's statement in the *Saddharmapuṇḍarīka-sūtra* that Ajita was desirous of fame and hence delinquent in his career as a bodhisattva, then Maitreya's present action would seem to be highly commendable.[21] We may assume that Ajita's ardent exertions on his own would have led him into the irreversible (*anivartika*) phase of his career. He would have then obtained his much awaited *abhiṣeka* (anointment) as the next Tathāgata from the Buddha Gautama himself. The precise circumstances leading to their meeting, however, as well as the crucial scene of Gautama's public anointment of Maitreya as his immediate successor, are for some reason never revealed in any canonical text.[22]

In the *Cakkavattisīhanāda-sutta* of the *Dīghanikāya*[23] as well as the *Maitreya-vyākaraṇa*, the Buddha addresses the monks and tells them that in the future there will appear a Buddha named Maitreya. There is no indication in either text that the two had ever met or that Maitreya was ever known by any other name. In the *Mahāvastu*, where Maitreya is referred to as many as eleven times, his personal name is given as Ajita and he is fifth in the list of the one thousand Buddhas who are destined to appear[24] (according to the Mahāsāṅghikas, as opposed to only five in the Theravāda tradition) in the current *bhadrakalpa*. But at no time does the text describe the two meeting or engaging in conversation.[25]

The name Ajita, however, seems to have gained recognition among the Theravādins toward the end of the sixth century, since it is known to the *Anāgatavaṃsa*, and its *Aṭṭhakathā*, the *Samantabhaddikā*, as well as to the *Dasabodhisattuppattikathā* mentioned above. The *Anāgatavaṃsa* appears to be the first Pali text to refer to Maitreya by his name Ajita, who was said to have been a son of King Ajātasattu of Magadha, a contemporary of the Buddha.[26] According to the *Anāgatavaṃsa-Aṭṭhakathā* Ajita became a monk and was the recipient of two priceless pieces of cloth that Mahāpajāpatī Gotamī, the foster mother of Gautama, had presented to the Buddha himself.[27] The author of the *Samantabhaddikā* is here undoubtedly drawing upon the canonical *Dakkhiṇāvibhaṅga-sutta* of the *Majjhimanikāya*. In this *sutta*, Gotamī presents two pieces of cloth to the Buddha, but the Lord asks her thrice to donate them not to himself but to the community (Sangha) of monks.[28] There is no mention in this *sutta* of any particular monk being chosen for the honor of receiving them.

Further elaboration of this story is to be found in a (sixteenth-century?) Sinhalese work called *Śrī Saddhammāvavāda-saṅgrahaya*.[29] According to this work Ajita was the son of a rich merchant named Sirivaḍḍhana of Saṃkissa, in the neighborhood of Sāvatthi. He witnessed the Buddha's descent from the Tāvatiṃsa Heaven (after preaching Abhidhamma to his mother there) at Saṃkissa and decided to renounce the world. He joined the Sangha and became a very learned monk and an expert in the Tipiṭaka. In recognition of his erudition, Gautamī, after listening to the aforementioned *Dakkhiṇāvibhaṅga-sutta*, offered him two lengths of cloth. The elder Ajita, however, made canopies out of them for the chamber occupied by the Buddha. Knowing his true disposition, the Buddha called the monks together and announced to them that the monk Ajita would, in this very *bhaddakappa*, become a Buddha by the name of Metteyya. Since according to the Theravāda tradition only five Buddhas may appear in a *bhaddakappa*, and since Gautama was the fourth, it followed that Ajita would be the next Buddha, even if Gautama had not specifically used such expressions as "the next" or "my successor."

The Thai *Phra Pathomsomphōthikathā* (nineteenth century) introduces still more innovations to the Sinhalese version. It follows the *Anāgatavaṃsa* in maintaining that Ajita was a son of King Ajātasattu and furnishes the name of his mother as Kañcanadevī. It differs, however, from the Sinhalese tradition in several details. Here Ajita is said to be a *sāmaṇera* (novice) and not a fully ordained monk. After narrating the story of Mahāprajāpatī's request to the Buddha to accept the pieces of cloth she had brought and his admonition to present them not to him but to the Sangha, the Thai version adds that Gotamī became very unhappy with the thought that the Lord had rejected her gift and went around the Nyagrodhārāma monastery offering her gift first to Sāriputta, Moggallāna, and then the other great elders. Each of them, however, refused her offer, pleading that they were unworthy of so great a gift. Gotamī finally had no choice but to give it to a novice, who happened to be none other than the novice Ajita, who accepted it quietly. Gotamī's heart was filled with sorrow, and she shed tears thinking that her store of merit was so low that a mere novice was the appropriate recipient of her gift. When the Buddha saw her weeping, he called Ānanda and asked him to fetch his alms bowl. Addressing the congregation of the great disciples, he said, "Disciples, do not carry this alms bowl of the Tathāgata; let this young Ajita carry it." He then threw it up in the air, whereupon the alms bowl disappeared into the clouds. At that point Sāriputta obtained the permission of the Buddha to retrieve it and floated up into the air to find it but returned empty-handed. All the other great disciples also tried to recover it, each equally unsuccessful. Then the Tathāgata commanded Ajita to bring back the alms bowl. Ajita realized that he lacked the miraculous power to fly, but with his heart filled with joy, he made an asseveration of truth (*sacca-adhiṭṭhāna-kiriyā*): "If I am leading the holy life (*brahmacariya*) as a novice in order to attain the Enlightenment which can destroy the Four Deadly Floods . . . then may the alms bowl of the Tathāgata descend into my hands!" Instantly, the alms bowl descended and, as if it were a sentient being, declared to the assembly of the elders: "I did not come into the hands of the *mahāsāvakas*, but I come to the novice monk, because he will become not a *sāvaka*, nor a *paccekabuddha*, but a *sammāsambuddha*." Gotamī was greatly pleased by this miracle and worshipped Ajita with deep reverence. Ajita thought, "What good are these high gifts for me?" and made a canopy over the ceiling of the Buddha's residence with one piece of cloth and curtains with the other. The Buddha watched this act of worship and looked down upon the novice with a smile. Then the venerable Ānanda, perceiving the smile of the Buddha, inquired as to the cause, and the Buddha replied: "Lo! Ānanda, the novice Ajita will become a lion among the Jinas, a Buddha by the name of Metteyya in this *bhaddakappa*."[30]

These extracanonical stories of the monk Ajita have led scholars to search for an individual among the known disciples of the Buddha with whom he could be identified.[31] There are indeed two monks by the name of Ajita and Tissametteyya, both mentioned in the "Pārāyaṇavagga" of the

Suttanipāta.[32] They were formerly pupils of the brahman Bāvari living on the banks of the Godāvarī (in the South), who later visited the Buddha and became his disciples. However, both attained arhatship during that lifetime[33] and hence could not be identified with a future Buddha.

Maitreya's *Vyākaraṇa* in the Mahāyāna Sūtras

As already stated, Maitreya's name appears in almost all of the Mahāyāna Sūtras. In some of them he is side by side with Mañjuśrī and participates in the discourses and is looked upon by everyone as the heir apparent to the Buddha Śākyamuni. We saw that he figures prominently in the introductory section, the "Nidāna-parivarta," of the *Saddharmapuṇḍarīka-sūtra*. He appears subsequently in four more Parivartas: the fourteenth, fifteenth, seventeenth, twenty-sixth. In the fourteenth, a large number of bodhisattvas appear from other Buddha fields and beg Lord Śākyamuni's permission to write down the *Saddharmapuṇḍarīka-sūtra*. But the Buddha tells them that they need not engage in this task, since he has at his service a great many bodhisattvas of his own Buddha field. At once, from all sides of the Sahā world, countless bodhisattvas materialize in a miraculous fashion and surround the Buddha. Maitreya is puzzled at the sudden appearance of this large congregation of bodhisattvas and, expressing his perplexity (*vicikitsā*), begs the Lord to dispel his doubts concerning this matter.[34] The sight also produces doubts in the minds of the lay disciples of the countless Buddhas from other worlds, and they too want to know how so many bodhisattvas could manifest from the Sahā world. The Buddhas then call their disciples to attention and ask them to remain silent, saying:

> "O sons of good families, wait a while. Maitreya bodhisattva, who has been proclaimed to be the successor to the Lord Śākyamuni, is asking questions concerning this matter to the Lord Śākyamuni. He will explain this matter. Listen to him."[35]

Two significant points are noticeable in this passage: (1) Maitreya's prophecy is alluded to as if that event had taken place long ago; (2) Maitreya is still subject to doubts and perplexities and hence has a long way to go before the prophecy of his Buddhahood is fulfilled. Maitreya, for example, wonders how Gautama could have brought so many bodhisattvas to maturity in the less than forty years since his own attainment of Buddhahood.[36] The fifteenth Parivarta, called the "Duration of Life of a Tathāgata," is a sermon preached in answer to this question. The sixteenth and seventeenth Parivartas, called, respectively, "The Merits" and "The Meritoriousness of Joyful Acceptance," are also addressed to Maitreya and describe in detail the merit accumulated by listening to the *Saddharmapuṇḍarīka-sūtra*.

Maitreya's induction into the Tantric tradition must have taken place several centuries after his appearance in the *Saddharmapuṇḍarīka-sūtra*. Even a casual look at Tantric literature shows that he plays a very minor role compared with such peers as Mañjuśrī and Avalokiteśvara. He is not mentioned at all in such major works as the *Hevajra-tantra*, and ritual manuals like the *Sādhanamālā* devote only a paragraph to him.[37] One significant passage in the *Guhyasamāja-tantra* shows that Maitreya was considered even by the Tantric tradition to be undeveloped in the mysteries of the Vajrayāna. The passage occurs in the seventeenth chapter, the "Sarvasiddhimaṇḍalavajrābhisambodhi," in which several Tathāgatas give short sermons on the nature of the *vajra-citta*, at the end of which the Lord Sarvatathāgatakāyavākcittavajra enters into a *samādhi* called *sarvatathāgatasamatāvihāra* and falls silent. It is at this stage that Maitreya greets all Tathāgatas and asks, "O Lords! How should a Vajrācārya, who has been anointed (*abhiṣikta*) by the Guyhasamāja consisting of all the Tathāgatas who have transformed their body, speech, and mind into *vajra* be seen by all the Tathāgatas and all the bodhisattvas?"[38]

All the Tathāgatas reply:

> "O son of good family, the *bodhicitta* should be seen as *vajra* by all the Tathāgatas. And why is that? *Bodhicitta* and the [Vajra]ācārya are not two; there is no duality between them. . . . All those Buddhas and bodhisattvas who live in the ten directions of the Lokadhātu visit the *ācārya* three times each day and worship him with the honor due to all the Tathāgatas, and utter these potent words: 'He is the father of all of us Tathāgatas; he is the mother of all of us Tathāgatas.' Moreover, O son of good family, the amount of the aggregate of merit born of the *vajras* of the lords, the Buddhas who live in the ten directions, does not surpass the amount of the aggregate of merit that occupies a single strand of hair of that [Vajra]ācārya. And why is that? O son of good family, the *bodhicitta* is the essence of the cognition of all the Buddhas and the source of the omniscient knowledge of all the Buddhas."[39]

These solemn words must have come as a great shock to Maitreya, who obviously considered himself to be an anointed person, and the text tells us that he became frightened (*bhītaḥ*) and deeply agitated (*saṃtrasta-mānasaḥ*) and remained silent after hearing these words.[40]

Maitreya suffered from doubts and perplexities unbecoming a truly advanced bodhisattva in the above episodes of the *Saddharmapuṇḍarīka-sūtra* and the *Guyhasamāja-tantra*. That he lacked confidence in his achievements and also needed to be reeducated in the deep mysteries of the Mahāyāna is made clear by his encounter with the indomitable Vimalakīrti described in the celebrated *Vimalakīrtinirdeśa*. It is understandable that the Great Disciples (*mahāśrāvakas*) would recognize their inferiority to the bodhisattva Vimalakīrti with regard to their achievement of wisdom (*prajñā*) and, therefore, would decline to visit him to inquire about his illness. It is extraordinary, however, that Maitreya as well hesitated and begged to be excused from performing this task when specifically ordered to do so by the Buddha. In disobeying the Buddha's command, Maitreya related to him an account of his past encounter with Vimalakīrti. He was once discoursing on the irreversible stage of a bodhisattva with the gods of the Tuṣita Heaven. At that time Vimalakīrti approached him and respectfully addressed him concerning his prediction:

> "Honorable Maitreya, the Blessed One predicted to you that after only one birth you will come to supreme and perfect enlightenment. With regard to which birth (*jāti*) did you receive this prediction (*vyākaraṇa*)? Is it the past (*atīta*) birth, the future (*anāgata*), or the present (*pratyutpanna*) one? If it is the past birth, it is already exhausted; if it is the future birth, it has yet to come; if it is the present birth, it is without foundation. . . . How then, O Maitreya, would you receive the prediction?"[41]

Maitreya, we are told, was reduced to silence and could not reply. He therefore pleaded with the Lord that he was incapable of inquiring about Vimalakīrti's illness. The revelation that Maitreya did not consider himself fit to visit Vimalakīrti must come as a surprise, since Maitreya, as Vimalakīrti admitted, was predicted to be the next Buddha. Even so, it is significant that, in the last chapter, the bodhisattva Maitreya is summoned to take over the task of transmitting this noble sūtra to future generations. In this connection, the Buddha narrates to Śakra, the king of gods, his own story of the distant past when he served the Buddha Bhaiṣajyarāja. At that time the bodhisattva Gautama was known as Candracchatra and was one of the one thousand sons of the *cakravartin* king Ratnacchatra. Describing the bodhisattva career of all those one thousand sons, the Buddha declares that they were destined to be the one thousand Buddhas of this *bhadrakalpa* and entrusts Maitreya with the guardianship of this sūtra.[42] The story appears to be an attempt to legitimize Maitreya's successorship and to place him in the exalted family of the Buddhas.

Maitreya in the *Prajñāpāramitā-sūtra*

The next important canonical text in which Maitreya matures as a propounder of the perfection of wisdom doctrine is the *Aṣṭasāhasrikā-Prajñāpāramitā-sūtra*. In the sixth Parivarta of this sūtra, called "The Supreme Merit of Dedication and Jubilation," Maitreya engages in a long discussion with the venerable Subhūti on the merit accumulated by others, the jubilation of a bodhisattva over that merit, and his dedication of the merit produced by that jubilation to the attainment of perfect enlightenment by all beings. Subhūti raises some important metaphysical questions concerning the foundations – that is, the "objective supports" (the *skandhas*) and points of view (*dṛṣṭis*) – that underlie the meritorious actions of others, over which the bodhisattva rejoices. He then points out that, if the bodhisattva rejected those subjective supports as nonexistent, there would arise the perverted perception of rejoicing over something that does not exist. If, however, he accepted these supports as real, he would be no better than an ordinary person who is devoid of even rudimentary wisdom. Maitreya's words to Subhūti in this context are spoken in the spirit of skill in means:

> "O Subhūti, this should not be taught or expounded in front of a bodhisattva who has newly set out in the faith, for he will lose what little faith he has, and what little affection, serenity, and respect which are his. In front of an irreversible bodhisattva should this be taught and expounded."[43]

Maitreya then proceeds to expound at length on the proper way in which a bodhisattva can skillfully transform the meritorious work founded on jubilation into omniscience.

Hitherto we have examined texts in which Maitreya participates in various discussions instigated by others, for example, by Subhūti or Vimalakīrti. But there are certain Mahāyāna Sūtras in which he initiates a dialogue by asking the Buddha a question or propounds a doctrine with great confidence on his own, as if he were vindicating his claim to future Buddhahood. In the *Samādhirāja-sūtra*, for example, the householder Candraprabha makes a resolution (*praṇidhāna*) to become a Buddha in the presence of Śākyamuni, and the latter, in his characteristic manner, bestows a smile upon him. Normally in sūtras it is the privilege of Ānanda to question the Lord concerning the reason for his smile and thus provide an occasion for the elucidation of an extraordinary event. In the *Samādhirāja-sūtra*, however, Maitreya is accorded this honor and elicits the Lord's prophecy (*vyākaraṇa*) about Candraprabha's future Buddhahood as described in the "Smitavyākaraṇa-parivarta" (no 15).[44] Similarly, in the last chapter of the *Lalitavistara*, called the "Dharmacakrapravartana," it is Maitreya who is singled out to request the Tathāgata Gautama to display a miracle called the Turning of the Wheel of Law on behalf of the countless bodhisattvas who were gathered at the Deer Park of Vārāṇasī. Using several hundred adjectives, the Tathāgata describes to Maitreya the true nature of the *dharmacakra*, which was not revealed to his earlier audience of the group of five monks.[45] The *Lalitavistara* itself does not allude to Maitreya as the successor to Gautama, but in the last Parivarta the Buddha specifically entrusts this sūtra to Maitreya, thus elevating him to a higher status than other bodhisattvas.[46]

The Bodhisattva Maitreya as a Preacher of the Doctrine

To be acceptable as a bodhisattva to both the Hīnayāna and the Mahāyāna schools, Maitreya would have to be an advocate of teachings that are free of sectarian bias. The *Śālistamba-sūtra* is a perfect example of such a teaching, since it is devoted entirely to the doctrine of *pratītya-samutpāda* (conditioned coproduction). The sūtra begins as follows. Once when the Lord was living in Rājagraha at Vulture's Peak, the venerable Śāriputra approached the place where the bodhisattva Maitreya was mindfully pacing back and forth (*caṅkrama*). They exchanged greetings and sat down together on a stone slab. Then the venerable Śāriputra spoke:

> "O Maitreya, having seen today a sheaf of corn (*śālistamba*) the Lord uttered the following: 'Whosoever, O monks, perceives the *pratītya-samutpāda* perceives the Dharma; whosoever perceives the Dharma perceives the Buddha.' Having spoken thus the Lord fell silent. O Maitreya, what is the meaing of these words of the Lord? What is *pratītya-samutpāda*? What is Dharma? Who is the Buddha? How is seeing *pratītya-samutpāda* [the same as] seeing the Dharma? How is seeing the Dharma [the same as] seeing the Buddha?"[47]

When asked thus, Maitreya expounded at great length on the doctrine of the *pratītya-samutpāda* and explained how perceiving the Dharma was identical to perceiving the Buddha. Although it is considered to be a Mahāyāna Sūtra, the *Śālistamba-sūtra* contains no doctrine that would be unacceptable to non-Mahāyāna schools and indeed was considered canonical by the Sarvāstivādins and the Mahīśāsakas, as we know from Yaśomitra's eighth-century commentary on Vasubandhu's *Abhidharmakośa-bhāṣya*, the *Sphuṭārthā-vyākhyā*. The *Kośa-bhāṣya* examines a view (attributed to the Mahīśāsakas by Yaśomitra) that the *pratītya-samutpāda* itself was an unconditioned (*asaṃskṛta*) dharma like *nirvāṇa*. This view was said to have been supported by the following sūtra passage:

> Whether the Tathāgatas appear or whether the Tathāgatas do not appear, the Law [of *pratītya-samutpāda*] does exist, the Thatness, the Dharmaness, the invariable nature of dharmas, the unchangeableness of the Law.[48]

Yaśomitra in his *Vyākhyā* identifies this text as the *Śālistamba-sūtra* and states that these were the words of Lord (Bhagavān) Maitreya spoken to Śāriputra.[49] Although this passage is missing in the extant editions of the *Śālistamba-sūtra*, it has a parallel in the Pali *Saṃyuttanikāya*[50] and is quoted by Candrakīrti in his *Prasannapadā*[51] commentary on Nāgārjuna's *Mādhyamika-kārikā*. It may certainly be regarded as a great utterance spoken by a future Buddha on the impersonal nature of the Law that prevails regardless of his appearance! It is significant that, at the conclusion of his discourse, Maitreya tells Śāriputra that whosoever understands properly the *pratītya-samutpāda* receives the prophecy of his future Buddhahood from the Lord: "You shall become a fully enlightened Buddha."[52] Such an utterance claimed to have issued from Maitreya seems to be an attempt on the part of the compiler of the sūtra to vindicate his claim to future Buddhahood.

The most important scripture revealing the true majesty of Maitreya's insight into the Law and his mastery over the meditational trances is the *Gaṇḍavyūha-sūtra*. An entire chapter (no. 54), some sixty pages long, describes his meeting with the pilgrim Sudhana. Following Mañjuśrī's command, Sudhana had traveled all over the South (Dakṣiṇāpatha) and had visited more than fifty *kalyāṇa-mitra*s in search of instruction in the bodhisattva path. Finally, he arrived at Samudrakaccha, probably a port city, where Maitreya was residing in a gabled palace called Vairocanakūṭālaṃkāra-garbha. He approached Maitreya and sang his praises in 55 beautiful verses, calling him the eldest son of the Jina, the "anointed one" (*abhiṣeka-prāpta*). Maitreya received him with honor and instructed him in the bodhisattva career in no less than 121 verses. At the conclusion of his speech Sudhana respectfully addressed Maitreya:

> "The Noble Maitreya has been proclaimed by all the Buddhas to be the one who will attain to Buddhahood after only a single rebirth. Such a person must have passed through all the stages (*caryā*) of a bodhisattva, must have fulfilled all the *pāramitā*s; . . . he is anointed (*abhiṣikta*) for omniscient cognition. . . . May he please instruct me: How should a bodhisattva conduct himself in following his career?"[53]

Then Maitreya praised Sudhana for his aspirations, took him to the gate of his gabled palace, opened its gates with a snap of his fingers, and led Sudhana in. By the majesty of Maitreya's resolution (*adhiṣṭhāna*) Sudhana was able to see instantly all the halls and chambers of that great palace. He witnessed in a trance state the place where Maitreya had first conceived the thought of enlightenment (*bodhicitta-utpāda*) and saw the numerous Buddhas under whom he had practiced the *pāramitā*s. He also saw the place where Maitreya had initially attained mastery over the Maitrasamādhi, which earned him the name Maitreya,[54] a derivation supported by the *Samādhirāja-sūtra*[55] and accepted by Haribhadra in his *Ālokā*[56] commentary on the *Abhisamayālaṅkāra* and the *Prajñāpāramitā-sūtra*. He then saw those places where, in the course of his manifold transmigrations, Maitreya had been born as a *cakravartin* king, as Śakra, the king of gods, and the place where he would be reborn, namely, the Tuṣita Heaven. He also witnessed the extraordinary scenes of Maitreya's birth in Jambudvīpa out of the petals of a lotus flower, his first seven steps as an infant, his youth in the harem, his renunciation, his self-mortification followed by his partaking of food, his approach to the *bodhi* tree, his victory over the forces of Māra, his enlightenment, and finally his turning of the Wheel of the Law at the request of Brahmā. When Maitreya realized that Sudhana had had the vision of the entire bodhisattva career of the future Buddha, he withdrew his magic power, snapped his fingers, and awakened Sudhana from his trance.

Sudhana then discovered that the palace was no longer there and that everything he had seen was nothing more than a supernatural vision. He then begged Maitreya to reveal the true location of the palace and of Maitreya himself who had conjured it. Maitreya engaged for a while in enigmatic answers but finally returned to a more conventional level and, apparently anticipating that future generations would be curious about his place and parentage, told Sudhana that his birthplace (*janma-bhūmi*) was called Kūṭagrāma in the country of Mālada in the South (Dakṣiṇāpatha). There, he had chosen to be born in a family of brahmans in order to remove their vanity of high birth. While living in his hometown he had established his parents, a large number of his clansmen, and a merchant named Gopālaka in Mahāyāna. He had left that area recently and was now living in Samudrakaccha in his gabled residence called the Vairocanavyūhālaṃkāra-garbha.[57] He added that after his death he would "display" his rebirth in the Tuṣita Heaven in order to bring to maturity both the gods of that abode and those who would arrive there later through the inspiration of the Lord Śākyamuni. He assured Sudhana that, in the company of Mañjuśrī, he would see Maitreya again after the latter had attained Buddhahood.[58] Maitreya then bid Sudhana farewell and directed him to return to Mañjuśrī for further instructions.

The Bodhisattva Maitreya and the Buddha Amitābha

The last Mahāyāna text that sheds light on the irreversible aspect of Maitreya's career before his rebirth in the Tuṣita Heaven is the *Sukhāvatīvyūha*. This sūtra, as is well known, is preached by Śākyamuni to the venerable Ānanda and contains a glorious description of the Land of Bliss (Sukhāvatī) presided over by the Buddha Amitābha. As the sūtra comes to a close, Ānanda expresses a wish to have a vision of the Lord Amitābha and of the bodhisattvas inhabiting his land. His wish is instantly granted by the Lord Amitābha, who produces a ray of light by which the entire Buddha land shines with great splendor. Maitreya, the only other person privileged to share the vision, also sees this miracle. The Lord Śākyamuni addresses him, saying:

> "Do you see, O Ajita, the perfection of that Buddha country and the bodhisattvas who never stop meditating, as well as those gods and

> men who are dwelling within the calyx of lotus flowers and others who are born miraculously sitting cross-legged in the lotus flowers?"[59]

Ajita Maitreya saw all these and spoke to the Lord:

> "O Lord, will the bodhisattvas who have left this Buddha country or departed from the company of other blessed Buddhas be born in the world Sukhāvatī?"[60]

The Lord's answer to Maitreya's question is an emphatic one. He even gives a list of hundreds of crores of bodhisattvas who at different times and different places served different Buddhas and managed by their devout faith to be born in the blessed land of the Buddha Amitābha. We are not told whether Śākyamuni wished Maitreya also to be born there. In all probability, Maitreya could have chosen to be reborn in Sukhāvatī, in the presence of the Buddha Amitābha. The sūtra is silent on this matter, and the Buddha is content merely to ask Maitreya to guard the sūtra and not let it perish or disappear. The Mahāyāna tradition agrees unanimously that Maitreya did not seek Amitābha's company, but instead was born in the Tuṣita Heaven, awaiting the time for his descent to earth as the next Buddha.

Lest we wrongly assume, however, that the path of Maitreya will not lead to Amitābha's paradise, it must be added that at least one text, the *Samādhirāja-sūtra*, declares emphatically that, by worshipping Maitreya and by holding to the good law, a person may be reborn in Sukhāvatī, presided over by the Buddha Amitābha. Then, having served Lord Amitābha, he will strive for the attainment of perfect enlightenment.[61] Consequently, these two goals are not in conflict.

The Bodhisattva Maitreya in the Tuṣita Heaven

Buddhists recognize a law (*dharmatā*) that an "anointed" bodhisattva must be born in the Tuṣita Heaven before descending to earth for his final incarnation. Since Maitreya is such a person, it is assumed by all Buddhists that he is at present dwelling in Tuṣita, although there is no canonical reference to his death while in the company of the Buddha Śākyamuni. The first canonical reference to his residence in Tuṣita is to be found in the *Saddharmapuṇḍarīka-sūtra*, in the twenty-sixth chapter called the "Samantabhadra-utsāha-parivarta." This Parivarta describes the arrival of the bodhisattva Samantabhadra and a great congregation of other bodhisattvas at the assembly of the Buddha Śākyamuni after the latter has completed his preaching of the *Saddharmapuṇḍarīka-sūtra*. The bodhisattva Samantabhadra approaches the

Lord and announces to him that his congregation has arrived from the eastern Buddha country of Lord Ratnatejābhyudgatarāja for the purpose of listening to the sermon called the *Saddharmapuṇḍarīka*. He begs Śākyamuni to explain in detail once more the entire sūtra. The Lord gives a brief exposition to the new audience, at the end of which Samantabhadra responds by saying:

> "O Lord, in the future I shall protect those who recite this sūtra and those who write it down.... Such people will never be born in purgatories nor in lower destinies. They will certainly be born in the company of the heavenly beings in Tuṣita, where the bodhisattva Maitreya, the great being, resides, endowed by the 32 marks, and surrounded by hundreds and thousands of other bodhisattvas and heavenly damsels (*apsaras*), preaching the Law."[62]

We saw earlier that Maitreya figures prominently in the first Parivarta as well as in several of the middle Parivartas of the *Saddharmapuṇḍarīka-sūtra*. This reference to his residence in the Tuṣita Heaven, coming in the last Parivarta, would indicate that Maitreya had died at some point before the conclusion of the twenty-fifth Parivarta (called the "Pūrvayogaparivarta"). It is likely, however, that the twenty-sixth Parivarta was a much later addition and that the compilers took the opportunity to introduce Maitreya's birth in Tuṣita by means of this Parivarta. The *Mahākarma-Vibhaṅga*[63] and the *Mañjuśrī-Mūlakalpa*[64] are the only two other Mahāyāna texts surviving in Sanskrit that mention, though in no more than a single line, Maitreya's residence in Tuṣita.

Among the Pali texts, the earliest reference to Maitreya's heavenly abode is to be found in the noncanonical *Mahāvaṃsa*. In this chronicle of the island of Sri Lanka, King Duṭṭhagāmaṇi Abhaya (101–77 B.C.), the hero of that island and the builder of the great stūpa at Anurādhāpura, is said to have been reborn in the Tuṣita Heaven, "where the bodhisattva Maitreya, the Compassionate One, awaits his time [to descend on earth] for attaining Buddhahood."[65]

In the late medieval period, the cult of Maitreya must have gained great popularity among the Theravādins of Sri Lanka and Thailand, as witnessed by the story of a monk named Malaya-Mahādeva, who is said to have visited heaven and gained an audience with Maitreya. According to the eleventh-century Pali narrative entitled *Rasavāhinī*,[66] by means of his supernatural powers the elder Malaya-Mahādeva took a devout layman to the Tāvatiṃsa Heaven to worship at the Cūḍāmaṇi-cetiya. There they met Maitreya, who was also paying his respects to the shrine, and the bodhisattva very graciously presented the layman with a set of divine clothes. The elder and the layman then returned to the island, where the layman enshrined the divine clothes in a *cetiya* and was subsequently reborn in Tuṣita in the company of the bodhisattva.

A similar story about the elder Malaya-Mahādeva's encounter with the bodhisattva Maitreya appears in the Thai *Phra Malai sutta*, written in Chieng Mai in the sixteenth century. Here the elder questions the bodhisattva concerning the means by which beings can ensure meeting him when he comes into the world. Maitreya advises the elder that recitation of the *Vessantara-jātaka* will provide the necessary merit to yield a human birth that coincides with the auspicious occasion of the advent of the new Buddha![67]

Maitreya the Tathāgata

The bodhisattva career of Maitreya, leading to his birth in the Tuṣita Heaven, is of importance to the Buddhist tradition because it establishes his succession to Gautama after the latter's teaching (*śāsana*) disappears from the world. This apocalyptic event is believed to take place five thousand years after Gautama's *parinirvāṇa*[68] (circa A.D. 4456!), as the world regresses toward evil days, when human beings will live no longer than ten years.[69] But the advent of Maitreya will not take place immediately after the end of the five-thousand-year period.[70] Buddhists envisage a long interval of thousands of chaotic years before the world gradually moves into the ascending half of its cycle. It will reach its apex when human beings will have attained a life expectancy of more than eighty thousand years.[71] The conditions will have improved so much by then that the earth will be a paradise, with wish-fulfilling trees yielding fruits and the people needing no government to rule over them.[72] In the course of time, with the increase in population, evil and greed will increase, longevity will begin to decrease, and the production of food and protection of the weak will become necessary. Such a time is considered to be most auspicious for the rise of a universal monarch, the *cakravartin* king, the first lawgiver, who will set in motion the Wheel of Command by Law (*dhammena eva cakkaṃ vatteti*)[73] and bring the world under his domain (*āṇaṃ pavatteti*). [74] With the rule of law firmly established, there will appear a Buddha who, by turning the other wheel, the Wheel of the Sacred Law (*dharmacakra*), will usher in a new period in which human beings will follow his noble path.[75] The turning of these two wheels at the same time is an extraordinary event that takes place once in a long while, at the start of each new ascension within an intermediate eon (*antarkalpa*) in a given time cycle (*mahākalpa*).[76] At other times, a Buddha may arise without a *cakravartin* preceding him, as in the case of our own Buddha, who appeared at the tail end of an *antarkalpa*, which is moving rapidly toward a minor apocalypse. Maitreya's advent is distinguished from that of Gautama because he resolved to become a Buddha precisely at a time when human beings will live for eighty thousand years, as we have seen in the *Mahāvastu* and the *Divyāvadāna*. Moreover, his way will be paved by a *cakravartin* who, according to the *Divyāvadāna* account, also resolved to attain that high office. The karmic forces generated by their volitions will thus combine to inaugurate in the distant future a civilization supported by the two wheels of law, one leading by way of meritorious deeds to heaven, and the other by way of renunciation to *nirvāṇa*, the two complementary goals of human life.

Despite the unanimity of the Buddhist tradition concerning Maitreya's succession as the next Buddha, no Mahāyāna text has even given the details of the future Buddha's place of appearance or of his family life. Our sources of information on these points are exclusively non-Mahāyānist. The *Dīghanikāya* (*Cakkavattisīhanāda-sutta*), the *Divyāvadāna*, the *Mahāvastu*, the *Anāgatavaṃsa*, the *Maitreya-vyākaraṇa*, and the still later Sinhalese and Thai texts treat this topic very seriously and seem to draw upon a common tradition, unmarred by sectarian dissensions. Because Maitreya's advent, for the reasons outlined earlier, must be preceded by that of a *cakravartin* king, the canonical accounts of Maitreya the Tathāgata uniformly begin with a narrative of the *cakravartin* Śaṅkha, who will rule from his capital city of Ketumatī (the present Vārāṇasī). Because a *cakravartin* must be a kshatriya, it is apparently imperative that the Buddha be a brahman, and Maitreya is made the son of the *cakravartin*'s chaplain, the brahman named Brahmāyu, and his wife Brahmavatī. In some accounts his family (*gotra*) name is Maitreya and his first name is Ajita. According to the *Anāgatavaṃsa*, the bodhisattva Maitreya will live a householder's life for eight thousand years with his wife Candramukhī and will have a son named Brahmavaḍḍhana. His renunciation will parallel that of Gautama, but after seeing the four sights, he will spend only a week practicing the austerities, in contrast to Gautama's six years.[77] He will sit under a *nāga* tree and will attain enlightenment.[78] According to the *Divyāvadāna*, on the day of his enlightenment the seven royal gems (the wheel gem, etc.) of the *cakravartin* will disappear, and King Śaṅkha will renounce his kingdom and become a disciple of Lord Maitreya.[79] Subsequently, surrounded by the vast multitude of his disciples, Maitreya will visit a mountain named Gurupādaka, where the remains of the venerable Mahākāśyapa are lying undisturbed. After the mountain pass opens by itself, the Lord will approach the remains of the elder; taking them in his hands, he will address his congregation:

> "O monks, these are the bones of the elder Mahākāśyapa, who was born when the Lord Śākyamuni appeared in this world, when the life expectancy of men was no more than a hundred years. This elder has been declared to be the chief among those who are satisfied with little, content with little, foremost in ascetic practices (*dhutaguṇa*).

When the Lord Śākyamuni entered into *parinirvāṇa*, this elder held a recitation of the teachings of the Lord (*śāsana-saṅgītiḥ*)."[80]

The *Divyāvadāna* story of the Tathāgata Maitreya's noble act of honoring the remains of the elder Kāśyapa was no doubt motivated by a desire to establish a physical connection, if not a direct line of transmission, between the Buddha of the present and the Buddha of the future. This narrative, however, is conspicuously absent in the *Dīghanikāya*, the *Mahāvastu*, the *Maitreya-vyākaraṇa*, and in the later Theravāda literature.[81] Is it possible that the Mūla-Sarvāstivādins, who inhabited Kashmir and Gandhāra, introduced this story into the Maitreya legend through the influence of the Indo-Greeks and the Persians who ruled these lands? This conjecture is strengthened by the evidence of a further elaboration of this story that is found in both the Khotanese *Maitreya-samiti* and a *Maitreya-sūtra*, extant only in several Chinese translations closely related to it.

According to the *Maitreya-samiti*, after becoming the Buddha, Maitreya will climb a mountain called Kukkuṭapāda. Thereupon, the elder Mahākāśyapa, who has apparently sat in meditation (probably a *samādhi* called *nirodhasamāpatti*) on that very spot since the time of the Buddha Gautama, will arise from his trance and, having bowed to the Buddha Maitreya, will say:

> "Never before has there been a monk who, like me, has known two Buddhas and who experiences as much happiness as I am now at being able to impart these words of the Buddha.... The former Ahur Mazda (whose name was Śākyamuni) has disappeared from all regions.... Śākyamuni asked me just before his death to tell you [that] ... an evil age his risen, which is devoid of Buddhist monks. I have a few more moments of my life to spend." ... [And Śākyamuni said further,] "At the beginning of this eon Krakucchanda was the Buddha. He was followed by Kanakamuni, and then by Kāśyapa. Those who became monks in their *śāsana* but were not able to attain perfection will achieve release through me, the fourth [successor]. The fifth will be Maitreya, my equal; may he too release many beings."[82]

Havng uttered these words, the text adds, the elder Mahākāśyapa will perform many miracles and will then enter *parinirvāṇa*.

The Chinese translation of the *Maitreya-sūtra* provides an additional detail about the episode. It relates that the elder Mahākāśyapa will offer Maitreya a robe (*saṃghāṭī*) of the Buddha Śākyamuni, saying that the Lord had entrusted it to him to be given to the future Buddha. When Lord Maitreya takes the *saṃghāṭī*, it will barely cover two fingers of his right hand and two fingers of his left. All will then marvel, "How small the past Buddha must have been!" The Lord Maitreya will then ask the elder to demonstrate his supernatural powers and to teach the *Sūtra of the Past Buddha.*[83]

The Theravādins, as noted earlier, have no canonical tradition of any such contact between a disciple of Gautama and the Buddha Maitreya. They have aspired, however, to establish a close connection between the two dispensations by claiming a family relationship between their Sinhala hero, King Duṭṭhagāmaṇi Abhaya, and the future Buddha Metteyya. According to the *Mahāvaṃsa*, Kākavaṇṇatissa and Vihāramahādevī, father and mother of Duṭṭhagāmaṇi, will be Metteyya's parents, Duṭṭhagāmaṇi himself will be the chief disciple of the Buddha, and his son Prince Sāli will be the Buddha's son.[84] The great lay devotees of the Buddha will be fortunate to have a vision of the Lord Maitreya, and the benefactor Anāthapiṇḍika will even redonate the sacred Jetavana to the new Lord![85] Both the *Anāgatavaṃsa* and the *Maitreya-vyākaraṇa* promise that anyone who has served the Sangha, repaired a *cetiya*, or even raised a flagpole will meet and serve the future Buddha. Although the texts do not mention them specifically, there need be no doubt that the great commentators like Buddhaghosa[86] or the noble kings like the imprisoned Burmese monarch Siritibhuvanādicca of Pagan[87] or the numerous scribes and copyists of the Tipiṭaka, who have fervently aspired to be reborn during the time of the Buddha Metteyya, will do so and will be blessed with his vision and will attain *nibbāna*.

The Concept of a Future Buddha and a Future Jina

This survey of the South and Southeast Asian literature on Maitreya helps us to trace the traditional stages of his bodhisattva career, which culminates in his attainment of Buddhahood. No survey, however, can turn a legendary figure into a historical person, regardless of the number of Mahāyāna Sūtras or Theravāda apologists who have tried to present him as a contemporary of the Buddha Gautama. His overwhelming presence in the Mahāyāna Sūtras seems to imply that it was the Mahāyānists who were responsible for anointing him as Śākyamuni's successor. But a close examination of the material discussed in this chapter does not bear this out. It must be remembered that of the dozen or so great Mahāyāna bodhisattvas, including Mañjuśrī and Avalokiteśvara, who have been described as *ekajātipratibaddha* (those who are able to attain Buddhahood in a single rebirth),[88] only Maitreya is accepted as a bodhisattva by the non-Mahāyāna traditions. His investiture as the future Buddha, overriding the claims of all other bodhisattvas, suggests that Maitreya might originally have been a bodhisattva of the non-Mahāyāna variety, or was at the very least introduced by a pre-Mahāyāna school. This idea could not have originated in the Theravāda school, however, if only because no more than a single paragraph in the entire Pali Tipiṭaka is dedicated to Maitreya, and that, too, in the context of a long narrative concerning the future *cakravartin* Śaṅkha. The Mahāsāṅghika *Mahāvastu* is far more likely to have been the source of the cult of Maitreya. Although it refrains from mentioning Mañjuśrī, Avalokiteśvara, or any other bodhisattvas, it refers to Maitreya as many as eleven times, recognizes his first name Ajita, alludes to his past *caryās*, and proclaims his future Buddhahood through the mouth of the Buddha Gautama. But whereas the bodhisattva Gautama of the *Mahāvastu* stands out as a supernatural being (*lokottara*), the depiction of Maitreya is surprisingly free of any Lokottaravāda influence. Maitreya's succession could therefore be accepted unreservedly by the Theravādins of the South, as well as the Mūla-Sarvāstivādins of the North and correlated with their legend of the future *cakravartin* Śaṅkha. But apparently neither school made any attempt to make Maitreya a contemporary of the Buddha Gautama by introducing him as the latter's disciple in the existing sūtras. Only the Mahīśāsakas appear to have been bold enough to proclaim this, by first making Maitreya the chief preacher of the *Śālistamba-sūtra* and by then making the further claim that Maitreya was anointed by the Tathāgata as the future Buddha because he had correctly understood the doctrine of *pratītya-samutpāda*. Having assimilated Maitreya into the canon, the Theravādins (as well as *ācāryas* of other schools) must have found it necessary to identify him with a canonical person worthy of this singular honor. Who could such a person be who would answer to the name Ajita? The *mahāśrāvakas*, because of their having attained arhatship, were disqualified from receiving the title of bodhisattva. Nor would it have been proper to confer so great an honor on a layman, even if he were one as generous as Anāthapiṇḍika, because monks would then have been obligated to treat a layman deferentially. Given these parameters, the choice of a young novice must have appeared an attractive compromise for the position of bodhisattva. The Theravādins therefore came up with the most plausible story of a novice named Ajita,[89] who received first a gift of cloth meant for the Buddha and then a prophecy of his future Buddhahood. The name Metteyya itself, which expressed mastery over the *mettā-bhāvanā*, a favorite form of meditation among the Theravādins, might have also contributed to the popularity of this bodhisattva among the mendicants and the laity alike.

The hypothesis that the legend of the bodhisattva Maitreya was a Mahāsāṅghika innovation is supported by his portrayal in the Mahāyāna Sūtras. Despite his status as the "anointed one," Maitreya is repeatedly shown to be inferior not only to the bodhisattva Mañjuśrī, but even to the householder Vimalakīrti. His image improves gradually, however, and is fully matured in his encounter with the pilgrim Sudhana. Thanks to the author of the *Gaṇḍavyūha*, we are allowed a brief glimpse of Maitreya, the human being, emerging out of the legendary mist. It is significant that the author of the *Gaṇḍavyūha* chose to make him not a resident of Kashmir or Gandhāra, which might have suggested possible western influences, but of the South (Dakṣiṇāpatha). By his own account, as he tells Sudhana, Maitreya was a South Indian brahman born in a small place called Kuṭigrāma (Hut Village), in the (as yet unidentified) Mālada country. At the time Sudhana met him, he was living in Samudrakaccha, probably a port city. Before he left his native place, he had converted his parents and a large number of clan members to the Mahāyāna. Such a statement could very well be taken to mean that he was born in a non-Mahāyāna family and was himself a convert to Mahāyāna, a significant piece of information that adds credence to his assimilation into Mahāyāna from the Mahāsāṅghika.[90]

We will never know if the novice Ajita of the Pali texts and the brahman Maitreya of the *Gaṇḍavyūha* are identical, or if they are both purely legendary figures. One thing, however, is certain: The idea of a future Buddha need not be attributed to foreign influence. Buddhist canonical texts, as well as the texts of other Śramaṇa sects, such as the Ājīvikas and the Jainas, are full of references that anticipate the rise of a new Tīrthaṅkara, Jina, or Tathāgata. As is well known from the *Sāmaññaphala-sutta* of the *Dīghanikāya*, at the time of the Buddha there were six other prominent leaders of ascetic communities who had long established themselves as *tīrthaka*s, the builders of bridges (for the crossing of the river of *saṃsāra*).[91] Makkhali-Gosāla, the Ājīvika saint, a senior contemporary of Gautama, was probably the first to proclaim himself a Jina (spiritual victor), a claim that was hotly disputed by his rival, the Nigaṇṭha Nāṭaputta, popularly known by his title Mahāvīra (the Great Hero), who was and still is recognized by his followers, the Jainas, as the twenty-fourth and last Tīrthaṅkara of the current cycle.[92] The first book of the *Vinayapiṭaka*, which describes the events following the Buddha's enlightenment, indicates that the Buddha himself must have been aware of the existence of such rivalries for the title of savior. We are told that the Buddha was in search of disciples who might be able to accept him as a teacher (*satthā*), and so proceeded from Bodhgayā to Vārāṇasī on foot. The first person to encounter him was the naked ascetic Upaka, a member of the Ājīvika community, who accosted him and asked not so much about him as about his teacher: "On account of whom have you, your reverence, gone forth? Who is your teacher? Whose *dhamma* do you profess?"[93] This question brought a most extraordinary reply from the Lord: It was he himself who was an omniscient person without a teacher, who had no equal in the world, who was the Perfected Being, the Teacher Supreme, the One who had attained to *nirvāṇa*.[94] Upaka seems to have taken this claim as the boast of an upstart, for as he departs he says tauntingly, "According to your claim, your reverence, you ought to be Anantajina?"[95] The last term, which is attested to nowhere else in the entire Buddhist canon, has been explained by the commentators as "a victor of the unending, namely, of *nibbāna*."[96] It is more likely that the term referred to an exalted Jina, the founder of a new mendicant community and, if taken literally, to an eternally free soul (*sadā-mukta*), someone like the Īśvara of the *Yoga-sūtras* of Patañjali.[97] The title Jina was the one most coveted at that time and was claimed by all three historical teachers, Makkhali-Gosāla, Nigaṇṭha Nāṭaputta, and Siddhārtha Gautama. It is therefore quite likely that there was an anticipation at that time of the appearance of a Jina, Tīrthaṅkara, or Tathāgata to coincide with the approaching end of a great eon. As a matter of fact, the Jainas believed that the long period stretching across countless eons that witnessed the rise of the twenty-four Tīrthaṅkaras of the current descending (*avasarpiṇī*) half of the time cycle ended exactly three years, eight and a half months[98] after the death of Mahāvīra in 527 B.C. They also believed that no new Tīrthaṅkara would arise during the remainder of the *antarkalpa*s, until the world began its ascendancy, and reached a state identical to the one described in the Buddhist texts as the time destined for the arrival of the Buddha Maitreya.[99] The Jainas have even compiled a list of the twenty-four Tīrthaṅkaras of the future time cycle, and their first Tīrthaṅkara of that period will be known as Mahāpadma, who will no doubt be a contemporary of the Buddha Maitreya.[100]

It is not merely adventitious that this Mahāpadma, the future Jina, was identified by the Jainas with a historical person who was a contemporary of both Mahāvīra and the Buddha. This person belongs to a royal family and is known as Śreṇika Bimbisāra,[101] the father of King Ajātasattu of Magadha. It is well known, as the Pali *Sāmaññaphala-sutta* relates, that Ajātasattu was a patricide, who subsequently became a lay follower of the Buddha.[102] The Jainas have claimed that Śreṇika had become a devout Jaina through the influence of his wife Celanā, an aunt of Mahāvīra. As a great devotee of Mahāvīra, he had accumulated enough meritorious karma to be the first Jina of the next cycle. Unfortunately, he was imprisoned by his son Ajātasattu, who kept him in chains and even lashed him daily himself. Later, Ajātasattu had a change of heart and approached his father, carrying an iron club, in order to free him from his chains. But the old king, misunderstanding his son's motives for approaching him with club in hand and fearful that he would cruelly inflict upon him an ignominious death, ingested poison and died instantly.[103] Despite his status as a future Jina, he was reborn, as retribution for this act of suicide, in hell, where he awaits his time to appear on earth as the next Jina, as surely as does the bodhisattva Maitreya in the Tuṣita Heaven.[104]

It is no small irony that the author of the *Anāgatavaṃsa*, allegedly an Indian Theravādin,[105] should choose a person from King Śreṇika Bimbisāra's family as the future Buddha. Members of the royal family, as is well known from the court histories of Buddhist kingdoms, were destined for high honors, especially when they embraced the yellow robes in their youth. The novice Ajita, as described in the *Anāgatavaṃsa*, was a prince, the son of the King Ajātasattu. The Buddhists could not be expected to appoint Śreṇika, a *sotāpanna* and victim of patricide, as a suitable candidate for bodhisattvahood. As for Ajātasattu, his act of patricide disqualified him from claiming any such honor. Whether or not there was indeed a prince named Ajita, there seems little doubt that this royal house, which has been credited with destroying several small "republics" (*janapada*s) of the Gangetic Valley and with founding the Magadhan empire, stood in some special relationship to both Buddhists and Jainas and was probably regarded by all as a family of minor *cakravartin*s (*dhammarājā*s; see note 104) ruling at the termination of a great salvific era that had seen the advent of numerous Buddhas and Jinas.

NOTES

1 The terms "Buddha" and "Tathāgata" are virtually synonymous in Buddhist materials. In choosing to refer to Maitreya as a Tathāgata rather than as a Buddha, however, I am following a distinction first noted in *Dharmasaṃgraha*, ascribed to Nāgārjuna. This work distinguishes between the five Buddhas – Vairocana, Akṣobhya, Ratnasambhava, Amitābha, Amoghasiddhi – and the seven Tathāgatas – Vipaśyi, Śikhī, Viśvabhū, Krakucchanda, Kanakamuni, Kāśyapa, and Śākyamuni. The former are celestial Buddhas who never appear on earth, whereas the latter advent from heaven for the weal of human beings in Jambudvīpa. Although Amitābha is referred to as Tathāgata in the *Sukhāvatīvyūha* and elsewhere, this does not negate the reasons for the classification itself. Hence, Maitreya is called Tathāgata to indicate his direct salvific role.

2 For example, "Among the doctrines of Zoroastrianism, which has strongly influenced other religions both East and West, is that of the savior (Saošyant), who, at the end of the world, will lead the forces of good and light against those of evil and darkness. Under the invading rules of N.-W. India Zoroastrianism and Buddhism came in contact, and it was probably through this that the idea of the future Buddha became part of orthodox belief" (A. L. Basham, *The Wonder That Was India* [New York: Grove Press, 1954], 274). For a discussion of the possible connection between Ajita Maitreya and Mithras Invictus, see Etienne Lamotte, *Histoire du bouddhisme indien des origines à l'ère Śaka* (Louvain, 1958), 782*ff.*

3 It is difficult to determine the period during which Maitreya would have been fully accepted by both the pre-Mahāyāna and the Mahāyāna schools. He must have reached his status as the successor to the Buddha Gautama by the time of the Kuṣāṇa King Kaniṣka (ca. 125 A.D.), since he is depicted in one of the king's copper coins bearing the Greek inscription "Metrauo Boudo." See Joe Cribb, "Kaniṣka's Buddha Coins – The Official Iconography of Śākyamuni & Maitreya," *Journal of the International Association of Buddhist Studies*, 3, no. 1 (1980): 79–87.

4 *Mahāvastu*, 1: 46.

5 See *Paññāsa-jātaka* (no. 35, "Padīpadāna-jātaka"), 2: 396–402, and *Jinakālamālī*, 5.

6 *Buddhavaṃsa*, 2: 51–6.

7 Maitreya is mentioned in the *Buddhavaṃsa* only in an appendix called the "Buddhapakiṇṇakakhaṇḍa" in the list of the five Buddhas of this *bhaddakappa*. *Buddhavaṃsa*, xxvii, 18–19.

8 *Mahāvastu*, 1: 67–8.

9 Ibid., 1: 69.

10 *Divyāvadāna* (no. 3, "Maitreyāvadāna"), 40.

11 For a pictorial depiction of these five Buddhas with their animal emblems in a Cambodian temple, see the *Pañcabuddhabyākaraṇa*, plate 14.

12 *Divyāvadāna*, 202.

13 *Dasabodhisattuppattikathā*, 127. The rebirth of King Śaṅkha in Tuṣita need not necessarily refer to Maitreya's present (and final birth) in that heaven, because one can be born any number of times in the world of gods (*devaloka*) by deeds of merit.

14 The editor of the *Anāgatavaṃsa* (Professor J. Minayeff) does not reproduce the text pertaining to Maitreya's past career but summarizes it as follows: "Then follows a history of the previous existence of Metteyyo, with the three Buddhas, Sumitto, Metteyyo, and Muhutto, during twenty-seven Buddhas, and finally at the time of the Buddha Gotama, when he was born as son of Ajātasattu, prince of Ajita" (*Anāgatavaṃsa*, 34).

15 *Suvarṇaprabhāsa-sūtra*, 108, 122.

16 The *Jātakamālā* does not mention Maitreya but calls the attendant (of the bodhisattva) by the name Ajita (*Jātkamālā* [no. 1, "Vyāghrī-jātaka"], 1–6).

17 *Jinakālamālī*, 4.

18 *Saddharmapuṇḍarīka-sūtra*, 1: 57, 90–4.

19 Ibid., 1: 95–6.

20 *Mahākarmavibhaṅga*, 39–40. See p. 39, n. 6, where Sylvain Lévi observes that the *Purvāparāntaka-sūtra* survives only in Chinese translation and that this passage is not found there.

21 A very interesting discussion of the virtue of leading the Sangha is recorded in the *Milindapañha* in connection with the Buddha's prediction regarding the Lord Metteyya's leadership of a large Sangha consisting of thousands of monks (*Milindapañha*, 159). Note that this is the only reference to Metteyya in the *Milindapañha*.

22 The only canonical text surviving in Sanskrit in which the Buddha directly addresses Maitreya and predicts his future Buddhahood is to be found in the "Pudgala-viniścaya" chapter at the end of the *Abhidharmakośa-bhāṣya* of Vasubandhu. There the Vātsīputrīya states that the Buddha does not make declarations regarding future existences lest he be accused of admitting the doctrine of eternalism (*śāśvatavāda*). The Vaibhāṣika encounters the Pudgalavādin by quoting the following passage, in which the Buddha does indeed speak of a future existence: idam tarhi kasmād vyākaroti – "bhaviṣyasi tvaṃ Maitreyānāgate 'dhvani tathāgato 'rhan samyaksambuddhaḥ" iti? evam api hi śāśvatatvaprasaṅgaḥ? (*Abhidharmakośa-bhāṣya*, 9: 471). Unfortunately, both Vasubandhu and his commentator Yaśomitra fail to indicate the source of this quotation, and it has yet to be traced in the extant canonical texts.

23 *Dīghanikāya*, 3: 76.
24 *Mahāvastu*, 3: 330.
25 Several passages in the *Mahāvastu* refer to the Buddha's prediction of Maitreya's future Buddhahood (e.g., *Mahāvastu*, 1: 51).
26 See note 14.
27 *Anāgatavaṃsa-Aṭṭhakathā*, p. 38.
28 *Majjhimanikāya* (no. 142, *Dakkhiṇāvibhaṅga-sutta*), 3: 253.
29 See M. Saddhatissa's summary of this version in his introduction to the *Dasabodhisattuppattikathā*, 31.
30 *Phra Pathomsomphōthikathā*, chap. 20. I am indebted to Christopher Court, instructor of Thai at the University of California, Berkeley, for a summary of this chapter, entitled "Metteyabyākaraṇa-parivatta."
31 See Lamotte, *Histoire du bouddhisme indien*, 776.
32 Ajitamāṇavapucchā and Tissametteyyamāṇavapucchā (*Suttanipāta*, 197–9).
33 *Suttanipāta-Aṭṭhakathā*, 5: 2.
34 *Saddharmapuṇḍarīka-sūtra*, 182.
35 Ibid., 84.
36 Ibid., 186.
37 In an iconographic depiction of the bodhisattva Maitreya in a *maṇḍala*, he has three faces, three eyes, and four arms of golden hue; he is seated in a cross-legged position with his two upper arms in the teaching (*vyākhyāna*) *mudrā*, his lower right hand in the *abhaya-mudrā*, and his lower left hand holding a blossom of *nāgakeśara* flowers; cf. *Sādhanamālā* (no. 283, "Maitreyasādhanam"), 560.

For a sketch of Maitreya based on the *Sādhanamālā*, see B. Bhattacharya, *The Indian Buddhist Iconography*, 2d ed. (Calcutta: Firma K. L. Mukhopadhyay, 1958), figure 47. It should be noted that the description of Maitreya given here is conspicuously silent on the characteristic feature of Maitreya's image as found in Tibet: the depiction of a stūpa in his crown. Nor does it make even the slightest hint of the depiction of Maitreya in Korean images, in which he has a huge square platform stūpa on top of his head. Even later Tantric texts like the *Niṣpannayogāvalī* by Abhayākaragupta of Vikramaśīla monastery, which is dated ca. 1114 A.D., are silent on this prominent feature of Maitreya's iconography, indicating that this style of depiction may not be of Indian origin.

38 *Guyhasāmaja-tantra*, 137. It should be noted that this is the only occasion where the term *vajrācārya* occurs in the *Guyhasamāja-tantra*.
39 Ibid., 138.
40 Ibid., 138.
41 *Vimalakīrtinirdeśa*, 85–8.
42 Ibid., 265–70.
43 *Aṣṭasāhasrikā-Prajñāpāramitā-sūtra*, 71.
44 *Samādhirāja-sūtra*, 14: 41, 74.
45 *Lalitavistara* (no. 26, "Dharmacakrapravartanaparivarta"), 306–13.
46 Ibid. (no. 27, "Nigamaparivarta"), 318.
47 *Śālistamba-sūtra*, 100 (i.e., a, 1–2).
48 *Abhidharmakośa-bhāṣya* (chap. 3, v. 28a), 137.
49 *Sphuṭārthā-Abhidharmakośa-Vyākhyā* (chap. 3, v. 28a), 293.

50 *Saṃyuttanikāya*, 2: 25.
51 *Prasannapadā* (*Mādhyamika-Kārikā-Vṛtti*), 40.
52 *Śālistamba-sūtra*, 106 (i.e., a, 19).
53 *Gaṇḍavyūha-sūtra*, 392–3.
54 Ibid., 408.
55 *Samādhirāja-sūtra* (tenth Parivarta), 1: 121–2.
56 *AbhisamayālaṅkārĀlokā-prajñāpāramitā-vyākhyā*, 385. For references to a *Maitreyavimokṣa-sūtra* (named after Maitreya?), see *Śikṣāsamuccaya*, 9, 177. For a discussion of the derivation of the name "Maitreya," see Sylvain Lévi, "Maitreya le Consolateur," in *Etudes d'Orientalisme publiées par le Musée Guimet à la mémoire de Raymonde Linossier* (Paris, 1932), 2: 355–402.
57 *Gaṇḍavyūha-sūtra*, 416–17.
58 Ibid., 418.
59 *Sukhāvatīvyūha*, 65.
60 Ibid., 69.
61 *Samādhirāja-sūtra* (18th Parivarta), 271. 52–3.
62 *Saddharmapuṇḍarīka-sūtra*, 266.
63 *Mahākarmavibhaṅga*, 40.
64 *Mañjuśrī-Mūlakalpa*, 489.
65 *Mahāvaṃsa*, 32, 73.
66 *Rasavāhinī*, pt. 2, 163.
67 See Frank E. Reynolds, "Buddhism as Universal Religion and as Civic Religion," in *Religion and Legitimation of Power in Thailand, Laos and Burma*, ed. B. Smith (Chambersburg, Pa.: Anima Books, 1978).
68 *Anāgatavaṃsa*, 34–6.
69 *Dīghanikāya*, 3: 73. For a Theravādin description of the destruction of the *mahākappa*, see F. E. Reynolds and M. B. Reynolds, *Three Worlds According to King Ruang: A Thai Buddhist Cosmology* (Berkeley, Calif.: Asian Humanities Press, 1982), chap. 10. For the Vaibhāṣika view, see the *Abhidharmakośa-bhāṣya* (chap. 3, v. 89–93), 178–81.
70 Contrary to the canonical tradition, Burmese and other Southeast Asian Buddhists often appeared to have anticipated the advent of the new Buddha soon after the 5,000th anniversary of the Buddha's *parinirvāṇa*, as noticed by E. Michael Mendelson: "In Burmese history, roughly from the time of King Bodawpaya onward, we can observe the interplay of two contradicting beliefs: one in the inevitable decline, and another in the nativistic and revivalistic forces that a messianic dispensation would be granted much sooner than the texts would have it" (*Sangha and State in Burma*, [Ithaca, N.Y.: Cornell University Press, 1975], 276).
71 *Dīghanikāya*, 3: 76 and *ĀryaMaitreya-vyākaraṇam* (verse restored from the Tibetan), 6.
72 *Dasabodhisattuppattikathā*, 121. On the millenarian visions linked to the future Buddha Metteyya in the political life of the Southeast Asian Buddhist countries, see S. J. Tambiah, *World Conqueror and World Renouncer* (Cambridge University Press, 1976), chap. 19.
73 *Aṅguttaranikāya*, 1: 101–10. For a full discussion of the ethic of *dharma* in early

Buddhist thought, see S. J. Tambiah, *World Conqueror and World Renouncer* (Cambridge University Press, 1976), chap. 4.

74 Compare "yathā, mahārāja, mahiyā rājāno honti samajaccā, samajaccānam pi tesaṃ eko sabbe abhibhavitā āṇaṃ pavatteti . . ." (*Milindapañho*, 189).

75 For further discussions of the interplay between the monarchy and the Sangha in India and Sri Lanka, see Frank Reynolds, "The Two Wheels of Dhamma: A Study of Early Buddhism" in *The Two Wheels of Dhamma*, ed. G. Obeyesekere, F. Reynolds, and B. L. Smith, American Academy of Religious Studies in Religion, Chambersburg, Pa., 1972; and Bardwell L. Smith, "Kingship, the Sangha, and the Process of Legitimation in Anuradhapura Ceylon: An Interpretative Essay," in *Buddhism in Ceylon and Studies on Religious Syncretism in Buddhist Countries*, ed. Heinz Bechert (Abhandlungen de Akademie der Wissenschaften in Gottingen, 1978), no. 108.

76 The *Divyāvadāna* begins the account of Maitreya with the question, What is the reason for the simultaneous appearance of these two jewels? (ko bhadanta hetuḥ ko pratyayo, dvayo ratnayor yugapal loke prādurbhāvāya? bhagavān āha: praṇidhānavaśāt; p. 37). The text then narrates the story of the two kings, Vāsava and Dhanasammata, who had in the past resolved to become a *cakravartin* king and a Buddha, respectively (see note 10 above). According to the Vaibhāṣikas, a *cakravartin* king arises only when the life span of human beings remains above eighty thousand years, and parallel to the rule pertaining to the appearance of the Buddhas, only one *cakravartin* king may rule at one time: atha cakravartinaḥ kadotpadyante? . . . amite cāyuṣi manuṣyāṇāṃ yāvad aśītisahasrake cotpattiś cakravartinām, nādhaḥ, tasyāḥ sasyasampadas tadūnāyuṣām abhājanatvāt. . . . na ca dvau saha buddhavat (*Abhidharmakośa-bhāṣya* [chap. 3, v. 95], 184).

77 *Anāgatavaṃsa*, v. 47, 54. According to the *Divyāvadāna*, Maitreya will attain enlightenment on the same day he renounces the world: yasminn eva divase vanaṃ saṃśrayiṣyati, tasminn eva divase . . . anuttaraṃ jñānam adhigamiṣyati (*Divyāvadāna*, 61).

78 *ĀryaMaitreya-vyākaraṇam*, 18, v. 54. This explains the association of the *nāgakeśara* flower with the iconographic representation of the bodhisattva Maitreya.

79 *Divyāvadāna*, 37. From this account, as well as that in the *Cakkavattisīhanāda* of the *Dīghanikāya*, it would appear that according to the Mūla-Sarvāstivādins even a Buddha and a *cakravartin* king cannot coexist! The role of the *cakravartin* king would seem to be solely that of establishing the rule of law and thus pave the way for the commencement of a Buddhist community at the beginning of the descending half of a new eon.

80 Ibid.

81 H. Saddhatissa notes that there is an unpublished Pali work named *Mahāsampiṇḍinidāna* in the Colombo Museum that contains a description of the cremation of the elder Mahākassapa's dead body in the presence of the future Buddha Metteyya. See *Dasabodhisattuppattikathā*, 43.

82 *Maitreya-samiti*, vv. 282–92.

83 Dr. K. Watanabe's translation of the *Maitreya-sūtra* in *Maitreya-samiti*, 227. For further discussions of the legend of the elder Mahākassapa's exchange of robes

with that of the Buddha Gautama, see G. P. Malalasekera, *Dictionary of Pali Proper Names* (London: Pali Text Society, 1960), 2: 478. For further discussion of this legend, see Lamotte, *Histoire du bouddhisme indien*, 226, and H. Saddhatissa's introduction to the *Dasabodhisattuppattikathā*, 43–5.

84 *Mahāvaṃsa*, 32: 81–3. The Pali *Anāgatavaṃsa* appears to be unaware of this Sinhalese tradition; according to this text Aśoka and Brahmadeva would become the two *agga-sāvaka*s of the Buddha Metteyya: Asoko Brahmadevo ca aggā hessanti sāvakā (v. 97). The *ĀryaMaitreya-vyākaraṇa* does not contain any information on the chief disciples of the Buddha Maitreya.

85 *Avadānakalpalatā* (no. 21, "Jetavanapratigrahāvadānam"), 1: 158, v. 83.

86 *Visuddhimagga*, 614.

87 G. H. Luce, "The Shwegugyi Pagoda Inscription, Pagan, 1141, A.D., " *Journal of the Burma Research Society*, 10, no. 2 (1920); 67–72.

88 *Samādhirāja-sūtra* (10th Parivarta), 119.

89 The *Dhammapada-Aṭṭhakathā* (2: 240) narrative of Sāriputta's disciple Saṃkicca the Novice (*sāmaṇera*), who is said to have attained arhatship the moment the razor touched his hair, might have served as a model for the story of Ajita-sāmaṇera's elevation to future Buddhahood.

90 Though we cannot be sure of his original religious affiliation, at the very least this information confirms that Maitreya was not a follower of Mahāyāna by birth.

91 The six *titthiya*s, namely, Pūraṇa Kassapa, Makkhali Gosāla, Ajita Kesakambali, Pakudha Kaccāyana, Sañjaya Belaṭṭhiputta, and Nigaṇṭha Nāṭaputta (the last identified with the Jaina teacher Mahāvīra), are all described in the following manner: ayaṃ deva ... saṅghī c'eva gaṇī ca gaṇācariyo ca ñāto, yasassī, titthakaro, sādhusammato bahujanassa, rattaññū, cirapabbajito, addhagato, vayo anuppatto (*Dīghanikāya* [2, *Sāmaññaphala-sutta*], 2: 48.

92 For a detailed account of Makkhali Gosāla's claim to the status of a Jina and to "omniscience," leading to his confrontation with the Jaina teacher Mahāvīra, see A. L. Basham, *History and Doctrine of the Ājīvikas* (London, Luzac, 1951), chap. 4.

93 *Vinayapiṭaka-Mahāvagga*, 1. 8.

94 Idid.

95 Ibid. The Buddha retorts with words that explain why he is entitled to be a Jina: mādisā ve Jinā honti ye pattā āsavakkhayaṃ / jitā me pāpakā dhammā tasmā 'haṃ Upaka, jino ti // (ibid): "Like me, they are victors indeed, / Who have won to destruction of the cankers; / Vanquished by me are evil things, / Therefore am I, Upaka, a victor" (*Book of Discipline*, 1: 12).

96 I. B. Horner's note: "*anantajina. Vinaya-Aṭṭhakathā* merely says, 'You are set on becoming a victor of the unending.' *Ananta*, the unending, may refer to *dhamma*, also to nibbāna" (*Book of Discipline*, n. 4).

97 kleśakarmavipākāśayair aparāmṛṣṭaḥ puruṣaviśeṣa īśvaraḥ / ... sa tu sadaiva muktaḥ sadaiveśvara iti (*Pātañjala-Yogasūtra* with the *Vyāsabhāṣya*, 1: 24).

98 imīse osappiṇīe dusamāsusamāe [samāe] bahuvīikkantāe tīhiṃ vāsehiṃ aḍḍhanavamehi ya māsehiṃ sesehiṃ Pāvāe ... kālagae ... parinivvuḍe (*Kalpasūtra*, no. 146. See Hermann Jacobi, *Jaina Sūtras*, Sacred Books of the East, vol. 22, pt. 1, London, 1884, p. 269.

99 For a description of the Jaina cosmology and the Jaina belief regarding the appearance of twenty-four Jinas in the ascending and descending halves of each time cycle, see P. S. Jaini, *The Jaina Path of Purification* (Berkeley and Los Angeles: University of California Press, 1979), 29–33.

100 For a list of seventy-two Jinas (the twenty-four of the past, present, and future), see Jinendra Varni, *Jainendra-siddhānta-kośa* (Varanasi: Bharatiya Jnanapitha, 1944), 2: 376–91.

101 The Jaina *Mahāpurāṇa* (of the ninth-century Guṇabhadra) contains the following prediction about King Śreṇika's future Jinahood: "Ratnaprabhāṃ praviṣṭaḥ san tatphalaṃ madhyamāyuṣā / bhuktvā nirgatya bhavyāsmin Mahāpadmākhya-tīrthakṛt // āgāmyutsarpiṇīkālasyāditaḥ kṣemakṛt satām / tasmād āsannabhavyo 'si mā bhaiṣīḥ saṃsṛter iti" // (*Mahāpurāṇa*, bk. 2, chap. 74, vv. 451–2).

In the Theravāda tradition King Śreṇika is known by the name of Bimbisāra; he is considered to be a devotee of the Buddha. See Malalasekera, *Pali Proper Names*, 2: 284–9. For further details on Śreṇika in the Śvetāmbara Jaina canon, see "Seṇiya," in M. L. Mehta and K. R. Chandra, eds., *Prakrit Proper Names* (Ahmedabad: Institute of Indology, 1971–2), 2: 856–7.

102 *Dīghanikāya*, 1: 80. In the Jaina tradition, King Ajātasattu is known by the name of Kūṇika. See Mehta and Chandra, *Prakrit Proper Names*, 1: 196.

103 Hemacandra describes the last days of Śreṇika in the *Triṣaṣṭiśalākāpuruṣacaritra*, 10: 12. 161–7. The Theravādins, however, have preserved a different version of the king's death. According to them, he was a *sotāpanna* (one who has "entered the stream") and submitted patiently to the torture perpetrated upon him by the men dispatched by his patricide son; he died peacefully and was reborn in the Cātummahārājika Heaven in the company of the regent king Vessavaṇa. See Malalasekera, *Pali Proper Names*.

The Jaina claim that King Śreṇika committed suicide and the Buddhist claim that his son confessed to the crime of killing him cannot be easily reconciled. Is it possible that the Jainas considered it politically advantageous to absolve the new King Kūṇika (i.e., Ajātasattu) of patricide or that the Buddhists found it doctrinally unacceptable to allow a *sotāpanna* to commit suicide? Whatever the case, there is no doubt that both traditions considered the dead king a righteous ruler, the Buddhists going as far as calling him *dhammiko dhammarājā*, a designation normally applied in the canon only to a *cakravartin* king.

104 Ordinarily, the Jainas also depict their would-be Jinas as being born in the heavens before their final incarnations as human beings. The case of Śreṇika is treated therefore as an extraordinary event that may take place only once in a long while. What is remarkable, however, is the Jaina refusal to make an exception to the operation of the laws of karma, even for so distinguished a person as a would-be Jina! Even assuming that Śreṇika had resorted to suicide only to save his son from his *ānantarya-karma*, an act that would seem appropriate for a bodhisattva, the Jainas cannot accept the taking of life in any form and had no choice but to consign him to purgatory. For a comparison of the careers of a bodhisattva and a would-be Jina, see P. S. Jaini, "Tīrthaṅkara-prakṛti and the Bodhisattva path," *Journal of the Pali Text Society*, 9 (1981): 96–104.

105 Attributed to an elder named Kassapa, an inhabitant of the Coḷa country. See Malalasekera, *Pali Proper Names*, 1: 66.

BIBLIOGRAPHY

TEXTS AND TRANSLATIONS

Abhidharmakośa-bhāṣya of Vasubandhu, Sanskrit text ed. by P. Pradhan. Patna: K. P. Jayaswal Research Institute, 1967.

AbhisamayālaṅkarĀlokā-Prajñāpāramitā-vyākhyā of Haribhadra, 2 vols., ed. U. Woghihara. Tokyo, 1932–5.

Anāgatavaṃsa, ed. J. Minayeff. *Journal of the Pali Text Society*. London, 1886, 33–53.

Anāgatavaṃsa-Aṭṭhakathā, ed. J. Minayeff. *Journal of the Pali Text Society*. London, 1886, 33–53.

ĀryaMaitreya-vyākaraṇam, ed. P. C. Majumder. Calcutta: K. L. Mukhopadhyaya, 1959.

Aṣṭasāhasrikā-Prajñāpāramitā-sūtra, ed. P. L. Vaidya. Buddhist Sanskrit Texts, no. 4. Darbhanga, 1960.

Avadanākalpalatā, 2 vols., ed. P. L. Vaidya. Buddhist Sanskrit Texts, nos. 22–3. Darbhanga, 1959.

Buddhavaṃsa, ed. R. Morris. London: Pali Text Society, 1882.

Dasabodhisattuppattikathā, text ed. together with trans. entitled *The Birth-Stories of the Ten Bodhisattvas*, by H. Saddhatissa. Sacred Books of the Buddhists, no. 29. London: Pali Text Society, 1975.

Dhammapada-Aṭṭhakathā, 4 vols., ed. H. C. Norman, London: Pali Text Society, 1914.

Dharmasaṃgraha, ed. M. Muller and H. Wenzel. Anecdota Oxoniensia, Aryan Series, vol. 1, pt. 1. Oxford, 1855.

Dīghanikāya, 3 vols., ed. T. W. Rhys Davids and J. E. Carpenter. London: Pali Text Society, 1890–1911.

Divyāvadāna, ed. E. B. Cowell and R. A. Neil. Cambridge, Eng., 1886.

Gaṇḍavyūha-sūtra, ed. P. L. Vaidya. Buddhist Sanskrit Texts, no. 5. Darbhanga, 1960.

Guyhasamāja-tantra, ed. B. Bhattacharya. Gaekwad's Oriental Series, no. 53. Baroda, 1967.

Hevajra-tantra, ed. and trans. by D. Snellgrove. London Oriental Series, no. 6. London, 1959.

Jātakamāla of Ārya Śūra, ed. by H. Kern. Harvard Oriental Series, no. 1. Cambridge, Mass., 1890.

Jātakatthavaṇṇanā, 2d ed., 6 vols., ed. V. Fausboll. London: Pali Text Society, 1964.

Jinakālamālī, ed. A. P. Buddhadatta. London: Pali Text Society, 1962. Translated as *The Epochs of the Conqueror*, by N. A. Jayawickrama. Translation Series, no. 36. London: Pali Text Society, 1968.

Kalpa-sūtra (Prakrit *Kappasuttaṃ*). Jayapur: Prakrit Bharati, 1977. Translated as *Lives of the Jinas*, by H. Jacobi in *Jaina Sutras*, Sacred Books of the East, no. 22, pt. 1. London, 1895, 217–311.

Lalitavistara, ed. P. L. Vaidya. Buddhist Sanskrit Texts, no. 1. Darbhanga, 1958.

Mahākarma-vibhaṅga, ed. and trans. S. Lévi. Paris, 1932.

Mahāpurāṇa of Guṇabhadra, ed. P. Jain. Varanasi: Bharatiya Jnanapitha, 1965.
Mahāvaṃsa, ed. W. Geiger. London: Pali Text Society, 1958.
Mahāvastu, 3 vols., ed. E. Senart (Paris, 1882–97). Translated as *The Mahāvastu*, 3 vols., by J. J. Jones. Sacred Books of the Buddhists, nos. 16, 18, and 19, London: Pali Text Society, 1949–56.
Maitreya-samiti, ed. and trans. E. Leaumann. Strasbourg, 1919.
Maitreya-sūtra, trans. by Watanabe, in the *Maitreya-samiti*, 227–80.
Maitreya-vyākaraṇa, ed. and trans. S. Lévi, "Maitreya le Consolateur," in *Etudes d'Orientalisme publiées par le Musée Guimet á la mémoire de Raymonde Linossier*. Paris, 1932, vol. 2.
Majjhimanikāya, 3 vols., ed. V. Trenckner and R. Chalmers. London: Pali Text Society, 1888–1902.
Mañjuśrī-Mūlakalpa, ed. T. Ganapati Shastri. Reprinted in the Buddhist Sanskrit Texts, no. 18. Darbhanga, 1964.
Milindapañho, ed. V. Trenckner. London: Pali Text Society, 1880.
Niṣpannayogāvalī, ed. B. Bhattacharya. Gaekwad's Oriental Series, no. 109. Baroda: Oriental Institute, 1949.
Pañcabuddhabyākaraṇa, ed. and trans. G. Martini, in *Bulletin de l'Ecole Française d'Extrême-Orient*, 55 (1969): 125–44.
Paññāsa-Jātaka or Zimme Paṇṇāsa (in the Burmese Recension), 2 vols. ed. P. S. Jaini. London: Pali Text Society, 1980–1.
Phra Malai suttta (known by the title *Dika Malaideva sut*). Bangkok: Thambanakhan Press, 1971.
Phra Pathomsomphōthikathā, by Paramanuchit Chinorot (1790–1853). Bangkok: Ministry of Education, 1962.
Prasannapadā-Mādhyamikakārikā-vyākhyā by Candrakīrti, in *Madhyamakaśāstram*, ed. P. L. Vaidya. Buddhist Sanskrit Texts, no. 10. Darbhanga, 1960.
Rasavāhinī of Vedeha, ed. by Saranatissa Thera, 2 parts. Colombo: Jinalankara Press, 1928.
Saddharmapuṇḍarīka-sūtra, ed. P. L. Vaidya. Buddhist Sanskrit Texts, no. 6. Darbhanga, 1960.
Sādhanamālā, 2 vols., ed. B. Bhattacharya. Gaekwad's Oriental Series, nos. 26 and 41. Baroda, 1925–8.
Śālistamba-sūtra, no. 8 in the *Mahāyāna-sūtrasaṅgraha*, ed. P. L. Vaidya. Buddhist Sanskrit Texts, no. 17. Darbhanga, 1961, 100–6.
Samādhirāja-sūtra, 2 vols., ed. N. Dutt, *Gilgit Manuscripts*, vol. 2, pts. 1 and 2. Srinagar-Kashmir, 1941 and 1953.
Saṃyuttanikāya, 4 vols., ed. Leon Feer. London: Pali Text Society, 1884–98.
Śikṣāsamuccaya, ed. C. Bendall. Indo-Iranian Reprints. The Hague: Mouton, 1957.
Sphuṭārthā-Abhidharmakośa-vyākhyā of Yaśomitra, 2 vols., ed. U. Woghihara. Tokyo, 1932–6.
Śrī-Saddhammāvavāda-saṅgrahaya, by Siddhartha Buddharakshita. Panadura, 1930.
Sukhāvatīvyūha, ed. M. Muller and B. Nanjio. Anecdota Oxoniensia, Aryan Series, no. 1, part 2. Oxford, 1883.
Suttanipāta, ed. D. Anderson and H. Smith. London: Pali Text Society, 1948.

Suttanipāta-Aṭṭhakathā (*Paramatthajotikā*), ed. H. Smith. London: Pali Text Society, 1916–18).

Suvarṇaprabhāsa-sūtra, ed. S. Bagchi. Buddhist Sanskrit Texts, no. 8. Darbhanga, 1967. Translated as *The Sūtra of Golden Light*, by R. E. Emmerick. Sacred Books of the Buddhists, no. 27, London, 1970.

Triṣaṣṭiśalākāpuruṣacaritra of Hemacandra. Bombay, 1956, chap. 10. Translated as *The Lives of Sixty-three Illustrious Persons*, by H. M. Johnson. Gaekwad's Oriental Series, no. 140. Baroda, 1962.

Vimalakīrtinirdeśa or the teaching of Vimalakīrti, by E. Lamotte. Sacred Books of the Buddhists, no. 32. London, 1976.

Vinayapiṭaka, 3 vols., ed. H. Oldenberg. London: Pali Text Society, London, 1979–83. Translated as *The Book of the Discipline*, 6 vols. Sacred Books of the Buddhists, vols. 10, 11, 13, 14, 20, 25. London, 1938–66.

Visuddhimagga of Buddhaghosācariya, by H. C. Warren and D. Kosambi. Harvard Oriental Series, no. 41. Cambridge, Mass., 1950.

Yoga-sūtras of Patañjali with Vyāsa-bhāṣya: See *Pātañjala-Yogadarśanam*, ed. by R. S. Bhattacharya (Bharatiya Vidyaprakashana). Varanasi, 1963.

MODERN WORKS

Basham, A. L. *History and Doctrine of the Ājīvikas*. London, 1951.

The Wonder That Was India. New York: Grove Press, 1954.

Bhattacharya, B. *The Indian Buddhist Iconography*, 2d ed. Calcutta: Firma K. L. Mukhopadhyay, 1958.

Cribb, J. "Kaniṣka's Buddha Coins – The Official Iconography of Śākyamuni & Maitreya." *Journal of the International Association of Buddhist Studies*, 3, no. 1 (1980): 79–87.

Jaini, P. S. *The Jaina Path of Purification*. Berkeley and Los Angeles: University of California Press, 1979.

"Tīrthaṅkara-prakṛti and the Bodhisattva Path." *Journal of the Pali Text Society*, 9 (1981): 96–104.

Lamotte, E. *Histoire du bouddhisme indien des origines à l'ère Śaka*. Louvain, 1958.

Lévi, S. "Maitreya le Consolateur," in *Etudes d'Orientalisme publiées par le Musée Guimet à la mémoire de Raymonde Linossier*. Paris, 1932, vol. 2.

Luce, G. H. "The Shwegugyi Pagoda Inscription." *Journal of the Burma Research Society*, 10, no. 2 (1920): 67–72.

Malalasekera, G. P. *Dictionary of Pali Proper Names*, 2 vols. London: Pali Text Society, 1960.

Mehta, M. L., and Chandra, K. R. *Prakrit Proper Names*, 2 vols. Ahmedabad: L. D. Institute of Indology, 1971–2.

Mendelson, E. M. *Sangha and State in Burma*. Ithaca, N.Y.: Cornell University Press, 1975.

Reynolds, F. E. "The Two Wheels of Dhamma: A Study of Early Buddhism." In *The Two Wheels of Dhamma*, ed. G. Obeyesekere, F. Reynolds, and B. L. Smith. American Academy of Religions Studies in Religion, Chambers, Pa., 1972.

"Buddhism as Universal Religion and as Civic Religion." In *Religion and Legitimation of Power in Thailand, Laos, and Burma*, ed. B. Smith. Chambers, Pa.: Anima Books, 1978.

Three Worlds According to King Ruang: A Thai Buddhist Cosmology. Berkeley, Calif.: Asian Humanities Press, 1982.

Smith, B. "Kingship, the Sangha, and the Process of Legitimation in Anuradhapura Ceylon: An Interpretative Essay." In *Buddhism in Ceylon and Studies on Religious Syncretism in Buddhist Countries*, ed. H. Bechert. Abhandlungen de Akademie der Wissenschaften in Gottingen, no. 108. 1978.

Tambiah, S. J. *World Conqueror and World Renouncer*. Cambridge University Press, 1976.

Varni, Jinendra. *Jainendra-siddhānta-kośa*, 4 vols. (in Hindi). Varanasi: Bharatiya Jnanapitha, 1944.

Maitreya in China, Korea, and Vietnam

Introduction

ALAN SPONBERG

The preceding chapter sets the stage for all the studies that follow. There Maitreya is depicted as a long-striving bodhisattva who will eventually be born as the next Buddha at the peak of the material and spiritual development of the present cycle, a figure who ensures the continuity of the Dharma after the *parinirvāṇa* of Śākyamuni Buddha and one who guarantees the aspiration of all beings to attain enlightenment during the golden era of some future time when the glories of the past have been regained. Following the tradition through a sample of the transformations that occur as it migrates out of its South Asian homeland, we shall see in the following chapters how Maitreya retains those early associations while also assuming a number of new guises, some implicit in the core tradition and some wholly new, the result of assimilation into local traditions and accommodation to local needs. We shall see Maitreya's role take on new nuances as the various potentials in the tradition are played out in new cultural contexts.

The four chapters making up this second section of Part II focus on the development of the legend in continental East Asia: in China proper, as well as in Korea and Vietnam. The first seeks to establish more accurately the parameters of early East Asian Maitreya devotionalism before the development of distinctive Chinese, Korean, and Vietnamese traditions. Drawing on the exegetical writing of a seventh-century Buddhist monk who was heir to the orthodox or mainstream Maitreya tradition, this study shows that Maitreya-related beliefs and aspirations within monastic institutions were thoroughly integrated into the standard Mahāyāna soteriology and that they fit into that soteriology in a way that combines both the "now" and "later" dimensions of the Nattier typology (see Chapter 2) while minimizing the here/now dichotomy.

With that foundation in mind we are in a position to appreciate both the common and the distinctive features of the picture that emerges from

Daniel Overmyer's study of Maitreya in the *pao-chüan* literature of popular religious sects dating from the fourteenth century in China. Overmyer shows Maitreya to be one of a constellation of salvific figures assimilated into millenarian aspirations that sometimes include militantly political and catastrophically apocalyptic notions. Far more often, however, his role is otherworldly; he is the one who "comes to rescue the lost from the profane world, by reminding them of their sacred roots and showing them the way home to the Eternal Mother."

This assimilation of indigenous traditions is an important theme in the studies of Korea and Vietnam as well. Lewis Lancaster surveys the roles of Maitreya in Korea – warrior, guardian figure, symbol of fertility, spirit of possession in shamanist practice, leader of a new world order – drawing on both textual and artistic sources that span a period from the time of the Three Kingdoms to the present. Hue-Tam Ho Tai then turns to Vietnam, another region that took much from early Chinese developments in formulating its own distinctive Maitreya tradition. Tai discusses in particular two twentieth-century millenarian movements there, considering them in the context of modern Vietnamese social history but with attention to their historical antecedents as well.

An important issue in the study of Maitreya in East Asia is the problem of tracing the incorporation of overtly apocalyptic and eventually even eschatological elements into the core tradition. Recent research has indicated Taoist origins for many of these elements, and further data important to this complex issue are provided by all of the studies in this section. Overmyer shows that Maitreya's role in the *pao-chüan* literature was only rarely millenarian in an overtly political sense, and even the implicitly apocalyptic theme introduced with the incorporation and elaboration of the three-cycle motif still lacks any developed eschatological dimension. Tai shows that apocalyptic elements seem to appear relatively late in Vietnam but then goes on to argue that the millennium of Maitreya does seem to represent an eschatological telos in the distinctly Vietnamese version of the three-cycle time scheme of the Hoa Hao movement, a development she seeks to trace back to the influence of one particular *pao-chüan* type of text said to have been introduced into Vietnam from China in the late nineteenth century.

Another theme that became very important in East Asia is the notion of Maitreya securing the welfare of the state as well as that of the individual, a notion that seems to contrast sharply with the focus of the Central Asian Maitreya cult on the individual. Did this idea originate in East Asia and, if so, following what model? This has been the topic of recent research by Antonio Forte (cited below), and a possible source that has been suggested were developments during the Northern Wei period. Lancaster's comments on Maitreya belief during the Three Kingdoms period in Korea support that thesis. He notes the prominence of the theme as a distinctive characteristic of the Korean Maitreya tradition, pointing out also that Maitreya beliefs were introduced into the area under the influence of the Northern Wei. In the following section we shall see how important this theme became in Japan after being introduced there from Korea. Another important theme, and one that also recurs in Japan, is the appearance, under special circumstances, of Maitreya to individuals here on earth. Both Lancaster and Tai note the prominence of this theme. Still further links to the study of Maitreya in Japan can be seen again in the popularity of the smiling or pensive Buddha image in Paekche and later in Vietnam.

As a group, the chapters in this section demonstrate that, as the Maitreya tradition in East Asia developed historically, Maitreya's appeal shifted increasingly from a locus in the monastery-based institutional religion to lay-based popular religion, gaining there new representations in popular art and literature and showing an ever greater degree of assimilation and adaptation under the influence of local traditions. That observation sets the stage, in turn, for the final section of Part II, for we shall see in those chapters how the continuation of the same trend dominates the history of Maitreya in Japan, even while the particular forms he takes there become distinctly Japanese.

4

Wŏnhyo on Maitreya Visualization

ALAN SPONBERG

Introduction

Recent scholarship on the place of Maitreya in Chinese Buddhism has provided valuable insight into several important areas of concern. Daniel Overmyer and Susan Naquin have documented the role of Maitreyan messianic belief in Chinese popular movements,[1] and Eric Zürcher, Anna Seidel, and Michael Strickmann have begun to explore the influence of indigenous Taoist eschatological thought on Buddhist millenarianism.[2] Although this research has begun to fill one significant gap in our knowledge of early Maitreya beliefs in China, there are other facets of the Maitreya cult that must be examined more closely as well.

For some in early China, Maitreya did indeed become the focus of militantly millenarian aspirations anticipating an imminent and apocalyptic transformation of the existing social order. For many more, however, Maitreya remained a cult figure of rather different dimensions, the focus of future aspirations certainly, but aspirations conceived in more personal and far less revolutionary terms. The latter, nonrevolutionary form of Maitreya belief, the orthodox cult or what we might refer to as the core tradition, had solid roots in the Buddhist canonical scriptures. Its practices drew on South and Central Asian precedents, and although it was based in the more learned strata of the monastic elite, it appears to have been a significant part of popular lay Buddhism as well, at least during the period up through the seventh century, when it came to be gradually eclipsed by the newer and more exclusive Pure Land cult of Amitābha.

In his article on Prince Moonlight, Professor Zürcher presents an excellent analysis of early Maitreya themes in China, distinguishing two quite different Maitreya cults. He speaks of a Taoist-influenced eschatological and messianic conception of Maitreya that emerged out of, yet differed significantly from the older canonical tradition of the bodhisattva Maitreya.[3] To explore this useful distinction, we must develop in more detail our picture of the mainstream or orthodox Maitreya cult in early China, especially in the period up through the first century of the T'ang. At this stage in the study of Maitreya in China it appears, rather ironically, that we know more about the militantly apocalyptic minority tradition than we do about the much more influential, canonically based cult from which the former was, at least in part, derived. This is particularly true with respect to the question of cult practice, the range of rituals and techniques that were associated with the orthodox Maitreya cult in China. We need a better sense of the way in which the Maitreya cult fit into the broader picture of mainstream Buddhist praxis.

Pioneering work on the canonically based Maitreya tradition in East Asia was done more than seventy years ago by Matsumoto Bunzaburo 松本文三郎.[4] His seminal study, which has had much influence on most subsequent Japanese Maitreya scholarship, remains an invaluable introduction to the Maitreya Sūtras of the East Asian tradition. It is limited, however, both by the restrictions of its scope and by presuppositions arising from Matsumoto's familiarity with the later Pure Land tradition in East Asia. Matsumoto's primary concern was to document the scriptural tradition for Maitreya devotionalism and then to show the parallels and differences between Maitreya's "Pure Land" in Tuṣita Heaven and Amitābha's Sukhāvatī. Although we have learned a good deal from this type of textual research about the scriptures read by those involved in the mainstream Maitreya cult, we nonetheless know relatively little about what these Maitreya devotees actually did in terms of praxis, and even less about how they understood the aspiration involved in that praxis, the aspiration to be reborn in Tuṣita Heaven. What were the parameters of their belief? How did they see the traditional goal of enlightenment in relation to their vow to gain rebirth in the splendor of Tuṣita Heaven? How did they see the goal of enlightenment in relation to the even more immediate aspiration of gaining a vision of Maitreya while still in the body? What sort of specific practices did they employ, and toward what specific goals? How were the different goals associated with the Maitreya cult interrelated, and how were they reconciled, one with another? Was it more important, in terms of soteriological efficacy, to seek a vision of Maitreya now or to secure the prospect of rebirth in Tsuita later – or should one rather focus on Maitreya's future career back here in this realm of human existence after his rebirth as the future Buddha? Were these, indeed, seen as different, mutually exclusive aspirations, as alternative orientations, or rather as variations or stages of the same goal?

All of these questions are extremely important in any effort to understand the mind of medieval Chinese Buddhists, especially since the Maitreya cult appears to have involved many attitudes and practices common to both monastic and lay Buddhists. These are not the kind of questions, however, that a study of the scriptural sources alone will directly illuminate. More work on the scriptural tradition is certainly necessary, but we also need to know what the East Asian Buddhists were making of those scriptures, how the various Maitreya-related themes were actually shaping the lives and attitudes of Buddhist practitioners. Although attitudes of contemporary religious practitioners are relatively accessible, through interview and direct observation, we are much more limited when undertaking such a study of a community of practice so far in the past. Even so, in the case of the medieval Chinese Maitreya cult a surprising variety of sources can be employed. In addition to the various Maitreya Sūtras and apocrypha themselves, there is much to be gleaned, for example, from biographical sources, from Buddhist art, from the Tun-huang records of lay associations, and from the many miracle stories associated with Maitreya.

It will take some time before the data available from these rather disparate sources can be integrated, but I suspect that eventually a surprisingly rich and detailed picture of early Chinese Maitreya belief will begin to emerge. The present chapter seeks to contribute to this effort by examining the explanation of Maitreya practice and attitudes presented in a seventh-century work written by a prominent Buddhist exegete actively involved in the assimilation of Chinese Buddhism in the Korean kingdom of Silla.[5]

Wŏnhyo's Description of Maitreya Cult Practice

The two textual passages discussed here are drawn from a commentary on one of the principal Maitreya Sūtras in the East Asian tradition, a commentary written in the mid–seventh century by Wŏnhyo 元曉 (617–86), a Korean monk from Silla.[6] Wŏnhyo was a very erudite, if equally eccentric scholar, and though he never studied at any of the main monastic centers around Ch'ang-an in China, there is no question that he was quite conversant with the Chinese Buddhism of his day. Perhaps the most prolific exegete among his compatriots, he is considered a key figure in the systematization of an indigenous Korean Buddhism. This pivotal role makes him an especially valuable source for my purposes here, both because of his broad knowledge of pre-T'ang Chinese Buddhism and also because of his motivation to organize that tradition for presentation to an audience living outside of China proper.

We can get some idea of the range of Wŏnhyo's scholarship and also of his special interests if we review briefly the topics covered by his written works, including those that have not survived.[7] Aside from one or two essays, most of Wŏnhyo's writing appears to have been exegetical, commentaries written on a particular sūtra or treatise for the most part. Besides commentaries on the Maitreya Sūtras and the Pure Land scriptures, his corpus includes works on the *Avataṃsaka Sūtra*, the *Lotus*, the *Vajrasamādhi Sūtra*, the *Sandhinirmocana*, the *Vimalakīrti Sūtra*, the *Mahāyāna-saṃgraha*, the *Yogācāra-bhūmi*, and a number of others. We can see that his background was quite broad, and though later Japanese historians often associate him with Hua-yen thought, it is clear that he had a special interest in the Maitreya cult practice and also a thorough familiarity with the Yogācāra works current in seventh-century China. Wŏnhyo is credited with two Maitreya works, a *Commentary on the Maitreya Sūtra[s?]* 彌勒經疏, which has not survived, and the *Doctrinal Essentials of the Sūtra on Maitreya's Rebirth Above [in Tuṣita Heaven]* 彌勒上生經宗要,[8] which contains the passages of interest here. Although the lost work was probably a line-by-line commentary on one or more of the Maitreya Sūtras, the work at hand is a broader discussion of different exegetical problems connected with the Maitreya tradition.

In addition to the apocryphal Maitreya works discussed by Zürcher and others, there were a number of different Maitreya scriptures available to Wŏnhyo.[9] Following a tradition that appears to have been well established by the seventh century, he takes three of these Maitreya works as the canonical standard, usually citing them by their short titles: the *Sūtra on Maitreya's Rebirth Above* (T 452), the *Sūtra on Maitreya's Rebirth Below [on Earth]* (T 453), and the *Sūtra on [Maitreya] Achieving Buddhahood* (T 456). Eponymously related to the first but actually referring to all three of these sūtras, Wŏnhyo's surviving Maitreya commentary is divided into ten sections, each on a different topic. In the first section Wŏnhyo discusses the general purpose 大意 of the sūtra, moving on in the second section to consider the various practices that were involved in the Maitreya cult. He continues, in the subsequent sections, to consider first the differences and the similarities among the three Maitreya Sūtras and then the question of whether the Maitreya teaching is a Hīnayāna or a Mahāyāna doctrine. Next he reviews various theories on the number of eons before Maitreya's advent and Buddhahood, and he concludes with a reconciliation of various scriptural pronouncements on the temporal relation between the career of Śākyamuni and that of Maitreya.

It is the second section of the commentary that is of special relevance to the questions raised above. Wŏnhyo provides there an unusually detailed discussion and explanation of Maitreya cult practice and also of the specific results one can expect to achieve from practicing the different techniques mentioned. The specificity of Wŏnhyo's comments warrants a translation of the passage in full.[10]

> Section Two: Elucidation of the Doctrinal Themes and the Intention 明經宗致 [of the Sūtra]
>
> This sūtra rightly takes the means and results 因果 of visualization and practice 觀行 as its doctrinal themes 宗, while having as its intention

意致 to cause beings to be born in [Tuṣita] Heaven, there to be forever without relapse [from the bodhisattva path].

Visualization here is of two kinds. The first is to visualize the majestic adornments (*alaṃkāra*) of [Tuṣita] Heaven as the setting for rebirth, and the second is to visualize the superiority of receiving rebirth [there] as a bodhisattva.[11] One concentrates one's thoughts in a detailed visual examination 專念觀察 and so this [technique] is called *samādhi* 三昧. Nevertheless, it is not a [*samādhi* that produces] the wisdom of meditative cultivation 修慧, as it consists only of learning [about Maitreya's heaven] and reflecting upon it 唯在聞思. [Even so,] it is still called the "Lightning-bolt Samādhi." Not having serenity (*praśrabdhi*) 輕安 [as a prerequisite], moreover, it is an effective means 因 for [use even in] this world fraught with desire, the *kāmadhātu*.[12]

The practice spoken of here is of three kinds: (1) hearing the name Great Benevolence 大慈 [i.e., Maitreya] and repenting with reverent mind the transgressions previously committed; (2) hearing the name Benevolent One 慈氏 and respectfully trusting 仰信 in the virtues manifested by this name; (3) undertaking the practice of the ritual acts of cleaning stūpa shrines, replastering them, offering incense and flowers, etc., as taught in a subsequent passage [of the this Sūtra].

This visualization and these practices together make up a single foundation. The results generated thereby are of four kinds: (1) the sprouting shoot, (2) leaves and flowers in the shade, (3) the blossoming of fine flowers, and (4) the ripening of fragrant fruit.

The "sprouting shoot" result subdues and extinguishes all the transgressions previously committed. This is the result attained by means of the first of the practices. With the "leaves and flowers in the shade" result, one no longer falls into the three undesirable paths of rebirth[13] or into the false views (*dṛṣṭi*) of untenable extremes [as opposed to the correct view of the middle path]. This is the result attained by means of the second practice. The "blossoming of fine flowers" result is to attain the fine recompense of being personally present there in Tuṣita [Heaven].[14] This is what one attains by means of the third practice. The "maturing of fragrant fruit" result is to attain [the stage of] nonrelapse on the supreme path. This is what one attains from the twofold visualization discussed above.

Why is this so? By virtue of having thoroughly visualized the circumstances of receiving rebirth as a bodhisattva [in Tuṣita Heaven], when one is then born in that Heaven one personally receives sacred instruction 聖導 and one never relapses from supreme, perfect enlightenment (*anut[tara-samyak-saṃ]bodhi*). Therefore [I say that] it is on the basis of the twofold visualization that one attains the fourth result.

By hearing the name of the Benevolent One, one trusts in the virtue of his humane excellence 仁賢之德. Far removed from any place that the holy name 聖名 is not heard and ever in accord with correct views, those of [Maitreya's] retinue achieve spiritual maturity 成就. Therefore [I say that] it is on the basis of hearing his name that one attains the second result.

The remaining two results and their respective means should be understood in corresponding manner. You should know that, having brought to maturity the means and the results of this visualization and practice, supreme enlightenment will occur quite naturally. And it is just this that is intended as the result of being reborn above [in Tuṣita Heaven].

This second section of Wŏnhyo's commentary is followed, in section three, by a long discussion of theories on whether Maitreya devotion is a Hīnayāna or a Mahāyāna practice, Wŏnhyo favoring the arguments that it was originally a Hīnayāna practice that came to be included in the Mahāyāna.

Wŏnhyo returns to the topic of the practices involved in Maitreya devotion in section four, while discussing the ways in which the three Maitreya Sūtras are similar and the ways in which they differ. The first of the differences that he raises is that the audiences for which the sūtras were intended differ, and this difference, as we shall see, is related to the type of practice employed.[15]

What I have spoken of as a difference with regard to those for whom [the sūtras were taught] refers to the fact that the people who cultivate the visualization are of three grades. The highest grade of people 上品之人 are those who either cultivate the *samādhi* of Buddha visualization 觀佛三昧 or who take repentance as their method of practice 因懺悔行法. In their present body they will succeed in seeing Maitreya 見彌勒.[16] According to the quality of their mind 心優劣, the image 形 they see will be either great or small. This is as is taught in the *Sūtra on the Sea of the Samādhi of Buddha Visualization* and the *Expanded Dhāraṇi*.[17]

The middle grade of people are those who either cultivate the *samādhi* of Buddha visualization or who [practice] by performing pure deeds (*karma*). After having given up this [present] body, they will be reborn in Tuṣita Heaven, there to see Maitreya and attain the stage of no relapse. This is as is taught in the *Sūtra on Rebirth Above*.[18]

The lowest grade of people cultivate the various good deeds – generosity (*dāna*), morality (*śīla*), etc. – and, upon that base, produce a vow (*praṇidhāna*) wishing to see Maitreya. After giving up their [present] body, they incur rebirth in accord with their past deeds until the time when Maitreya completes the path 成道 [and is reborn on earth]. They will see Maitreya then and attain deliverance 得度 as part of the three assemblies. This is as is taught in the *Sūtra on Rebirth Below* and the *Sūtra on Achieving Buddhahood.*

Thus those for whom the *[Sūtra] on Rebirth Above* was [taught] are people of the middle grade, whereas the other two sūtras are for the benefit of the people of the lowest grade.

These two passages tell us a great deal about Wŏnhyo's understanding of Maitreya cult practice. First of all he recognizes several distinct practices. These include performing *pūjā*-type ritual acts at a shrine, hearing or being mindful of Maitreya's names, having confidence or trust (*śraddhā*) in Maitreya's virtues, repenting past sins, and meditating with a special twofold "visualization" technique. Conspicuously absent here is any specific mention of collective devotional activity.[19] Proceeding to consider the effectiveness of these practices, Wŏnhyo arranges them in a hierarchy, relating each to the different result it produces. Finally, in the second passage, Wŏnhyo goes on to elaborate this schema of practice and result by correlating it with a hierarchy of Maitreya practitioners who are distinguished on the basis of the speed with which their practice will result in gaining a vision of Maitreya and attaining the stage of no relapse on the path to supreme, perfect enlightenment. With each grade of practitioner he indicates a specific textual source for the particular practices employed.

Analysis of Wŏnhyo's Views

Let us look more closely at some of the details in Wŏnhyo's discussion of the practices and goals of Maitreya belief. Most immediately striking is Wŏnhyo's emphasis on visualization 觀, a cult activity apparently of such importance that he explicitly distinguishes it from the other, more traditional forms of practice 行.[20] Although the different forms of practice (including visualization) can be combined, according to the second passage, Wŏnhyo asserts that it is specifically the visualization technique that ensures the most desirable result. In his discussion of the technique, moreover, Wŏnhyo makes it clear that what is involved is an active visualization of a specific scene in carefully reflected, eidetic detail. Thus in this context, "visualization" (rather than simple "contemplation," for example) seems to be the most appropriate rendering of the Chinese *kuan* 觀.

This Chinese character, which means literally "to see" or "to regard," is also a frequently encountered technical term in Buddhist Chinese, one with several distinct meanings. In its most common technical usage it renders the Sanskrit *vipaśyanā*, discernment or insight, one of the two components of Buddhist meditation. Wŏnhyo's comment that this technique involves "concentrating one's thoughts in a detailed visual examination" suggests that here the term has yet another specialized meaning, one that as we shall see below links this Maitreya work to a series of other "visualization" sūtras and one more probably derived from the practice buddha-mindfulness or recollection (*buddhānusmṛti*).

Another aspect of this visualization technique is also noteworthy. What is the practitioner told to visualize? It is not Maitreya per se. The procedure, in Wŏnhyo's understanding at least, is twofold; it is a visualization of both "one's conditioned and one's direct recompense" 依正報 – of the setting of one's next rebirth and of the body one will then have. This means that one is to visualize oneself, personally present, amidst all of the splendors of Tuṣita Heaven, splendors that certainly include, but are not limited to, Maitreya. The figure of Maitreya would, of course, dominate any vision of Tuṣita, but the objective of the twofold technique is not simply to produce an image of Maitreya himself. It is rather to place *oneself* in the presence of Maitreya and his heaven. This detail may be of particular significance in considering East Asian iconographic depictions of Maitreya and Tuṣita, especially those in settings thought to have been meditation chapels.

Next Wŏnhyo considers the question of whether this visualization technique is technically speaking a *samādhi*, an advanced technique of concentrated mental absorption. He observes that, although it is generally referred to as a *samādhi*, it is not an advanced *samādhi* in the most technical Abdhidharma sense, which is to say not a *samādhi* that directly produces wisdom (*prajñā*), nor one that requires having attained a substantial degree of serenity. "Serenity" 輕安 here renders *praśrabdi*, a specific mental factor (*caitta*) referring to the functional integration of mind and body that counteracts the normal state of intellectual and emotional agitation or restlessness. Such a prerequisite would have put this practice out of the reach of lay Buddhists and even many monks.

Moreover, Wŏnhyo seems to suggest not only that proficiency in the more advanced meditative practices is unnecessary, but that it could even be counterproductive. More advanced meditation techniques could put one quite out of reach of Maitreya. Buddhist cosmology portrays a universe comprising countless world systems, each divided into three interconnected spheres: the desire realm (*kāmadhātu*), the realm of form (*rūpadhātu*), and the formless realm (*arūpadhātu*). Tuṣita Heaven is only the fourth of six heavens in the desire realm – still very close to the level of human existence and surpassed by more than twenty higher heavens in the other two realms, all of which are attainable by meditative practice. Cultivation of the more advanced degrees of *samādhi* would quickly take the practitioner out of the desire realm altogether and thus beyond the abode of Maitreya in Tuṣita.

If this is, in fact, what Wŏnhyo had in mind with his rather elliptic comments on the nontechnical nature of this visualization practice, we can infer that he placed some importance on establishing the Maitreya cult as a path open to all beings regardless of their station or vocation in life. It was a practice accessible even to lay devotees, not one limited only to professional, monastic meditation specialists. This observation is all the more significant in light of the fact that Wŏnhyo does not introduce into this discussion the eschatological ideas associated with the three stages of the decline of the Dharma, ideas that were certainly current and popular in the Chinese Buddhism of his time, though probably more in the context of the new Pure Land cult than in that of the older visualization tradition. In the subsequent polemic initiated by Pure Land devotees against the Maitreya cult practice, the relatively low cosmological status of Tuṣita became a crucial point. Advocates of Amitābha's Pure Land argued that being reborn there was better than rebirth in Tuṣita, which was still rife with all the impurities of the desire realm, the *kāmadhātu*. Women were still to be found in Tuṣita, they pointed out. Maitreya devotees had a quick rejoinder, however: They noted that even though Sukhāvatī might be more pure and refined than the desire realm of this world, it was nonetheless a separate world system and thus far more remote and far more difficult of access than Tuṣita, which is right here immediately at hand.

With this understanding of Wŏnhyo's view of Maitreya visualization in mind, we can now look at what he has to say about the goal or objectives of this practice. I want, in particular, to draw attention to the way in which Wŏnhyo integrates several different aspirations associated with the Maitreya cult. In his list of the results one can expect, Wŏnhyo mentions the goals of (1) ameliorating the negative karma accrued as the result of past sins, (2) avoiding undesirable rebirths in the future, (3) being reborn in Tuṣita Heaven as a bodhisattva, and (4) attaining the degree of nonrelapse on the bodhisattva path. Although there is clearly a hierarchy here, the four levels do not appear to be necessarily sequential. In other words, one can aspire directly to the highest result even from one's current state, and it is precisely that goal that is brought about by visualization as the preeminent practice.

The interesting thing about the fourth and highest level of aspiration is that the ultimate goal is to ensure nonrelapse from supreme, perfect enlightenment (*anuttara-samyak-saṃbodhi*), the goal already long established as the summum bonum of Mahāyāna Buddhism. For Wŏnhyo the value of rebirth in Tuṣita Heaven lies in the fact that close association with Maitreya speeds one's progress on the bodhisattva path. Thus rebirth in Tuṣita is not strictly speaking an end in itself, especially when we take into account the fact that the distinguishing characteristic of supreme, perfect enlightenment is its efficacy in working for the benefit of other beings, at all levels of this world.

This observation is particularly significant when we begin to consider the soteriological orientation of Maitreya cult practice in its various historical and cultural manifestations. In Chapter 2, Jan Nattier proposes a morphological typology by which she contrasts different instances of the myth according to whether the aspirant's encounter with Maitreya takes place in the present or the future (now vs. later) and whether it takes place on earth or in Tuṣita Heaven (here vs. there). These two axes yield a matrix comprising four logically possible combinations (here/later, there/later, there/now, and here/now). If, however, we attempt to plot the tradition Wŏnhyo represents onto this matrix, we find that it does not fall neatly under any one of these headings. It can be understood only as a composite of three of the four types. Wŏnhyo says that the aspirant provisionally seeks rebirth in Tuṣita Heaven (there/later) by cultivating a particular visualization practice (there/now) in order to perfect bodhisattva skills and understanding that will subsequently be of use on earth (here/later). The unifying idea is the doctrine that Maitreya is the next Buddha and that he is currently dwelling in Tuṣita Heaven before his rebirth as Śākyamuni's successor. (Also operative, of course, is the general notion that enlightenment is most easily achieved at a time when there is a Buddha active in the world.)

Now there is certainly no note of here/now urgency in Wŏnhyo's view, but the other three typological motifs are so intertwined that it would be a distortion to try to characterize the tradition described by Wŏnhyo under any single one of the four headings suggested by Nattier. The value of such a typology, however, lies not just in the extent to which it exactly mirrors the data we have. Indeed, we should be suspicious whenever that appears to be the case. As hermeneutic tools, typologies are often the most useful when they draw our attention to what is *not* present in the data even though we might have expected it to be. That is the value of this typology. Logically, the typology allows for four mutually exclusive orientations, although what I actually see in the historical data is more a marked contrast between only *two* basic positions. On the one hand, there is the postmillenarian core tradition, which focuses on Maitreya's Buddhahood in the distant future and, on the other, there is a repeatedly manifested premillenarian minority view, one often militantly apocalyptic and revolutionary in its expectation of Maitreya's imminent advent. Note, however, that both of these share a concern with what is of this world. "Here" or "there" is not the primary focus of concern; the crucial distinction lies on the now versus later axis.[21] What most sharply demarcates these two traditions is the temporal setting of their respective expectations: Does one expect to realize the goal later in another lifetime, or now in this lifetime? Within the core tradition, which looks to later lifetimes, the there/later (rebirth in Tuṣita) and the there/now (visualization of oneself in Tuṣita) elements are secondary elaborations, developments that make sense only in the context of an expectation to be reborn later with Maitreya at the time most auspicious for achieving enlightenment. In terms of the typology outlined above, we might call this developed version of the core tradition a here/even-later orientation. Even so, we must remember that the ultimate objective remains the orthodox Mahāyāna goal of supreme, perfect enlightenment – an achievement that by definition is to be employed for the benefit of all sentient beings at all levels of the universe and one that is most easily attained during Maitreya's future tenure as the next Buddha.

What we have, then, in the tradition as presented by Wŏnhyo is an aspiration that subsumes three of the four aforementioned morphological types, though all effort remains directed ultimately toward enlightenment, an enlightenment that is achieved later and one that is attained *in* – and *for the benefit of* – this world. If the basic dichotomy between this tradition and the militant movements is that plotted on the now versus later axis, we must recognize that the here versus there distinction, where it can be identified at all, remains secondary and not, in fact, definitive. This lack of emphasis on the here versus there axis is not as surprising as it might first seem, actually – not if we remember that for the Buddhists Tuṣita was the fourth of six heavens in the *kāmadhātu* and thus still very much a part of *this* world, still very much a part of the "here." Tuṣita was not some remote or ontologically transcendent other realm, not really a "there." The cosmology operative in Buddhism is one that presupposes a rather fluid continuity between the human realm and the heavens, certainly a greater continuity than we are used to in the Judeo-Christian tradition. To find a here versus there dichotomy in Buddhism comparable in metaphysical magnitude to that between heaven and earth in the Semitic traditions, we would have to turn to the contrast between nescience (*avidyā*) and enlightenment (*bodhi*), between *saṃsāra* and *nirvāṇa*; but then the spatial metaphor might not be as appropriate. Perhaps an even more useful and revealing typology could be constructed by adding a corporate versus individual axis to the matrix. This would allow a further contrast between the individualistic core tradition and the communal/here/now apocalytic movements. It would also allow some interesting cross-cultural comparisons to be made, particularly given the tendency toward a corporate orientation in the mainstream of Judeo-Christian millenarianism. For our present purposes, in any case, we must at least note the prominence of the now versus later axis in the complex of aspirations outlined in the text translated above.

Wŏnhyo's exegesis provides one clear example of this composite orientation, but it is by no means an isolated instance.[22] Indeed, the frequency with which this combination of objectives is encountered leads me to suspect that it was the dominant form of Maitreya belief in China. I wonder, in fact, if there are *any* cases in which the there/later or the there/now orientations do occur independently – standing on their own, exclusively and without the underlying here/later assumption of eventual rebirth on earth with Maitreya. The interior logic of Buddhist doctrine and of the myth itself leads one to question whether the former two orientations could stand on their own, and I have seen no conclusive evidence for any instance in which they did occur outside the context of the basic here/later assumption. Rather than actually occurring as independent morphological types, it seems far more likely to me that the notions of rebirth in Tuṣita Heaven and visualization of Maitreya were consistent (if not necessary) developments or elaborations of the core idea, the here/even-later orientation. But at what point were the latter elaborations added to the core idea? And where? We have seen that the fully developed composite orientation was well established as orthodox by the beginning of the T'ang. But whether this composite tradition was a development that originated in China or whether it is one going back to South Asian (or perhaps Central Asian) sources is a question that requires further research. Wŏnhyo's discussion in the text translated here does suggest to me, however, that this combination of Maitreya-related aspirations was one established very early in China as the orthodox tradition and thus one that was very likely established, at least in part, on the basis of some non-Chinese precedent.

The second passage translated above provides a few more details of interest as well as one significant addition to Wŏnhyo's initial comments that will help establish the antiquity of the tradition he represents. In the latter passage he speaks more generally of seeing or gaining a vision of Maitreya rather than of the more elaborate visualization technique he had already outlined. Perhaps here he is drawing on the language of an older, less specific tradition. We see again the association of the immediate goal with the longer-term objective of gaining nonrelapse in one's pursuit of supreme, perfect enlightenment. Also both visualization and repentance are mentioned together as practices characterizing the highest grade of devotees, those who will succeed in gaining a vision of Maitreya even now while still in this lifetime.

Of much more interest in this passage, however, is Wŏnhyo's correlation of specific sūtras with each of the levels of aspirants. Somewhat surprisingly perhaps, the two sūtras that Wŏnhyo specifies for the highest group of practitioners are not among the three standard Maitreya Sūtras; indeed, they are not even part of the broader group of Maitreya-related works. Why are two works, neither dealing particularly with Maitreya, given such a prominent place in Wŏnhyo's presentation of Maitreya cult practice? Why, indeed, are they elevated to a position even above that of the Maitreya Sūtras themselves? That Wŏnhyo gives them such prominence in his commentary on the most important of the Maitreya Sūtras indicates that he saw them as extremely important to Maitreya cult practice and also very closely linked to the Maitreya Sūtras. This requires a closer look at the two works in question.

We shall see that the association with these two sūtras links the Maitreya group to a tradition of visualization practice introduced into China, perhaps from Kashmir, as early as the beginning of the fourth century. There is a group of sūtras, all recorded as having been translated by figures from the northwestern frontier of India and all bearing in their title the term *kuan* 觀, or "visualization." Alexander Soper studied these works in his *Literary Evidence for Early Buddhist Art in China*,[23] noting their importance to East Asian iconographic traditions. The full title of the Maitreya Sūtra commented on here by Wŏnhyo is in fact the *Sūtra Taught by the Buddha on Visualizing Maitreya Bodhisattva's Rebirth Above in Tuṣita Heaven* 佛說觀彌勒上生兜率天經. Noting the presence of *kuan* in the title of this work, Soper tentatively included it in his list of "visualization sūtras." He retained some doubts, however, and preferred to render the *kuan* in this case as "meditation" rather than "visualization," pointing out the following:

> Actually the *kuan* factor is touched on only lightly in the Tuṣita *sūtra*. No technique of visualization is offered; the goal of mystical seeing is described in a routine way; and the figure drawn for the reader of the Bodhisattva in glory is composed of conventional attributes.[24]

Soper is quite correct in this assessment, though he was looking only at the sūtra text itself[25] and not examining the way in which the text was understood and used. The nature of the visualization technique Wŏnhyo describes suggests a much closer link between the visualization tradition and the practice associated with this Maitreya Sūtra.

The two works that Wŏnhyo cites as sources for the highest grade of Maitreya practice are the *Sūtra on the Sea of the Samādhi of Buddha Visualization* (T 643) and the *Expanded Dhāraṇi Sūtra* (T 1339). The first of these is a work translated by Buddhabhadra between 398 and 421 and one that Soper includes in his group of "visualization sūtras."[26] This work is, in Soper's opinion, probably the earliest of the visualization series. That being the case, it is not surprising that Wŏnhyo would take it as the locus classicus for the visualization technique he presents, even though it is of much more diverse content than the later visualization sūtras.

The second work, the *Expanded Dhāraṇi Sūtra*, is not one of the titles that Soper includes in his list of texts associated with the visualization tradition. However, this work does appear to be, at least in part, a recension of the *Pratyutpannabuddhasammukhāvastitasamādhisūtra*, a text better known in China as the *Samādhi Sūtra of Bhadrapāla* (T 416, 417, 418, 419). It is the latter recension of the work that became the most popular, and in that form it *is* recognized as a text associated with the visualization tradition. Under the latter title it is, in fact, one of the works that Soper includes in his list, pointing out that it is even more closely related to the *Sūtra on Visualizing Amitāyus* than is the *Sūtra on Buddha Visualization*.[27]

We can conclude, then, that Wŏnhyo's comments on the eidetic nature of the visualization technique and his association of the Maitreya Sūtras with the *Sūtra on Buddha Visualization* and the *Expanded Dhāraṇi Sūtra* clearly establish that the Maitreya cult was considered to be very much a part of the older visualization tradition. Wŏnhyo's time, the seventh century, marked the beginning of the Pure Land polemic directed against Maitreya devotion, an important feature of the later Pure Land tradition. Now that the seventh-century Maitreya cult can be seen to have roots in the older visualization tradition, it is important to note that, unlike the Pure Land movement, this tradition was characterized not by an exclusive focus on one particular cult figure, but rather by its emphasis on a particular technique. In that light, it is much less surprising, for example, that many of the figures associated with the Maitreya cult also wrote commentaries on the Pure Land Sūtras, and especially on the *Sūtra on Visualizing Amitāyus*, a text already central to the visualization tradition long before it was taken up by the more exclusive Pure Land movement.

When we speak of the Maitreya cult in this period, we are thus referring to something quite different from the slightly later and much more exclusively focused Amitābha cult of the East Asian Pure Land tradition. Maitreya-related activities were still, I think, simply one part of a much broader tradition of Buddhist practice. The differentiation of cult figures in the visualization tradition appears to have been a matter of functional specificity. Cult activities directed specifically to Maitreya, for example, were given precedence over those directed toward Śākyamuni or Mañjuśrī in certain life situations, not because he was considered to be a superior cult figure generally, as Amitābha came to be, but because Maitreya was associated with particular aspects of one's life. Maitreya cult activities were given preference, for example, when one was considering one's future rebirth or, in an even more particular situation, when the Buddhist scholar was in need of exegetical inspiration.[28] In other situations, when the practitioner was about to undertake a hazardous journey, for example, or when he was ill, similar techniques were employed to address an equally specialized and functionally specific cult figure, in this case Avalokiteśvara or the Medicine King Buddha.[29]

The later sectarian polemic that set Maitreya up as a rival of Amitābha has made it difficult to see the Maitreya cult of early China in this more comprehensive light. Wŏnhyo's comments can help us begin to sort out Chinese notions regarding Maitreya before the emergence of Amitābha exclusivism. By indicating more precisely the composite nature of the devotee's aspiration to be reborn in Tuṣita and by clearly linking Maitreya devotion to the early visualization tradition, Wŏnhyo gives us some very important pieces to the complex puzzle of early Buddhist thought and practice in China.

NOTES

1 Daniel L. Overmyer, *Folk Buddhist Religion* (Cambridge Mass.: Harvard University Press, 1976) and Susan Naquin, *Millenarian Rebellion in China: The Eight Trigrams Uprising of 1813* (New Haven Conn.: Yale University Press, 1976).

2 See especially E. Zürcher, "Prince Moonlight," *T'oung Pao*, 68 (1982): 1–75; Anna K. Siedel, "The Image of the Perfect Ruler in Early Taoist Messianism: Lao-tzu and Li Hong," *History of Religions*, 9 (1969/70): 216–47; and Michael Strickmann, "Chinese Views of the End of the World," unpublished paper.

3 Zürcher, "Prince Moonlight"; see esp. 13*ff*.

4 *Miroku jōdo ron* 彌勒浄土論 (Tokyo: Heigo shuppansha, 1911) with a summary and review by Noël Péri in the *Bulletin de l'Ecole Française d'Extrême-Orient*, 11 (1911): 439–58.

5 For further research in a similar vein, see my chapter, "Meditation in Fa-hsiang Buddhism," in *Traditions of Meditation in Chinese Buddhism*, ed. Peter Gregory (Honolulu: Kuroda Institute and University of Hawaii Press, 1986), 15–43.

6 On Wŏnhyo see Motoi Nobuo 本井信雄, "Shiragi Gangyō no denki ni tsuite" 新羅元暁の伝記について, *Ōtani Gakuhō*, 41, pp. 33–52, and also Robert Buswell's forthcoming article, "The Biographies of the Korean Monk Wŏnhyo," in *Biography as a Genre in Korean Literature*, ed. John Jamieson and Peter Lee (Berkeley, Calif.: Center for East Asian Studies).

7 My summary is based on the list provided by Mochizuki Shinkō 望月信京, *Bukkyō daijiten* 佛教大字典, rev. ed. (Tokyo: Sekai Seiten Kankō Kyōkai, 1954–71), 783.

8 T 1773: 38. 299a–303a.

9 A summary list is provided by Zürcher in "Prince Moonlight," 12 n. 16. For a thorough study of thirty-seven Maitreya texts in East Asia see chap. 2 of Matsumoto's *Miroku jōdo ron*.

10 The text is found at T: 38. 299c1–24; in revising this translation for publication I was thankful for several helpful suggestions offered by Sung-bae Park.

11 The phrase *yi-cheng-pao* 依正報 is a technical term referring to the "conditioned and the direct recompense" one receives after death as the result of one's deeds (karma) in this life. The direct recompense is the body one receives, and the conditioned recompense is the setting into which one is reborn. I have rendered the terms more freely in the translation here and below.

12 *Praśrabdhi* is a positive mental quality (*caitta*) listed as part of the general class of mental factors in Buddhist Abhidharma psychology. It is the factor conducive to and required for the higher levels of meditation, attainments that take one out of the *kāmadhātu* and thus beyond Tuṣita Heaven.

13 Rebirth as an animal, as a ghost, or as a denizen of hell.

14 Lit. "the fine recompense, conditioned and direct, of Tuṣita," that is, being there oneself (direct recompense) in those surroundings (conditioned recompense).

15 This passage is found at T: 38.300b12–22.

16 Here and below one might also render this phrase "gaining a vision of Maitreya."

17 T 643: 16 and T 1339: 21, respectively; these will be discussed below.

18 The *ku* 故 here is probably a *Taishō* misprint for *ju* 如, which would make this phrase parallel to the rest of the text.

19 Repentance may have been done publicly following the Indian *upoṣadha* tradition, but even in that case there would seem to be little emphasis on the collective orientation of the activity.

20 The Chinese term *kuan-hsing* 觀行 would be understood more naturally as a compound term, one that originally would probably have rendered *anusmṛti-bhāvanā*, the generic designation for the sixfold mindfulness or recollection of the Buddha, Dharma, Saṅgha, *śīla*, *tyāga*, and *devatā*. Wŏnhyo makes it clear in the following discussion, however, that he wants to contrast *kuan* with *hsing*. Even so, we should note that *buddhānusmṛti* is the most likely South Asian precursor of this visualization tradition, though the latter does seem to present a more developed and specialized understanding of the original practice.

21 It is very important to note that the distinction I refer to here thus does not correspond to the traditional Sino-Japanese typology of "ascent" versus "descent," an exegetical categorization that has become prominent in Japanese scholarship on the Maitreya tradition. The core tradition includes both ascent and descent motifs, whereas the militant, minority tradition focuses only on the imminent descent.

22 The close interrelation of these three elements is also well illustrated by a famous incident from the life of Hsüan-tsang, one that I have discussed at some length in the article cited in note 5. During his travels in India, this seventh-century Chinese pilgrim was set upon by river pirates. Learning that the pirates planned to sacrifice him to Durgā, he requested time to perform a highly structured Maitreya visualization exercise, hoping that this would ensure his rebirth in Tuṣita Heaven, where he could perfect his knowledge of the Dharma under Maitreya's instruction. He also vowed to be reborn with Maitreya "to this world again, where he would teach these same pirates [in their later lives], bringing them to practice good deeds and to abandon all evil acts, and where he would propagate the Dharma widely for the benefit of all beings" (T 2053: 50.233c31–234a21).

23 Alexander Soper, *Literary Evidence for Early Buddhist Art in China* (Ascona: Artibus Asiae, 1959), 143*ff*, 184*ff*, 215*ff*, 222*ff*.

24 Ibid., 216.

25 T: 14.419c–420a.

26 Soper, *Literary Evidence*, 184*ff*.

27 Ibid., 143; note that the title of T 417 should be transcribed *Pan-chou San-mei Ching* rather than *Po-chou San-mei Ching* as in Soper's text.

28 This aspect of the Maitreya cult has been well documented by Paul Demiéville in "Le *Yogācārabhūmi* de Sangharakṣa," *Bulletin de l'Ecole Française d'Extrême-Orient*, 44 (1954): 339–436; see esp. 376–95.

29 See Raoul Birnbaum's study, *The Healing Buddha* (Boulder Colo.: Shambala, 1979).

5

Messenger, Savior, and Revolutionary

Maitreya in Chinese Popular Religious Literature of the Sixteenth and Seventeenth Centuries

DANIEL L. OVERMYER

Introduction

Maitreya has played a variety of roles in different texts and circumstances. He is a symbol of hope for deliverance in the future who presents different facets to persons in diverse social and religious situations. Though Maitreya's basic promise is constant, the needs and interests of his devotees shape what they see. This is true as well for the roles of Maitreya in scripture texts produced by popular religious sects in China from the sixteenth century on. In these books Maitreya appears as a bodhisattva in paradise, a messenger bringing new revelation in the present or recent past, a preacher to sinful individuals, and a savior yet to come who will rescue the world from its confusion and suffering. In this last role he comes during a new period of time that will culminate in all returning to heaven or in the transformation of this world into a place of joy and long life. In some passages the Buddha Maitreya and his predecessors are described as "taking charge of the world" (*chang shih-chieh* 掌世界), but in most his coming task is called "taking charge of the religion" (*chang chiao* 掌教). What "taking charge of the world" means is spelled out in detail in only one of the texts I have collected, but in a few other books there are clear political implications, easily perceived and amplified by an aggressive sect leader. What gave force to these implications, for sect leaders and Confucian officials alike, was their foundation in an alternative world view, in which the world is created and directed by gods and Buddhas quite outside the pantheon of Confucian culture heroes. The mainstream of sectarian teaching is based on a distinctive creation myth, described below, concerning the origins of the world and human beings in primordial times. According to the myth, three successive cycles of time, each "controlled" by a Buddha, were established at the time of "creative chaos" (*hun-tun* 混沌). In China, as elsewhere, primordiality meant superior reality and authority. So it is that in these books the creation myth is referred to over and over again, and devotees are repeatedly told that they are *yüan-jen* 元人 (原人), "primordial ones," "people of the origin." In other words, the mythic foundations of their being and meaning have nothing to do with Confucian understandings, though the sectarians came to include in their teaching originally Confucian ethical principles and loyalist attitudes toward the ruler and state.[1]

However religious his basic task and intention, Maitreya could thus appear as a symbol of a different system of order and authority in the world, and hence it is not surprising that he was often viewed with suspicion by official investigators. Nonetheless, in the scripture texts themselves his role is predominantly otherworldly; he comes to rescue the lost from the profane world by reminding them of their sacred roots and showing them the way home to the Eternal Mother (Wu-sheng lao-mu 無生老母), chief deity of sectarian tradition. In her heavenly paradise they will enjoy felicity and long life forever or, more precisely, for eighty-one eons, or *kalpa*s. Considered in isolation, some of the language related to Maitreya in these books has a political "aroma," as the Chinese would say. But taken in the larger context of their teaching, Maitreya's fundamental task is to bring spiritual deliverance; it is this task that is explicitly and repeatedly promised and spelled out, constantly reinforced with exhortations to maintain pious diligence. With a few exceptions, what detail one finds is devoted to names of deities to whom prayers may be offered, descriptions of memorials and charms, and numerical lists of trigrams, the years of each Buddha's reign, and mythical sacred places. In the *Huang-chi chiu-lien pao-chüan,* discussed in the section on Maitreya in sectarian scriptures, there is apparently suggestive language about this text revealing ancient secrets concerning "important affairs of the latter realm" (the present world) (*hou-t'ien ta-shih* 後天大事). In secular writings *ta-shih,* "the great affair," often refers to attempts to claim the throne of China. But in this text it is soon clear that *ta-shih* refers to the new outpouring of revelation in the third period of world history, that of the "imperial ultimate," Huang-chi 皇極. Its content is the liberation from *saṃsāra* of the remaining children of the Eternal Mother, the creator of humankind. Its intention is the restoration of primordial unity (*shou-yüan* 收元) as the last act of salvation history (*mo-hou i-chü* 末後一舉), which takes place in heaven, beyond the world. The directional language employed is that of departure (*li* 離, *ch'ü* 去) and ascent (*shang* 上, *teng* 登), as well it might be, for at the end of the age the world is in utter chaos.

The sources for this chapter are Chinese vernacular texts called *pao-chüan* 寶卷, "precious volumes," material I have been collecting for some time, most recently on a research trip to China in 1981. These books were composed by the leaders of popular religious sects, which first appeared in their characteristic early modern form in the fourteenth century with their own types of leadership, organization, congregational rituals, beliefs, and texts.[2]

The first extant books of scripture produced by these groups that can be dated were composed in the early sixteenth century. From then on many hundreds of these books were written throughout the imperial period and continued to appear in China until the mid–twentieth century. Hundreds more have been composed on Taiwan since 1950. Though there are various types and styles, and they have developed over time, the term most commonly used to designate these books is *pao-chüan,* a name often found in the titles of the texts themselves. They can be distinguished from the scriptures of monastic Buddhism and priestly Taoism by their use of the vernacular and by their teachings, deities, and relatively eclectic approach.[3]

A common theme in these books is the creation of the world by a mother goddess, Wu-sheng lao-mu, the Eternal Venerable Mother, who sends down to earth ninety-six myriads of her children. Though they are originally all "Buddhas and immortals," once on earth they forget their true home in paradise and become attached to fame, profit, and sensual pleasures. Trapped by their desires, they are immersed in *saṃsāra,* the "sea of suffering," repeatedly encountering death and rebirth and suffering punishments in purgatory. The Venerable Mother, grieved by this, sends down messenger deities to remind her lost children of their true nature and the way home.

According to this myth, time is organized into three great cycles, each succeeding the last and presided over by three Buddhas. The Buddha of the past is Jan-teng 燃燈 (Dīpaṇkara), the Lamplighter; that of the present is Śākyamuni; and that of the future is Maitreya, referred to as the "Buddha who has not yet come" or is "about to arrive." The passage of each cycle is accompanied by disasters, in some texts described as the end of the world for each cycle. But hope remains, because the Buddha of the next time period will soon descend, and those with karmic potential, who believe sect teaching and practice the proper rituals, will be saved. In sectarian texts of the Ming and Ch'ing dynasties (1368–1912) the second cycle, that of Śākyamuni, is about to end, and Maitreya is soon to arrive. In fact, he or his heralds may have already come to reveal texts and religious practices that will enable the faithful to survive. At the end of their trials is the "last act," the "recovery of original wholeness" (*shou-yüan*), when the Mother and her children will be reunited, and the sacred and profane merged together. In most texts this reunion takes place in paradise, but in a few the language indicates hope for changing this world itself into a "realm of utmost bliss."[4]

This myth of creation and salvation provides the background for all the roles Maitreya plays in Chinese sectarian scriptures. I shall discuss these roles as depicted in several early *pao-chüan,* after first reviewing briefly the historical background. This discussion proceeds according to the chronological appearance of the texts, the better to discern any development of ideas and themes. At the end I summarize what this material tells us and discuss its implications for our understanding of the place of Maitreya in Chinese popular religion.

All of the books presented here were produced by popular religious sects, but in most cases precise organizational connections are unclear. There were variations in sect form and activities, dependent on both individual traditions and local circumstances, and these variations could influence attitudes toward the surrounding society. Ideally, then, this discussion should proceed on a case-by-case basis, relating *pao-chüan* content to sect situation as much as possible. Here, however, my purpose is to discuss a theme in *pao-chüan* literature as such in an attempt to order this literature as a genre in its own right. This is not a discussion of sect history, only of the major form of written material produced by some of these groups. Although in style and structure *pao-chüan* are a type, this type includes much variation in content, as I have discussed before. All the books discussed here expound religious teachings in a direct way, though in one or two instances short stories or vignettes are employed for this purpose. None are based on the more developed stories characteristic of the later stages of this literary tradition.

All references here to Maitreya in *pao-chüan* literature are based on the texts I have collected and read, a total of about one hundred. Since I have examined many more than this number, I am confident that my collection is representative, though it is far from complete. Li Shih-yü's bibliography of *pao-chüan* still extant in the twentieth century contains 774 entries, with some duplication. Sawada Mizuho's study lists 208 titles, and, of course, many more of these books were lost or destroyed over the centuries.[5]

Maitreya in Chinese Historical Sources

The role of Maitreya in orthodox Buddhist writings and iconography is discussed in the previous chapters. There he appears as a teacher and savior in heaven, waiting to descend as the next Buddha. His devotees aspire to go to his paradise after death or to be reborn on earth in the joyous time of his descent, when all who hear Maitreya's preaching will be saved. Maitreya will come when the world is flourishing, ruled by a wise and benevolent king who prepares Maitreya's way and then is converted by him. This association with a world-ruling king is important, because in some sources Buddha and king are conflated, and Maitreya becomes a figure royal and religious at the same time. As Professor Jaini discusses in Chapter 3, several accounts predict that it is a king who will be reborn as the future Buddha.

In some noncanonical Buddhist texts written in China in the sixth century, Maitreya and similar figures appear in a very different setting, as militant saviors who descend in a time of chaos and decay to cleanse the world of evil and establish a purified community of the elect. This cleansing involves cosmic warfare between demons and bodhisattvas, but in the end a "Magic City" will appear, in which the pious will live in peace, ruled by the Buddha. The social origin of these texts is not clear, but they include comments critical of monks and in praise of lay piety, so they appear to have been produced by groups in which literate lay persons were present.[6]

Historical sources note the existence of militant Buddhist groups in this same period, led by monks who claimed political authority, some in the name of future saviors. Some of these groups were involved in armed uprisings, the causes of which are ambiguous. By the early seventh century we find references to associations with monk leaders who proclaimed themselves Maitreya and evidently attempted to found new states of their own. In the eighth century a man named Wang Huai-ku 王懷古 stated that a new Buddha was coming to replace the decaying regime of Śākyamuni and that his arrival would coincide with the founding of a new dynasty. By this time there were Maitreya sects with leaders, followers, and scriptures of their own.

In the eleventh century a former military officer named Wang Tse 王則 led an uprising in the name of Maitreya during which he proclaimed, "Śākyamuni Buddha has declined. Maitreya Buddha shall rule the world." Fourteenth-century sources describe several Maitreya groups, some militant, others not. In the middle of that century powerful groups that venerated Maitreya took an active part in the civil wars leading to the overthrow of the Yüan (Mongol) dynasty.[7]

After the founding of the Ming dynasty in 1368, groups that venerated Maitreya continued to be active, though only some of them became involved in uprisings. Groups that looked forward to Maitreya understood him to be one of a series of three Buddhas, in some cases to be reborn in the family of a sect leader. For example, an account of an early nineteenth-century group in Hopei quotes one of its texts as follows:

> In the past the Lamplighter Buddha ruled the religion (*chang-chiao*), and [then] each year had six months, and each day [only] six [Chinese] hours. Now Śākyamuni Buddha is dominant, and the year has twelve months, with twelve hours to the day. In the future, the Buddha of the Future, Maitreya, will control the religion; then each year will have eighteen months and each day eighteen hours. The Buddha of the Future will be reborn in the Wang family of Shih-fo k'ou 石佛口 [a Hopei village].[8]

Susan Naquin discusses several other eighteenth- and nineteenth-century instances of claims that sect leaders were Maitreya incarnate.[9] In some cases such leaders became involved in militant uprisings, which further contributed to an aura of subversion around Maitreya in the eyes of officials and literati.

In the historical background of our texts, then, Maitreya originated as a Buddhist savior with a potential for radical, politically oriented interpretation. At the popular level traditions about him were carried on by sectarian groups, most of them concerned with promises of divine aid for believing individuals. Some sect leaders, however, saw in Maitreya a promise of world renewal, which they attempted to implement by direct, even violent, means. In the following, we shall look at the scriptural correlates of these different roles and interpretations.

Maitreya in Sectarian Scriptures

Before we proceed, we should attempt to clarify the quantitative place of Maitreya in the *pao-chüan* in order to avoid any temptation to see his roles as more important in this tradition than they really were. In fact, at a quantitative level, Maitreya is not an important figure in *pao-chüan* literature still extant in the twentieth century; quite the contrary. Li Shih-yü's bibliography lists more than 700 *pao-chüan* titles; only three of these titles include the name Maitreya, four if one counts a text referring to Pu-tai 布袋, considered to be a Sung dynasty reincarnation of this Buddha. In Sawada Mizuho's list of 208 titles, only two refer to Maitreya. To be sure, there are some texts devoted to Maitreya whose titles do not include his name. For example, my copy of the *Ting-chieh pao-chüan* 定劫寶卷 (Precious book establishing the last age) (to be discussed below) provides a longer title inside the cover, a common characteristic of *pao-chüan,* for which the cover title is often an abbreviation. In this case the longer title is *Fo-shuo Mi-le ting-chieh chao pao-chüan* 佛說彌勒定劫照寶卷 (Precious scripture in which the Buddha discourses on Maitreya establishing the last age).[10] The title of the *Chiu-lien huang-chi* scripture discussed below does not mention Maitreya, but he is the chief actor in this text. Nonetheless, from a survey of titles alone one can easily determine that Maitreya is only rarely a chief object of devotion in this literature.[11] In all but 5 of the more than 100 *pao-chüan* I have studied, Maitreya either is not present or plays a minor role, and in all cases the chief deity of sect mythology is superior to him, be it the Holy Patriarch of the Limitless, the Venerable Mother, or the Ancient Buddha. However, as part of a defining mythological tradition in sectarian scriptures, Maitreya has an important qualitative role. Wherever we find the three-stage time scheme noted above, with its promise of collective salvation, Maitreya's influence is present even if he is not mentioned.

The first *pao-chüan* composed by a sect founder to expound his own teachings were the five written by Lo Ch'ing 羅清 (1443–1527) in the early sixteenth century. Lo Ch'ing's books became the model for the later development of this type of scripture. However, Maitreya is completely absent from his teachings and appears only once, in a negative context, in the *Cheng-hsin ch'u-i wu hsiu cheng tsu-tsai pao-chüan* 正信除疑無修証自在寶卷 (The precious book [containing the truth] which is of sovereign independence, needing neither cultivation nor realization, and which rectifies belief and dispels doubt). Chapter 19 of this book is entitled "The Evil Spirit of the Maitreya Sect" ("Mi-le chiao hsieh-ch'i" 彌勒教邪氣), the theme of which is "the Maitreya sect is really an evil and heretical tradition" (*cheng shih hsieh-feng* 正是邪風). This tradition is attacked for writing charms and for being bound to "the realm of name and form, which is empty." Its adherents are told, "If you believe in heresy, and are not diligently pious, you will go to hell," a term I use advisedly here, because for Lo Ch'ing such people are doomed to stay in purgatory forever. This condemnation is part of a larger attack on older, rival sectarian traditions, which Lo Ch'ing rejects because of their image worship and use of folk rituals. It is important to note that although Lo Ch'ing evidently knew of the Eternal Mother myth, he did not incorporate it or its three-stage time scheme into his teachings. He was not concerned about collective destruction at the end of a world cycle and so had no need for a dramatic rescue by a savior such as Maitreya. His teaching centers on individual release from *saṃsāra* through insight into one's potential for enlightenment. The most important orthodox sources of his thought are Ch'an and Pure Land Buddhism.[12]

However, in another very old *pao-chüan,* evidently composed not long after those by Lo Ch'ing, Maitreya has a very important role indeed. This is the *Huang-chi chin-tan chiu-lien cheng-hsin kuei-chen huan-hsiang pao-chüan* 皇極金丹九蓮正信皈真還鄉寶卷 (The precious book of the golden elixir and nine lotuses of the imperial ultimate period, which [leads to] rectifying belief, reverting to the real and returning to our true home), which was reprinted in 1523.[13] This text, which repeatedly refers to the Chin-tan tao 金丹道, or "Way of the Golden Elixir," represents a stream of *pao-chüan* thought much more influenced by Taoism and the Maitreyan tradition in Buddhism. In it the Eternal Mother myth and three-stage time scheme are already basically complete, with a Buddha presiding over each period. The future Buddha, Maitreya, is explicitly identified as such in the interior of the book (chaps. 7, 10, 11, and 12), but in the opening chapters this bearer of new revelation is called Mi-t'o 彌陀, Amitābha, not Mi-le 彌勒, Maitreya. Since his task is that of Maitreya and he is equated with the Wei-lai Fo 未來佛 (e.g., chaps. 2 and 3), the Buddha not yet come, there is no doubt that is who he is. Presumably the author of the *Huang-chi chiu-lien* book used the name of the more innocuous Amitābha to avoid immediate association with Maitreyanist "subversion." For our purposes this idiosyncracy may be ignored; the chief actor in this book is Maitreya, here incarnate as Wu-wei tsu-shih or Wu-wei chiao-chu 無爲祖

師(教主), "The patriarch of noninterference" or "Master of the religion of noninterference."

The first four chapters of the *Huang-chi chiu-lien pao-chüan* focus on Mi-t'o/Mi-le's resistance to the Venerable Mother's instructions that he descend to the profane world to save the "injured souls" (*ts'an-ling* 殘靈), the ninety-two myriads of former "Buddhas and immortals" (her children) who have lost their way in *saṃsāra*. Mi-t'o/Mi-le protests that he is too much attached to the beauties and comforts of paradise, but finally relents and descends to the "vicinity of Shadowless Mountain" in "the Han land of nine divisions" (Chiu-chou Han-ti 九州漢地: China). There in the "Three-Minds Hall" (San-hsin t'ang 三心堂) of the "Palace of noninterference" (Wu-wei fu 無爲府), he manifests himself as the Wu-wei patriarch. His task is to reveal the *Chiu-lien* scripture, which he does in long, rambling responses to questions put to him by persons who appear at the hall. Within this sketchy narrative framework he discusses his teaching in the first person (*wo* 我, wu 吾), expounding a variety of topics in twenty-four chapters (*p'in* 品) in two *chüan*.

The Patriarch's message is a call to those with karmic potential (*yu-yüan jen* 有緣人) to realize their true nature and origin as children of the Venerable Mother of the Imperial Ultimate (Huang-chi Lao-mu 皇極老母) and recognize the true patriarch (*jen chen-tsu* 認真祖), here clearly indicating Wu-wei/Maitreya himself. Once they have awakened (*wu* 悟) to who they really are, their devotees are urged to believe, warned against backsliding, and told of the ritual practices that will guarantee their acceptance in heaven. These practices include exercises to enable the soul to pass through the mysterious aperture between the eyebrows (*k'ai hsüan-kuan* 開玄關) and "publishing one's name in the registry for returning home" (*kuei-chia pu piao ming-hsing* 皈家簿標名姓), by sending up the appropriate memorial (*piao* 表) (several types are listed; see chaps. 14, 17, and 18).

In this book Maitreya has a double role, the most important of which is as revealer of the *Chiu-lien* book in the recent past. This scripture is his legacy, but at the same time is described as a *wei-lai ching* 未來經 (scripture about the future) (chaps. 12 and 17), which reveals the secrets of the Imperial Ultimate stage that is soon to appear (*tang-lai* 當來). It is Maitreya who will usher in this new period, so his role is also that of a future savior. We are told near the end of the book that he will come again: "I am leaving now, but I will return to restore the original wholeness. Those with karmic potential I will see again" (chap. 22). In the meantime the proper attitude for devotees is *waiting* (*teng* 等) – "waiting for the time" (*teng-shih* 等時) (chap. 10); "waiting for the time when one will leave the profane body, and one's holy nature will return to the real" (chap. 21); "waiting for the last Dragon-Flower Assembly" (chap. 13); etc.[14] In chapter 17 we read, "The children of the Buddha are all refining themselves in lay households, waiting for the original patriarch to appear."

In chapter 12, the faithful are exhorted to "each day at home in the company of the worthy and good, discuss the mysterious and expound the wonderful. If the Way is late in coming (*tao wan lai* 道晚來), think on the patriarch's intentions, nourish your vital force, and preserve your spirit. Day and night, with minds not idle, while being in accord with the profane, respond to the holy" (*sui fan ying sheng* 隨凡應聖).

So this is a book filled with expectancy, but one which realizes that long periods of time may be involved. We are told that humankind has been in bondage to *saṃsāra* for eighteen *kalpa*s, and that each Buddha reigns for long periods: 108,000 years for the Lamplighter Buddha, 27,000 years for Śākyamuni, and 97,200 years for Maitreya (chap. 10). Furthermore, the pious are told that they must refine themselves for a long time (chaps. 23 and 24) before reaching perfection and the assurance of salvation.

The chief message of the *Huang-chi* scripture is a promise of personal salvation, a promise made repeatedly through a variety of metaphors: "going to Ling-shan" (a sacred mountain in paradise), "ascending to the precious land" (*teng pao-ti* 登寶地), "going home, and returning to one's origin and source" (*kuei chia ch'ü fan-pen huan-yüan* 歸家去反本還原). Such return leads to "seeing the Venerable Mother," "sitting in the lotus pavilion," and "living forever." These promises are intensified by their placement against the background of the terrible chaos at the end of the age. Chapter 11 describes the end of the world in great detail, alternating threats of warfare, black wind, and death with hope that "then the true Buddha [Maitreya] will appear," or that "then the ancient Buddha will establish the religion (*she chiao* 設教) . . . and lay out a street to the clouds," so that the Mother's children "can escape all forms of calamity and difficulty."

All this is summarized in chapter 24, where in a section praising the value of the *Huang-chi* book we are told:

> The worthy and good who encounter it apply themselves to make progress. After a long time, when their merit is complete, then parents and children (*fu tzu* 父子) meet together. Throughout the whole sky Buddhas and patriarchs sending down a bright light, welcome and guide them. Those who study the Way transcend both profane and holy, and together go to the city of clouds; they go to the golden elixir peach garden assembly and shed their profane bodies (*t'o-liao fan-t'i* 脱了凡躰) . . . .
>
> Those who preach this scripture will transcend the three realms of existence. Those who explain its meaning will escape death, and on the sea of suffering will float on a boat to the shore. There little

> children will be able to see their dear Mother (*chien ch'in niang* 見親娘), enter the Mother's womb (*ju mu t'ai* 入母胎), and fear no calamities. They will realize the eternal, and forever enjoy security and good health, and for eighty-one *kalpas* will not be moved. They will live for time without measure. I urge each of the worthy and good to believe and accept this, and to maintain the three refuges and five prohibitions [i.e., "moral principles"]. . . . Then all will enter the great ritual arena of the Imperial Ultimate period.

It is Maitreya's task to convey these promises in person, have them inscribed in a book, and then fulfill them in his return to earth.

The *Hauang-chi chiu-lien pao-chüan* is the earliest text I have found so far to expound these teachings. As such it is a key source of sectarian mythology and terms from then on and, for practical purposes, defines a major stream in this tradition.

Another early text, the *Yao-shih pen-yüan kung-te pao-chüan* 藥師本願功德寶卷 (The precious book of the merit of the original vows of the [Healing Buddha] Master of Medicine), 1543, discusses "the various Buddhas [who] are in charge of the religion. The Bodhisattva yet to come bestows compassion to enable all of every sort of living being to transcend the sea of suffering, and together realize enlightenment. He desires that at the three Dragon-flower assemblies they will all meet together" (p. 5).

Chapter 20 of this book is devoted to the "Bodhisattva Maitreya." In it we read:

> As for the Bodhisattva Maitreya, sentient beings on the great earth do not recognize him. He controls the wind and sends down the rain . . . [and manifests] a brilliant light that penetrates the clouds. He leads all to return [to their true] home, he leads all to return home. . . . So, sentient beings leave suffering behind, and do not fear the three types of disasters.

Maitreya tells the Buddha:

> Sentient beings in the last age of the Dharma (*mo-fa* 末法) are concerned only for wine, sex and wealth. They do not fear at all the fact that when one loses human form it is extremely difficult to obtain it again for a myriad ages. If we don't do something now, they will continue to revolve in *saṃsāra* and again fall into the wrong path.

The Buddha replies:

> Exhort all people; [tell them,] "Why don't you turn to the light and become concerned with obtaining your original face [understanding your true nature]?"

The discussion is followed by verse:

> The Bodhisattva Maitreya in the lower world, in this world of suffering, saves the worthy and good. With a "Dharma boat" he saves all of the Mother's children, and those who depart from the world see their dear Mother. (p. 24)

The basic characteristics of Maitreya in *pao-chüan* literature are established in these early texts. He is one of several messengers sent to earth by the Venerable Mother in a last effort to save sinful humankind. He is a symbol of a new outpouring of divine compassion, active here in the present but described in some books as coming in the immediate future. Those whom Maitreya saves are enlightened now and return to the Mother's paradise at death. The eschatology here is personal and otherworldly.

The next texts in my collection, those of the Hung-yang chiao 弘陽教, appeared about fifty years later, at the end of the sixteenth century. In those that I have examined so far, it appears that, although the three-stage time scheme is mentioned, Maitreya is not. Again, the emphasis is on the present. As we read in the opening pages of the *Hun-yüan hung-yang t'an-shih chen-ching* 混元弘陽嘆世真經 (The true scripture of sorrow for the world of the Origin in Chaos Vast Yang [sect]), ca. 1594:

> According to the teachings of the "Vast Yang" school, at present Śākyamuni Buddha is in charge of the religion, and is considered to be Master of the Hung-yang sect. The past was the time of Pure Yang (*ch'ing-yang* 清陽), and the present that of Hung-yang; only in the future will it be the White Yang [period]. All of you in proclaiming [this] should have no doubts or regrets; true teaching rarely appears, and it is difficult to understand and hear.

This formula is repeated in other Hung-yang texts, though in some other versions the characters for "vast" and "pure" are replaced by homophones meaning "red" and "blue-green." Richard Shek comments on "the rudimentary concept of a three-stage progression in human history" in Hung-yang texts:

> . . . this theory is not developed to its fullest extent yet, for there is no information given on who governs the past age of blue *yang* and the future age of white *yang* . . . [these texts] pay almost exclusive attention to the present age, when Śākyamuni Buddha is still very much in control of things, and the various deities are helping him retrieve the primal beings.[15]

An important seventeenth-century *pao-chüan* that describes Maitreya as harbinger of a third period of revelation and cosmic time was the *Ku fo t'ien-chen k'ao-cheng lung-hua pao-ching* 古佛天真考証龍華寶經 (the Dragon Flower scripture) first published in 1654. Chapter 13 of this book is titled "Three Buddhas Continue the Lamp of the Doctrine" ("San Fo hsü-teng" 三佛續燈). This is explained as "The three Buddhas of past, present, and future putting the world in order (*chih-shih* 治世) and continuing the lamp of long life. . . . At the beginning the Ancient Lamplighter Buddha (Jan-teng ku Fo; Dīpaṅkara) appeared first to put the world in order. At an assembly on Divine Mountain (Ling-shan 靈山), he arranged a Dragon-flower holy congregation."

Jan-teng's rule lasted for nine *kalpa*s (*chieh* 劫). He was succeeded by

> the Literary Buddha, Śākyamuni, who preached, undertook responsibility for our assemblies, and continued transmitting the lamp. He controlled this world of suffering for eighteen *kalpa*s.
>
> Next there appeared the Honored Buddha Maitreya, who preached, undertook responsibility for our assemblies, and continued transmitting the lamp. He was in charge of the "constellation world" (*hsing-su shih-cheih* 星宿世界) for eighty-one *kalpa*s [a reference to a future "age of constellations" when one thousand Buddhas will appear].

There is much fanciful imagery associated with each rule, such as the different colors and number of lotus-flower petals: blue-green with three petals for Jan-teng, red with five petals for Śākyamuni, and golden with nine petals for Maitreya. Except for undefined references to "putting the world in order," none of this imagery is explicitly political. Furthermore, in this text there are *five* stages of development; Maitreya is succeeded by the Venerable Patriarch T'ien-chen 天真, a central figure in *Lung-hua ching*. T'ien-chen is succeeded in turn by the leaders of religious sects and their branches. They "undertake responsibility for assemblies of disciples."

A subsequent recapitulation of this in verse concludes, "The three Buddhas controlled the religion and continuously transmitted the lamp; the five patriarchs appear in accord with the cycles of the world; lamp to lamp is passed on continually; surely this will never end. From patriarch to patriarch it has been transmitted until today."

In this series Jan-teng is described as a creator "who first apportioned the world, established the universe, and split open the mists of chaos." He and his successors "establish religion and save men and the gods" (*li-chiao hua-tu jen t'ien* 立教化度人天). Maitreya appears in the middle of the series, evidently in the past, since he is followed by sect masters who bring the tradition down to the present and will continue it in the future. The eschatological thrust of his mission has been absorbed by generations of sect building, a process described in more detail in chapter 14. It is interesting that in this important text the role of Maitreya has no direct political implications; even his "rule" is over a celestial realm.

The alliance of Maitreya with cycles of cosmic time influenced the writers of other *pao-chüan,* including some in the Lo chiao. The *San-tsu hsing-chiao yin-yu pao-chüan* 三祖行脚因由寶卷 (The religious activities of the three patriarchs and their causes and connections), 1682, is a text of the Lo sect in praise of three patriarchs of the tradition, surnamed Lo, Yin, and Yao, with one *chüan* devoted to each. In the chapter dealing with Patriarch Yin, there is a comment about the three successive Buddhas, with Śākyamuni clearly in the present: "The third age is the 'White Yang *kalpa*,' in which the Buddha Maitreya controls the heavens (*chang t'ien-p'an*). He sits on a nine-petaled lotus flower called the 'lotus flower of the ninth grade.' In the future (*wei-lai*) he will rule for 108,000 years" (1.29b).

The last *chüan* of this book, devoted to Patriarch Yao, begins with the following verse:

Maitreya, true Maitreya,
With a myriad transformation bodies,
In the last age you instruct all beings
The confused and blind cannot
recognize you. (3.1)

Here again, Maitreya controls an undefined heavenly realm, a stage in the process of salvation.

In the *Shih-wang pao-chüan* 十王寶卷 (Precious book concerning the ten kings of purgatory), ca. 1700, there is a fragment of Maitreya mythology with more tantalizing possibilities. Jan-teng and Śākyamuni are not mentioned; however:

> The Buddha Maitreya changes heaven and replaces earth, and all human beings in the world change their appearance. They understand the Great Way, and in the Golden City [enjoy] golden branches and jade leaves. In Heaven they accompany Buddhas and patriarchs and secretly sit on golden lotuses. Altogether they continue twenty-four important tasks of the latter realm (*hou-t'ien ta-shih*). The Buddha Maitreya is coming to gather up the primal ones and control the heavens (*t'ien-p'an* 天盤). These important tasks of the latter realm must not be leaked out. Confused people do not understand that in contributing funds and devoting one's mind one must base oneself entirely on a shared rejection of the earthly womb (*kung she liao fan-t'ai* 共捨了凡胎); as a result one will realize enlightenment,

> and on the highest grade of nine-leafed lotus attain eternal Buddhahood. (p. 20)

This ambiguous passage is not developed further in the *Ten Kings* text, which is a fine statement of sectarian mythology and paths to deliverance. Nonetheless, in this case a potentially political role for Maitreya is barely disguised and could easily have been built upon by those so inclined.

The *Book Concerning the Ten Kings* is the last *pao-chüan* in my collection that can reasonably be dated before the eighteenth century. The sixteenth and seventeenth centuries were the formative period of *pao-chüan* development. In this period Maitreya appears as an essentially religious figure, a messenger and preacher on earth, and a savior in heaven, precisely his roles in orthodox Buddhist scriptures, but with time spans radically foreshortened. The beginning point for a political interpretation is present in statements concerning his "controlling the world," but this beginning is not developed in the texts that have survived. This suggests that the radical political application of Maitreya mythology in some sectarian uprisings during these centuries was not directly supported by the scriptural tradition of these sects. This application, attested to in historical sources, was promoted by tracts for the times and oral teaching by aggressive sect leaders to their disciples. In addition, other eschatologies were available, derived from astrology, popular understandings of dynastic decline and renewal, and calculations of dates in the sixty-year cycle of "celestial stems and earthly branches." These eschatologies could be combined with that of Maitreya to reinforce its latent political implications. Nonetheless in sixteenth- and seventeenth-century *pao-chüan* themselves, Maitreya is not a revolutionary.

Later texts for the most part continue the tradition of Maitreya as one of a series of saviors. For example, an eighteenth-century text, the *Ta-sheng Mi-le hua-tu pao-chüan* 大聖彌勒化度寶卷 (The precious book of salvation brought by Maitreya), is in the form of vignettes concerning several incarnations of Maitreya, who adopts various guises to save people in different situations in the Soochow area.[16] Though in language and structure this is a sectarian book, its emphasis on Maitreya as a wandering messenger to erring individuals is unusual for this tradition. The theme of the *Hua-tu pao-chüan* is set in passages such as the following:

> The Buddha Maitreya took leave of the Venerable Mother and descended to the Han land of the nine divisions. City gods and locality gods received his carriage, bowed, and said, "We hope the Buddha in his compassion will save all sentient beings."
>
> The Buddha replied, "In obedience to the Venerable Mother's edict I have descended to the world to save all people. You should each with sincerity aid the task of universal salvation, [so as to]

> together attain the Buddha Way and sit on the heart of the lotus. . . .
> I have now descended into the world only so that people on the great earth can drive away heresy and return to orthodoxy, realize enlightenment and not reject the Venerable Mother's saving intentions. (pp. 10a–11a)

> Maitreya transformed himself to save living beings; holding a staff, he roamed about everywhere, observing how the people of the world piled up sins (*tsao tsui* 造罪) as high as the mountains and did evil (*tso-e* 作惡) as deep as the sea. (p. 14a)

To a crowd at the Tiger Hill monastery in Soochow, Maitreya says, "The last age approaches, but you good people do not understand [the significance of] this last age of the teaching (*mo-fa*), and still go on contending for fame and profit without cease. You have completely forgotten a hope for lodging temporarily in life and returning in death." The preacher urges his audience "to maintain a vegetarian diet, do good and practice religion according to the true Way" (p. 14b).

In another scene Maitreya transforms himself into a "Confucian physician" carrying a gourdful of medicine on his back and an elixir for restoring youth in his hand. He heals the illnesses of all who come to him "with one dose" and then preaches to them the virtues of a vegetarian diet, repentance, and doing good (pp. 19b–20a). He also appears as a ragged scholar who stations himself outside a wine shop, exhorting drunkards to change their ways. In the same form he visits the "flowery streets," where he preaches about lewd sexual behavior and engages in a debate with two prostitutes (who repent). He also converts an evil rich man, a butcher, a group of rowdy young men using high-pressure sales tactics in a marketplace, and selfish monks in a monastery.

Near the end of this book, Maitreya says, "I leave behind this *pao-chüan* to urge people to sincerely and quickly cultivate good karma. All those with karmic potential will together enter the Dragon-flower assembly. All those who listen will awaken to the Way, all those who hear will clarify their minds. [This book] points out clearly the path to heaven, and sweeps away the darkness of purgatory" (p. 93a). In sum, this is an interesting and lively book that presents Maitreya as an earnest preacher who meets people on their own terms and shows them a better way.

Another pre–nineteenth century text that mentions Maitreya is the *K'ai-hsüan ch'u-ku hsi-lin chüan* 開玄出谷西林卷 (The book of the Western Grove, which opens up the mystery and leads the way out of the valley), 1785. We are told that "the Western Grove" is Maitreya's paradise in the west, and, indeed, that is the savior's location in this text. He appears when the soul of the pious human hero of this book reaches heaven while he is in a trance state, sees a great congregation at worship, and is told that "this [is] the world of Maitreya in the palace of superior goodness" (p. 81a). It was, in fact, a "Dragon-flower assembly" presided over by Wu-sheng lao-mu. Here Maitreya greets the pious above rather than preaching to sinners below. Such pacific understandings of the Buddha's role have continued to be dominant in nineteenth- and twentieth-century texts, both *pao-chüan* and books composed by "spirit writing."

However, I know of two exceptions to this pattern – *pao-chüan* in which the political symbolism of Maitreya is taken more literally. The first of these is the *Ting-chieh pao-chüan,* noted above. My copy was reprinted in 1941, but Li Shih-yü says that it is mentioned in the *Tan-ching chai wen-ch'ao* 澹靜齋文鈔 (Documents from Tranquillity Studio), which was written in the eighteenth century. Susan Naquin informs me that she has come across several references to the *Ting-chieh* book in eighteenth-century discussions of sectarian activities.[17] Hence I shall treat it as a work of that period.

This book, *Establishing the Last Age*, is firmly within the tradition of *pao-chüan* piety, with its exhortations to practice devotion and engage in ethical living and its promises of blessings to those who respond. Maitreya is part of the three-stage structure: "Jan-teng in the past, Śākyamuni [in the present], and for the assembly of the future it is the Buddha Maitreya" (*chüan* 1; no pagination).

In a discourse between the Buddha and his disciples, a bodhisattva asks, "Who is Ju-t'ung 儒童?" (the Learned Youth Buddha, a Buddhist manifestation of Confucius). The Buddha replies, "Confucius is the Honored Buddha Maitreya who is just about to descend to be reborn (*tang-lai hsia-sheng* 當來下生) and appear in the world. He will be in charge of the religion for 108,000 years."

"When will the Honored Buddha Maitreya appear in the world?" The Buddha replies, "He will appear in 2,500 years in a tripartite sixty-year period, in the first year of a cycle in the lower *yüan* period." The Buddha then goes on to explain that "tripartite" here refers to division of the sixty-year cycle into three twenty-year periods. The first two are times of starvation, chaos, and demons, in response to which "a myriad holy ones descend to earth." The last twenty-year period is one of growth and prosperity. The precise point at which Maitreya descends is not specified. However, this passage is followed by an extended discussion of the disasters, demons, and gods that will appear in the last age and how the remaining ninety-two myriads (of the original ninety-six) of the Mother's children might be saved.

In a later section of this book there is a discussion of three vaguely defined "holy places" (*sheng-ti* 聖地), which serve as centers for the Buddhas of the three ages. That of Maitreya is located "south of Yen 燕 and north of Chao 趙," which would put it in North China. Here "Maitreya, the Honored

Buddha of the Future, will descend to be reborn. He will establish the third Dragon-flower assembly, of the White Yang period. He will produce a city of silver by transformation. This will be a place where he will save the sons and daughters of the imperial womb, shelter them from disasters and enable them to attain Buddhahood."

After a discussion of purgatory and its justified punishments for sinners, we read that after 2,500 years, when the time is fulfilled, the Buddha Maitreya will appear in the world, and purgatory in all its courts and departments "will be transformed into a Lotus pool. There will be no purgatory."

Near the end of this book there is another discussion of these Buddhas, with the first now Amitābha as a manifestation of Lord Lao (Lao-tzu deified). Maitreya as the Ju-t'ung Buddha will descend to the world, bestow the virtues of benevolence, righteousness, propriety, and so on, and establish the third, White Yang assembly. He will be in charge of the religion for 108,000 years, the period of "correct teaching in the last age of the dharma" (*mo-fa cheng-chiao* 末法正教).

A few lines later the Jade Emperor asks, "Now who shall be in charge of the religion?" The answer comes, "At present, because sentient beings in the last age are enduring great suffering, it is Maitreya of the White Yang assembly who descends to control the religion and the world." Maitreya leads a large number of deities and disciples to the world, where together with the Jade Emperor, he "establishes another universe and changes the world, and again lays down the principles of human relationships" (*pieh li ch'ien-k'un, kai-huan shih-chieh, ch'ung li jen-lun* 別立乾坤改換世界重立人倫).

Maitreya's coming will bring "years of great peace and prosperity" (*t'ai-p'ing chih nien* 太平之年). The wicked will forever be in purgatory and "will not see the Buddha Maitreya descend to earth," but the pious who worship him "will be able to see the years of great peace."

"The Buddha Maitreya said, 'When this time comes, in China of the central realm, if people without distinction between poor and rich will only recite the name "Honored Buddha Maitreya," they will all attain freedom and happiness. I fear only that people are unwilling to sincerely believe this.'"

The *Ting-chieh pao-chüan* is strongly oriented toward dramatic change in the future and contains material that obviously encourages active implementation: "In this year a 'Dragon-flower assembly' [sect congregation?] should help the Buddha Maitreya, and Kung Ch'ang 弓長 [a legendary sect leader] will aid Maitreya." All this is heightened by repeated references to struggle with unspecified barbarians (*hu-jen* 胡人; Manchus?) and to "establishing another world and changing the universe."

The text in my collection in which Maitreya is presented most explicitly as a revolutionary figure is the *Li-shih pao-chüan* 立世寶卷 (The precious book on establishing [a new] world), which was written in the late nineteenth or early twentieth century.[18] It is apparently a product of a branch of the Shou-yüan sect. It is a manuscript of ten leaves with no place, date, or pagination and can be found in the Shanghai Municipal Library. This text is so lively, militant, and rustic that it deserves to be quoted and summarized extensively. On the first page we are told that

> . . . the Buddha Maitreya comes to take charge of the religion, he has put aside his immortal clothing and descended to the secular world. When Śākyamuni Buddha saw him his mind was scorched (*hsin chiao-tsao* 心焦燥). . . . Now the time has come, the red flower withers, and the white flower blooms; only now does Śākyamuni withdraw from his position, and Maitreya laughs out loud. The great *kalpa* has arrived, and Maitreya has ascended to the throne (*teng liao chi* 登了基). He kept his hair, and changed his clothing. He put on the gauze hat and round-collared robe [of an official], . . . and has appeared in the world (*ch'u-shih* 出世). Who in the world knows this? Maitreya Buddha is in charge of the world (*chang ch'ien-k'un* 掌乾坤).

After stating that a wind will blow for seven days and seven nights, during which no doors will open and the whole world will be black, this dramatic little manuscript continues:

> Maitreya, obeying an imperial decree, decends from heaven. In front of Shadowless Mountain, he will secretly fish for the worthy [a line that appears in the *Huang-chi chiu-lien* scripture]. Those who understand his intentions, seeing the shore nearby, board the Dharma boat [of salvation].
>
> If one asks when the great *kalpa* will arrive, [one may say that] in the *kuei-ch'ou* 癸丑 year, fierce smoke [lit. "smoke from burning wolf dung"] will arise [as a warning]; [the *kalpa*] will begin in the *keng-tzu* 庚子 year, and appear in the *jen-tzu* 壬子. Only in the *chia-tzu* 甲子 year will it finally end. If you do not believe what I tell you, it will be most difficult for [you] confused folk to escape the "tiger *mao*" (*hu-mao* 虎卯) year.[19] Those who do pass through the *hu-mao* year are deities and immortals in heaven. When the Red Yang Buddha's rule of the world was completed, the venerable patriarch wanted to sweep the heavens clean and replace the earth (*sao-p'an kai-huan ch'ien-k'un* 掃盤改換乾坤). The Eternal Mother sent up a memorial, to which the patriarch agreed, and he sent Maitreya Buddha down to the red dust world.

Upon his descent, Maitreya was reborn in a Li 李 family of P'ang-chuang 龐庄 village, in Ning-chin 甯津 county (in Hopei province). He was very poor, with nothing to eat or wear, was orphaned at five, was uncared for by his brothers, and endured much suffering, even though "he originally descended to the profane world in obedience to a commission from heaven, and came to the red dust to rule the world" (*chang ch'ien-k'un, chih shih-chieh, lai tsai hung-ch'en* 掌乾坤治世界來在紅塵). Wearing ragged clothing, he begged for a living, sleeping in temples or monasteries or on the ground, "with the stars and planets as his companions, and a broken brick for a pillow." He was cold, hungry, and sick at heart. When he was fifteen he met the Venerable Mother in human form (*tang-jen lao-mu* 當人老母) and from her "obtained the Great Way, and encountered its true transmission, which he remembered in his saintly mind." The Venerable Mother told him that after a long time he would be the one to "restore the original wholeness." At age sixteen he concealed himself at Mt. Yen 燕 and "managed the Way" (*pan-tao* 辦道) with a multitude of followers.

> They stirred up the wind and waves, broke the law, and each fled to the wilds. [His associates?] "Little King Yama" and Chang Sung-yü 張宋雨 raised their arms and rebelled (*tso fan* 作反. Crossing the Yellow River, they hastened to Beijing, wishing to seize the world (*yao to ch'en-k'un* 要奪乾坤). When they and their followers rebelled, they were surrounded, those foolish fifty-one.[20] Behind their brains a blade was bared, which opened up the heavenly gates. One can only say that this blade killed them. Who understood that Maitreya Buddha had been commissioned to descend to the world?

At eighteen, young Li went to Mt. Wu-t'ai 五台, shaved off his hair, became a monk, and "looking up to the sky vowed to become enlightened." Here he devoted himself to spiritual cultivation, and he, Maitreya, was given the religious name Li Hsiang-shan 李向善, "Li who inclines toward goodness." "Possessed by the Venerable Mother, Li Hsiang-shan authorized [?] (*p'i* 批) a true scripture, which was written down by a local man." He also built a "Perfect Bliss monastery," where he settled, "the better to be established on the central plain" (North China). Then disaster struck, "for no reason," and the "Ch'ing Court sent troops to climb the mountain, to arrest Li Hsiang-shan and his brother [who was an incarnation of 'the Buddha of the Prior Realm']". The two brothers were taken to the capital, where the "Western Empress Dowager" (Hsi T'ai-hou 西太后) ordered that they be imprisoned. Hsiang-shan said to his younger brother, Hsiu-cheng 修正, "I am to rule the world on behalf of Heaven (*wei t'ien chih-shih* 爲天治世)." His brother replied, "I will return to the heavenly palace for you. You save the multitudes, manage the Great Way, and rule the heavens." He then committed suicide by taking poison.

Hsiang-shan was starved in prison for a month, but the Venerable

Mother responded to his needs, and he "ate four times a day, four bowls of rice each meal." For a whole month he neither defecated nor urinated. The Empress Dowager ordered officials to go and take a look, and they saw that "with the Venerable Mother's protection he had manifested supernatural powers." When "she saw his Buddha body, tall and large, the Empress Dowager was afraid," and "she personally allowed him, Maitreya Buddha, to quickly return to the mountains." As he was about to leave, the Empress Dowager gave him a placard inscribed with her own hand, *chen-ju tzu-tsai* 真如自在 (eternally real, of sovereign independence).

After his release he returned to the mountain again to "manage the Way," and the "Great Way became widely known." He saved "children of the Venerable Mother with karmic potential."

Later in this text we are told that Li Hsiang-shan saved eighteen disciples, who set up branch sects, whereas he himself is equated with the "patriarch who restores wholeness" (Shou-yüan tsu 收元祖). The imminent destruction of the world is described in some detail: "The world will be swept clean, heaven and earth will be replaced. Before one's eyes the city of Beijing will be in complete chaos; Niu Pa 牛八 [an old sectarian name][21] will come to the throne in Beijing and take revenge on his enemies." Blood and death will be everywhere, while all contend for power. But once again, violence fails. "When Niu Pa has swept the earth clean, his true nature will return to heaven." Competition among sects will lead only to further violence. In the midst of this, Maitreya urges the lost to quickly seek out his way of escape, which enables them to avoid calamity and participate in "the restoration of wholeness." "Li Hsiang-shan, Maitreya Buddha, is about to restore the original wholeness. From the heavenly palace a cloud city has been sent down, and in it all pious men and women can hide."

After a succession of threats and promises, we are told that "all the people of the Way one at a time knelt down and cried out to the Shou-yüan patriarch, 'We will obey your words.' Those who know that the Shou-yüan patriarch is Maitreya Buddha [already] come, and quickly take refuge in him, will not suffer disasters."

> The Shou-yüan patriarch has [re]established the sun and moon [which earlier he had taken away] and replaced the world. Here it is completely different from the Prior Realm. The heavens, earth, sun and moon have all been changed (*ch'üan tou kai-pien* 全都改變). All men and women, with no calamities or difficulties, came to the Latter Realm [here equated with the new world]. Here the sun rises in the south, and sets in the north, and the air is clear and bright. In one year there are eighteen months, in each month forty-five days, which makes 810 days for one year. The winds are harmonious and rains

> timely, with well-being and abundant harvest. In the capital, Lord Mu Tzu 木子[22] [Li] ascends to the golden palace, and invites Shou-yüan to come to the golden palace to support and protect the realm.

So Shou-yüan/Maitreya serves the ruler in the palace, "appointing Buddhas to their positions," rewarding each according to merit. The pious are warned:

> If he doesn't save you, you won't make it to the Latter Realm, where there are civil and military positions, [and one can be] an official or a high minister. There is wealth and noble rank, with blessings and long life matching those of heaven itself. Those left behind, who entered the Way late, and who have accumulated no merit, only fall into the midst of human life, there to farm the fields. The hearts of the people of the Way were glad and they laughed aloud. Who would have thought that farmers could become high officials! In the red dust world, enjoying worldly blessings, they will have descendants for 10,000 generations. After a hundred years they will enter the realm of the holy, and go to the Divine Mountain.

There in paradise the faithful will be appointed to positions according to their merit, as Buddhas, patriarchs, arhats, bodhisattvas, immortals, and princes and princesses. Ten ranks are named, the last five of which involve rebirth on earth as officials, wealthy persons, or farmers. In the concluding section of this account we are told that "when the Shou-yüan patriarch had taken care of the important affairs of the Latter Realm, he returned to the heavenly palace, before the Venerable Mother's throne." At the end there is a final warning: "those who do not take refuge in the Shou-yüan patriarch, when the great kalpic calamities come, will all regret it. If in this life one does not recognize the road home, then one must wait for another 108,000 years."

There are inconsistencies here, and descriptions of the world to come oscillate ambiguously between heaven and earth. Li Hsiang-shan as Maitreya incarnate at first is not directly involved in an uprising led presumably by some of his associates but later seems to be both ruler and chief minister of the new world. References to the overthrow of the Ch'ing dynasty are unmistakable. Here at last is a text that confirms the darkest suspicions of officials and scholars concerning sectarian subversion! Nonetheless, it is but one small manuscript near the end of a long scriptural tradition that was very rarely so politically explicit. As such it demonstrates one extreme possibility but does not characterize that tradition as a whole.

Concluding Comments

The richness of Maitreyan mythology in Chinese popular texts is a reflection of the complexity of the symbol of Maitreya elsewhere, as can be seen in the other chapters of this volume. It also reminds us that no single explanation of his significance will suffice; he is neither just a savior nor simply a revolutionary, but a potent combination of both, and the particular role he plays depends on the interests of the preachers and writers who have formulated the ongoing Maitreya tradition. Those of us whose spiritual roots are in Judaism or Christianity should take special care in treating a symbol from another culture like Maitreya, who in some of his roles is related to world renewal at the end of a cycle of time. Such dramatic hopes for the future are a central theme in the Judeo-Christian tradition and can easily lead us astray in our evaluation of what appears to be an analogous belief. The temptation is to read in too much, to respond instinctively, particularly in an age when our own technology makes the end of human time more possible than ever before.

For me the basic answer to this dilemma is to immerse oneself in the data and as much as possible let the sources speak for themselves. Given a chance, the complexity of human data will assert itself and will resist attempts at manipulation by the investigator. In the case of Maitreya this means to let each role have its turn but at the same time look for unifying themes that help make sense out of the phenomenon as a whole.

In a typology of Buddhas, Maitreya shares much with other figures such as Mañjuśrī or Amitābha. He can be an object of contemplation, a revealer of wisdom, or a compassionate savior in paradise. He shares with his model Śākyamuni a concern for life in this world and an easy familiarity with princes and kings. What Maitreya adds to all this is his association with a future age of bliss. He is a symbol of universal and collective hope, beyond individual aspirations, beyond the history of the present age, so that he offers general and transcendent renewal. This symbolism is given additional power by the fact that Maitreya has two bases of operation, one in heaven, one on earth, and in our texts he moves easily between them. He is the future "lord of history," but he can also be present now, as a preacher, sect leader, or peasant boy. As such his promises have a scope and depth beyond those of a Śākyamuni who is gone or an Amitābha who stays in paradise.

No doubt it is Maitreya's readiness to be reborn in the world and share its sufferings that so appealed to ordinary folk in China. It must have been comforting to be told that Maitreya said, as in the *Huang-chi chiu-lien pao-chüan*, "This cruel realm of suffering will become a lotus world" (chap. 2), and "You will personally see the world which is about to come" (chap. 11). Mahāyāna Buddhism is basically a gnostic system; in such a system Maitreya wandering around as a ragged monk or peasant is about as close to a human, historical savior as one can get. Kuan-yin (Avalokiteśvara) does the same, but Kuan-yin is a bodhisattva, not a world-conquering Buddha. Add to this a compassionate mother goddess and popular techniques of trance and spirit possession, and the sectarian Maitreya becomes a powerful figure indeed.

NOTES

1 On this see my article, "Attitudes Toward the Ruler and State in Chinese Popular Religious Literature: Sixteenth and Seventeenth Century *Pao-chüan*," *Harvard Journal of Asiatic Studies* 44 (December 1984): 347–79.

2 For recent discussions of Chinese sects see Susan Naquin, *Millenarian Rebellion in China: The Eight Trigrams Uprising of 1813* (New Haven, Conn.: Yale University Press, 1976); Daniel L. Overmyer, *Folk Buddhist Religion: Dissenting Sects in Late Traditional China* (Cambridge, Mass.: Harvard University Press, 1976); Daniel L. Overmyer, "Alternatives: Popular Religious Sects in Chinese Society," *Modern China* 7, no. 2 (April 1981): 153–90; and Richard Hon-chun Shek, "Religion and Society in Late Ming: Sectarianism and Popular Thought in Sixteenth and Seventeenth Century China" (Ph.D. diss., University of California, Berkeley, 1980) (University Microfilms International No. 8029585). See also the symposium "Syncretic Sects in Chinese Society," pts. 1 and 2, in *Modern China* 8, nos. 3 and 4 (July, October 1982). For a bibiliographical discussion of Japanese studies on this topic, see Noguchi Tetsurō 野口鐵郎, "Chūgoku shūkyō kessha-shi joshō – toku ni Byakurenkyō-shi o chūshin to shita kenkyūshi-teki dōkō" 中國宗教結社史序章一特白蓮教史を中心とした研究史的動向 (An introduction to the history of Chinese religious organizations – Trends in studies on the White Lotus sect), *Kindai Chūgoku*, 4 (October 1978): 63–88.

3 For general discussions of *pao-chüan* literature, see Daniel L. Overmyer, "Values in Chinese Sectarian Literature: Ming and Ch'ing *Pao-chüan*," in *Popular Culture in Late Imperial China: Diversity and Integration*, ed. David Johnson, Andrew J. Nathan, and Evelyn S. Rawski (Berkeley and Los Angeles: University of California Press, 1985), 219–54; Li Shih-yü, *Pao-chüan tsung-lu* 李世瑜 ,寶卷綜録 (Shanghai: Chung-hua shu-chu, 1961); and Sawada Mizuho, *Zōhō Hōkan no kenkyū* 澤田瑞穂,增補宝巻の研究 (Tokyo: Kokusho kanko kai, 1975). See also Shek, "Sectarianism and Popular Thought," 155–201.

4 For a discussion of this mythology, see Overmyer, *Folk Buddhist Religion*, 134–61, Naquin, *Millenarian Rebellion*, 7–24, and Overmyer, "Values in Sectarian Literature."

5 See note 3.

6 Antonino Forte, *Political Propaganda and Ideology in China at the End of the Seventh Century* (Naples: Istituto Universitario Orientale, 1976), 271–80, and E. Zürcher, "'Prince Moonlight': Messianism and Eschatology in Early Medieval Chinese Buddhism," *T'oung Pao* 48, no. 1–3 (1982):1–75.

7 Overmyer, *Folk Buddhist Religion*, 25–7, 80–5, 98–100. For a discussion of fourteenth-century Maitreya-related sects in their historical context, see Frederick

W. Mote, "The Rise of the Ming Dynasty, 1330–1367," forthcoming in *Cambridge History of China,* vol. 7.

8 Overmyer, *Folk Buddhist Religion,* 104–5, translated from the *Na Wen-i kung ch'u-jen Chih-li tsung-tu tsou-i* 那文毅公初任直隸總督奏議, ed. Jung An 容安 (b. 1788), vol. 42, pp. 18–19.

9 Naquin, *Millenarian Rebellion,* 21, 92–3; and Susan Naquin, *Shantung Rebellion: The Wang Lun Uprising of 1774* (New Haven, Conn.: Yale University Press, 1981), 52, 154–7, 190, 206. On Maitreya belief in Ming and Ch'ing sects see also Overmyer, *Folk Buddhist Religion,* 101–8, 120–3, 150–61.

10 I am not sure what to do with the character *chao* in this title. Its usage here is not defined in the book, and in yet another title this character is omitted. As a verb it means "to illumine," but as a noun, which it is here, it refers to a permit, pass, or document. Perhaps here it refers to a document for understanding and surviving the last age.

11 However, it should be remembered that in the minds of officials Maitreya was associated with heresy, so that texts with his name in the title would have been the first to be confiscated.

12 For recent discussions of Lo Ch'ing and his sect, see Daniel L. Overmyer, "Boatmen and Buddhas: The Lo chiao in Ming Dynasty China," *History of Religions,* 17, no. 3–4 (February–May 1978): 284–302; and Shek, "Sectarianism and Popular Thought," 202–51.

13 The date "second year of the Chia-ching 嘉靖 period" occurs three times in the *Huang-chi chiu-lien* book. In his *Pao-chüan tsung-lu* (p. 20), Li Shih-yü lists two Ming (1368–1644) editions of this text. However, Sawada Mizuho in his *Zōhō hōkan no kenkyū* (110) treats the *Huang-chi pao-chüan* as a Ch'ing dynasty book, on the basis of the two editions available to him. The first of these is incomplete, but he suggests a Ch'ien-lung 乾隆 (1736–95) date for it. The second, published in 1908, is attributed to a "Ninth Patriarch Huang 黄," whom Sawada describes as the founder of the Golden Elixir Way (Chin-tan tao). His dates are 1684–1750. However, there is no mention of a "Patriarch Huang" in the edition used in this chapter, though there are references to "nine patriarchs coming and going in response to the cycles of time" (chap. 1). The revealer of this text is repeatedly identified as the Wu-wei Patriarch, an incarnation of Maitreya. In chapter 12 he is quoted as saying, "I wrote this *pao-chüan* in the Han 韓 family home." So the editors of the 1908 edition or others before them added the name of Patriarch Huang to the introductory material of the book. If Sawada's dates for him are correct, Patriarch Huang must have built his teaching on our text, which repeatedly refers to the "Golden Elixir Way of the Imperial Ultimate Cycle." The name Chin-tan tao first appears as the name of a Taoist sect in South China in the twelfth century.

14 In the *Fo-shuo Mi-le hsia-sheng ching* 佛說彌勒下生經 (Sutra of the Buddha's discourse on the descent of Maitreya) (T 453:14. 421–3), translated in the late third century A.D., the term "Dragon Flower" is used to describe the tree under which the future Buddha attains enlightenment. This text also refers to ninety-six *i* (myriads) of disciples who are saved in these preaching assemblies (*hui*) led by

Maitreya. In sectarian texts "Dragon Follower Assembly" refers to the gathering of humankind at the end of each time period.

15 Shek, "Sectarianism and Popular Thought," 175.

16 A preface to this book is dated 1594. Li Shih-yü (*Pao-chüan,* 69) says merely that it is from the Ch'ing, whereas Sawada Mizuho (*Hōkan,* 216) discusses a 1900 reprint. The copy I read in Shanghai was reprinted in 1929, with a cover date of 1936. This *Hua-tu pao-chüan* describes itself as the teachings of the Hsüan-tun chiao 玄頓教 (Religion of mysterious and instantaneous [enlightenment]), which Sawada (*Hōkan,* 216) says was a branch of the Way of Yellow Heaven (Huang t'ien tao 黃天道), founded in the 1550s. See also Shek, "Sectarianism and Popular Thought," 252–75 on the Huang-t'ien sect. However, in both style and content this book appears to be from a later period of *pao-chüan* development, particularly in its use of the short-story form. Hence I tentatively date it to the eighteenth century.

17 The *Tan-ching chai wen-ch'ao* was written by Kung Ching-han 龔景瀚 (1747–1803). I have not yet been able to locate a copy. For references to the date of the *Ting-chieh pao-chüan* I am indebted to Li Shih-yü, *Pao-chüan,* 70, and to Susan Naquin, personal communication, March 18, 1983.

18 The *Li-shih pao-chüan* can be dated by its references to Hsi T'ai-hou, "Empress Dowager of the West," that is, Tz'u-hsi 慈禧 T'ai-hou (1835–1908), who ruled China, directly or indirectly, from 1862 until her death.

19 "*Hu-mao* year" does not make sense by conventional standards, because the character *hu,* "tiger," is not one of the "celestial stems" in the "stem–branch" cycle of terms. Perhaps *hu* refers to the fierceness of this year in the end time.

20 The characters for "those foolish fifty-one" are *sha wu-shih i ke*. One wonders if the character *sha* 傻, "foolish," is not intended to be read as *sha* 殺, "to kill," which would make these lines read "their followers rebelled, they were surrounded, and fifty-one were killed."

21 When combined, the characters *niu* and *pa* form the character *chu* 朱, the surname of the Ming royal house. It was an old sectarian practice to split surname characters in this way. During the Ch'ing it was, of course, considered subversive to evoke the name of the ruling clan whose dynasty the Manchus had overthrown.

22 When combined, the characters *mu* and *tzu* form the character *li,* which is Maitreya's human surname in this text.

6

Maitreya in Korea

LEWIS LANCASTER

Introduction

Korea received Buddhism at a time when the Maitreya cult was at the pinnacle of its importance in China, surpassing in some ways the interest being shown toward such figures as Śākyamuni and Amitābha.[1] Having first heard of Maitreya in the formative years of the Buddhist religion within its cultural boundaries, Korea continued to hold the Maitreya practice in high esteem long after the cult activities in China had given way to other Buddhist interests, especially those concerning Amitābha and Bhaiṣajyaguru. It was not until the end of the seventh century that Amitābha cult practices began to gain popularity in Korea and at least a century later before Bhaiṣajyaguru was accorded support that can be documented.[2] In China both figures were already prominent during the early T'ang period.

Korean scholars have been somewhat slow in dealing with the history of Maitreya; only one major work has been devoted to the subject, the *Han'guk mirŭk sinang ŭi yŏn'gu* 韓國彌勒信仰의 硏究 of Professor Kim Sam-yong 金三龍 published in 1983.[3] In this volume, he provides a chronological description and analysis of the advent and development of the Maitreya cult. The belief in Maitreya came to Korea during the Three Kingdoms period under the strong influence of the Northern Wei dynasty of China.[4] From the images of both Paekche and Koguryŏ, we can see that Maitreya was included in triad compositions. The Sŏsan 瑞山 triad from the Paekche period shows him together with Śākyamuni and Avalokiteśvara,[5] indicating that he was accepted as a bodhisattva to be seen as an attendant figure of the Buddha. Since Maitreya was considered to be the ruler of Tuṣita Heaven and the next Buddha to appear in a human body,[6] Korea, like many Buddhist societies, came to put special emphasis on the role of this coming Buddha as one who secures the welfare and benefit to individuals and the nation. Kim Sam-yong makes the point that the Maitreya pattern found in Paekche differed from that of the Silla area. In Paekche, the belief was centered on the concept that a Buddha land of Maitreya must be created within society, that it must be a special and perfected place for the new incarnate Buddha to be born. In Silla, in contrast, there was much more emphasis on the appearance of Maitreya in a variety of human and divine bodies in the ordinary world, imperfect and filled with problems.[7] Professor Ahn Kye-hyŏn supports the idea that the descent of Maitreya occupied a central place in both Paekche and Silla Buddhism.[8] Although Maitreya had been brought into Korea during the Northern Wei period, Professor Hwang Su-yŏng points out that the seated pensive Maitreya with crossed legs was being introduced as early as the mid–sixth century from the Southern dynasties and that of the Sui directly into Paekche.[9] From Paekche the image of Maitreya was sent to Japan, and a firmer understanding of Paekche Buddhism is necessary for the study of that introduction of art and teachings into the culture of Korea's neighbor.

In addition to the images from the Three Kingdoms period that still exist, which unfortunately are few in number, we have some anecdotal information from the ancient records. The beginnings of written history are not represented among the collection of extant documents, and so scholars must rely on the two earliest authorities, the *Samguk sagi* 三國史記 and the *Samguk yusa* 三國遺事. The *Samguk sagi* is the work of a Confucian Kim Pu-sik, who finished his compilation of old stories in 1145.[10] His history attempts to provide a study of the three kingdoms of Silla, Koguryŏ, and Paekche from their supposed foundations in the first century B.C. up to the founding of the Koryŏ dynasty. The sources available to Kim Pu-sik disappeared long ago, and there is not much known about them. We do know that he made use of the *Haedong kogi*[11] 海東古記 , but we have no copy of this work and do not even know the date of its composition. It is probable that no written chronicles were kept in Korea before the fourth century, and thus even the twelfth-century writer had to construct his work with limited resources. Because so little was known to exist in Korea for a project of this sort, scholars suggest that Kim based some of his early period work on the accounts contained in the histories of the Chinese dynasties and much of the rest on the oral tradition of his time.[12]

In 1215 a very different kind of history appeared, one devoted to the biographies of Buddhist monks. The *Haedong kosŭngjŏn*[13] 海東古僧傳 covered the lives of important monks starting with Sundo, who is said to have brought Buddhism to Koguryŏ in the fourth century. We can trace the model for this work back to such texts as the *Kao seng chuan* and other attempts by Chinese Buddhists to provide a history of the movement in East Asia.[14]

A third history of life within the Korean culture is available for these important centuries; it is a text written by a Buddhist monk, Iryŏn, in the thirteenth century. Unlike the *Samguk sagi,* which provides, by design, only data related to secular history, the *Samguk yusa* focuses on the Buddhist aspects of Korea's past.[15] Once again, the writer had before him documents that are no longer available to us. Included in the *Samguk yusa* is a section taken from the *Karak kukki* 駕洛國記, considered to be a 1076 composition giving the foundation story of the Karak state.[16]

From these documents, which are limited to be sure, we discern something of the interest in Maitreya and find information that can be matched to the images that have survived from the periods under consideration. One of the early concepts of Maitreya that diverged from the usual story of his future Buddhahood and his residence in Tuṣita Heaven was the idea that Maitreya appears in this world in the form of a Hwarang 花郎. This view of the actions of Maitreya appears to be purely Korean in origin.[17] During the Three Kingdoms period and the Unified Silla dynasty, there was an organization of young men known as Hwarang. From the histories, we have only a vague grasp of the events that led to the foundation of this organization and to its enormous importance in the military life and government of the Silla dynasty. By the sixth century the group was under the control of the court and had become part of the military organization.[18] Before this official recognition, it seems that the Silla aristocracy placed their sons in the movement, which provided training in ritual, music, archery, charioteering, writing, and mathematics[19]; it also required making arduous pilgrimages to sacred spots in the mountains. The Hwarang also studied those rules of social conduct that can be classified as Confucian, even though the histories tell us that the rules were put together by a Buddhist monk, Wŏn'gwang 圓光, in the sixth century.[20] The five rules were to serve the king with loyal heart, to give filial respect to one's parents, to share with one's friends a sincere affection, to fight without retreating, and never to take life without purpose. After the group was given official status, it was organized into military-like units whose troops may have numbered as many as one thousand men.[21] All of this was taking place as Buddhism was being absorbed into the culture, but the stories about the Hwarang indicate that it has a place in the life of the nation that was not limited to Buddhist or Confucian elements. The pilgrimages to the mountains and to the spots held sacred by virtue of the presence of magical powers or spirits would indicate that this group held to beliefs and practices that predate the coming of Buddhism to Korea.

Scholars have not yet reached complete accord about the nature of this Hwarang tradition. Yi Sŏn-gun, an ardent nationalist, has speculated that the Hwarang represented the highest example of love and support for the nation, and he has focused on the military events associated with these young men.[22] Others, however, question the emphasis on the military and see the major element in the movement as religious or shamanistic. Mishima Shoei's classic work makes a telling argument for seeing the Hwarang as groups of youth who performed within the religious dimension of society. He concludes that they functioned as shamans, and therefore we can look to similar activities in other parts of Asia and even Europe to see and understand the nature of these events in Korea.[23] Bishop Rutt has tended to follow the lead of Mishima, citing evidence that Yi documents do not refer to the military exploits of the Hwarang, only to their religious side. However, as we shall see later, there are earlier accounts of the warrior exploits of the Hwarang. Rutt contends that the Japanese control of Korea in this century and the glorification of the *bushido* cult aroused among Koreans the notion that their own Hwarang had in the past performed heroic acts, the equal of any that could be cited in Japan.

Many of the extant tales about the Hwarang that are found in the histories of the Three Kingdoms may come from the *Hwarang segi* 花郎世紀, a compilation of stories done in the eighth century by Kim Tae-mun 金大問; these stories were available to the writers of the extant histories but no longer exist.[24] In the *yusa* we find a story about the founding of the Hwarang, and it is from information such as this that researchers base their suppositions. Here we read that the twenty-fourth king of Silla was a great admirer of beauty and sought to surround himself with beautiful people and objects. Toward that end, he held contests and selected the most attractive young women to be known as *wŏnhwa* (essence of flowers). Unfortunately, a deadly game of competition emerged, and the two top contenders became jealous of each other. One of them, Chunjŏng by name, invited the other, Nammo, to a party and proceeded to get her drunk. While the unfortunate young woman was in this condition, she was led to the bank of the river, struck with a rock, and buried in the sand alongside the water. Each woman had a band of followers; the young men who were associated with the lost *wŏnhwa* mourned her disappearance and with sad laments disbanded. Revenge was not to be denied the murdered Nammo, for one of Chunjŏng's enemies came to know of the deed, made up a song about it, and taught it to the children, who began to sing it in the streets. The young men who had been supporters of Nammo found her grave and thus came to know of her sad end. The king was disturbed that his contest and organization had come to such an end, and so he abolished the position of *wŏnhwa* and created a new title of Hwarang for the bands of young men.[25]

On the basis of this story, it is apparent that the beginning and development of the Hwarang was separate from that of Buddhism. It was not until the sixth century that the histories explain the connection of this group with Maitreya and Buddhism.[26] We are told that a monk at Hŭngnyun monastery 興輪寺 was a devout follower of Maitreya and that he spent his days doing prostrations in front of the image of this bodhisattva. During this time, the monk prayed that Maitreya might be reborn as one of the noble youth who belonged to the Hwarang; then the monk could pledge to serve him. As is usual with many of these accounts, a dream played a major role in the unfolding of the story. The monk, named Chinja 真慈, saw an old man in a dream and was told by this dream personage that, if he would go to a certain monastery, he would find a Hwarang who would be Maitreya. Overjoyed that his wishes seemed to have been granted, the monk set out for the place indicated in the dream, and when he arrived he was met by a youth. The young man showed him about the monastery and helped the visitor get settled. Chinja went to the abbot's quarters and told him of his dream and the information that the monastery was to be the home of Maitreya in the form of a Hwarang. The abbot told him to climb up the mountainside; there in a sacred spot he would be able to meet with heavenly beings and receive instructions from them about how to locate the Hwarang Maitreya. Chinja followed the instructions and when he had come to the spot indicated by the abbot was met by a white-haired old man, who was none other than the spirit of the mountain, a deity of great importance to the Koreans. The old man asked the monk about his mission and, hearing that he was seeking the Hwarang Maitreya, sent him back to the monastery, informing the surprised monk that he had already met this person at the gate of the compound. Chinja hurried back to the monastery and told the other monks that Maitreya was already among them. They went together to the grove of trees near the buildings and saw the handsome youth who had greeted them. Chinja asked the youth to tell them his life history, and the young man replied that his name was Miri (var. Misi 未尸 ; see note 27) and that he had no other name, certainly no family name, since he had never known his parents. The monks were assured that here was the incarnate form of Maitreya who had appeared as a Hwarang. The youth was taken from the monastery back to the palace. There he won approval from the entire court and was appointed leader of the Hwarang. Thereafter, he instructed them in all of the necessary arts and sciences, until after seven years he disappeared. He was said to have gone to the land of the spirits (*sinsŏn* 神仙), leaving behind the grieving Chinja and all of the Hwarang. Chinja spent his time visualizing the departed youth until at long last he had a vision of the young man as Maitreya. These visions helped the monk to develop a pure mind and provided him with comfort until the time of his own rebirth into a spiritual world, which we might suspect was Tuṣita Heaven.[27]

This description of the founding of the Hwarang and the introduction of Maitreya into its midst provides us with a religious view of the group of youth who made up the organization. The *Samguk sagi* paints quite a different picture of these youth and their role in society, and it is this one that has found favor in Korea among those who would interpret the Hwarang as a military organization intended to defend the nation. This history includes a story illustrating the valor and the love of nation that was exemplified by the Hwarang activities. We are here reminded that Buddhism from the Northern Wei was also deeply involved in the notion that the religion could provide great protection to the nation. One of the Hwarang went forth to battle, rode his horse into the midst of the enemy lines, and killed many soldiers before he was captured. Ordered to appear before the ruler of the enemy, he carried himself with such poise and brave demeanor that the leader was greatly impressed, granted him a pardon, and ordered the guards to escort him back to the safety of his own lines. The youth, rather than being glad to have escaped with his life, only regretted that he had been in the presence of the head of the enemy's army and had not been able to kill him. With renewed purpose, he wheeled his horse about and charged directly into the enemy line once again and this time was killed. His head was severed from his body and carried back to his father, who lifted up the blood-soaked face, wiped the blood from it, and said, "My son looks just as if he were alive. He was able to die for our king, there is no regret."[28] The bloodied head of the Hwarang on the saddle horn is a depiction of the life of young men that must have been very realistic in a time when wars raged between Silla and its neighbors. The great contrast between the youth Miri wandering about the monastery grounds, teaching other young men the more elegant aspects of life, and the bloodied head of the young warrior indicates that there was no one depiction of the Hwarang in the early texts.

These differing accounts of the Hwarang suggest that the term and those using it were associated with at least two different types of activities, the one being a shaman-like role of dancer and musician or that of an individual specially trained in rituals and ceremonies and the other being a military role enacted by young men who trained as warriors and were able to perform great feats of bravery with little regard for their individual safety and life. It is probable that in the Silla dynasty the two careers were followed by the same youths. Training in cultural matters did not rule out the possibility of national need forcing the same young men to take to the field of battle as well.[29]

The subsequent history of the Hwarang is of interest but difficult to trace. When Silla had unified the peninsula under one court, military needs were not as pressing and the Hwarang organization was not as important in the military scene. One scholar has speculated that the Hwarang tradition can still be traced to the Nong Ak 農樂 bands, which are all-male groups of entertainers in the Kyŏnggi provinces.[30] The process by which the notion of the Hwarang as warriors came to be replaced by one in which they were renowned as entertainers can be found as far back as the Koryŏ period. During that time Buddhism was the national religion and the court held great festivals that combined Buddhist and shamanistic elements.[31] One part of the tradition was the performance of a Hwarang song called "Ch'ŏyong." This song is preserved in the fourteen pieces of poetry contained in the *Samguk yusa* and are called *hyangga* 鄕歌.[32] Written in the ninth century, the songs continued to be used and in the Koryo were considered magical talismans against disease. The Hwarang wrote *hyangga* as a part of their training, and from this we can see the combination of shamanic elements and Buddhism. The *Hunmong chahoe* 訓蒙字會 (sixteenth century),[33] referring back to older usage, gives the meaning of the Hwarang as the shaman or the husband of a shaman; a similar meaning occurs in the *Chibong yusŏl* 芝峰類説 of the seventeenth century.[34] The old idea that the Hwarang were reincarnations of Maitreya does not seem to have been extended to these masked dancers or "husbands of shamans," and thus we must make a clear distinction between the early years when this group was the source of leadership of the nation and included in their training music and poetry, which had a shamanic connection, and the later times when the name was applied to professional performers and shamans.

When we compare the artifacts of Buddhism with these stories, we can see that the cast and carved images of the youthful Maitreya with his right leg crossed on the left, and his handsomely featured face with a subtle smile playing on the lips, provide an excellent presentation of the Hwarang described in the histories of the Three Kingdoms. It is understandable that this motif of the meditative pose of a young man, which had found such admirable expression in the Northern Ch'i statuary of China, would be used by the Koreans and viewed as Maitreya appearing among the group of Hwarang. It may be that the dance groups still found in the southern part of Korea are a dim echo of the Hwarang tradition, but the images of Maitreya from the ateliers of Silla captured a magical moment in the history of Maitreya in Korea, a moment that has passed and is now only reflected in the art.

The Koryŏ period brought many changes to Korea and to Buddhism. One was the growing belief in the various periods of the Buddhist teachings. According to this belief, the worst period was to be the time when the true teaching disappeared and was replaced by a false or misunderstood one. In the year 1052, fifteen hundred years after the death of Śākyamuni, this evil age was thought to have begun.[35] Events of the time made this evil age seem quite real. During the twelfth century, there was social disorder led by men such as Yi Cha-gyŏm (1126) and Myoch'ŏng (1135) and a military coup (1170).[36] During these anxious times, there was a growing belief in the appearance of Maitreya as a protector and defender. This is the view of Maitreya that is perhaps more traditionally Buddhist, for it is the concept of the bodhisattva or, as he is sometimes called, the Tathāgata Maitreya. There had been for a long time stories about the strange and sudden appearances of

Maitreya. In particular, monks who were tempted to break their vows were often saved by the intervention of some person who was later found to be none other than Maitreya.

In the Diamond Mountains, there is an image of Maitreya that tradition says ascended to Tuṣita Heaven and then returned again to the monastery. As the image returned, the footprint was left on the stepping stone in front of the hall. The idea of Maitreya ascending and descending is a theme in paintings and in texts,[37] but this may be the one instance in which the trip was said to have been made by Maitreya's image. Because of the miracle that had occurred, the image was considered to have great magical powers, and pilgrims would come to it in order to pray for wishes and good health.

Kim Sam-yong has recorded the presence of 370 images of Maitreya in Korea, and it is interesting that 221 of these belong to the Koryŏ period.[38] After the Silla period, the pensive-youth image of Maitreya was no longer popular, and in its place newer images of the bodhisattva-Tathāgata were to be seen. Of special note regarding these Koryŏ images was the appearance of a headpiece that was attached to the top of the figure. Headpieces such as this seem to have no corresponding model in either China or India, and the purpose of this iconographic form is not clear. If the images have a Korean model, we must look to the non-Buddhist elements of the society. Choi Nam-sŏn, in his article "Asi chosŏn,"[39] has pointed to some activities in the later period that may have been part of the Koryŏ artistic vision. There had been a long tradition of the native religion of the peninsula in which people believed in the spirits of a certain spot, spirits who could be approached in prayers or in rituals of propitiation. There were altars erected at these spots; sometimes stone slabs were planted in the ground and used in this erect position for the focus of the rituals. In other spots, unusual stones that appeared naturally were looked upon as divine objects. These menhir-like stones (*ipsŏk* 立石) were to be found scattered across the nation, and Choi believes that later during the Buddhist era the stones were carved with heads and faces. The figure of the carved *ipsŏk* was often thought to be or identified as Maitreya. He has applied this approach to one of the most famous of these giant Koryŏ standing Maitreyas, the Kwanch'ok monastery 灌燭寺 statue in Ŭnjin 恩津. Choi says that this image was originally Avalokiteśvara, later changed to a Maitreya with a headpiece. He speculates that this image is a carved *ipsŏk,* which had been on the spot and revered by pre-Buddhist devotees. Other examples of such stone carvings can be seen in a number of sites located near Kuwŏlsan in Hwanghae-do.[40] This use of stones already standing provides one explanation for the many uncontoured images with heads as big as the body, arms and clothing being only roughly indicated by relief rather than fully in the round. Such images are found in a variety of places: Ch'ungch'ŏng nam-do, Chŏlla buk-do, Kyŏng-gi-do, and Cheju-do.

In yet another example of Korean models being used for Maitreya images, we find that guardian figures (*changsŭng sinang*) became associated with this Buddhist bodhisattva. In Cheju-do there are two stone images named Maitreya: One is called the western Maitreya and the other the eastern. Their placement seems to have been determined by geomancy, and each has a separate function with regard to the community. The eastern one is approached when Maitreya is asked to give the supplicant a son, and the western one is associated with the Dragon King and good fortune.[41] This pattern of looking to Maitreya for protection and assistance is borne out by the survey of images made by Kim Sam-yong. He found that local people were using the 370 images of Maitreya for the following purposes: 32 for good fortune, 73 for securing a son, 23 for curing illness, and 40 for giving protection in times of trouble.

The presence of the dual Maitreya guardian figure types in Cheju-do brings up the question of the double images in Buddhist art. Suggestions for it go back to the ancient histories, where Maitreyas appear to give aid to people. In one tale, as early as the Unified Silla period, two monks left their homes and retired to the mountains to practice meditation without distraction. They occupied huts next to one another and proceeded with their meditation practice night and day. One night a beautiful young woman appeared at the door of one of the huts and begged the monk to allow her to rest because it was getting dark and she had lost her way and was very weary. He saw how attractive she was and told her, regretfully, that he was unable to allow her to enter his cell because he should not do anything that would arouse his passions. The weary woman went next door and was finally admitted by the second monk, who took compassion on her state even though he knew he was running the risk of succumbing to such beauty. After she had bathed, she asked him to step into the tub. When he did so, he was amazed to find that his mind was fixed in a state of concentrated bliss, his skin became the color of the golden liquid that had replaced the water, and the tub appeared as a lotus petal platform. The woman announced that she was Avalokiteśvara, and the test of this compassion for her condition had proved that he was worthy of the exalted state he had reached.

Next door his companion meditator heard the voices and in righteous indignation burst into the room ready to denounce the monk for his fall from grace, only to find his friend seated on a high pedestal with a golden-colored body and having the form of Maitreya. He was invited to step into the golden liquid and was also transformed and became Amitāyus. The villagers flocked to see the two figures and to hear them preach the Dharma. After they had finished speaking, the two rose into the air and were seen by the assembled to be riding away into the heavens in chariots.[42]

The idea of dual figures can be found in a number of places and in several aspects. Two Maitreyas, for example, can be viewed at Yŏng'am (hermitage). These images are said to have been constructed during the reign of Sŏnjong in the Koryŏ dynasty (eleventh century). The wife of the king had a dream in which she saw two monks coming to beg at the palace. She willingly gave them offerings and as a result conceived a son. In commemoration of this event, the king had the two images constructed, and since the visitation had resulted in the birth of a son, he made both of them in the form of Maitreya. The statues remain today in the monastery as National Treasure 93.[43]

Dual figures are not limited to Korea; the theme can be found in Central Asia as well. Preserved in a fresco in the deserts of western China is a depiction of a two-headed Buddha. This two-headed image is said to be related to an event in which two devout believers wanted to make images but lacked sufficient funds for separate constructions and so were forced to make only one. The Buddha's compassion was aroused by this situation, and so he transformed the image into a two-headed one, thus securing greater merit for the donors.[44] In the Pohai region, dual images of seated Buddhas were being made at the time when the Maitreya cult practices were strong in Korea. These enthroned dual images are related to a story in the *Lotus Sūtra* in which the Buddha shares the teaching seat. We see that the doubling of images is closely tied to Maitreya lore, but nowhere is this more dramatically depicted in art forms than in Korea with its giant standing twin Buddha images.[45] The use of the guardian figures, who often stand on either side of entrances, as models for Maitreya may be one reason for the ready acceptance of the double presentation. If Maitreya's role is one of protection, then he should have some of the attributes of other protecting deities.

The most distinctive images of this pantheon that grew out of the Koryŏ remain those with heavy headpieces. A great variety of images throughout Korea can be found with these headpieces, which have become an accepted iconographic form for Maitreya. In some cases, it is obvious that the headpieces have simply been added to an image. This apparent willingness to put the iconographic mark of Maitreya on images of all sorts makes it difficult to judge their importance or the intent of those who made the additions. Griffis was one of the first to publish his impression that the head of the Maitreya was often surmounted by a platform, and the objects placed on that platform resembled stūpas and pagodas.[46] We know that Maitreya had an epithet, "the one who wears the stūpa on the head,"[47] and this could be one explanation for the headpieces. In Tibetan art, the crown of Maitreya is adorned with a stūpa, and it is a generally accepted identifying mark for images of this bodhisattva. Although the ephithet of "stūpa on the head" is known, it seldom appears in the texts of the Buddhist canon. We do find it in the Tantric texts of China as a name associated with the Buddhas and bodhisattvas placed within the mandala.[48] There are other textual references to the role of the stūpa and Maitreya; one example is the statement that Maitreya bears in his hand a lotus pedestal on which is located a stūpa that is dedicated to Vairocana Buddha.[49] It is possible that the artisans in Korea took this epithet of Maitreya quite literally and placed on his head a platform that supported a stūpa or pagoda. Once this pattern had been estalished, later people added these heavy platforms or included them when constructing images but may have had no idea of the origin of the decoration.

The complexity of the Maitreya cult in Korea is shown by the great variety of images and the uses made of them. In part, this complexity results from the persistence of interest in the stories and practices associated with Maitreya. For example, in the Yi dynasty, Buddhism underwent rather severe proscriptions and began to decline. Because monastic institutions held less power and were not so numerous as in the halcyon days of the Koryŏ dynasty, incorporation into folk religious practices tended to be the way in which Buddhism was given a place in the life of lay followers. The Yi dynasty was from time to time beset with serious political troubles, especially the invasions of Japan and, later, troops of the Ch'ing dynasty. During these tumultuous times, Maitreya belief became more popular; people prayed to Maitreya to appear and to give aid and comfort. The suppression of Buddhism was accompanied by the destruction of its images; many of the statues of the Buddha were partially damaged, in some cases the heads being hacked off. People used these destroyed statues as objects of their Maitreya belief and attached newly made heads, which often show the platform or a large headpiece. Kim Sam-yong points out that during this time images of Maitreya were being constructed in the old Paekche area with their bases buried in the ground.[50] He believes that this pattern was connected to the thought that Maitreya ascends to Tuṣita and descends to the earth. There is a good example of a buried-base Maitreya at the standing triad found at the An'guk monastery 安國寺 site. Here we are strongly reminded of the *ipsŏk* stones that are partially buried so that they stand erect. There is one other example of buried Maitreyas. In the later Koryŏ, a famous monk named Sindon 辛旽 declared that Maitreya would appear from beneath the earth. Indeed, an image of Maitreya made a miraculous appearance, slowly rising up from the ground. It was discovered that the miracle had been staged, for underneath the image sacks of beans had been buried, and as they sprouted and swelled they lifted the image out of the earth. The writers in the Koryŏ used this as an example of the evil that occurs during the age of the bad teaching.[51]

The continued following that Maitreya enjoyed can in no small measure be attributed to the fact that he had become a major part of the fertility practices in Korea, where children and especially sons were of great importance. Even today the Maitreya image is the one before which women pray for the birth of a son, and if a boy is born to one of these devotees it is not unusual for the child to be given the name of Mirŭk.[52] The role of Maitreya in the fertility cult practice is most easily seen in the Cheju-do practice. There is one spot on the island where in the past an image of Maitreya was placed next to a phallic stone. Women would come to that spot to touch the stone in the hope that the act would result in the birth of a son. The fact that prayers for sons are directed toward the Dragon King, the Mountain Spirit, the Seven Stars, and Maitreya indicates that it was Maitreya, of all the Buddhist pantheon, who was thought to be efficacious in the ceremonies directed toward birth.

We have discussed the fact that in the earlier dynasties the Hwarang, who were associated with the belief in Maitreya, had strong ties to shamanism. Maitreya still holds a place in the world of the *mudang,* women who are possessed by a series of deities during their ritual trance ceremonies. Among the deities that possess the shamans are Buddhist ones, such as Maitreya, Bhaiṣajyaguru, and Avalokiteśvara.[53] When we consider that Maitreya is a giver of sons, it is easy to see why he, above other Buddhist figures, would continue to play a role in the shamanic tradition dominated by women.

In the Chogye order monasteries, only minimal attention is paid to Maitreya, except in those places where special stories and images attract the attention of lay people. True, Maitreya figures are still being constructed in the monasteries: Ssangyong monastery built a fifty-foot-high concrete Maitreya in the 1960s; Yangnyŏng hermitage commissioned a stone Maitreya that was made from local rock and completed in 1968; a large image of Maitreya as a bodhisattva was constructed at the Wŏnhyo monastery by the nuns who occupy that institution. Although some monasteries devote time and money to the promulgation of the lore about Maitreya and provide, for the devotees, images of this bodhisattva, the greatest attention is given not by the clerics of Buddhism but by the lay people. Thus the Maitreya cult that must once have occupied an important place in the monastic life of Korean Buddhism has faded from this central focus and retains a place of honor mainly among women followers.[54]

Just as in Japan, new religions have arisen in Korea to meet the needs of current generations. In Korea many of these religions, whether related to folk practice, Christianity, or Buddhism, emphasize a messianic vision. Perhaps the most famous example for Westerners has been the controversial claim of Rev. Moon that he is the Messiah.

Maitreya has been an important part of the messianic groups in Korea. One such new religion is Chŭngsan-gyo 甑山教, and in it we see elements that characterize a number of these modern movements.[55] The individual for whom this group is named, Chŭngsan, believed that a disease would appear in Kunsan district and from there spread throughout the world.

Unchecked, it would wipe out all of humankind. Chŭngsan maintained that he alone had the magical power necessary to keep this disaster from occurring. His followers dedicate themselves to the practices that continue to ward off total destruction, and upon their shoulders has descended the responsibility for the safety of all of human life. Chŭngsan was thought to have had two incarnations – the first when he descended in 1840 to the Eiffel Tower (built in 1870) and the second when he took lodging in a Maitreya image and lived for thirty years in the present century. The leaders of the groups that were formed on the basis of this teaching believed that the image gave forth power and illumination and for those thirty years was the center of Buddhist power. By 1945, there were eighty sects of Chŭngsan-gyo in Korea and among these were a number of Maitreya cults. Since these Maitreya organizations were not officially recognized by the government when it designated the members of a League of Folk Religions (Tongdo-hoe),[56] they have not been listed as religious organizations. Of great importance to the Chŭngsan-gyo is a mantra that is said to have been heard by Ānanda when it was given to Śākyamuni by Maitreya. This mantra is the most powerful talisman against disease and destruction, and as we have seen the group is dedicated to the task of controlling the ultimate epidemic.

Another group that includes Maitreya in its practice is the Pongnam-gyo founded by Kim Yŏng-gŭn (1898–1950), a native of Cheju-do. This leader urged all to worship Maitreya as the central deity and to work toward the construction of the Dragon Flower Realm in which Maitreya will rule when he comes to earth.[57]

An interesting development has grown up around Yi Yu-song, who stresses that Korea, in particular the southern part, has been chosen as the place for the salvation of humankind. This is in part due to the weather, for in the southern region of the peninsula the four seasons are clearly distinguished and seasonal rhythm is essential for a complete and happy life. It is believed that, after a cosmic disaster, the elite – of any religion – will be saved and will dwell in Korea. Hananim, the primordial deity of Korean epics, the ruler of heaven, will descend in the form of Maitreya Buddha. This Maitreya will not wear the robes of the Buddhists but will be wearing the traditional clothes of the Koreans. He will establish the new order, a utopia in which people will be pure of heart and will live in peace for sixty thousand years, the length of time usually attributed to one of the three periods of the teaching of Maitreya.[58] This is another example of the age-old notion that the land of Maitreya can be constructed out of the merit and practice of those who believe in his birth.

The Maitreya groups have never been in close contact with one another and have tended to splinter into small, selective bands of believers.[59] Because of the lack of organization and the tendency to remain aloof, the movement has not been very visible. Division into many sects has been one method of spreading particular brands of teaching concerning Maitreya, but this tendency toward fragmentation has kept the groups from being a major political or social force. During the Japanese occupation the Maitreya groups were frowned upon by the authorities because they were potential sources of organized opposition. The teaching that proclaimed that Korea was to have a key influence on the future of the world was not appreciated by the military governors, who were trying to assimilate Korea into the orbit of Japanese control. It must have been upsetting to hear that Japan would be destroyed by fire (interpreted later to be the atomic bomb) and that peace would come only when Korea had achieved her place as the center of power and control of the world. The opposition of the Japanese government to the Maitreya cults and the fact that some of these groups were not recognized as regular parts of the organized religion by post-Japanese administrations of Korea itself are examples of the fear that arises in reaction to such cults. The Hwarang were strong supporters of the rulers of their times, and thus the Maitreya practice was welcomed and made a part of the national system during the Silla period; the new religions that adopt Maitreya as their messiah have not elicited a similar response in twentieth-century government offices.

The Maitreya images in Korea have long puzzled and moved Westerners as well as the natives of the country. The search by Westerners for an explanation of the forms that Maitreya has assumed in Korea has been going on for more than a century and is likely to continue for a long period. G. C. Foulke of the U.S. Navy recorded the first account of a Westerner seeing the Ŭnjin image, the 64-foot-high granite sculpture with a large platform on its head; he expressed his initial glimpse from some miles away within the context of his profession – he thought he was looking at a lighthouse rising above the trees. Another navy man, Lt. Bernadon, was the first to make note of the dual images, and he wondered about the fact that one had a round platform and the other a square one.[60] It is surprising how little study has been devoted by either Koreans or outsiders to these giants that still stand and are still being constructed.

Of this we can be sure: Maitreya has had a long and interesting career in Korea. He has been a Hwarang warrior, a guardian figure, a symbol and source of fertility, a deity possessing the *mudang,* a future leader of the new society that will emerge in Korea. His images are just as varied, for we can see him as a bodhisattva in triad with Śākyamuni, a young princely figure sitting in pensive pose, a towering giant carved from an ancient menhir, a composite with a body of one type and a later head, a supporter of platforms on which rest mysterious shapes, a huge-headed image called "baby Buddha." His name is spread across the countryside, designating monasteries, bridges, lighthouses, castles, walls, mountains, rivers.[61] People turn to him for the birth of a son, a cure for illness, protection, and personal merit; he is the guardian of sailors, the bestower good fortune. Even in the twentieth century he has not been forgotten – twenty-seven new images have already been constructed, compared with sixty-three during the entire Yi dynasty.[62] The giant images of Maitreya rise above the tree tops of the monasteries, and although the monks and nuns may pay little attention to them, they continue to represent to the lay community a promise of help and to the members of the Maitreya groups a hope for the coming new age of peace. The scholar can find here a rich resource for studying the development of Buddhism as it spread across East Asia and became adapted to the local environment and culture. It is difficult to imagine a study of Korea that does not in some way touch on the beliefs that surround Maitreya.

NOTES

1 The research of Professor Zenryū Tsukamoto, *Chūgoku bukkyō tsūshi* 中國佛教通史 (Tokyo: Suzuki gakujutsu azidan, 1968), and Professor Shinko Mochizuki *Chūgoku jōdō kyōri shi* 中國浄土教理史 (Kyoto: Hozokan, 1964), regarding the use of images of Amitābha and Maitreya as proof of cultive activity is convincing evidence of this shift of interest in China.

2 Jonathan Best has provided much that is new in the study of art history in Korea. See his "Malanda's Legacy: A Social and Cultural History of Buddhism" (forthcoming).

3 Kim Sam-yong, *Han'guk mirŭk sinang ŭi yŏn'gu* 韓國彌勒信仰의研究 (Seoul: Tonghwa Ch'ulpan kongsa, 1983).

4 Ibid., 53–5.

5 The seminal studies of these images have been done by Hwang Su-yŏng. See especially his "Meditating Maitreya Statues of the Three Kingdoms," *Proceedings of the First International Conference on Korean Studies* (Seoul: Academy of Korean Studies, 1980), 1025–7. Also his article "Silla pan'ga sayu sŏksang" 新羅半跏思惟石像, *Han'guk pulsang ŭi yŏn'gu* 韓國佛像의研究 (Seoul: Samhwa ch'ulpansa, 1973), 201–30, where he discusses three cross-legged bodhisattva figures of the seventh century and emphasizes that Buddha statues were used in connection with Maitreya as an attendant in the Three Kingdoms period. Additional reference to these matters can be found in Tamura Encho, *Chōsen bukkyō to nihon bukkyō* 朝鮮仏教と日本仏教 (Tokyo, 1980).

6 These ideas are discussed at some length by Yi Ki-baek in "Samguk sidae ŭi pulgyo chŏllae wa kŭ sahoe chŏk sŏnggyŏk," Yŏksa hakpo 歴史學報, 6 (1954): 128–205. The issue is also found in A. Soper, *Literary Evidence for Early Buddhist Art in China* (Ascona, 1959), 211.

7 Kim, *Han'guk mirŭk*, 55. For more details on Silla see note 18.

8 Ahn Kye-hyŏn, "Han'guk pulgyosa sang kodaep'yŏn" 韓國佛教史,上,古代篇 *Han'guk munhwasa daegye* 韓國文化史大系 (Seoul: Korea daehakkyo minjok munhwa yŏn'guso, 1970), 6:179–267. He states that the belief in Maitreya seems to have been introduced and flourished with Kongju as its main center. During the

reign of Muwang, the famous Mirŭk monastery 彌勒寺 was constructed near Yonghwasan, and the legends about the construction of that monastery indicate that there was a strong belief in the descent of Maitreya into the world.

9 Hwang Su-yŏng, "Paekche pan'ga sayu sŏksang sogo" 百濟半跏思惟石像小考, in *Han'guk pulsang ŭi yŏn'gu* 韓國佛像의硏究 (Seoul: Samhwa ch'ulpansa, 1973), 47–72. Professor Hwang also thinks that Kongju was a center of sixth-century Maitreya cult activity. There is some problem with the identification of the image under consideration in this article. Professor Hwang originally, and in this reference, regarded the image as the work of Paekche. Professor Kim Won-yong thinks that the statue designated as National Treasure 83 (see note 43) is indeed a Paekche artifact, but recently Professor Hwang has changed his mind and now thinks that it belongs to Silla. For other information on Maitreya in Paekche see Kim Sam-yong, "Mirŭksa ch'anggŏn e taehan mirŭk sinangjŏk paegyŏng" 彌勒寺創建에對한 彌勒信仰的背景, *Mahan paekche munhwa* 馬韓百濟文化, 1 (1975): 11–30. Also his work "Paekche mirŭk sasang ŭi yŏksajŏk wich'i" 百濟彌勒思想의歷史的位置, *Mahan paekche munhwa* 馬韓百濟文化, 4–5 (1982); Kim Yŏng-t'ae 金煐泰, "Paekche ŭi mirŭk sasang" 百濟의彌勒思想, *Mahan paekche munhwa* 馬韓百濟文化, 4–5 (1982); Tamura Encho, "Paekche ŭi mirŭk sinang" 百濟의彌勒信仰, *Mahan paekche munhwa*, 4–5 (1982). A survey of some of this is presented in W. Watson, *The Earliest Buddhist Images of Korea: Transactions of the Oriental Ceramic Society* (London: Oriental Ceramic Society – Transactions, 1957–9), vol. 31.

10 *Samguk sagi* (Seoul, 1978), 2 vols.

11 See Kenneth Gardiner, *The Early History of Korea: The Historical Development of the Peninsula up to the Introduction of Buddhism in the Fourth Century A.D.* (Honolulu: University of Hawaii Press, 1969), app. 2, for a good description of the sources of these histories.

12 Questions about the use of Chinese materials have been discussed in detail by John Jamieson, "The *Samguk Sagi* and Unification Wars" (Ph.D. diss. University of California, Berkeley, 1968).

13 Gardiner, *Early History*, 67.

14 The hagiographic literature in Chinese Buddhism is extensive and includes material found in the catalogues of *Taisho* 大正, vol. 55.

15 Although it is true that more Buddhist lore is found in the *yusa*, we can judge the value of the material only by carefully interpreting its content. Legends and tales are the basis of much of our knowledge of these formative years in Korea, but they are at best echoes of a distant past and in many cases are fragments of material that was once available in a more comprehensive collection.

16 The best study of this text has been done by S. Mishina in a two-part work, "Sankoku-iji koshō" 三國遺事考証, *Chōsen Gakuho* 朝鮮學報, 29 (October 1962) and 30 (January 1963). He has extracted the relevant passages from the *Yusa* and made an extensive study of the fragmentary remains of the *Kukki*.

17 See R. Rutt, "The Flower Boys of Silla," *Transactions of the Korea Branch of the Royal Asiatic Society*, 38 (1961), for a good discussion of the work done by Waley and others who have tried to find parallels.

18 Several scholars have dealt with the military nature of the Hwarang, among them Kim Kwang-yŏng, "Hwarangdo ch'angsŏle taehan sogo" 花郎道創設에 對한小考, *Tongguk sasang* 東國思想, vol. 1 (1958); Kim Sang-gi "Hwarang-kwa mirŭk sinang e taehayŏ" 花郎과 彌勒信仰에對하여, *Yi Hong-jik paksa hwagap kinyŏm hanguk sahak nonch'ong* 李弘稙博士華甲紀念韓國史學論叢 (Seoul: Singu munhwasa, 1969), 3–12; Kim Yŏng-t'ae "Silla ŭi mirŭk sasang" 新羅의彌勒思想, *Dongguk daehakkyo nonmunjip* 東國大學校論文集, 14 (1975); Lee Min-yong, "Silla sahoe ŭi mirŭk sinang" 新羅社會의彌勒信仰, *Dongguk sasang* 東國思想 5 (1970); Seo Yun-gil, "Silla ŭi mirŭk sasang" 新羅의 彌勒思想, in *Hanguk pulgyo sasangsa* 韓國佛教思想史 (Iri: Wŏn'gwang taehakkyo, 1972), 81–108.

19 The major work of S. Mishina, *Shiragi karō no kenkyū* 新羅花郎の研究 (Tokyo, 1943), is a standard for all research on the Hwarang institution.

20 J. Joe Wanne, *Traditional Korea: A Cultural History* (Seoul: Chung'ang University Press, 1972), 83.

21 E. Henthorn, *A History of Korea* (New York: Free Press, 1971), 44–6; Rutt, "Flower Boys," 31.

22 See note 18.

23 See note 19; also Mishina, *Shiragi,* 125.

24 Jamieson, "*Samguk Sagi,*" 306.

25 SGY 234. For use of SGY see Yi Hong-Jik, "Samguk yusa saegin" 三國遺事索, *Yŏksa hakpo* 歷史學報, 5 (1953).

26 SGY 236.

27 SGY 237. For a discussion of the word "Miri" see Kim Sang-gi, "Hwarangkwa mirŭk sinang e taehayŏ" 花郎과 彌勒信仰에 對하여, *Yi Hong-jik paksa hwagap kinyŏm hanguk sahak nonch'ong* 李弘稙博士華甲紀念韓國史學論叢 (Seoul: Sin'gu mumhwasa, 1969), 3–12.

28 Jamieson, "*Samguk Sagi,*" 195–6.

29 Henthorn, *History*, 45.

30 Alan Heyman, "Folk Music and Dance," in *Folk Culture in Korea,* ser. 4 (Seoul: International Culture Foundation, 1974).

31 Ibid., 97.

32 Rutt, "Flower Boys," 31*ff*. See photo reprint of the 1814 edition of Yi Che-hyŏn's *Ikchae chip* 益齋集 (Seoul, 1961), which contains *Yŏgong p'aelsŏl* 櫟翁稗說 (poetry and tales).

33 *Hunmong chahoe* 訓蒙字會, by Ch'oe Se-jin (1433–1542), a reprint of the Enryakuji print of the University of Tokyo Library.

34 *Chibong yusŏl* 芝峰類說, by Yi Su-gwang (1563–1628), photo reprint of 1634 print.

35 Kim, *Han'guk mirŭk,* 155–6.

36 See note 35.

37 The triad of Maitreya Sūtras deals with this aspect of Maitreya. See T 452, T 453, T 454, and T 1774 for comments.

38 Kim, *Han'guk mirŭk,* 248. Some characteristics of these Maitreya images that Professor Kim has noted are the following. They are out-of-doors rather than

housed in the image halls of the monasteries, the pose is standing, the images are constructed from local stone, the face of the images is pointed toward the south, and many of the images were not originally Maitreya but have been given a later attribution. He also notes examples of some natural stones that are revered as images of Maitreya.

39 Choi Nam-sŏn, "Asi chosŏn" 兒時朝鮮 in *Yuktang Ch'oi Nam-sŏn chŏnjip* 六堂崔南善全集 (Seoul: Hyŏnamsa, 1973), 2: 177–8. He states that the people performed their rituals on an altar called *sindan* (the altar of the spirits), usually found in the mountains. The group in charge of these rituals were called *tanggul* and the sacred spot was *sodo* 蘇塗.

40 Choi, "Asi chosŏn," 177.

41 See *Han'guk minsok chonghap chosa pogosŏ* 韓國民俗綜合調査報告書, vol. 5: *Cheju do* (Seoul: Ministry of Culture and Information, 1971), 171–2. Both have rounded headpieces.

42 SGY 239. For a discussion of the combination of the cult of heaven and Buddhism, see Hwang P'ae-gang, *Silla pulgyo sŏlhwa yŏn'gu* 新羅佛教說話研究 (Seoul, 1972), 286*ff*.

43 The Korean government has designated certain art objects to be national treasures, and they are assigned numbers in sequence of adoption.

44 Simone Gauber et al., *Buddhism in Afghanistan and Central Asia: Iconography of Religions,* vol. 13, no. 14, pt. 1 (Leiden: Brill, 1976), 9, 245. Examples of two-headed images are shown.

45 Mikami Tsugio, "Panrajō shutsudo no nibutsu zazō to sono rekishiteki igi" 半拉城出土の二仏並座像とその歴史的意義, *Chosen gakuho* 朝鮮學報 , no. 49 (October 1968): 333–48.

46 W. E. Griffis, *Corea: The Hermit Nation* (New York: Scribner's, 1907), 39.

47 This is a name for Maitreya that was most popular among the T'ien t'ai sect.

48 One such example is found in T 2401. 748 and 751b, a Tendai document of the tenth century.

49 See *Taishō*, 9:285, for this iconographic description. This passage has been noted by Lee Yu-min in her work on Maitreya being done at Ohio State University, Department of Art History.

50 Kim, *Han'guk mirŭk,* 175

51 Ibid., 66.

52 Cha Jae-ho, "Boy Preference Reflected in Korean Folklore," in *Virtues in Conflict: Tradition and the Korean Woman Today,* ed. S. Matielli (Seoul: Royal Asiatic Society, 1977), 115–16. See also her article on the same topic, "Boy Preference," *KIRBS Research Bulletin,* no. 1 (1973): 1–14. Kim Sam-yong, *Han'guk mirŭk,* 175, describes the fertility connection. Some women ingest the stone dust that is made from the carving of the Maitreya images, believing that it will be of aid in giving birth to a son.

53 The work of Laurel Kendall is generating a great deal of new interest in the content of the *mudang*'s performance. See her *Restless Spirits* (forthcoming from University of Hawaii Press). See also Paul Pai's *Les croyances populaire en Coree* (Lyon, 1956).

54 This problem is discussed in some detail in Lewis Lancaster, "Buddhism and the Family," in *Religion and Family in East Asia,* ed. G. Devos and Sofue (Osaka: National Museum of Ethnology, 1984).

55 Kim, *Han'guk mirŭk,* 214–15.

56 See the extensive study of the issue in S. Palmer, "The New Religions of Korea," *Transactions of the Korea Branch of the Royal Asiatic Society,* 43 (1967): 5*ff.*; also Lee Kang-o, "Chŭngsan-gyo: Its History Doctrine and Ritual," *Transactions of the Korea Branch of the Royal Asiatic Society,* 43 (1947): 44.

57 Kim, *Han'guk miruk,* 214.

58 P. Gernot, "New Religions in Korean Society," *Proceedings,* p. 1080. Also see his "Current Trends in New Religions in the World and Thought of Chŭngsangyo," in *Chŭngsan sasang yon'gu* 甑山思想研究 vol. 4 (Seoul, 1979). Similar material is found in Mun Sang-hi, "Fundamental Doctrines of the New Religions in Korea," *Korea Journal,* 11, no. 12 (1971). Yoo Pyŏng-dŏk, *Han'guk sinhŭng chonggyo* 韓國新興宗教 (Iri: Wŏn'gwang University, 1974), 306–10, points out that the founder of Chŭngsan-gyo, Kang Chŭngsan, took advantage of the strong belief in Maitreya that existed in the Kŭmsan monastery area and stated, "To see me in the future, go to see the Maitreya Buddha at Kŭmsan monastery 金山寺." In *Han'guk minsok* 韓國民俗, vol. 2, *Chŏllabukto,* 154–9, the writer reports that the interest in Maitreya among the monastic community at Kŭmsan is not very evident, but he is very popular among the people who live nearby.

59 B. Earhard, "New Religions of Korea: A Preliminary Interpretation," *Transactions of the Royal Asiatic Society of Korea,* 49 (1974): 24.

60 The famous pair, according to the oral tradition of the village people, is a male and female. The round hat is the male and the square one the female. The small image that has been placed between them was constructed in 1953.

61 See thc *Sinjŭng tongguk yŏjisŭnggram* 新增東國輿地勝覽 (Seoul: Minjok munhwa ch'ujinhoe, 1969). There are six monastery names, five mountain rivers, as well as the other designations.

62 Kim, *Han'guk mirŭk,* 248.

7

Perfect World and Perfect Time

Maitreya in Vietnam

HUE-TAM HO TAI

Introduction

The Maitreya theme inspired two recent millenarian movements in Vietnam, both founded in the first half of the twentieth century. Known respectively as the Cao Đài 高台 and Hòa Hảo sects, each claimed at the height of its popularity and political involvement more than a million followers. The religious doctrines of the two sects were based on the familiar East Asian conflation of Confucian, Taoist, and Buddhist teachings and practices and thus contained many elements that were either identical or at least very similar. Nonetheless, the Cao Đài and Hòa Hảo sects represented two distinct and opposing trends within East Asian popular religion. The Cao Đài sect provided a splendid example of unrestrained doctrinal eclecticism, complex and highly hierarchical organization, and elaborate rituals. But the Hòa Hảo sect was animated by the spirit of reform and simplicity both in its teachings and in its ritual practices; and for much of its early history, it was without an infrastructure of any kind. These two opposing tendencies are neatly illustrated by the relative importance of the millenarian dimension, and more particularly of the Maitreya theme, in their respective doctrines.[1]

Cao Đài, the earliest of the two sects, was founded in 1926 by a group of people brought together by their shared belief in spiritism. They self-consciously set about the task of amalgamating the teachings of not only the three major religious currents of East Asia, but also of the world religions known to them. Within this religious admixture, the most important dimension was not millennial, but spiritist. The ultimate source of doctrinal authority was a figure called Cao Đài, or Supreme Being, from whom emanated prophecies and religious commands via the agency of teen-age mediums. Cao Đài was represented by a highly naturalistic rendition of a human eye, designed to symbolize his omniscience. Maitreya himself was not the object of a special cult, but was merely one among a crowded pantheon of deities that incorporated figures as diverse as Jesus Christ, Joan of Arc, Confucius, and Victor Hugo. Even when the leaders of the sect spread apocalyptic propaganda, as they did on several occasions during the 1920s and 1930s, they did so in the name of Cao Đài, not Maitreya.

The Cao Đài sect represented the coming together of too many disparate ideas and preexisting sectarian groupings for its genealogy to be traced to any particular source. Although its founders tried to present it as an entirely new religion, its doctrine was an uneasy blend of preexisting beliefs, of which Maitreyan eschatology was but one. Popular familiarity with this eschatology made southerners receptive to their dire warnings of impending cataclysm without their having to spell out in detail the source of their belief.

A clearer idea of the role of Maitreyan eschatology in Vietnamese history can be gleaned from studying the Hòa Hảo sect and its antecedents. The sect took its name from the village of Hòa Hảo in the province of Châu Đốc near the Cambodian border, where its founder, Huỳnh Phú Sổ, was born in 1919. In 1939, after undergoing a religious crisis, Huỳnh Phú Sổ proclaimed the founding of his sect; within months, a large number of people were flocking to him. They believed in Maitreya eschatology but had been unwilling to join a sect as eclectic as Cao Đài. Unlike the Cao Đài leaders, Huỳnh Phú Sổ had no aspiration to be the founder of a new religion. Instead, he wanted to be considered an orthodox Buddhist and always insisted on his sect being called Hòa Hảo Buddhism. However, his political activities, his willful simplification of Buddhist teachings, and his emphasis on laicization and collective (as opposed to individual) salvation earned him the hostility of most mainstream Buddhists.

The Hòa Hảo sect was more overtly millenarian than the Cao Đài sect. Its eschatology was presented in a purer form, shorn of spiritist overlay. Its genealogy was clearer, and it was readily acknowledged by Huỳnh Phú Sổ as an updated version of a millenarian tradition that could be traced to the previous century.

This tradition was the Bửu Sơn Kỳ Hương religious sect, which was possibly the first organized millenarian movement in Vietnam. Its roots lay in the pioneer society of the Mekong Delta and the southwestern frontier where Huỳnh Phú Sổ was born. The Bửu Sơn Kỳ Hương (Pạo-shan ch'i hsiang) 寶山奇香 doctrine was a mixture of Confucian, Taoist, and Buddhist teachings. The Confucian contribution was most pronounced in its ethical dimension; Taoism provided a rationale for the emphasis on faith healing and various kinds of magic, which leaders of the sect used to support their claims to charismatic authority. Its Buddhism was of a lay-oriented type, highly reminiscent of Chinese folk Buddhism such as was illustrated by the White Lotus religion.

The core of the Bửu Sơn Kỳ Hương doctrine was the idea that Maitreya's descent into the world was imminent. It was an article of faith among the sectaries that Maitreya would be reborn in the Seven Mountains of Châu Đốc province, hence the idea that these were precious mountains (*bửu sơn*). It was believed that, in these mountains, Maitreya would convene a Dragon Flower Assembly (*Hội Long-Hoa* 會龍華) to proclaim the new Dharma that was to govern his millennium. The Bửu Sơn Kỳ Hương doctrine was presented as a set of guidelines to teach those who wished for salvation and rebirth in Maitreya's millennium how to perfect themselves in order to attain their goals; it was therefore likened to a strange, wonderful fragrance (*kỳ hương*) emanating from the precious mountains – hence the name of the sect.

Although it is easy to trace the evolution of the Bửu Sơn Kỳ Hương sect into the twentieth-century Hòa Hảo sect, it is more difficult to trace the history of the Maitreya theme in its various forms or to explain the late appearance of organized millenarianism in Vietnam.

The Role of Maitreya Before the Nineteenth Century

Buddhism was already popular in the commandery of Chiao-chih 交趾 (as northern Vietnam under Chinese rule was known) by the late second century. Chiao-chih was then a major trading center, attracting merchants from India, Southeast Asia, Central Asia as well as North China. Shih Hsieh 士燮 (137–226), who was prefect of Chiao-chih in the late second century, was said to move among the populace "to the sound of bells, musical stones, drums and whistles" and accompanied by "scores of Hu people bearing lighted incense."[2] These "Hu people" were probably monks of either Indian or Central Asian origin. Mou-tzu 牟子, who lived in Chiao-chih during Shih Hsieh's tenure as prefect, became a convert to Buddhism, having previously been a Taoist, and in turn converted other Chinese residents.[3]

Mou-tzu is traditionally considered to be one of the two founders of the Vietnamese *āgama* school; the other is K'ang Seng-hui 康僧會 (d. 280), a Sogdian whose family had moved to Chiao-chih from India. K'ang Seng-hui is credited with having translated numerous Buddhist scriptures into Chinese both while living in Chiao-chih and after moving to Wu.[4] In 1096, the monk Thông Biện 通辨 asserted that, at the time of Mou-tzu and K'ang Seng-hui, about twenty stūpas had already been erected in Chiao-chih and that there were some 500 monks who were able to recite fifteen sūtras.[5] These included those translated by K'ang Seng-hui, and the *Sūtra in 42 Sections,* which was popular in China as well.[6] Given the presence in Chiao-chih of Central Asian monks and traders, it is highly likely that Pure Land sūtras were among those in circulation.

Very little is known of the evolution of Vietnamese Buddhism during the period of disunity in China, for while the Chinese empire was plunged in turmoil, Chiao-chih was able to survive in a state of quasi independence at the margin of political strife. Thus few of the events that took place in Chiao-chih found their way into the Chinese historical records. When Emperor Kao of Ch'i 齊高帝 (479–482) announced his intention to send missionaries to Chiao-chih to spread Buddhism, he was dissuaded from doing so by T'an Ch'ien 曇遷, a Buddhist of Central Asian origins, on the ground that the religion of Buddha was already flourishing in the South.[7]

In 544, Lý Bí 李賁 took advantage of continued turmoil in China to found a short-lived independent kingdom. He then ordered the building of a temple decorated by a seated statue of Amitābha, eight feet in height and in the style of the Lung-men carvings, possibly to commemorate his new dynasty.[8] But in 546, he was betrayed by Lao tribesmen to the Chinese. After his death, his kingdom fell prey to political strife. In 555, a kinsman of Lý Bí, who was known as Lý Phật Tử 李佛子 (Lý "Son of Buddha") became leader of the Lý forces. He was able to defeat his rivals one by one before submitting to Sui rule in 590.

It was during the reign of Lý Phật Tử that the first Thiền (Ch'an) Buddhist school was founded in Vietnam. The founder was Vinitaruci, an Indian convert from Brahmanism. Seeking greater knowledge of his new faith, he had gone to China, arriving in Ch'ang-an in 574, the year when Emperor Wu of Northern Chou (561–577) launched his persecution of Buddhism. Vinitaruci fled from Ch'ang-an toward Hunan, where he was accepted as a disciple by Seng-ts'an 僧璨, the third patriarch of Ch'an Buddhism. Advised by Seng-ts'an to go farther south, he moved on to Canton and from there to Chiao-chih, where he remained from 580 to his death in 602.[9] Members of his sect, which endured until the twelfth century, acted as advisers to Vietnamese kings after the country became independent of China in 939. Another Ch'an school was founded by Vô Ngôn Thông (Wu-yen-t'ung) 無言通, who came from China in 820, and like the Vinitaruci school, supplied advisers to the Vietnamese throne, until its disappearance in the thirteenth century.[10]

The first reference to a Maitreya cult in Vietnam comes from I-ching 義淨, *Biographies of Eminent Monks of the T'ang Who Sought the Dharma in the Western Regions (Ta-t'ang hsi-yü ch'iu-fa kao-seng chuan* 大唐西域求法高僧傳). I-ching made two trips to India, one in 671 and another in 689. During one of these trips, he met a Vietnamese monk from Ái 愛 prefecture (present-day Thanh Hóa) named Đại-Thặng-Đăng (Ta-ch'eng-teng) 大乘燈. By the time Đại-Thặng-Đăng joined I-ching's group, he had already gone to Ceylon and India and had been living in Tamralipti for twelve years. Đại-Thặng-Đăng by that time wanted to go to China to spread the teachings of Buddhism but died in Kuśinagara. According to I-ching, Đại-Thặng-Đăng's "constant preoccupation was with the Tuṣita Heaven; he hoped to rejoin the Compassionate One [Maitreya]. Everyday, he painted one or two trees with dragon-flowers to show the deepest wish of his heart."[11] By the time of I-ching's pilgrimage, the cult of Maitreya in China had been eclipsed by the cult of Amitābha. It is possible that Đại-Thặng-Đăng was holding onto a cult that had also flourished in Chiao-chih earlier. It would seem that, for Đại-Thặng-Đăng, the cult of Maitreya was exclusive and that it was also purely devotional, devoid of eschatological overtones.

Buddhism reached its apogee in Vietnam during the Lý dynasty (1010–1226). Although it continued to flourish under the Trần (1226–1397), there were already signs that Confucianism was gaining ground. An idea of the popularity of Buddhism under these two dynasties can be had from a popular saying of the times: "The soil belongs to the king, the pagoda to the village, and the landscape to Buddha" (*đất vua, chùa làng, phong cảnh Bụt*);[12] yet it is impossible to assemble an accurate picture of Buddhist practices among the population from the historical records, which focus overwhelmingly on details of court life. Periodically, the court would order stūpas to be built by the hundreds throughout the country.[13] The more important temples were endowed with generous gifts of land and were lavishly decorated. Gold and copper statues were cast in such numbers that only when they were of truly imposing magnitude was their casting noted. Thus we learn that, in 1041, copper from the royal treasury was set aside for a large statue of Maitreya flanked by two bodhisattvas.[14]

King Cao-tông of the Lý 李高宗 (1173–1210) ordered his subjects to call him Buddha.[15] However, royal claims to Buddhahood did not prevent monks from leading rebellions that shook the very foundations of the throne. None of the recorded rebellions indicates that Maitreya provided a theme for challenging dynastic rule as it did in China.

The historical records available for the next few centuries yield scattered evidence of a devotional cult dedicated to Maitreya. But during the Ming occupation of Vietnam (1407–28) a large number of documents were destroyed, making it impossible to gain a fuller picture of the state of Vietnamese Buddhism at the time. The Lê 黎 dynasty (1428–1786), which was founded when Chinese occupation came to an end, continued the effort begun by the Ming toward greater Confucianization. Buddhism thus lost the court patronage it had previously enjoyed, although it continued to flourish among the people. During the seventeenth and eighteenth centuries, when the country was divided, the Trịnh 鄭 lords held sway north of the eighteenth parallel, and the Nguyễn 阮 lords to the south; there was a limited revival of court patronage of Buddhism. In 1601, Nguyễn Hoàng 阮皇 ordered the construction of a seven-story stūpa dedicated to the Heavenly Mother (Thiên

Mụ 天母) on the bank of the Perfume River in Huế. Among the many statues that decorated the temple was one of a smiling Maitreya located in a hall set aside for his cult.[16]

In 1742, monk Liễu Quán held a giant Dragon Flower Platform Convocation (Đàn Long-Hoa 壇龍華) in front of the temple of the Heavenly Mother. Since 1740 at least, the Nguyễn territory had been awash with rumors of impending disaster, but Liễu Quán merely wanted to signal to the world his firm intention of retreating behind the walls of his monastery.[17] Liễu Quán was an important figure in the Nguyễn territory, for he was the first Vietnamese-born monk of the Lin-ch'i 臨濟 branch of Ch'an Buddhism. Previous Lin-ch'i monks had been Chinese and had come to Vietnam at the invitation of Nguyễn lords to spread their brand of Buddhist teachings.

None of the entreaties of the Nguyễn lord succeeded in changing Liễu Quán's mind. It was being prophesied that the country would be plunged in disaster, both political and natural. Members of the nobility would rebel against Nguyễn rule, and the country would fall under foreign rule. People would be swallowed up by fire or die of the plague. Trees would lose all their leaves, and mountains would change location. Such was the panic caused by these predictions that the Nguyễn lord ordered his subjects to change their style of clothing to avert the calamity of foreign rule by pretending it had already happened. Against other predicted disasters, he had no cures.[18]

In the 1770s, disaster finally did strike the country. A peasant rebellion deposed the Nguyễn, then the Trịnh, and finally the Lê dynasty, which since the early seventeenth century, had reigned only in name. A scion of the Nguyễn house united the country in 1802 and founded the Nguyễn dynasty.

The paucity of historical evidence poses problems of interpretation. How safe is it to extrapolate from the meager data? Was the cult of Maitreya purely devotional, or did it carry eschatological overtones as in some cases in China? The stories of Đại-Thặng-Đăng and Liễu Quán suggest that the cult of Maitreya was purely devotional and was also exclusive. But it had to vie for popularity with other cults devoted to Amitābha, and even Bhaiṣajyaguru and Avalokiteśvara in his East Asian guise as the female bodhisattva Kuan Yin.

Apocalyptic prophecies were given credence, but it is impossible to determine whether they formed part of a specific eschatology. However, it seems that the idea of Maitreya's rebirth and rescue of humankind, so prevalent in Chinese millenarianism, was absent from the rumors that circulated in the mid–eighteenth century.

With the return of peace in 1802, Chinese immigration into Vietnam, which had slowed down during the decades of unrest, resumed with added momentum. Many of the new arrivals were fleeing from the turmoil caused by the two White Lotus rebellions of 1796 and 1813. Vietnamese officials, whose knowledge of domestic events in China was usually gleaned on tribute missions and was therefore of a highly specific and restricted nature, seem to have had little knowledge of the White Lotus religion and its adherents. This is evident from an observation made by a nineteenth-century historian, in which White Lotus sectaries were confused with the Triads, with whom the Vietnamese were more familiar as they operated off the coasts of South China and Vietnam.[19] Furthermore, the sectaries known to the Vietnamese came from Ssu-chuan rather than from North China, which was the area of greatest White Lotus strength and activity. It is possible that only with the two large-scale rebellions of 1796 and 1813 did knowledge of the White Lotus ideology spread among the pool of potential immigrants into Vietnam. This would explain the specific form the Maitreya theme took within the Bửu Sơn Kỳ Hương doctrine, for by the nineteenth century, White Lotus millenarianism embraced far more than Maitreyan eschatology.

The Origins of Vietnamese Millenarianism

The founder of the Bửu Sơn Kỳ Hương religion was a native of Sa Đéc province in the Mekong Delta. Named Đòan Minh Huyên, he became known by generations of his followers as the Buddha Master of Western Peace (Phật Thầy Tây An).

Both Đòan Minh Huyên and his followers were products of the pioneer society that grew out of the process of colonizing southern Vietnam. This process had begun in the late seventeenth century under the Nguyễn lords after the arrival in 1679 of three thousand Chinese refugees from the Manchu conquest of China. These refugees settled in the area that was later to be known as Saigon and opened the way for more immigrants to join them. Peasants from the central provinces were sent by the Nguyễn lords to add to their numbers. As the early settlers began to clear the wilderness and occupy more territory, they came into contact with Cambodian peasants who lived in scattered villages throughout what later became the border region. This region was thus highly heterogeneous, both ethnically and culturally. It was also a battleground in which Vietnamese and Thai rulers fought for supremacy over Cambodia.

Whether Chinese, Vietnamese, or Cambodians, the inhabitants of the area had only tenuous connections with the mainstream culture of their respective societies. The brand of Buddhism practiced by the Cambodian peasants of the border bore little resemblance to the religion practiced at court. The Vietnamese had come for a wide variety of reasons. Some were lured by promises of prosperity; others had been banished as criminals; still others had come to escape the ideological straitjacket that the early nineteenth-century Nguyễn emperiors sought to impose on the country as a means of unifying it after two centuries of strife. Many of these self-imposed exiles were defrocked monks, victims of the court's attempt to regulate the size of the Buddhist clergy and to impose greater control over both the teachings and the practices of Buddhism.

The Chinese who poured into southern Vietnam in the nineteenth century were different from those who had preceded them. Whereas the earlier immigrants had been welcomed either because they were versed in Confucian scholarship or, in the case of Lin-ch'i monks, because they were expected to spread orthodox Buddhist ideas, the new arrivals were often considered undesirable by the local authorities, an indication that few of them were imbued with Confucian virtues or learning of any kind.

It was in this volatile environment that Đòan Minh Huyên was born in 1807 in the village of Tòng Sơn.[20] Although his father had been prosperous, he died while his son was still young, whereupon his widow and son were hounded out of the village by envious relatives. Not until 1849, when he was already 42, did Đòan Minh Huyên return to his native village, claiming that in the intervening years he had received a thorough religious training while remaining silent about the specifics of this training.

The year 1849 seems to have been a highly propitious time for millenarian movements. A cholera epidemic swept through Vietnam, leaving indescribable devastation in its wake. Court records put the death toll at nearly 600,000.[21] Entire villages were decimated. The ravages of the epidemic were particularly grim in the pioneer society of the Southwest, where the scattered settlers were struggling to establish a foothold against the wilderness and create viable communities. Village institutions and kinship networks were destroyed; families were separated, and peasants were left destitute and utterly devoid of support in an area already burdened with the effects of ethnic heterogeneity and cultural anomie. Hit by disaster, the pioneer world became an extraordinarily fertile ground in which the seeds of a millenarian movement might grow.

As Tòng Sơn lay in the path of the epidemic, its villagers began to take measures to protect themselves against the worst of its depredations. They performed ceremonies that featured the slaughter of much of their precious cattle in sacrifice. It was at that point that Đòan Minh Huyên suddenly announced that he was the Buddha who had descended into the world to rescue humankind. Calling a halt to the ritual slaughter of the animals, he told his fellow villagers that he would protect them against the dreaded epidemic and began distributing cures and amulets inscribed with the characters *bửu sơn kỳ hương* (*pao-shan ch'i hsiang*). Over time, these amulets became a badge of allegiance to the teachings of Đoàn Minh Huyên. Members of the Hòa Hảo sect were the most famous wearers of these amulets, but there were other, smaller twentieth-century groups whose adherents also claimed to be following the teachings of Đòan Minh Huyên without recognizing the authority of Huỳnh Phú Sổ.

In addition to dispensing cures and amulets, Đoàn Minh Huyên disseminated advice on how to achieve salvation and rebirth in the millennium of Maitreya. When news of his proselytizing activities reached the provincial authorities, he was arrested and brought to the prefectural town of Long Xuyên to await trial. But further investigation having failed to disclose seditious intent, he was released. The provincial governor insisted on his being ordained into the Lin-ch'i branch of Buddhism and that he be sent to the Temple of Western Peace (Tây An tự) in Sam Mountain. Even though his religious affiliation was not of his own choosing, he became known as the Buddha Master of Western Peace.

None of the scanty sayings attributed to Đòan Minh Huyên or his immediate disciples attempts to lay out in detail the millenarian scheme on which the Bửu Sơn Kỳ Hương ideology was built. Instead, there was an underlying assumption that the population of southern Vietnam was already familiar with the basic ideas of Maitreyan eschatology. It must therefore be inferred that, despite the absence of historical records indicating belief in the imminent descent of Maitreya into the world, such a belief was already widespread in the mid–nineteenth century, thus facilitating the emergence of a millenarian movement such as the Bửu Sơn Kỳ Hương. What brought about the transformation of the purely devotional cult of Maitreya of Đại-Thặng-Đăng and Liễu Quán into the eschatology of Đòan Minh Huyên and his followers? One possible explanation is the influence of White Lotus ideology.

Given the long enmeshment of Buddhism and politics and, in particular, royal authority, it is significant that, although Đòan Minh Huyên's teachings were highly apocalyptic, they were also basically apolitical. They did not suggest the need for a great political leader to prepare the ground for Maitreya's descent. Đoàn Minh Huyên's teachings, which preached a lay type of folk Buddhism, were not intended to foster rebellion against the state as a prelude to the establishment of a new millennium. Instead, they urged the creation of new communities. These were to form a refuge where those who heeded Đòan Minh Huyên's message would flock in order to perfect themselves so as to achieve salvation and rebirth in the millennium of Maitreya. Those who did not were warned that they would perish in the coming apocalypse. The refuge to which the faithful were directed was the Seven Mountains of Châu Đốc province, near the Cambodian border. They came there to await the descent of Maitreya, who was due to be reborn into the world to hold his Dragon Flower Assembly and to reign over a new millennium of peace, virtue, and prosperity.

The early Bửu Sơn Hương sect thus represented a holistic effort at reintegration on several planes: individual, social, cultural, and, by extension, cosmic. It was designed to create a new moral universe on the basis of the diverse cultural values and religious ideas that vied for the allegiance of the heterogeneous population of the border area; it was an effort to overcome the anomie of that milieu. Despite the religious context of the community-building effort, it was also part of a larger scheme promoted by the Vietnamese court to colonize as quickly as possible the border area. Even though Đòan Minh Huyên preached loyalty to the ruler, his teachings were heterodox. But the court was willing to turn a blind eye to this fact, subordinating ideological considerations to geopolitical concerns, for the settling of the frontier was proving an arduous task, beset by obstacles of all sorts.

But if the obstacles to the success of this effort were many, the rewards, both for the court and for the peasants who became involved in it, were equally tempting. The secret of success lay in sufficiently motivating peasants so that they would be willing to struggle through untold hardships. Purely economic reasoning was not sufficient to dissuade peasants from giving up when difficulties mounted. The appeal of Đòan Minh Huyên's teachings seems to have been their capacity to invest new significance in human life and the sufferings of the pioneers and to hold out the promises of a better future in which they would be the chosen ones. At the same time, Đòan Minh Huyên gave practical guidance on how to run new communities. Through his predictions that Maitreya would descend into the Seven Mountains, this region was transformed in the eyes of his followers from a frightening wilderness into a promised land. A number of villages were built in that area during the lifetime of Đòan Minh Huyên. These villages, and those built after his death in 1856, formed the geographical core from which the Bửu Sơn Kỳ Hương religion fanned out in the late nineteenth century.

Colonial conquest brought another alteration of the Maitreya theme. Although it was predictions of a coming apocalypse that brought Đòan Minh Huyên's followers into the Seven Mountains, theirs was essentially an optimistic vision of the future, emphasizing salvation and rebirth in a perfect world. However, the turmoil that accompanied French conquest in the 1860s prompted a shift of emphasis away from the idea of the Dragon Flower Assembly of Maitreya to the much darker and terrifying vision of the coming apocalypse. With this shift of emphasis came the need for a new soteriological strategy that stressed militant political action rather than quiet devotion. New villages continued to be built, but now the sectaries were at war with the colonial state. Through the late nineteenth century, they remained in a state of repeated, if sporadic and ineffectual, revolt against it.

The Bửu Sơn Kỳ Hương Eschatology

It was the successors of Đoàn Minh Huyên and particularly twentieth-century members of the Hòa Hảo sect who provided elaborate explanations of the Bửu Sơn Kỳ Hương eschatology. It is built on a central idea, the idea of the Three Eras (Tam Ngươn 三元). Although couched in Sino-Vietnamese, it has no exact equivalent in Chinese popular religion and seems to be a composite of various theories of history of both canonical and noncanonical origins. It bears some resemblance to the idea of the Three Stages as set out by the sixth-century monk Hsin-hsing 信行 (whose sect was later banned) and was also heavily influenced by Taoist cosmogony, as was the White Lotus millenarian time scheme. According to the Bửu Sơn Kỳ Hương doctrine, the cosmos evolves in a series of eras, beginning with the high era (*thượng ngươn* 上元), followed by the middle era (*trung ngươn* 中元) and finally the low era (*hạ ngươn* 下元).[22] Each era is considered the equivalent of a *kalpa,* and each series or cycle corresponds to a *mahākalpa*. Each era is further divided into three periods, which correspond to the establishment of the Dharma (*lập pháp* 立法; Ch. *li fa*), its apogee (*tượng pháp* 嚮法; Ch. *hsiang fa*), and, finally, its decay and destruction (*mạt pháp* 末法; Ch. *mo fa*). This is accompanied by the decline from a high point of moral virtue and material well-being to utter chaos and misery brought about by man-made and natural disasters. The end of each era is punctuated by even greater cataclysm, and at the end of a *mahākalpa* comes an apocalyptic event in which the universe is purified of everything that is wicked and evil, and the forces of the cosmos rearrange themselves in a new "creation of heaven and establishment of earth" (*tạo thiên lập địa* 造天立地; Ch. *ts'ao t'ien li ti*).

In the Bửu Sơn Kỳ Hương world view, heaven, earth, and human beings are linked together in a holistic configuration. The moral behavior of the individual affects not only the well-being of society as a whole, but also the workings of the universe; conversely, any natural calamity is a reflection on the turpitude of humankind on earth and a sign of heaven's displeasure. Unlike the Confucian and Taoist world views, the mediating force in this cosmogony is not the Son of Heaven. Each individual bears a measure of responsibility for the proper functioning of the universe and consequently has a religious role to perform. Yet the importance of free will is limited; ultimately, all that the individual can achieve through self-effort is salvation. The bodhisattvas and Buddhas can alleviate only the worst sufferings of humankind; they cannot halt the inexorable progression from the high era of peace and plenty to the final apocalyptic conflagration that will wipe out most of humankind and change the face of the universe.

Certain texts that are used by Hòa Hảo writers to support the millenarian argument borrow from the theme of the three heavens: the former heaven of the Dīpaṅkara Buddha, the middle heaven of the historical Buddha Gautama, and the later heaven of the Maitreya Buddha. The concordance between the idea of the three heavens and that of the three eras is not absolute. The later heaven of Maitreya would seem to correspond to the high era of the cycle following that in which Gautama figures, so that the middle heaven would correspond to the low era. The Dīpaṅkara Buddha is associated with the idea of the Lotus Pond Assembly (Hội Liên Trì 會蓮池), Gautama with the idea of Mount Meru (Hội Linh Sơn 會靈山), and Maitreya with the Dragon Flower Assembly (Hội Long-Hoa). Each assembly corresponds to the time immediately following an apocalypse when the survivors gather to receive the new Dharma for the coming age from the appropriate Buddha. Although the idea of the three eras is implicitly cyclical, the millennium of Maitreya seems to be the telos of this time scheme.

The best description of Maitreya's role in the Bửu Sơn Kỳ Hương eschatology comes from a text that is said to have originated in the late 1880s in Shansi province in China. First written in Chinese, this text is now available only in Vietnamese translation. It appears to belong to the type of *pao-chüan* literature that was widely used by the White Lotus religion. The first translation into Vietnamese under the title *True Sūtra of Maitreya's Rescue of the World (Di-lặc độ thế chơn kinh 彌勒度世真經)* was published in 1939,[23] a few months before Huỳnh Phú Sổ underwent the religious crisis that led to his founding the Hòa Hảo sect. The translation carried a preface claiming that the sūtra had suddenly appeared from under a rock that had been split apart by thunder in Shansi. The sūtra was intended to show the way to earn salvation in these dying days of the low era. It promised wonders for those who heeded its message and helped propagate it by making copies of its text, and threatened dire retribution for those who disregarded it.

According to this sūtra, in previous incarnations, Maitreya and Gautama had been brothers.[24] In the natural scheme of things, Maitreya should have been the logical choice to descend into the world and rescue humankind, since he was the elder of the two. But Gautama, being young and rather impetuous, badly wanted a chance to shine; he thus proposed that they hold a contest to determine who would go first. They sat in meditation, eyes closed, each with his staff in front of him. Gautama cheated by opening his eyes; he saw that on Maitreya's staff a red flower had grown, a sign that Maitreya had been chosen. He plucked off the flower and transferred it to his own staff, but once there, the flower withered. Maitreya, who had been quite aware of Gautama's doings, allowed him to descend into the world, but predicted that, because the flower had not bloomed properly, during the whole of Gautama's time on earth the fortunes of sentient beings would be inequitably distributed and that much misery would befall them. After 3,000 years, it would be necessary for him to descend into the world to bring order and virtue. By now, 2,500 years had passed, and the world, as he predicted, was plunged in vice, misery, and chaos. Maitreya could not bear the spectacle of so much human suffering. He went to Mount Meru, where the Buddhas congregated, and asked for permission to begin his own mission ahead of time. He also asked for volunteers to precede him and act as his messengers. The Jade Buddha agreed to be reborn into the world, and Maitreya then described to him the kinds of wickedness he would have to fight against and how they should be punished. The list of evils is more detailed than can be found in canonical scriptures such as *The Lion-Roar on the Turning of the Wheel,* probably because it drew on nineteenth-century realities. The text concludes with a description of the delights of the Maitreyan millennium that carries echoes of the first Maitreya Sūtra to be translated into Chinese, the *Sūtra on Maitreya Descending to Be Reborn (Mi-le hsia-sheng ching* 彌勒下生經).

Maitreya and Vietnamese Millenarianism

The *True Sūtra of Maitreya's Rescue of the World* is virtually the only text used by either Bửu Sơn Kỳ Hương or Hòa Hảo authors to explain their vision of history in which Maitreya is the central theme. Most other texts focus either on the idea of the low era and the imminent end of the world or on the Dragon Flower Assembly. They infrequently mention Maitreya by name; instead, they speak vaguely of the Buddha. Other texts do not focus on Maitreya at all, but on the various messengers who will precede him into the world. At least, Maitreya has not been made subordinate to another figure of cult such as the Eternal Mother (Wu-sheng Lao Mu 無生老母) as in the White Lotus religion after the sixteenth century. He continues to be the most exalted deity, but attention has become focused on intermediaries.

In the Bửu Sơn Kỳ Hương and Hòa Hảo doctrines, the Maitreya theme has been made largely implicit. The figure of Maitreya has been swallowed up in the imagery associated with his mission and in the time scheme in which he remains only a sort of signpost. The rallying cry of rebelling sectarians was not that Maitreya was reborn, but that the low era had come to an end and that utter chaos was imminent.

A variety of arguments can be adduced to explain the apparent eclipse of Maitreya in Vietnamese eschatology. The one preferred by sectarian authors is based on the iconoclasm of the Bửu Sơn Kỳ Hương and Hòa Hảo sects. This iconoclasm was more apparent than real. Both Đoàn Minh Huyên and Huỳnh Phú Sổ objected to devotional cults dedicated to specific deities, not on the ground that these deities did not exist, but on the ground that the cults would entail ruinous expenses. In order to discourage the faithful from worshipping countless gods, the sect leaders refrained from mentioning any by name.

However, another possible explanation centers on the role of intermediaries and messengers whom Maitreya sends down into the world to prepare his mission. Đoàn Minh Huyên claimed in 1849 to be a living Buddha sent into the world to rescue humankind. But it is unclear whether he was thus laying claim to being Maitreya or one of his messengers, for both the Bửu Sơn Kỳ Hương and Hòa Hảo writings are extremely vague on this point. Some of his successors claimed to be living Buddhas in their own right, others to be his reincarnation, as did Huỳnh Phú Sổ. With the availability of flesh-and-blood prophets such as Đòan Minh Huyên and Huỳnh Phú Sổ, the thwarted urge of their followers to worship idols found an outlet in the deification of the sect leader.

When Huỳnh Phú Sổ set himself up as the latest reincarnation of Đòan Minh Huyên in 1939, he gave himself the task of reinvigorating the tradition he had inherited and of updating its practical teachings to make them more relevant to the changed conditions of southern Vietnamese society in the late colonial period, as well as more competitive with the secular ideologies that came from the West. One result of Huỳnh Phú Sỗ's preoccupations was an unprecedented outpouring of tracts designed to explain the Bửu Sơn Kỳ Hương millenarian time scheme to a public that was no longer readily conversant in the language of apocalypse and salvation.

Many of these tracts were written in self-conscious reaction against the determinist view of history propounded by Western-educated intellectuals who had fallen under the spell of either communism or social Darwinism. In the extremely crude forms in which they were known to Hòa Hảo writers, both presented history as an inexorable process in which the weak were ruthlessly trampled by the stronger in the name of progress. Both views held a kind of dismayed fascination for the Vietnamese, who were quick to cast their whole country in the role of the weak species that was probably doomed to extinction. Whereas some reacted by embracing Western ideas as the only key to progress, others took refuge in the familiar cosmogony that linked moral self-cultivation to salvation and posited a totally different view of the evolution of humankind. The persuasiveness of this world view lay not only in its reassuring familiarity, but also in its equally reassuring appearance of inexorability, a weapon against the certitudes of both communist and social Darwinist teleologies. This aspect allowed the Hòa Hảo writers to turn the tables ideologically against the Westernizers. Instead of allowing the history of their country to be used as an example of weakness in a Western-centered world view, they would use the history of the West to reinforce their own millenarian interpretation of the universe. Hòa Hảo tracts are replete with examples culled from the Bible or Western history. Noah's flood is presented as a cataclysm that signaled the end of an era. The French Revolution was the traumatic end of a subperiod within our present era. As for the coming apocalypse, tracts dating from the 1960s predict it will take the form of a nuclear holocaust.

Maitreya is a Buddha of many faces. Which one his devotees concentrate their gazes on depends on their particular needs and aspirations. The career of Maitreya highlights a few of these faces, showing in the process that they can easily blur into one another.

For many centuries, Maitreya was the object of devotion of Vietnamese who aspired only to be reborn at some later time into his Tuṣita Heaven. To them, he symbolized above all compassion; they did not expect him to descend among them to remake the world. As such, he had to compete with other symbols of compassion, such as Amitābha, Avalokiteśvara, and Baiṣajyaguru.

With Đòan Minh Huyên and the early adherents of the Bửu Sơn Kỳ Hương sect, Maitreya became the center of an eschatology that predicted cataclysm but also offered hope of salvation on a collective scale through quiet devotion and social action. Members of the sect could hope both to ascend into the Tuṣita Heaven and to be present at the Dragon Flower Assembly here on earth. With this orientation, the Bửu Sơn Kỳ Hương doctrine did not preach a message of rebellion. Instead, it taught acceptance of hardship. Building on the pioneer world of the Cambodian border region, it also offered a new moral, cultural, and social vision. In the name of that vision, later sectaries, confronted by a colonial state, became more militant. Acting on the belief that Maitreya's descent was imminent, they engaged in frequent, if sporadic and ineffectual, rebellion against the colonial state.

Thus whereas to the early Vietnamese Maitreya had symbolized compassion, to the sectaries of the nineteenth and twentieth centuries, he symbolized their aspirations for a perfect world that came from their utter hopelessness.

Yet neither despair nor fervor can be sustained at a high pitch for long periods of time. Outbursts of revolt were thus interspersed with periods of quietude, during which the sectaries fixed their gazes once more on Maitreya the compassionate, hoping to ascend into his Tuṣita Heaven.

Depending on circumstances, Maitreya was thus thought to be in his distant heaven, or about to be reborn, or even already moving among humanity. Despite the endless calculations that the Maitreya myth had engendered throughout Asia, considerations of time and space were rendered infinitely elastic by the shifting needs of his devotees.

NOTES

1 For a fuller discussion of the two sects, see Hue-Tam Ho Tai, *Millenarianism and Peasant Politics in Vietnam* (Cambridge, Mass.: Harvard University Press, 1983); for the Cao Đài sect in particular, see also Victor L. Oliver, *Caodai Spiritism: A Study of Religion in Vietnamese Society* (Leiden: Brill, 1976).

2 *San-kuo chih,* 49: 10a, quoted in Keith W. Taylor, *The Birth of Vietnam* (Berkeley and Los Angeles: University of California Press, 1983), 73–4; see also Paul Peillot, "Meou-tseu ou les doutes levés," *T'oung Pao,* 19, no. 5 (December 1919): 225–433.

3 Trần Văn Giáp, "Le bouddhisme en Annam des origines au XIIIe siècle," *Bulletin de l'Ecole Française d'Extrême-Orient,* 32 (1932): 214–15. The author follows the account by monk Thông Biện (1096), which in turn was based on the sixth-century Central Asian monk T'an Ch'ien.

4 Ibid., 207–8.

5 Ibid., 209.

6 Nguyễn Lang, *Việt Nam Phật giáo sữ luận* (Essays on the history of Vietnamese Buddhism) (Saigon: Lá Bối, 1974), 30.

7 Trần Văn Giáp, "Bouddhisme," 210. See his discussion of the textual problems of T'an Ch'ien's account.

8 Taylor, *Birth,* 139.

9 Trần Văn Giáp, "Bouddhisme," 231–6.

10 Ibid., 234–44.

11 Ibid., 226–7; for a biographical sketch of I-ching, see Kenneth Ch'en, *Buddhism in China* (Princeton, N. J.: Princeton University Press, 1964), 238–9.

12 Nguyễn Huệ Chi, "Các Yếu tố Phật, Nho, Đạo được tiếp thu và chuyển hoá như thế naò trong đời sống tư tưởng và văn học thời đại Lý-Trần" (How were Buddhist, Confucian, and Taoist factors integrated and how did they evolve in the intellectual and cultural life of the Lý-Trần period?) in Viện SửHọc (Institute of History), *Tìm hiểu xã hội Việt Nam thời Lý-Trần* (Understanding Vietnamese society in the Lý-Trần period) (Hanoi: nhà xuất bản Khoa Học Xã Hội, 1980), 610.

13 Details of court patronage of Buddhism during the Ly dynasty appear in Viện văn Học (Institute of Literature), *Thơ văn Lý-Trần* (Literature of the Lý-Trần period) (Hanoi: nhà xuất bản Khoa Học Xã Hội, 1977), 1: 575–81.

14 Ibid., 577.

15 Trần Văn Giáp, "Bouddhisme," 258.

16 For a description of the temple of the Heavenly Mother and the various cult rituals performed there, see Thái văn Kiểm, *Cố Đô Huế* (Imperial Huế) (Saigon: Bộ Quốc Gia Giáo Dục, 1960): 76–9.

17 Thích Mật Thể, *Việt Nam Phật giáo sử lược* (Summary history of Vietnamese Buddhism) (Đà Nẵng: Bộ Quốc Gia Giáo Dục, 1960): 198.

18 Léopold Cadière, "Le changement de costume sous Võ Vuong ou une crise religieuse à Huế au XVIIIe siècle," *Bulletin des Amis du Vieux Huế,* 4 (October–December 1915): 417–24; see also Jean Koffler, "Description historique de la Cochinchine," *Revue Indochinoise* 12 (December 1911): 582–607.

19 Trịnh Hoài Đức, *Gia Định Thành thông chí* (Gia Dinh Gazetteer), trans. into modern Vietnamese by Nguyễn Tạo (Saigon: Phũ Quốc Vụ Khanh Đặc Trách Văn Hoá, 1972), 3: 102. The gazetteer was originally written between 1820 and 1825.

20 For details of the life of Đoàn Minh Huyên and of his sect, see Tai, *Millenarianism and Peasant Politics,* 3–43.

21 *Quốc Triều chính biên toát yếu* (Summary of the primary compilation of the present dynasty) (Saigon: Nhóm Nghiên Cứu Văn Sử Đia, 1972) 286.

22 The Bửu Sơn Kỳ Hương millenarian time scheme is most usefully compared with the time scheme of the White Lotus religion rather than with the theory contained in canonical scriptures such as the *Lion-Roar on the Turning of the Wheel (Cakkavatisīhanāda-suttanta)* because of the blending of Taoist with Buddhist ideas.

23 *Di-lặc độ thế chơn kinh* (True sūtra of Maitreya's rescue of the world), trans. into Vietnamese by Vũ Xuân Tăng (Saigon: Đức Lưu Phương, 1939).

24 Other scriptures depict Maitreya and Gautama as having been playmates in earlier lives, but the idea that Maitreya was the elder, and therefore superior to Gautama, seems to be specific to this text. See Chapter 3, this volume.

Maitreya in Japan

Introduction

HELEN HARDACRE

As pointed out in Chapters 1, 2, and 5, there is probably no simple way to summarize the numerous, complex religious aspirations expressed through Maitreya. The chapters in this volume show how different societies and periods particularize the figure, and in each appropriation of Maitreya we find that the application of indigenous motifs to the figure adds further nuances. Japan's historical record regarding Maitreya is perhaps the most complete of the Asian records treated in this volume, and in Japan as nowhere else we can begin to investigate variations on the tradition's core themes in greater detail.

In Chapter 8, Miyata introduces the spectrum of Japanese Maitreyan phenomena, and from it we can identify three themes of indigenous tradition with which Maitreya is particularly associated. First, there are agrarian utopian ideas based on the horizontal cosmology found in pre-Buddhist myths, a cosmology in which a world of spirits and ancestors exists across the sea, in the same plane as the human world. Among other expressions based on this utopianism, the idea developed that Maitreya's ship would appear from across the sea, bringing abundant harvests and other boons in the Year of Maitreya, which would come after a famine.

Second, Japan's cult of sacred mountains, examined in detail in Chapter 11 by Collcutt provided fertile ground for the development of new Maitreyan phenomena. The mountain cult was based on an indigenous vertical cosmology in which ancestors, deities, and spirits lived above the human world, a cosmology found in mythic compilations alongside the horizontal cosmology. Most important, the saint Kōbō Daishi left an enduring mark on the cult when he expressed in his will the desire of "waiting to see Maitreya." Thereafter the legend spread that he never died but remained atop a mountain, suspended in a state of deep meditation from which he will awaken when Maitreya descends to rule over the earth. Kōbō Daishi's aspiration was copied by many future ascetics and "self-mummified Buddhas," who ascended Japan's numerous sacred mountains in a quest for spiritual powers and visions of Maitreya. These cases add a nuance to Nattier's here/later category (see Chapter 2), since the devotee hopes to meet Maitreya millions of years hence, but without experiencing death in the interim.

Third, Japan's indigenous tradition of world renewal, or world mending, has been associated with Maitreya. The idea of Maitreya as a savior who will bring about the renewal of the world is one variation on this theme. Examples of it are seen in Fujikō, treated in Chapter 11, whose leader prophesied in 1733 the advent of the world of Maitreya after his own self-mummification, and in Deguchi Ōnisaburō, founder of the new religion Ōmotokyō, who proclaimed in 1928 that he was an incarnation of Maitreya. More commonly, however, we find an association between world mending and Maitreya in which lay devotees establish a perfected world over which Maitreya presides, as in the Buddhist lay group Reiyūkai, the subject of Chapter 12 by Hardacre.

Japanese traditions of agrarian utopias, sacred mountains, and expectations of world renewal thus have powerfully shaped the cult of Maitreya in Japan. By the time it entered Japan, however, the cult was already a compendium of many motifs accumulated as the tradition moved through China and Korea.

In Chapter 9, Guth takes up the problem of identifying the "Pensive Prince of Chūgūji," the famous seated statue of a youth in the nunnery adjacent to Hōryūji in the ancient capital of Nara. Though it ranks among Japan's best-known works of art and though Korean influence has long been surmised, its identity has remained a mystery until now.

The Korean cult of Maitreya exerted a very direct influence on early Japanese Buddhism. Maitreyan devotionalism was at its height in the three kingdoms of the peninsula, especially Silla, at the very time that Buddhism was gaining a foothold in Japan through the sponsorship of the Soga clan under Prince Shōtoku. The Korean Hwarang tradition documented in Chapter 6 by Lancaster was undoubtedly well known. During the seventh century, many images of Maitreya were created in Japan, some by Korean artisans. Around the same time, between 621 and 643, a group of temples and images was dedicated to Shōtoku, possibly through the patronage of Soga women who retired to nunneries after the Soga defeat coinciding with Shōtoku's death.

By examining the Chūgūji statue in the context of Buddhism's transmission from Korea into Japan, Guth is able to identify the statue as a seventh-century representation of Shōtoku in the guise of Maitreya. The choice of Maitreya to represent Shōtoku was most likely based on the association of

Maitreya with the *cakravartin* and Ajita, an identification also treated by Kitagawa in Chapter 1.

In Chapter 10, Brock shows how the desire of eighth-century ascetic monks to retain the purity of the Sangha led them to construct a monumental image of Maitreya in a particular pose: receiving Śākyamuni's robe from Kāśyapa. Maitreya was the focus of these monks' hopes to adhere to the precepts and to practice meditation as canonical texts say that the arhats in the mountains near Vulture Peak did. The devotionalism expressed in the rock-cut Maitreya at Kasagidera seems to parallel that seen in Wŏnhyo (Jap. Gangyō), described by Sponberg in Chapter 4. To these Japanese monks Maitreya represented the unbroken lineage of Dharma transmission and the hope of restoring simplicity to monastic life, freeing it from the political entanglements of life in the capital. Taking to the mountains, they venerated Maitreya in the expectation of his reign.

In Chapter 11, Collcutt documents a Maitreya who is far removed from canonically based ideas about the figure. Perhaps more than any other chapter in this volume, Collcutt's demonstrates the power of indigenous traditions to appropriate and completely transform Maitreya.

In Fujikō, a cult of Mt. Fuji, Miroku (the Japanese name for Maitreya) has become essentially a bringer of abundant rice harvests, and Mt. Fuji itself has become the vestibule of the Tuṣita Heaven. As mentioned earlier, Fujikō's leader proclaimed the advent of Maitreya's world, but he did not anticipate precisely the state of affairs predicted in canonical sources, such as those surveyed by Jaini in Chapter 1. The coming of Maitreya's (Miroku's) world would mean harmony among the four estates of Tokugawa society (samurai, cultivators, artisans, merchants), material plenty, and individual moral perfection in honesty, sincerity, and other conventional values. This sort of earthly utopia is reminiscent of the delights envisioned by some of the cults surveyed by Overmyer in Chapter 5. Maitreya of the Buddhist canons remained in the background while Fujikō focused its devotion on the deity of Mt. Fuji, developing into a comprehensive cult functioning apart from monastic and canonical tradition. Indigenous themes here are associated more with the name of Maitreya than with the canonical substance.

Even in modern times Maitreya cults retain a distinct vitality. Read in combination, Chapters 6, 7, 8 (to a lesser extent), and 12 show that, in Vietnam, Korea, and Japan, new religious groups continue to find Maitreya an appropriate symbol for their goals. While the Vietnamese association Bửu Sơn Kỳ Hương and Japan's Ōmotokyō prophesied an imminent millennium to be brought about by Maitreya or a leader proclaiming himself to be Maitreya, more frequently found is the idea expressed in Reiyūkai, that lay believers must perfect themselves and the world, whereupon Maitreya's reign will be inaugurated. This result will come entirely from the religious practice of the laity, Reiyūkai holds, without priestly intercession and irrespective of the evolution of the world cycle. This idea stands in contrast to the emphasis on the world cycle's evolution seen in Nattier's exposition in Chapter 2 and in the Paekche belief documented by Lancaster in Chapter 6.

The idea of lay people's self-cultivation resulting in the perfection of the world and the manifestation of Maitreya is the focus of Reiyūkai's Maitreya pilgrimage. Reiyūkai has also developed a text called the *Maitreya Sūtra,* a compilation of canonical excerpts regarding Maitreya, but the actual beliefs and practices of the group remain peripheral to this text, which members recite in order to repent, to transfer merit to ancestors, and to cultivate discipline. In Reiyūkai, as in Fujikō, there is a definite separation between textual tradition and the beliefs of ordained clerics, on the one hand, and actual lay practice, on the other.

Thus in Japan we see not only a considerable variety of Maitreyan motifs but their combination with indigenous traditions in many different ways. The power of indigenous traditions to shape and transform Maitreya is remarkable and distinctive, and the relative abundance of historical data on all periods makes Japanese Maitreyan phenomena a rich field for further study.

8

Types of Maitreya Belief in Japan

MIYATA NOBORU

Introduction

The cult of Maitreya entered Japan in the early sixth century bearing elements of Buddhist millenarianism and messianism, following the eastward transmission of Buddhism through Southeast Asia, China, and Korea. Because this process of transmission differed according to the acceptance of Buddhism in each society, the form taken by the cult of Maitreya also differed. This is an instance of interaction of Buddhist doctrine with the ethnic character and traditional world view of each of the peoples involved. In Japan, the cult of Maitreya merged with traditional concepts of messianism and millenarianism; conversely, these native concepts were expressed through Buddhist millenarianism and messianic movements.

There are two major scholarly approaches to the Maitreya cult in Japan. One is that of the historian or Buddhologist who attempts to grasp the Maitreya cult through the analysis of the transmission and transformation of Buddhist doctrine and images (icons) through history. Thus the transformation of Buddhism through its transmission from China to Japan and the history of Buddhism in Japan itself are of central concern. The second approach is that of the folklorist and anthropologist. These scholars attempt to grasp the Maitreya cult as a datum of folk religion. This chapter adopts the latter standpoint in its discussion of the Maitreya cult in Japan.

It is often pointed out that the Maitreya cult manifests aspects of Buddhist messianism in relation to mass millenarian movements. In Japanese religion and society, however, this is only rarely the case. Seldom do we encounter the expectation of a future messiah combined with a detailed or concrete vision of the millennium. Furthermore, movements prophesying Maitreya's advent as a messiah are almost never found. The discipline of the history of religions is highly suited for the comparative analysis that might explain this anomaly. In this chapter, however, the scope of discussion is limited to a presentation of the characteristics of the Japanese cult of Maitreya from the standpoint of the study of folk religion in Japan.

The Maitreya Cult and the Ancient Nobility

This section attempts to describe concretely the special characteristics of the Maitreya cult in Japan from the standpoint of the study of folk religions. In order to undertake that task, however, it is necessary to have an adequate knowledge of the Buddhist cult of Maitreya. No folklorist analysis of the cult can ignore this historical context.

Buddhism was not at first readily accepted in Japan, but instead stood in opposition to the traditional concept of *kami* 神. The first Buddhist statues to come to Japan represented Maitreya, and these images were perceived as "foreign *kami*." A certain image was worshipped by the Soga clan, but they were opposed by the imperial clan and by the Otomo, and the statue was eventually thrown into the Naniwa Canal. A highly significant episode concerning the Buddha Maitreya is related in the *Nihon ryōiki* 日本靈異記. It is recorded that Soga Umako ordained three women as nuns to serve the Maitreya statue received from the Korean kingdom of Kudara.[1] These three were the first to take the tonsure in Japan. The fact that the first Buddhist clerics in Japan were women is especially noteworthy. The eldest of them was seventeen at the time. We may suppose that all of them were premenstrual girls. Just as the unmarried girls acting as mediums (*miko* 巫女) traditionally served the *kami*, these pure females served the Buddha Maitreya. These three nuns lived in the residence of the Soga clan and, while observing abstinences and purifications (*mono imi* 物忌), worshipped the Buddha Maitreya.

Ascent and Descent Motifs

It is well known that, within the East Asian textual traditions regarding Maitreya, two basic motifs inform the cult of Maitreya: a motif of ascent (*jōsho* 上生) and a motif of descent (*geshō* 下生). The ascent motif derives from the text known in Japan as the *Miroku jōshō kyō* 彌勒上生經 (T 452), in which it is related that the bodhisattva Maitreya is presently practicing spiritual cultivation in the Tuṣita Heaven. If devotees acquire sufficient merit, they may be reborn there. So doing, they will descend with him in the fullness of time as members of his assembly. The descent motif derives from those scriptures known in Japan as the *Miroku geshō kyō* 彌勒下生經 (T 454) and the *Miroku jōbutsu kyō* 彌勒成仏經 (T 456). In these texts it is related that 56,740,000 years after the death of Śākyamuni, Maitreya will descend from the Tuṣita Heaven and preach three sermons on the Dharma. In these texts, Maitreya is a future Buddha.

There are significant differences between the two motifs. In the ascent motif we find a clear expression of the ideal of a pure land in the notion of rebirth in the Tuṣita Heaven and in the notion of participation in the three assemblies at which Maitreya will preach the Dharma (*sann'e chigu* 三會值遇). However, we do not find this notion of rebirth in a pure land in the descent motif. Instead, the predominant notion is that of the future Buddha as a savior here in this world. Obviously, these two motifs must be clearly separated.[2]

Cultic developments exemplifying either the ascent or the descent motif had not yet appeared in Japanese Buddhism of the sixth century. Instead, the Buddha Maitreya was worshipped by the Soga clan as a powerful *kami* of foreign origin for their personal good fortune, long life, and this-worldly benefit. In the seventh-century reign of Emperor Tenchi, data regarding the Buddha Maitreya and the Maitreya Sūtras suddenly proliferate. By the Nara period (710–94), the expressions "Maitreya's pure land" (*Miroku Jōdo* 彌勒浄土) and "the pure land of the Tuṣita Heaven" (*Tosotsu ten jōdo* 兜率天浄土) were known. This shows that the motif of ascent had taken form. According to the traditional view of historians of Buddhism, the ascent motif was central in the society of Ritsuryō 律令 Japan (the early governmental system closely patterned on Chinese administration), and the descent motif did not yet exist. In the latter half of the Nara period, the cult of Amitābha gradually gained strength. Inoue Mitsusada expressed the difference between the two cults in this way. The cult of Amitābha proclaimed the possibility of rebirth in a pure land for the dead through the merit transferred by their descendants. In the Maitreya cult, however, each individual could achieve rebirth in the pure land through his or her own accumulation of merit. Inoue wrote that the Amida cult was easily accepted by the Japanese.[3] In Japan the popularity of the Amitābha cult surpassed that of the Maitreya cult some forty or fifty years after a comparable change in China, and thereafter the notion of ascending to the Tuṣita Heaven gradually disappeared from Japanese aristocratic society.

It is generally believed that the descent motif had not yet assumed a concrete expression at this time. However, Maekawa Akihisa has suggested that we see in the *Konjaku monogatari* 今昔物語 and the *Eiga monogatari* 栄花物語 a foreshadowing of the descent motif.[4] In these works it is recorded that, in the year before Tachibana Naramaro 橘奈良麻呂 raised a revolt, he held a "Maitreya assembly" (*Miroku e* 彌勒會). Hayami Tasuku has a different view of the matter.[5] According to Hayami, the idea of Maitreya's descent in ancient times was that, after achieving rebirth in the Tuṣita Heaven, the devotee would participate in Maitreya's three assemblies and achieve supreme, perfect enlightenment. Thus behind the descent motif lay a concept of individual salvation. Therefore, Naramaro's *Miroku e* could not possibly have envisioned a world revolution in the same way that such a conception emerged in China.

In the Heian period (794–1133), the idea of Maitreya's descent gradually became prominent within Saichō's 最澄 Tendai 天台 school and also within Kūkai's 空海 Shingon 真言 school. It should be noted, however, that this development cannot be attributed to influence from Empress Wu's uprising at the end of the T'ang. Rather, we can best account for the Japanese situation by pointing to the notion of *chigu ryūge sann'e* 值遇龍華三會, which developed from the conception of rebirth in the Tuṣita Heaven, which was already prominent in the Nara period.[6] This idea corresponds to that of the Latter Days of the Dharma (*mappō* 末法). During the Heian period, nobility who believed that they had entered the Latter Days (following the periods of True and Counterfeit Teachings after the death of Śākayamuni) came to believe that Maitreya (presently in the Tuṣita Heaven) would come and preach three sermons beneath the Dragon Flower Tree (the idea of *ruȳge sann'e*). This was to be the advent of "the merciful lord long hidden since the days of Śākyamuni." In these words of Saichō we can sense anticipation of Maitreya's three sermons beneath the Dragon Flower Tree.

Waiting for Maitreya

A sense of expectation of Maitreya is even stronger in Kūkai (Kōbō Daishi), who proclaimed the notion of "waiting to see Maitreya" (*taiken miroku* 待見彌勒). It is well known that, when he died in 835, his dying words were preserved in the *Go yuigo nijū-go kà jō* 御遺告二十五箇條, in which he proclaimed that after he died he would be reborn in the Tuṣita Heaven, and after waiting before Maitreya for 56,000,000 years, he would surely descend with Maitreya to this world. Kūkai's seclusion on Mt. Kōya 高野山 suggested that this mountain was in fact Maitreya's pure land.[7] On the basis of Kūkai's writings, his fervent disciples spread the idea that Kūkai had not really died, but instead was interred upon the mountaintop in a state of deep meditation (*nyūjō* 入定). In this way they gave a concrete form to the idea of Maitreya's descent, which in later eras was widely promulgated in the course of proselytization of the Shingon school. This idea found its way into folk society as well.

However, no data attesting to the presence of the idea of Maitreya's descent among the people have yet been found for the Heian period itself. At that time the cult of Maitreya was limited to aristocratic society. Typical of the cult members in that era were Fujiwara Michinaga 藤原道長 and Nakamikado Munetada 中御門宗忠. Michinaga believed that Kimpusan 金峰山, a mountain in the Yoshino area, was the Golden Pure Land of Maitreya and made a pilgrimage to Kimpusan. In 1007 he had buried a gilt sūtra cylinder. The nearby mountain Kasagizan 笠置山 was known as a spirit mountain on which a giant Maitreya image was carved, and pilgrimage to this site was frequently made in aristocratic society. The conception of Maitreya held by Munetada, author of the *Chūyu-ki* 中右記, has been studied in detail by Hiraoka Jōkai.[8] Munetada recorded his hope to be present when, after the death of the Emperor Horikawa, that emperor became the first to be reborn in the Tuṣita Heaven and then descend with Maitreya. Heian aristocrats were not satisfied with rebirth in a pure land (e.g., Amida's Pure Land) alone. Instead, their conception of Maitreya's descent was linked to their desire to achieve final salvation through participation in Maitreya's three sermons beneath the Dragon Flower Tree. In the background were the confused conditions of politics and economy in their society as well as the notion of the Latter Days of the Dharma.

Maitreya's World and the Year of Maitreya

The *Genji monogatari* 源氏物語, which reflects aristocratic society of roughly the eleventh century, records in the "Evening Faces" chapter that Genji earnestly cultivated virtue in preparation for a pilgrimage to Kimpusan.[9] There he worshipped Tōrai Dōshi 當來導師 and Maitreya and prayed that he would be reborn in "Maitreya's world" (*Miroku no yo* 彌勒の光) and that his love of Evening Faces would continue forever. It appears that this notion of Maitreya's world had become commonplace in aristocratic society. The term used is not drawn from the Buddhist canon. Instead, it seems to represent a latent notion of a utopia found in certain areas of Japan.

The notion of utopia dimly reflected here is that of the eternal world, the *tokoyo* 常世. This concept of an unchanging eternal world underwent change, but it is certain that in ancient times it existed in the area called Hitachi no kuni 常陸國. In the *Hitachi no kuni fudoki* 常陸國風土記 it is stated, "The ancients looked on Hitachi as the greatest paradise on earth." This passage presents Hitachi as a great and abundant country possessing the fruits of land and sea and a happy, joyous populace. The word "Hitachi" itself means "the place where the sun rises," thus an eastern area. From the point of view of the central Yamato court, this was an important area for sea transport, which was necessary for the pacification of the Ezo in the northeast. At the entrance to the territory of Hitachi, the deity Kashima no kami 鹿島の神 was worshipped. This powerful deity had been worshipped since the establishment of the court. As the *Hitachi no kuni fudoki* admonishes, "When entering the country for the first time, first purify the mouth and hands, and then, facing to the east, worship the Kashima deity."

Since Hitachi was the homeland of the Nakatomi 中臣 and Urabe 卜部 clans, forebears of the Fujiwara, it was to this deity that the Fujiwara went to divine their fortune. Thus Hitachi and Kashima were important sites for aristocratic society. In the twelfth and thirteenth centuries, pilgrimages to

Kashima were frequent occurrences. *Waka* poetry found in the *Fubokushō* 夫木抄 reveal that Kashima was regarded as the eastern edge of the world. It is for this reason that folklorists such as Yanagita Kunio and Origuchi Shinobu understood the *tokoyo* as a latent notion of utopia.[10] Maitreya's pure land, the Tuṣita Heaven represented in the Buddhist texts, is a heavenly world, not a land across the sea. The Japanese concept of utopia is based on a world view positing a realm across the sea.

The Ship of Maitreya

One of the most important characteristics of Japan's Maitreya cult can be observed in the area around Kashima in Ibaragi Prefecture. There it is believed that the ship of Maitreya (*Miroku no fune* 弥勒の舟) will return one day from a paradise across the sea, heavy-laden with rice. Even now this notion of the coming of Maitreya's ship is found in the area from Ibaragi to Shizuoka Prefecture in the towns and villages along the seacoast. There one can find songs like the following:

Maitreya's ship is coming!
The deities of Kashima, Ise, and Kasuga are at the helm.

On a cloud come thirteen princesses from India.
They come scattering rice, much rice before them,
And after them will come Maitreya, also scattering rice.

The earth is abundant, and the harvest is rich.
The five grains are ripening, and the people of the world rejoice.
Shall we go forward or back?
Afterwards, Maitreya is coming!

Maitreya dances (*Miroku odori* 彌勒踊) are traditionally performed in the precincts of temples and shrines in June and July. The songs quoted above seem on linguistic grounds to derive from the Edo period (1600–1868). They are probably popular songs of the eighteenth century. However, on folkloristic grounds they appear to represent the traditional Miroku[11] notion held by the people of these areas.

Returning to the notion of Miroku's ship, it is believed that not only Maitreya himself but also a *miko* (a shamaness or priestess) is on board. She is to return with Maitreya. This belief is sustained by the cultic milieu of the Kashima Shrine, in which the priestess of the shrine, called Ōmono imi 大物忌, delivers an oracle. In a ritual possession, she foretells each year's fortune, which itself is believed to evoke the World of Maitreya. That world will be one of fertility and abundance, a prediction couched in the language of agrarian tradition. There, the folk tradition of song and dance was developed as a means of spreading the prophecy of abundance. The aim of the dance was to purify the world and to ward off evils and epidemics. These dances and songs prevailed widely during the early years of the Edo era. This tradition might be called a popular religious movement centered around the sacred act of oracle and dance.

Historically speaking, this popular movement was clearly different from the ascent motif that had developed earlier among the aristocracy. The folk conception became popular in the peripheral areas of the eastern provinces, such as the middle Kantō provinces and the northeastern provinces, far from the Yamato court. One of the most important elements that gave rise to this popular movement was a private calendar of Miroku, which foretells his descent or return.

The Latter Days and Private Era Names

The idea of Maitreya's world developed in an intellectual milieu colored by the idea of the Latter Days of the Dharma. The aristocrats dreamed of participating in Maitreya's *sann'e akatsuki* 三会の暁, "the dawn of Maitreya's three assemblies," which would be held after the descent. However, in 1171 in one part of Kyoto, we find the word "Miroku" in private use as a name for that year, as a *shinengo* 私年號. *Shinengo* were used privately and represented a denial of the era name established by the emperor. These *shinengo,* which can be found in some records, represent a denial of the "world" represented by the official designation. The aristocrats' use of the word "Miroku" for a period that they believed to be the Latter Days means that for the first time the idea of Maitreya's world took a concrete form among them. However, other than this use of private era names, we have no knowledge of Maitreyan thought in the twelfth century.

It was during the period of disunity in the sixteenth century, the Sengoku era and the Eishō (1504–21), Kyōroku (1528–32), and Tenbun eras (1532–55), that the use of the Miroku *shinengo* became prevalent. This was the time of the greatest civil strife in Japanese history. It seems that the use of the Miroku *shinengo* was most prevalent in eastern Japan.[12] Apparently, these private designations for the year were used to ensure good fortune. It was believed that one could, in fact, change fortune by changing the designation of the year to an auspicious phrase. It is significant that the popularity of Maitreya as a year name was bound up with the Kashima Shrine.

Scholars of the Edo era are investigating the use of Maitreya as a year name by the priests of the Kashima Shrine. They have suggested that these priests disseminated the practice. The Kashima dance and the Maitreya dance mentioned earlier were performed for the purpose of magically warding off evil. These shamanic dances were performed by the priests of the shrine called Kashima kotofure 鹿島事觸, in which they communicated oracles. We can well imagine that talismans inscribed with the Miroku *shinengo* could have spread among the people of the Sengoku period who sought salvation from the present world. They did not record their feelings, but we can understand their sentiment about Maitreya's world through the folk dances perfomed even now.

Maitreya and the Folk Calendar

Japanese agricultural society went through cycles of abundant harvests and famine. However, there was great regional variation related to differences in geography and climate. Japan's agricultural society never experienced a crisis of nearly total extinction. According to the lunar calendar popular among the Japanese, the Year of the Snake is that in which the Day of the Snake is repeated three times during the sixth month. According to folk belief the Year of Maitreya will come in the Year of the Snake, and this notion provided the basis for the compilation of private calendars of Maitreya.

A popular belief in the "Year of Maitreya" existed during the Edo age. It was believed that in that year disasters were especially likely to occur, and thus it was necessary to repeat the rites of the New Year. Extant records show that a repetition of the New Year's ritual was performed in 1667, 1759, 1771, 1779, and 1814. These observances were called *torikoshi shōgatsu* 取越正月. None of these years was a Year of the Snake. However, they were years of bad economic circumstances or times of epidemic disease. This belief was centered in the large cities of Edo, Kyoto, and Osaka.

The idea of the snake day is based on the dating system originating in China called the "stems and branches." It was a product of calendrical lore of the educated classes that came down to the people. To the farming population a famine represented a misfortune of great magnitude. It was popularly believed that a great famine would occur once every twelve years. *Miroku jūnen* 彌勒十年, *tatsu no toshi* 辰の年 was a phrase prophesying that, in the Year of the Dragon or in the following year (that of the snake), the Year of Maitreya would surely come. Both snakes and dragons are related to water, and it was believed that just as the snake sheds its skin and is "reborn," so the Year of Maitreya would surely bring a renewal of life and good fortune.

There was an ambiguous notion in folk belief that the Year of Maitreya returns every twelfth year according to the popular lunar calendar. That year, according to the belief, is one of famine, and a year of good harvest follows. It might be hypothetically stated that, since the year of Maitreya is a year of terror and famine, people expected the coming of a fantastic utopia in the following year.

Maitreya and the Cult of Sacred Mountains

The cult of Maitreya centered in Ibaragi Prefecture envisions a utopia across the sea from which Miroku will bring a good harvest. This notion is very different from the ideas of Maitreya found in Buddhist texts. The cult of Maitreya found in the Shingon school of Kūkai developed on the sacred mountain Kōyasan and through the cult of sacred mountains. The cult of sacred mountains is related to the Japanese idea that the other world exists in the mountains, not across the seas. During the Edo period the cult of sacred mountains, based on the idea that the mountains represented the other world, spread to all areas of Japan. The *yamabushi* 山伏, who practiced austerities in the mountains, came into close contact with the people. They were respected because of the discipline and austerities they practiced in the mountains, where ordinary people dared not go.

Maitreya and Mummies

This type of Japanese Maitreya belief is related to mountain worship, especially worship of Mt. Fuji, typical of Japan's sacred mountains. It was propagated by Shingon priests and therefore is a Buddhist belief of Maitreya's ascent. According to this belief, the world of Maitreya is called *sann'e no akatsuki,* "the dawn of Maitreya's three assemblies." This world will manifest on the peak of Kimpusan, which is called the Golden Pure Land (Ōgon jōdo 黄金浄土). In order to be reborn in the Golden Pure Land, one has to wait and live until the advent of the world of Maitreya. This notion led to a belief in the *nyūjo miira* 入定ミイラ, "self-mummified priest."

The myth and legend of ascetic Shingon priests came to dominate the spiritual life of the masses in rural areas of eastern Japan. The idea of self-mummification is rooted in belief in Mt. Kōya as a sacred mountain, combined with the concept of the Latter Days of the Dharma toward the end of the Heian period. Kūkai was said to have died and been cremated, but he was also believed to be physically alive, a notion confirmed by his empty tomb. Of course, this belief is structurally similar to that surrounding the empty tomb of Jesus.

The Shingon sect, consisting of holy men and ascetics practicing austerities in the mountains, developed in close relationship to the traditional mountain worship of Japan. In mountain worship, the pure land of Maitreya was metaphorically taken to be the pure land of Kimpusan. Many ascetic priests, who practiced in Kimpusan waiting for the appearance of Maitreya's world, went down to agricultural villages and propagated the belief in Maitreya's coming. The villagers regarded these priests as messiahs themselves. Many legends of Kūkai and his miracles represent the legacy of these priests. The images and symbols of the other world deep in the mountains were reinforced and enriched by the expectation of Maitreya's world. In other words, clearly independent of the Kashima type of belief based on the notion of the other world beyond the sea, Shingon's notion of Maitreya is based on the belief in a paradise in the depths of the mountains.

Fujikō

Various types of popular belief in Maitreya were developed under the strong influence of the cult of sacred mountains. In the Edo period, a new type of ascetic priest appeared. Kakugyō 角行 was an early example of this type. Descending from Mt. Fuji to Edo, he was believed to have the power to ward off evil and to defeat the power of epidemics. He wandered around the capital city of Edo, became popular with the masses, and formed a cult group called the Fujikō 富士講. According to legend, Kakugyō was born in Nagasaki and performed extended austerities in a cave while sitting on a pile of logs. He is said to have been an ascetic of the Shingon school, but this is uncertain. He went to Edo to spread the word of his supernatural powers, a proselytization campaign he called *ofusegi*, the pacification and subduing of all evils. He compiled his teachings in a book called the *Otaigyō no maki* お大行の巻.[13] It is written in a secret language that only believers of Fujikō could read. This secret language is preserved even in present-day Fujikō. However, in Kakugyō's time Fujikō's Maitreya cult elements had not yet taken concrete form.

It was in June 1773 that the appearance of a savior called Miroku on the top of Mt. Fuji was proclaimed. This group thus had as its sixth leader a messiah-savior called Miroku. He foretold the advent of the "world of Miroku" before his own death by self-mummification. By this act, Fujikō or Fujidō (the Peerless Way) developed among the masses of the eastern provinces in the mid–eighteenth century.

The Fujikō leader wrote the name Miroku with an eccentric choice of characters: 身録 instead of 彌勒, the traditional way of writing "Maitreya." He upheld the values of the merchants and told people to "work hard and make money." Miroku himself came from a tradesman's family that had come to Edo from Ise and become rich in a single generation. Miroku's given name was Itō Ihei. While managing an oil business, Miroku became a disciple of the fifth-generation leader 月行 Gatsugyō and climbed Mt. Fuji many times. While learning the teaching of Fujikō, he gradually came to have more confidence in his own powers. He decided to abandon all the wealth he had accumulated and to become a Fujikō ascetic. He received an oracle from the deity of Mt. Fuji, Sengen Bosatsu 淺間菩薩, and entering a deep meditative trance on the top of Mt. Fuji, he proclaimed the advent of Maitreya's world. Throughout the mid–seventeenth century when the *bakufu* government was weakening, famine continued and society was greatly disturbed. The first peasant uprisings in Edo occurred in 1773. The peasants wanted a stable price for rice and broke into the establishments of rice merchants. Seeing this, Miroku entered his trance.

From the time of Kakugyō, Fujikō had been a small group centering on magical asceticism. However, the number of followers increased when the news came that Miroku had extinguished his life in a rock chamber he had built, drinking only water until he died in a trance.[14]

At the beginning of the nineteenth century, Fujikō had 808 branches, one in each of the wards of Edo, and the group was also recruiting in agricultural areas around Edo. After Miroku's death, his daughter Hana 花 and Itō Sankō 伊藤參行 streamlined the organization and called it Fujidō 不二道. Fujidō was based on the motif of Maitreya's descent; it was not an antiauthoritarian movement. The intent of making the state recognize the proclamation of Maitreya's descent was foremost. But from the government's standpoint, Fujidō was a heterodoxy that could not be tolerated, and government leaders tried to suppress Fujidō many times. To counter this suppression, Fujidō chose a leader from the Kyoto aristocracy and took other measures of compromise that gradually brought the group within the sphere of official toleration. It is significant that Fujidō proclaimed Maitreya's descent in concrete terms and also that they preached a harmony between the rhythms of agriculture and human sexuality.

Among the important ideas of Fujidō was the equality of the sexes. Members were urged to perform sexual intercourse in a spirit of equality so as to maintain the succession of agricultural cycles. By reversing the usual hierarchy of the sexes, they believed, it would be possible to evoke a true sexuality, which would bring forth the power of procreation. In this sense, they believed that sexuality could enrich both agriculture and society. Ritual transvestism symbolized an androgynous ideal, and this practice was accompanied by specific formulas for performing sexual intercourse in such a way as to recover the primordial unity of the sexes. These practices were rather widely accepted among the masses of Tokugawa agricultural society.

Yonaori and Yonaoshi

Maitreya and Peasant Rebellion

There is a great volume of research on Edo period peasant rebellions, but the bulk of it is written from the standpoint of social and economic history. Yasumaru Yoshio's is the only work that treats the religious basis of these uprisings.[15] He addresses the connection between the Edo period Maitreya cult and popular movements. We saw earlier that the motif of Maitreya's descent was contained in Fujikō's doctrine. However, this movement was limited to Fujikō's believers. Comparing peasant rebellions and folk movements, we may mention the *okage mairi* おかげ参り (thanks pilgrimage) and the *eejanaika* ええじゃないか (the "ain't it grand?" pilgrimage). The latter was especially connected wth ecstatic behavior and is known for having involved masses of people from the end of the Edo period to Meiji.

Wakamori Tarō[16] has pointed out the importance of Maitreya elements in the *eejanaika*. In the *eejanaika*, great numbers of believers went off to the Ise Shrine, caught up in ecstatic song and dance. The songs proclaimed that Japan would be turned upside down and that dances celebrating abundant harvests would be performed – an expression of the Fujikō desire that the world be reformed. The songs also proclaimed that through Maitreya the five cereals would be abundant and that myriad *kami* and Buddhas would manifest along with Maitreya. That is, the songs prophesied a coming utopia. Some talismans that were reported to have fallen from the sky had Maitreya's name written upon them. As discussed earlier, there was a belief that, when misfortune continues, the rites of the New Year must be performed again. The notion of reforming the world (*yonaori* 世直り) was based on the idea of overturning continuing misfortune. It was natural for people to expect that Maitreya's descent would occur with the reformation of the world.

However, the expression *yonaoshi* 世直し also existed in popular consciousness. As an active, transitive construction, *yonaoshi* carries the implication that there is some active, human agent taking the initiative in bringing about reform. In contrast, the intransitive expression *yonaori* suggests a suprahuman flow of nature, a natural outcome of the workings of the universe. Thus when the expression *yonaori* was used in the *eejanaika,* it implied that changes would take place naturally, bringing about a utopia of abundant harvests without the need for any revolutionary intervention. *Yonaoshi,* however, expressed a straightforward desire to change the world. It is important to note that the Maitreya cult was connected with *yonaori,* but not with *yonaoshi*.

Maitreya and the Earthquake Catfish

The Japanese islands have always experienced earthquakes. According to popular legend, whenever a large earthquake struck, people chanted the magical formula "*Yonaoshi, yonaoshi!*" This chanting, it was believed, helped quiet the earth.

The notion of *yonaoshi,* "world mending," had been held by the people for a long time. The idea was that the world must be transformed someday but not made radically new. That is, the people longed for a change that was moderate and reformative, not a full-scale eschaton, millennium, or revolution. The chanting of "world mending" at the time of an earthquake reveals the longing of the people for this sort of change. However, it does not signify a desire for a total extinction of the world by some calamity. In other words, the people did not want a decisive end to this world in order to bring about the new. Instead, they hoped for a gradual realization of Maitreya's world. This can be clearly seen in the now famous ethnological data of *namazu-e* 鯰繪, pictures of the earthquake catfish, produced mainly at the time of an earthquake in the beginning of the nineteenth century.

Research on *namazu-e* has been carried out by Ouwehand,[17] who has pointed out that just after the Edo earthquake of 1855, in which much of the city was burned, about 400 types of catfish pictures were distributed in Edo. Some of these represented "*yonaoshi* catfish," or catfish in the form of large men who appeared out of the Tokyo Bay and destroyed the city, rounding up the rich and beating them, pulling money out of their mouths. These pictures represented an uprising, and they were well received by the urban lower classes. However, the number of *yonaoshi* catfish was extremely limited. Most of the paintings portrayed ordinary catfish punishing the catfish responsible for the earthquake. There are many pictures of the Kashima deity threatening the catfish with a large sword and forcing him to vow never again to cause such a disaster.

In eastern Japan, songs such as the following were found: "Even if an earthquake comes, the Kashima deity will pacify it with his sword, so we will not be destroyed." This song expresses a desire to avert an earthquake. It is evident that the people wanted a basic change in the world order but not a catastrophe like the earthquake. Even if some people profited from uprisings, most uprisings were of the *yonaori* type, and they may have anticipated the advent of Maitreya.

Maitreya and the New Religions

From the religiocultural background of folk religion and its world view, new Japanese religions in the nineteenth century emerged as popular religious movements. For instance, modern Japanese religions such as Konkōkyō 金光教 and Ōmotokyō 大本教 embrace the notion of world mending.

Professor Michio Araki states that Konkōkyō internalized an ethical, eschatological vision of the kingdom of Kami, where people help and save one another. But this kingdom is to come after the end of the world of humans, in which humans control and dominate all. The timing of the eschaton is unspecified, since it is to be achieved when all humans realize the *kami* in themselves. World mending is the gradual process already initiated by the founder, Konkō Daijin 金光大神.

Ōmotokyō expressed the notion of world mending in the phrases *tatekae* 立替 (reconstruct) and *tatenaoshi* 立て直し (rebuild). This reconstruction was to be sustained by Maitreya, incarnate in the body of one of the founders of Ōmoto, Deguchi Ōnisaburō 出口王仁三郎. Ōnisaburō was the second man in Japanese religious history to proclaim himself an incarnation of Maitreya. He was profoundly influenced by the woman founder of Ōmoto, Deguchi Nao 出口なお. She received an oracle from deities while in a trance in 1892. It was as if she were recapitulating the life history of the founder of Tenrikyō 天理教, Nakayama Miki 中山ミキ. While in the trance, she prophesied that the world of the deity Ushitora no Konjin 艮の金神, "which brings the plum flower that blooms only once in 3,000 years," was at hand. She proclaimed a new world and assembled followers who were to be the nucleus of a religious group. However, at this stage there was not yet any connection with Maitreya. Eventually, the world of Ushitora no Konjin was identified with Maitreya's World. It was not until Ōnisaburō had been named Nao's successor that unmistakable Maitreya imagery was found. In 1916 he proclaimed Maitreya's advent at Takazuna City in Hyōgo Prefecture, where he received an oracle from the Kashima deity, who appeared upon the waves.

Ōmoto developed as a religion of prophecy. The group prophesied the Russo-Japanese and Sino-Japanese wars, as well as World War I. It prophesied, moreover, that a change of the entire world would take place in or around the Year of the Dragon. This notion was deeply supported by folk belief. All of the wars prophesied occurred in or near the Year of the Dragon.

On the third day of the third month of the third year of the Shōwa era (March 3, 1928), when Ōnisaburo was fifty-six, he proclaimed that he was Maitreya incarnate. He strongly believed that great change would occur around the Year of the Dragon. In folk beliefs there was also fear of the advent of this year, and hence there was probably no opposition to the idea of joining Maitreya's descent to the traditional notion of the Year of the Dragon.

The Year of the Dragon occurs naturally in the twelve-year cycle; thus there is no implication that some individual must instigate the events associated with it. In this sense it was natural that *yonaori* and the Year of

Maitreya were joined in popular conception. This also corresponds to the natural, agricultural calendar of crop production, especially that of rice. Ōnisaburō preached world transformation not by a radical eschaton but by many small renewals, eventually to bring forth the world of Maitreya.

In other words, the world view we see here is continuous with the traditional folk-religious concept of Maitreya's world. From a comparative standpoint, an important characteristic of Japanese Maitreya beliefs is their passive *yonaori* nature. In some Chinese and Korean popular movements connected with Maitreya, there was a much more radical, revolutionary orientation advocating the total renewal of the world and urging the complete replacement of the existing political system.

Maitreya and the Imperial System

A final type of Maitreya belief found in Japan is related to the imperial court. In contrast to private calendars, which were informally produced among the masses and specified the time of Maitreya's advent, the imperial system traditionally maintained the prerogative of producing the official calendar. By this system it controlled and organized the entire nation. The official calendar traditionally had the strongest appeal, and Japan was unique among Asiatic societies in that it never experienced the displacement of the imperial system nor the domination of a foreign nation. Here we find a strong contrast with the radical, revolutionary religious movements of Southeast Asia, where native religions seek to restore the world through resistance to colonial domination.

Control of the calendar was traditionally one of the emperor's most important ceremonial functions. Annual ceremonies performed by the imperial family had the aim of renewing the world in order to ensure the coming of the New Year. According to folk belief, the emperor was a magicoreligious figure capable of achieving a world mending within the structure of the imperial system. The fact that there was little radical sentiment in *yonaori* movements derives from the people's assumption that the emperor was in control of world mending. However, there were several instances in which people who were not satisfied with *yonaori* sought true *yonaoshi*. Here, appropriation of Maitreya symbolism never went beyond the prophecy of Maitreya's descent. Historical experience probably decreed that, even if *yonaoshi* failed, the possibility of averting a true cataclysm still remained in *yonaori*. But the masses have also had the will to renew the world, seeking the realization of Maitreya's world. Imperial Maitreya belief and folk-religious beliefs, sometimes in opposition, sometimes in harmony with each other, constitute a dynamic whole, characterizing the Japanese Maitreya cult.

NOTES

1 See Kyoko Nakamura, trans., *Miraculous Stories from the Japanese Buddhist Tradition* (Cambridge, Mass.: Harvard University Press, 1973).
2 Matsumoto Bunzaburō 松本文三郎, *Miroku jōdoron* 彌勒浄土論 (Tokyo: Hinoeuma shuppansha, 1911), 143–64.
3 Inoue Mitsusada 井上光貞, *Nihon jōdo kyō seiritsu-shi no kenkyū* 日本浄土教成立史の研究 (Tokyo: Yamakawa shuppansha, 1962), 8–9.
4 Maekawa Akihisa, "Tachibana Naramaro to miroku e" 前川明久 *Shoku nihongi kenkyū* 続日本紀研究, vol. 7, no. 7.
5 Hayami Tasuku 速永侑, "Ritsuryō shakai ni okeru miroku shinkō no juyō" 律令社会における弥勒信仰の受容, *Nambu bukkyō* 南部仏教, 10.
6 Hiraoka Jōkai 平岡定海, *Nihon miroku jōdo shisō tenkai-shi no kenkyū* 日本弥勒浄土思想展開史の研究 (Tokyo: Nihon gakujutsu shinkokai, 1958–60), 521.
7 Ibid., 529.
8 Ibid., 550–3.
9 Murasaki Shikibu, *The Tale of Genji,* trans. Edward Seidensticker (New York: Knopf, 1981).
10 Yanagita Kunic 柳田國男, *Kaijō no michi* 海上の道 (Tokyo: Chikuma shobō, 1961).
11 The folklorist records this word in phonetic transcription, not in Sino-Japanese characters, to avoid confusion with the homonym of strictly Buddhist provenance. "Miroku" is the Japanese word for Maitreya, but in the Japanese writing system it is possible to write this word with any of several character combinations, each of which has visual associations having nothing to do with Buddhism's Maitreya.
12 Kubo Tsuneaki 久保常晴, *Nihon shinengo no kenkyū* 日本私年号の研究 (Tokyo: Yoshikawa kōbunkan, 1967).
13 Iwashina Koichirō 岩科小一郎, "Fujikō no keifu" 富士講の系譜, *Nihon jōmin bunka kenkyūjo kiyo* 日本常民文化研究所紀要, 2 (1973).
14 Miroku's teachings are compiled in the *Sanjū-ichi nichi no maki* 三十一日の巻 and *Ichiji fusetsu no maki* 一字不説の巻.
15 Yasumaru Yoshio 安丸良夫, *Nihon no kindaika to minshū shisō* 日本の近代化と民衆思想 (Tokyo: Aoki shokan, 1974).
16 Wakamori Tarō 和歌森太郎, ed., "Kinse miroku shiñkō no ichimen" 近世弥勒信仰の一面, *Shichō* 史潮, 48 (1941).
17 Ouwehand, C., *Namazu-e and Their Themes* (Leiden: Brill, 1964).

9

The Pensive Prince of Chūgūji

Maitreya Cult and Image in Seventh-Century Japan

CHRISTINE M. E. GUTH

Introduction

Few works of art in Japan are as familiar to art historians and the general public alike as the main image in Chūgūji 中宮寺, a nunnery adjacent to Hōryūji 法隆寺 in the historic Asuka district of Nara Prefecture. Reproduced as often in travel guides and posters as in scholarly publications, this evocative statue represents a slender, youthful being seated in a pensive attitude with the fingers of his right hand supporting his head and his bent right leg resting across the left knee (Figures 1 and 2). Images in this distinctive posture are known in Japan as *hanka shiyui-zō* 半跏思惟像 (figure seated in meditation with one leg crossed over the other).

Because of its exceptional aesthetic and religious importance, the Chūgūji statue has generated interest among scholars since the very beginnings of art historical research in Japan.[1] Despite the voluminous corpus of writings about it, however, there is still no consensus as to its identity or to the date and circumstances of its creation.

The identity of the Chūgūji statue is problematic because images of the *hanka shiyui* type may represent several bodhisattvas.[2] Figures seated in meditation with one leg crossed over the other first appearing in the art of the Gandharan region of northwest India around the second or third century A.D. generally represent unidentified bodhisattvas in attendance on the Buddha.[3] In China, where this iconographic type was popular between the fifth and eighth centuries, the meditating pose symbolizes a turning point in the spiritual career of both Prince Siddhārtha and Prince Ajita – usually the moment immediately preceding enlightenment.[4] Since the events of the teaching career of Prince Ajita, the future Buddha Maitreya, are modeled after those of Prince Siddhārtha, the Buddha Śākyamuni, it is often impossible, without inscriptions or contextual evidence, to distinguish between images of these two bodhisattvas.

Figure 1. Meditating bodhisattva. Camphorwood; height, 133 cm; second half of seventh century. Chūgūji, Nara. Photograph courtesy of Asuka-en, Nara.

The special popularity of Maitreya Bodhisattva in the states of Paekche and especially Silla during the sixth and seventh centuries makes it likely that the majority of images of deities in the pensive pose found on the Korean peninsula represent Maitreya rather than Śākyamuni.[5] The same holds true in early Japan, where monks from Paekche and Silla were influential in the diffusion of the Maitreya cult.

Scholars do not dispute that the *hanka shiyui* statue housed in Chūgūji was created during the seventh century, when the cult to Maitreya Bodhisattva was especially popular in Japan. However, opinions differ on whether this exceptional image belongs in the first or second half of the century. The answer to this question is important for determining both the statue's meaning and its place within the development of early Japanese sculpture.

This chapter seeks to cast light on these three issues by examining the

Figure 2. Meditating bodhisattva (detail). Chūgūji, Nara. Photograph courtesy of Asuka-en, Nara.

traditional literary sources pertaining to the Chūgūji statue, by comparing the statue with other *hanka shiyui* figures, and by reconstructing the religious and political milieu in which it was created and worshipped. A study of Chūgūji's statue illuminates many of the distinctive features of Maitreya worship in seventh-century Japan.

The Soga Clan and Maitreya Worship in the Seventh Century

The beginnings of Maitreya worship in Japan are closely linked to the Soga 蘇我, the clan in power from 587 until 643 that was instrumental in gaining official recognition for Buddhism in Japan. An entry dated 584 in *Nihonshoki* 日本書記 (Chronicles of Japan) referring to the installation in their family temple of a stone statue of Maitreya from Paekche indicates that, from the outset, this deity assumed a special role in Soga family devotions.[6] Because

Buddhism during this era was practiced on a private, family basis it is likely that Maitreya was regarded as a special guardian deity of the Soga and their dependents.

Prince Shōtoku 聖徳太子 (552–621), regent under Empress Suiko 惟古 (r. 593–629) and unquestionably the most charismatic member of the Soga family, was among the first members of the ruling elite to see Buddhism's potential as an instrument of the state. Like his forebears, the pious prince, widely regarded as the founder of Japanese Buddhism, was probably a devotee of Maitreya. Shōtoku's efforts to assert Soga authority over the entire nation contributed to the spread of Maitreya worship. In 603, when he offered a statue of Maitreya from the Korean peninsula to the leader of the Hata clan, he was advocating the clan's worship of this powerful deity, as well as seeking their allegiance.[7]

Like rulers elsewhere, the Soga sought pragmatic benefits from Buddhism. The worship of Maitreya appealed to them because, as lord of Tuṣita Paradise and the next Buddha to appear on earth in human form, he offered benefits both in this world and in the next. Initially, prayers were addressed to him for good health, longevity, and, especially, happiness in the afterlife. Thus when Prince Shōtoku died in 621, his mother prepared an embroidery thought to depict Maitreya's Tuṣita Paradise in the hope that he might be reborn there.[8] However, over the course of the seventh century, especially after 643, when all Soga males were massacred by their political rivals, the worship of Maitreya acquired expanded spiritual and political meaning. Growing contact with monks from China and Silla and the introduction of new scriptures and images led to a more sophisticated understanding of Maitreya's distinctive character. Internecine strife in the wake of the Soga massacre combined with threats to Japan's autonomy from Silla and T'ang China made the promise of Maitreya's advent, and the return to peace, prosperity, and rightful political order attendant on it, especially attractive. Influenced by beliefs of Silla origin, Maitreya Bodhisattva was visualized as the handsome, princely leader of a new world order. This confluence of beliefs added new levels of suggestion and richness rather than superseding or negating the earlier Soga-related image of Maitreya. The *hanka shiyui* statue in Chūgūji was created and worshipped in this religious and political milieu.

The Pensive Prince of Chūgūji

Carved of aromatic camphorwood now darkened with age and a little less than life size, the Chūgūji statue represents a slender youth attired in a skirt the ample folds of which cascade about the round seat that supports him. His chest, modeled with considerable subtlety, is bare, and his head, with elongated ears and two knots of hair, is unadorned. A few tendrils of hair fall ribbon-like over his shoulders. Setting off the elegant simplicity of his head with its dreamy, half-closed eyes and faint hint of a smile is a flaming aureole attached to a wooden pole behind him. This aureole, the lotiform pedestal on which his seat rests, and his elongated ears are the only features that proclaim his divinity.[9]

The meditating youth of Chūgūji does not project an aura of solemnity and awe, nor does he impose himself on the viewer by the directness of his gaze, towering scale, or sumptuous attire. He speaks instead in the familiar language of the manifest world: Spirituality is expressed intuitively through the emotional suggestiveness of his pose. The remarkable grace and pliancy of its pose make this a penetrating evocation of a being in a state of profound introspection. Through the humility of this attitude, the viewer is led to see something of the human condition. This sense of humanity, almost unique in seventh-century Japanese sculpture, gives the statue its universal appeal.

The statue in Chūgūji was created by means of an unusual technique. Wooden images of the seventh century are generally made of solid blocks of wood, usually camphor, but this one comprises at least twenty-four interlocking pieces held in place with nails and wooden pegs.[10] This is the earliest instance of the use of what has come to be known by art historians as the assembled wood block, or *yosegi zukuri* 寄木造, technique.

In all likelihood, the Chūgūji statue was not designed to be seen as it is today. Like other seventh-century works such as the Kudara Kannon 百濟観音 (Paekche Avalokiteśvara) and the four Guardian Kings in Hōryūji, it probably wore a metal crown and other ornaments. These, however, were lost before the nineteenth century.[11] The statue also may have been gilded as was its *hanka shiyui* counterpart in Kōryūji 広隆寺 (see Figure 4). Although camphor was the wood preferred for statuary in the seventh century, it seems to have been appreciated more for its practical and symbolic value than its natural appearance. The aromatic camphorwood, impervious to insects, was doubtless thought to be a suitable native alternative to sandalwood, the material from which the first image of the Buddha is said to have been carved.[12]

Although they do not specifically mention the statue, early records about the origins of Chūgūji help to establish both a *terminus ad quem* and a probable context for its creation. The eighth-century *Hōryūji garan engi narabi ryūki shizaichō*, a record of Hōryūji's origins and treasures, is the first document to mention the nunnery. It claims that it was one of seven temples founded by Prince Shōtoku.[13] However, the ninth-century *Jōgū Shōtoku hōō teisetsu*, a biography of the prince, states that the nunnery was founded only after his death in 621 on the site of his mother's palace.[14] Archaeological studies made over the course of this century indicate that the present Chūgūji is a fifteenth-century structure built on a site slightly to the east of the original building. Old roof tiles, some dating to the seventh century and believed to have belonged to the original building, were used in this reconstruction.[15] On the basis of this combined archaeological and textual evidence, it can be assumed that Chūgūji was founded some time in the seventh century and that its founding, if not actually ascribed to Shōtoku himself, was intimately connected with him.

There are no temple records identifying the main image in Chūgūji as Maitreya Bodhisattva. First mentioned in the thirteenth-century *Taishi mandara koshiki*, it is identified as Guze Kannon (Avalokiteśvara World Savior) 求世觀音 and likened to a now lost statue in Shitennōji 四天王寺, the appearance of which is recorded in a twelfth-century iconographic drawing (see Figure 8) discussed below.[16] The *Taishi mandara koshiki* gives instructions for the performance of a ceremony honoring Prince Shōtoku in which a seventh-century embroidery showing the Prince's rebirth in paradise, possibly Maitreya's Tuṣita Heaven, is hung as the chief object of devotion.[17] This embroidery, known as the *Tenjukoku mandara* 天壽國曼荼羅 (Mandala of the realm of long life), and the pensive statue are Chūgūji's two greatest treasures.

The statue's identification as Guze Kannon reflects the belief, widespread by the thirteenth century, that Shōtoku was an avatar of Avalokiteśvara Bodhisattva, embodiment of charity and compassion.[18] The correlation between Prince Shōtoku and this bodhisattva appears to have originated in the late seventh or eighth century. The earliest recorded evidence is in eighth-century Hōryūji documents, where a statue of Avalokiteśvara in the Yumedono 夢殿 (Hall of dreams) on the Hōryūji compound is described as being of the prince's size.[19] Subsequently, the title Guze Kannon appears to have been applied to many images associated with the prince. Through its identification as Guze Kannon, the Chūgūji statue was assimilated into the popular cult of Shōtoku: Its worship was tantamount to worshipping Prince Shōtoku himself. Despite later identification as Cintāmanicakra or Ārya Avalokiteśvara, the statue's intimate connection with Prince Shōtoku remains a dominant theme in all premodern documents.[20]

The Chūgūji statue's identification as Guze Kannon vividly illustrates a phenomenon common in the history of Japanese art wherein the meaning of an ancient image is reinterpreted in keeping with prevailing religious beliefs. This occurs especially often in connection with images whose iconography is ambiguous or whose original significance is forgotten. Generally, the process of reinterpretation involves fusing rather than simply discarding the old for the new. Consequently, it is very difficult to chart.

The Date and Identity of the Chūgūji Statue

The Chūgūji statue is one of some thirty figures of the *hanka shiyui* type ascribed to the seventh and eighth centuries. After this period, the production of seated pensive figures ceases abruptly. All the figures are nearly identical in pose but vary considerably in details of attire and style, and especially in the success of their rendering of the pensive attitude. Three are relatively large wooden statues, but the remainder are all small, portable gilt bronzes, thirty centimeters or less in height. Two of the bronzes are dated; one also bears an inscription identifying it as Maitreya. A comparison of the Chūgūji figure with four other *hanka shiyui* statues makes its position within this genre of imagery and within seventh-century sculpture as a whole clearer.

By far the largest number of seated meditative figures belongs to a collection of gilt bronze statuary in Hōryūji known to art historians as the *shiju hattai butsu* 四十八体仏 (forty-eight Buddhas).[21] This anachronistic name is an allusion to Amida's forty-eight vows to save humanity and has no meaning in relation to the images in question. It does, however, illustrate the way images gain new connotations consonant with prevailing beliefs and practices. Although the *shiju hattai butsu* differ considerably in style and iconography, all belong to the seventh or eighth century. Some may be of Korean provenance.[22] Most are rather small in scale, indicating that they were originally made for private devotion rather than for installation in a temple.

How this diverse group of statues entered the Hōryūji collection is not entirely clear, but at least thirty are believed to have been transferred in the eleventh century from the nearby Tachibanadera 橘寺, which had fallen into disrepair. The tradition that Tachibanadera had been founded by Prince Shōtoku probably prompted their transferal to Hōryūji. By the eleventh century, Hōryūji had become the most prestigious of the temples associated with him. Other statues also may have been donated over the centuries by individuals or provincial temples to honor the memory of the sainty prince.

One of only two dated pensive figures belonging to this Hōryūji collection is now in Tokyo National Museum (Figure 3). The cyclical year *hinoe tora* 丙寅, also read *heiin*, appearing on its base provides a date of 606 or 666.[23] This statue's most striking feature is its pencil-thin, almost concave torso, offset by a disproportionately large head and massive rectangular base. Despite its lack of balance, the image has an ethereal elegance and serenity. The inscription, revealing that it was dedicated by a woman with the family name Takaya 高屋 on behalf of her deceased husband, raises many questions. The woman's given name is not legible, but the adjacent character *Kara* 韓, probably denoting a small kingdom in the southern part of the Korean peninsula, has led several scholars to propose that the statue was imported.[24]

If a date of 606 were accepted, this would be one of the earliest dated

Figure 3. Meditating bodhisattva. Gilt bronze; height, 41.5 cm; 606 or 666. Tokyo National Museum.

Buddhist icons in Japan, antedating by nearly a quarter of a century the key monument of early-seventh-century sculpture: Hōryūji's Śākyamuni trinity of 623 made by the official Soga sculptor Tori Busshi.[25] The gilt bronze statues of Śākyamuni flanked by two standing bodhisattvas exemplify the Tori school style, which derived from that practiced in sixth-century China as filtered through Paekche.[26] Its distinguishing features are elongated ovoid heads with sharply chiseled, severe features; flat, frontally oriented bodies with sloping shoulders; and abstract patterned garments. The seated Śākyamuni's robes form a rigidly ordered cascade of semicircular pleats. The standing attendants' garments fan out to the side, ending in sharp finlike projections.

Even when the disparity in subject matter is taken into account, the *hinoe tora* figure has little in common with this triad. Despite its slenderness, it is conceived more fully in the round and its facial expression is far less abstract. These features point to a date in the second half of the seventh century, when

Japanese sculpture is characterized by a greater preoccupation with plastic form and movement.[27]

A *hanka shiyui* image carved of red pine (Figure 4), one of two statues of this iconographic type housed in Kyoto's Kōryūji, furnishes important evidence of an imported stylistic model available to sculptors during the first half of the seventh century. Temple records identify it as Maitreya. Like its counterpart in Chūgūji, this nearly life size figure has captured the popular imagination owing to its pleasant youthful appearance and warm facial expression.[28] Unlike the gilt bronze with the *hinoe tora* inscription, there is no hint of clumsiness in the modeling of its body and no stiffness in the rendering of its limbs. Indeed, its gestures, especially that of the hand touching the chin, have remarkable subtlety and grace. Its torso, devoid of ornaments, is smooth and firm; the triple fold lines at the neck are a Buddhist convention of Indian origin. The skirt pulled taut over the legs forms elaborate vertical pleats over the round pedestal on which the figure sits. Their crisp, sharply chiseled surfaces set off the smooth flesh and gently rounded form of the body.

The Kōryūji statue's most unusual iconographic feature is its low triple-lobed crown. This crown, unique among *hanka shiyui* figures in Japan, has parallels in gilt bronze statues datable between 600 and 650 in Korea. The striking resemblance between the pensive figure in Kōryūji and a large gilt bronze image in the National Museum in Seoul (Figure 5) has led many scholars to believe it to be of Korean provenance.[29] This view finds both technical and documentary corroboration: Red pine is abundant on the Korean peninsula, especially in the region under Silla rule, but rare in Japan. Moreover, both temple and national chronicles refer to images from Paekche and Silla donated to Kōryūji. The interpretation of these documents, however, is problematic.

Entries in *Nihonshoki* 日本書記 (Chronicles of Japan) reveal that, in the twelfth year of Empress Suiko's reign (603), Hata Kawakatus 秦河勝, a member of a clan of Korean ancestry, received from Prince Shōtoku a Buddhist image and constructed a temple named Hachiokadera 蜂岡寺 to house it. Later in the twenty-second year of the same reign (623), the Hata clan temple received another Buddhist image, which had been sent by the king of Silla in Shōtoku's memory.[30] Both the Hachiokadera and the Hata clan temple are thought to refer to Kōryūji since this temple's ninth-century chronicle records that two golden statues of Maitreya Bodhisattva, one a gift from Prince Shōtoku, were installed in its Golden Hall.[31] Further support for the theory that Shōtoku's statue was of Korean provenance comes from a fifteenth-century temple record that refers to this image as having been sent by the king of Paekche.[32] From this body of evidence, the red pine statue has been widely accepted as a portrayal of Maitreya that originated in Paekche around 603. Following this line of reasoning, the other pensive statue in Kōryūji,

Figure 4. Maitreya bodhisattva. Red pine; height, 123.5 cm; first quarter of seventh century. Kōryūji, Kyoto. Photograph courtesy of Sakamoto Studios.

popularly known as the Naki Miroku 泣彌勒 (Crying Maitreya), is thought by many Japanese scholars to be the later gift sent in 623, although comparable works have yet to be found in Silla.[33]

Specialists of Korean art, however, take a different view.[34] They believe that the red pine statue, like its bronze counterpart in the Seoul National Museum, originated in the Silla Kingdom and is therefore the image sent in 623 by the king of Silla to honor Shōtoku's memory. In support of this claim they cite the special prominence in Silla of the worship of Maitreya, especially in the hope of being in attendance when, following his descent to earth and enlightenment beneath the Dragon Flower Tree, he will preach to the three assemblies.

A *hanka shiyui* figure in Yachūji 野中寺 (Figure 6), a temple in Osaka, exemplifies the new trend toward plastic form and movement characteristic of sculpture in the second half of the seventh century. This work bears an

Figure 5. Meditating bodhisattva. Gilt bronze; height, 90 cm; first quarter of seventh century. Seoul National Museum. Courtesy of the Korean Cultural Service.

inscription identifying it as Maitreya and its date as the cyclical year *hinoe tora*. The inscription also names the donors as a group of one hundred and eighteen *chishikisha* 知識者 affiliated with a temple generally thought to be Tachibanadera.[35] Unlike the inscribed statue discussed above, this work is universally accepted as a work of 666. *Chishikisha* is a term that designates a group of Buddhist devotees united in any pious endeavor, often the commissioning of an image. According to the inscription, this particular group dedicated the statue of Maitreya to ensure Emperor Tenchi's 天智 (or Empress Saimei's 齊明) recovery from illness. The detailed, dated inscription makes this work a valuable landmark in tracing both stylistic and religious developments in the second half of the seventh century.

Figure 6. Maitreya bodhisattva. Gilt bronze; height, 31.2 cm; 666. Yachūji, Osaka. Photograph courtesy of Sakamoto Studios.

The Yachūji Maitreya bears little resemblance to its dated counterpart in Hōryūji. Its compact, well-rounded body and hunched posture, though less pleasing to the eye than the elegantly attenuated Hōryūji statue, features a greater sense of mass. The rendering of its garment, conveying a sense of the weight and pull of the fabric over the legs and around the base, gives the whole a more tangible quality. The pearl-like border on the hem and floral bands over the legs draw further attention to this sense of corporeality. Both works, however, do have in common their disproportionately large heads, which unlike the perfect ovoid forms of the Tori school, are broad across the forehead and tapered to a point at the chin. In addition, both wear a three-part coronet, which is especially common in imagery of the second half of the seventh century.

The Yachūji Maitreya's dedication to Emperor Tenchi or Empress Saimei is one of several pieces of evidence testifying to the prominence of the Maitreya cult during the third quarter of the seventh century. Emperor Tenchi (r. 662–73) himself appears to have been devoted to Maitreya, for in the seventh year of his reign he constructed a temple in Omi Province (Shiga Prefecture) and installed there a statue of Maitreya.[36] The creation of the famous Kasagidera 笠置寺 rock-carved image of Maitreya is attributed in traditional sources to Emperor Tenchi's reign.[37] The thirteenth-century *Taimadera engi*, an illustrated scroll relating the legendary origins of Taimadera, ascribes the creation of its statue of Maitreya to Tenchi's reign.[38] The now lost main image in the Golden Hall of Shitennōji, to be discussed below, is also said to have been installed during this period.

Unusual since it was excavated from the vicinity of Mount Nachi 那智山 in Wakayama Prefecture, is a gilt bronze (Figure 7) now in Tokyo National Museum.[39] Traces of a green patina on its brilliant gold surface attest to its centuries-long burial. The naturalistic treatment of its body and easy fall of its garment give it considerable grace. The curve of its bare torso and especially the slight forward tilt of its head relieve it of the rigidity of its two *hinoe tora* counterparts. Its unadorned head and hairstyle, a double topknot and two strands of hair falling ribbon-like over the shoulders, approximate the Chūgūji statue's hairstyle. Although this work cannot be dated with precision, its naturalism clearly sets it in the second half of the seventh century.

In the absence of inscriptions or other documentation, it is impossible to be sure of this image's identity, but its discovery in a sūtra mound (*kyōzuka* 經塚) points to a connection with the worship of Maitreya.[40] In the Heian period (794–1185) it was widely believed that the year 1052 signaled the onset of the decline of the Buddhist Dharma (*mappō* 末法), an age leading to the disappearance of Buddhist teachings and concomitantly to lawlessness on earth. This apocalyptic belief prompted the burial of Buddhist scriptures, images, and other objects in holy spots, especially mountaintops, there to await the coming of Maitreya, whose appearance would initiate a new age of Buddhism. Inclusion of this pensive figure in such a sūtra mound suggests that, in the Heian period at least, it was thought to represent Maitreya.

Evidence identifying extant seventh-century *hanka shiyui* images as Maitreya is limited to the inscription on the statue in Yachūji, the Kōryūji chronicles, and, less reliably, the context in which the Tokyo National Museum statue was discovered. Yet this severely limited evidence must be weighed against a total absence of written testimony identifying meditative statues as Prince Siddhārtha. Iconographically, the Chūgūji statue conforms closely to the Kōryūji Maitreya. Its tufted hairstyle parallels that of the Tokyo National Museum figure. These features make it possible to identify the figure tentatively as Maitreya.

In style, the Chūgūji statue is also close to the Kōryūji Maitreya. Both statues are carved of wood, were once gilded, and are just under life size. Both have slender but pleasingly balanced bodies with well-modeled limbs and warm, even tender, facial expressions. Moreover, both feature a dramatic

Figure 7. Meditating bodhisattva. Gilt bronze; height, 30 cm; second half of seventh century. Tokyo National Museum.

contrast between the smooth bare torso above and the richly intricate garments below.

The loose, flowing treatment of the Chūgūji statue's garments, however, differs significantly from the taut linear treatment of the Kōryūji's. The ample, curvilinear pleats of the Chūgūji statue are in the Tori school idiom as seen in the Śākyamuni triad of 623. The Chūgūji statue's elongated, ovoid face, the sharp vertical indentation between its nose and mouth, and the slight upward curve of its lips also have precedents among Tori school works. The Chūgūji Maitreya thus appears to represent a synthesis of two stylistic traditions, one derived from the Kōryūji Maitreya and the other from the Tori school.

The more convincing sense of volume in the treatment of both the body and the drapery, however, suggests that the Chūgūji Maitreya was carved well after the Hōryūji Śākyamuni and Kōryūji Maitreya. The statue of Śākyamuni is conceived in an additive fashion, whereas the Chūgūji Maitreya forms a rhythmically flowing whole. The arrangement of garments in the latter is also freer and more naturalistic than the rigid, somewhat arbitrary system featured in its Kōryūji counterpart.

A survey of documents concerning now lost images of Maitreya in other temples throws light on the significance of the two stylistic sources noted in the Chūgūji statue. It also provides evidence that reinforces its proposed identification and date.

Lost Images of Maitreya

Today Chūgūji and Kōryūji are the sole temples in Japan still housing as their main icons statues of Maitreya in the *hanka shiyui* pose. Documentary evidence, however, indicates that six of the seven temples that, according to the *Hōryūji garan engi narabi ryūki shizaichō*, were founded by Prince Shōtoku also enshrined images of this deity in their main halls.[41] In addition to Chūgūji and Kōryūji, these include Shitennōji, Tachibanadera, Hokkiji 法興寺, and Katsuragidera 葛城寺. Only Hōryūji lacks one.

Shitennōji in Osaka is said to have been founded by the prince in 593 following his victory over the anti-Buddhist Mononobe clan. The *Shitennōji goshuin engi*, a record of the temple's holdings dating perhaps to the tenth century, describes its chief image as a golden statue of Guze Kannon donated by the king of Paekche.[42] But according to another, earlier source, the golden statue represents Maitreya and was installed during the reign of Emperor Tenchi.[43] The *Bessonzakki* 別尊雜記, a collection of iconographic drawings compiled in 1175 by the Shingon monk-artist Shinkaku 心覚, includes a detailed sketch of this now lost work (Figure 8).[44] Identified as Cintāmanicakra or Ārya Avalokiteśvara, it represents a fully clothed bodhisattva seated in *hanka* pose but without the right hand held to the chin. Instead, the hand forms the *abhāya mudrā*, "fear-not gesture."[45]

These three references to the Shitennōji statue represent three different stages in a process of reidentification made necessary by changing patterns of belief and facilitated by the statue's iconographic ambiguity. Like its counterpart in Chūgūji, the Shitennōji statue was designed to represent Maitreya, but as the worship of Maitreya waned in favor of that of Avalokiteśvara and the cult to Shōtoku gained popularity, it was renamed Guze Kannon. Still later, through the pervasive influence of Shingon Buddhism, the statue was identified as Cintāmanicakra Avalokiteśvara.

Three nunneries associated with the prince – Tachibanadera, Hokkiji, and Katsuragidera – also housed statues of Maitreya, probably of the *hanka shiyui* type. Evidence for the presence of such a figure in Tachibanadera is

Figure 8. "Shitennōji's Guze Kannon." Iconographic drawing by Shinkaku included in Bessonzaki; 1175. Photograph after *Daizōkyō zuzō*, vol. 3.

based on references in two late Kamakura period records. They identify the image in the temple's Golden Hall as Guze Kannon, liken it to the Chūgūji *hanka shiyui-zō*, and ascribe its creation to Shōtoku.[46]

According to temple tradition, Hokkiji was founded in 626, on the site of the palace of Yamashiro no Oe, Shōtoku's eldest son. Excavation of the temple's foundations give a date in the second half of the seventh century, however. According to the same tradition, in 638 the monk Fukuryō had a statue of Maitreya installed in the temple's Golden Hall to pray for Shōtoku's enlightenment.[47] There are no data on its appearance.

Reconstructing the history of Katsuragidera is complicated by the fact that it was moved from its original site in the Asuka district to the new capital of Heijō-kyō in 710. The present Katsuragidera is located to the east of Nara City. Therefore, it is not clear whether the old or new temple is referred to in a vignette included in the ninth-century *Nihon ryōiki* 日本靈異記, a collection of Buddhist didactic tales compiled by the monk Kyōkai 景戒. What is certain is that in the mid–eighth century, the temple housed a gilt bronze statue of Maitreya Bodhisattva as its chief devotional image.[48] Since the cult of Maitreya Bodhisattva had waned by this time, it is likely that the image in question had been transferred from the original seventh-century temple.

From the above, a pattern emerges. Six of the seven temples "founded" by Shōtoku, with the exception of Hōryūji, at one time housed statues of Maitreya. Like the Chūgūji Maitreya, some were later identified as Guze Kannon. Although traditional accounts claim Shōtoku as their founder, a careful reading of individual records combined with archaeological evidence indicates that the temples and their images were probably dedicated between the prince's death in 621 and the end of Tenchi's reign in 673. Moreover, they were not dedicated by the prince, but for him. The red pine statue sent by the king of Silla in 623 was the first of the Maitreya statues placed in these temples to commemorate the prince's memory. Because of its foreign provenance, early date, and installation in a temple associated with Shōtoku during his lifetime, it was seen as an appropriate model for later images such as the Chūgūji Maitreya. Through such replication, both the outward appearance and the spiritual aura of the image were preserved and disseminated.

Shōtoku Taishi and the Maitreya Cult

Veneration of Prince Shōtoku began soon after his death. In 621, the *Tenjukoku mandara* was created in his honor. The statue of Śākyamuni made, according to the inscription on its aureole, "to the size of the prince," now installed in Hōryūji's Golden Hall, was dedicated two years later.[49] The statues of Maitreya Bodhisattva in Chūgūji and related temples were made between the 620s and 670s in honor of the saintly prince. Thus by 670 when Hōryūji was rebuilt following a devastating fire, the cult to Shōtoku was firmly in place.[50]

The temples and images dedicated in Shōtoku's memory between 621 and 643 undoubtedly were commissioned from the Tori workshop by members of the Soga clan. The identity of those who continued to revere Shōtoku following the Soga decline is unclear, but they may well have been Soga women who retired after the deaths of their husbands to the three nunneries that figure among the seven temples associated with the prince.

Even more likely candidates, however, are the mothers of Empress Jitō 持統 (645–721) and Empress Gemyō 元明 (661–721), both of whom were of Soga descent. Their patronage may account, at least in part, for the continued production of Tori-style works during the latter part of the century. Both the creation of the statue of Maitreya in Chūgūji and the costly 670 reconstruction of Hōryūji, which included a revival of Tori-style images modeled after works made during Shōtoku's lifetime, must be viewed against this backdrop.[51] The religious and political prestige of the Soga imperial mothers surely conferred official sanction and national status on the worship of Shōtoku.

In the seventh century, Japan, unlike China, had no tradition of portraiture. The creation of a likeness of a living person was fraught with danger, and no special value was attached to recording for posterity the appearance of the deceased.[52] Even rulers were not celebrated in their own right. However, identification with a Buddhist deity, a practice with many illustrious precedents in China, offered a suitable alternative.[53] Shōtoku's identification with Śākyamuni, given expression in the creation of the statue "made to his size," offers the first instance of this phenomenon in Japan. The prince's association with the statue of Avalokiteśvara Bodhisattva in the Yumedono some time in the late seventh or early eighth century is another early example of this practice. The former image was created in the belief that Shōtoku Taishi, as founder of Buddhism in Japan, was the native equivalent of Śākyamuni, founder of Buddhism in India. The latter image, however, probably became associated with the prince only after its creation, because of his status as a Buddhist saint. The link between the prince and the various statues of Maitreya Bodhisattva discussed above follows the same pattern. Some works, such as the Kōryūji Maitreya, were identified with the prince only after their creation. Others, such as the Chūgūji image, may have been consciously made to give expression to the link between Maitreya and the prince.

If Shōtoku was Śākyamuni's successor, it followed that he was one and the same as Maitreya Bodhisattva, the future Buddha. Shōtoku's two identities were not mutually exclusive, but statements within different vocabularies of the same fundamental truth. The title Taishi 太子, "Prince Royal," by which Prince Siddhārtha, Ajita, and Shōtoku were commonly known in China and Japan, contributed to the merging of their identities.[54] Written with the characters for great and child or son, the term implies a prince with expectancy of succession. It may also denote a princely being who is not yet spiritually mature or fully enlightened – a bodhisattva. Thus Shōtoku Taishi, like Siddhārtha and Ajita, was seen as a prince in both the political and religious realms.

Because both Siddhārtha and Ajita meditated beneath a tree before attaining enlightenment, the meditating figure in Chūgūji and related *hanka shiyui-zō* could have been designed to commemorate Shōtoku Taishi's identification with Śākyamuni, Maitreya, or both. However, political and religious developments in the second half of the century when the statue was carved make it more likely that the pensive prince of Chūgūji was intended to represent Maitreya and, by extension, Prince Shōtoku.

In the late 650s, the T'ang government formed an alliance with Silla and in 660, with Silla's assistance, seized the Paekche capital. Silla and T'ang were thus aligned against Koguryo, Paekche, and Japan. Fearing a Silla invasion, in 661 Japan promised to aid Paekche, but in 663 the Japanese–Paekche coalition was defeated. During this period a strong sense of militant nationalism developed in Japan. After 663, under the rule of Emperor Tenchi, however, Japan was determined to make peace with T'ang and Silla and to abandon Koguryo, which in 668 was finally overcome. As part of an effort to cultivate good relations with former enemies, diplomatic and religious missions were encouraged. Between 665 and 707, fourteen ships carried monks to study in Silla and thirteen carried diplomatic missions to China. Both Japanese monks who had returned from Silla and immigrant Silla monks were influential in the development of Buddhism during this period.[55] The cult of Maitreya Bodhisattva was in place during the period of hostilities, but it saw further expansion during the subsequent era of intense exchange with Silla.

By the time it had reached the Japanese archipelago, the cult of Maitreya was a confluence of many beliefs.[56] As the Buddha who will appear at the end of this world cycle to reestablish a just order over the entire world, Maitreya was linked with the *cakravartin*, the ideal universal monarch who conquers with the Buddhist Dharma rather than with the sword. Maitreya's earthly name of Ajita, meaning "victorious," undoubtedly contributed a militant element to this image.[57]

Added to these were beliefs of Silla origins. The Maitreya cult was practiced at the Silla court by a group of young aristocratic warriors who formed a fraternity known as the Hwarang 花郎, "Perfumed Followers of the Dragon Flower." This name is an allusion to the Dragon Flower Tree under which Maitreya Bodhisattva is to attain enlightenment. Members of the Hwarang were thought to be incarnations of Maitreya.[58]

In view of its close contacts with Silla, it is likely that the multidimensional cult of Maitreya, culminating in Maitreya's identification with the Hwarang, was known and influential in Japan. Shōtoku's association with Maitreya was implicit in his status as Śākyamuni's successor as well as in his title of Taishi. As a devout Buddhist ruler who had ensured the future of Buddhism in Japan by his victory over the anti-Buddhist Mononobe 物部 clan, Shōtoku was undoubtedly perceived as a *cakravartin*. The *Hōryūji garan engi narbi ryūki shizaichō's* claim that the prince had founded seven temples is surely inspired by the tradition that the *cakravartin* has seven treasures with which he rules his state. The growth of nationalistic fervor combined with the emphasis on military might during the second half of the seventh century provided fertile ground for Shōtoku's association with the militant Hwarang perception of Maitreya and for the transformation of Shōtoku into a national culture hero. The uncertainty and fear of a Silla invasion surely underlay the belief that, through the veneration of Maitreya and his Japanese incarnation, peace and prosperity would be restored to Japan. Thus the statue of the pensive prince in Chūgūji bears silent witness to the way the Maitreya cult was appropriated and reshaped in keeping with the religious and political needs of seventh-century Japan.

NOTES

Research for this article was supported by a Japan Foundation Short Term Professional Fellowship during the summer of 1982.

1 For a historiography of the statue see Inoue Tadashi, "Chūgūji hanka shiyui-zō ni tsuite"井上正，中宮寺半跏思惟像についこ, *Kokka* 國華, no. 819 (June 1960): 205–20.

2 For an overview of the development of imagery of this type, see Francois Berthier, "The Meditative Bodhisattva Image in China, Korea, and Japan," in *International Symposium on the Conservation and Restoration of Cultural Properties: Inter-regional Influences in East Asian Art History* (Tokyo: National Research Institute of Cultural Properties, 1982), 1–13.

3 A notable example of this type of figure appears in a frieze in the Freer Gallery of Art. For reproductions, see Ashwin Lippe, *The Freer Indian Sculptures*, Smithsonian Institution, Freer Gallery of Art Oriental Studies no. 8 (Washington, D.C., 1970), figure 11.

4 On Maitreya cult and imagery in China see Alexander Soper, *Literary Evidence for Buddhist Art in China* (Ascona: Artibus Asiae, 1969), 211–21, and Matsubara Saburō 松原三郎, *Chūgoku bukkyō chōkoku-shi kenkyū* 中國仏教彫刻史研究 (Tokyo: Yoshikawa kobunkan, 1961), 129–47.

5 On the Maitreya cult and imagery in Korea see Tamura Enchō 田村圓澄, "Kodai Chōsen no Miroku shinkō"古代朝鮮の弥勒信仰朝鮮學報, *Chōsen gakuhō*, 162 (January 1982): 1–27, and Jonathan Best, "The Sosan Triad: An Early Korean Buddhist Relief Sculpture from Paekche," *Archives of Asian Art*, 33 (1980): 89–108.

6 W. G. Aston, trans., *Nihongi: Chronicles of Japan from the Earliest Times to A.D. 697*, 2 vols. in 1 (Rutland, Vt.: Tuttle, 1972), 2: 101. The same event, dated 538, is described in *Gangoji garan engi narabi ni ryūki shizaichō* 元興寺伽藍縁起并流記資財帳, compiled in 738. See *Dainihon bukkyō zensho* (hereafter *DNBZ*) (Tokyo: Kōdansha, 1972), 85: 1. It is probable that Maitreya was also worshipped by others not belonging to the Soga clan, but there is little documentary evidence that Buddhism was practiced during this early period by individuals or families who were not part of the ruling elite.

7 This statue, today in Kyoto's Kōryūji, is discussed more fully below (see Figure 4).

8 This is the so-called *Tenjūkoku mandara* discussed more fully below.

9 The aureole is probably a later addition. See Sherwood Moran, "The Statue of Miroku Bosatsu of Chūgūji: A Detailed Study," *Artibus Asiae* 21 (1958): 193–9.

10 On the construction of the Chūgūji statue see ibid., 180–6.

11 For reproductions of these works see Seiichi Mizuno, *Asuka Buddhist Art: Hōryūji*, trans. Richard Gage. Heibonsha Survey of Japanese Art 4 (New York: Weatherhill, 1974), plates 53 and 55.

12 For a discussion of the Chinese Buddhist attitudes toward sandalwood, which in turn influenced Japan, see Soper, *Literary Evidence*, 259–65.

13 *Hōryūji garan engi narabi ryūki shizaichō* 法隆寺伽藍縁起并流記資財帳, *DNBZ*, 85: 114.

14 *Jōgū Shōtoku hōō teisetsu* 上宮聖德法王帝説, *DNBZ*, 71: 120.

15 Ota Hirotarō 太田博太郎 et al., eds. *Hōryūji to Ikaruga no koji, Nihon koji bijutsu zenshū* 法隆寺と斑鳩の古寺,日本古寺美術全集 (Tokyo: Shūeisha 1979), 25: 115, 143.

16 The *Taishi mandara koshiki* 太子曼荼羅講式 is reproduced in *Shōtoku Taishi zenshū*, 聖德太子全集, ed. Ishida Mosaku 石田茂作 (Tokyo: Ryūginsha 1943), 5: 133.

17 For a brief discussion and reproduction of this embroidery, see Ota et al., eds., *Hōryūjji to Ikaruga no koji*, plate 78 and accompanying text.

18 On Shōtoku's identification as Guze Kannon see Hayashi Mikiya 林幹彌, *Taishi shinkō: Sono hassei to hatten.* 太子信仰: その発生と発展 (Tokyo: Heibonsha, 1972), 40–51.

19 On the Yumedono statue see Ota Hirotarō, comp., *Nara rokudaiji taikan: Hōryūji IV* 奈良六大寺太觀 (Tokyo: Iwanami Shoten, 1972), 7–13.

20 See Inoue, "Chūgūji hanka shiyui-zō ni tsuite," 205–7.

21 On the *shiju hattai butsu*, see Tazawa Yutaka 田澤坦 et al., *Hōryūji hōzō sho-kondō-zō* 法隆寺寶藏小金銅像 (Tokyo: Iwanami shoten, 1954). These works were donated to the Imperial Household in 1878 and are now housed in the Tokyo National Museum, but for clarity they will be referred to here as belonging to Hōryūji.

22 Kuno Takeshi 久野健 has proposed that at least three of this group, including one bodhisattva in meditation, are Korean. See his *Kodai Chōsen-butsu to Asuka-butsu* 古代朝鮮仏と飛鳥 (Tokyo: Higashi Shuppan, 1979), 7–15.

23 For a reproduction and transcription of the inscription, see Nara National Museum, comp., *Hōryūji kennō kondō-butsu* 法隆寺獻納金銅仏 (Nara: Nara kokuritsu hakubutsukan, 1981), 64.

24 See, for instance, Matsubara Saburō, "Shiju hattai butsu – sono keifu ni tsuite" 四十八体仏 - - その系譜について, *Kobijutsu* 古美術, 19 (October 1967): 31–2, and Francois Berthier, "Divers problèmes concernant la statuette en bronze doré datée de l'an Hinoe-tora appartenant au groupe statuaire dit 'les 48 Buddha,'" *Transactions of the International Conference of Orientalists in Japan*, no. 16 (1971): 66–80.

25 On the Hōryūji Śākyamuni triad, see *Nara rokudaiji taikan: Hōryūji II*, 11–28.

26 On the origins of the Tori style see Kuno Takeshi, "Asuka-butsu no tanjō" 飛鳥仏の誕生, *Bijutsu kenkyū*, 315 (December 1980): 1–16.

27 On the problems of stylistic development in the seventh century see Machida Kōichi 町田甲一, *Jōdai chōkoku-shi no kenkyū* 上代彫刻史の研究 (Tokyo: Yoshikawa kobunkan, 1977), 1–75.

28 On the Kōryūji statue see Chizawa Teiji 干澤楨治, "Kōryūji no hanka shiyui-zō ni tsuite" 広隆寺の半跏思惟像についこ, *Museum*, no. 116 (November 1960): 2–6 and no. 117 (December 1960): 2–6. The technique used is discussed in Kuno, *Kodai Chōsen-butsu to Asuka-butsu*," 4–5.

29 On the work on Seoul see Kang Woo-bang 姜友邦, "Chōkoku Tokujugū bijutsukan kyuzō no kondō sanzankan shiyui-zō ni tsuite" 朝国徳寿宮美術館旧蔵の金銅三山冠思惟像についこ, *Bukkyō geijutsu* 仏教艺術, 123 (March 1979): 11–44.

30 Aston, trans., *Nihongi*, 2: 127, 149–50.

31 *Kōryūji shizai kōtai jitsurokuchō* 広隆寺資財校替实録帳, *DNBZ*, 83: 230.

32 *Yamashiro no kuni Kadono gun Kaedeno oinogō Kōryūji raiyuki*, 山城州葛野郡楓野大堰郷広隆寺未由記, *DNBZ*, 83: 242.

33 Inoue, "Chūgūji hanka-shiyui-zō ni tsuite," 218, for instance, assumes this to be the case.

34 Kang, "Chōkoku Tokujugū bijutsukan kyuzō," 25–9, and Jonathan Best, personal communication.

35 On this and other inscribed statues of the period see Kuno Takeshi, "Asuka Hakuhō sho-kondō-butsu no hatsugansha to seisakusha" 飛鳥・白鳳小金銅仏の発願者と制作者, *Bijutsu kenkyū*, 309 (February, 1979): 26–7.

36 *Fusō ryakki* 扶桑略記, in *Kokushi taikei* 國史大系, comp. Kōen 皇圓 (Tokyo: Keizai zoshisha, 1897), 6: 520. See also Hayami Tasuku 速水侑, *Miroku shinkō: mō hitotsu no Jōdo shinkō* 弥勒信仰もう一つの浄土信仰日本人の行動と思想, Nihon no gyōdō to shisō 12 (Tokyo: Heibonsha, 1980), 58–60.

37 See Chapter 10, this volume.

38 *Taimadera engi/Chigo Kannon engi* 当麻曼荼羅縁起稚兜觀音縁起, in *Nihon emaki taisei* 日本絵巻大成, ed. Komatsu Shigemi 小松茂美 (Tokyo: Chūo Koronsha, 1979), 24: 15.

39 This work was recently published in Nishikawa Shinji and Emily Sano, *The Great Age of Japanese Buddhist Sculpture A.D. 600–1300* (Fort Worth Tex.: Kimbell Art Museum, 1982), entry 2. For a fuller discussion of the excavation of this work see Ishida Mosaku, *Nachi hakkutsu bukkyō ibutsu no kenkyū* 那智発掘仏遺物の研究 (Tokyo: Tokyo hakubutsu bijutsukan, 1927), 16–24.

40 On *kyōzuka*, see Hayami, *Miroku shinkō*, 135–62.

41 This section is based on documentation gathered by Tamura Enchō in his "Hanka shiyui-zō to Shōtoku Taishi shinkō" 半跏思惟像と聖徳太子信仰, *Shiragi to Asuka Hakuhō no bukkyō bunka* 新羅と飛鳥白鳳の仏教文化 (Tokyo: Yoshikawa kobunkan, 1975), 82–8.

42 *Shitennōji goshuin engi* 四天王寺御朱印縁起, *DNBZ*, 85: 305. This record is said to have been written by Shōtoku but was probably compiled after the 960 destruction of the temple.

43 The record in question, which may date to the Daidō era (806–10), no longer survives in independent form. It is contained in *Taishi-den kokonmokurokusho* 太子伝古今目録抄, *DNBZ*, 71: 274.

44 *Taisho shinshu daizōkyō* 大正新修大藏經 (Tokyo: Daizō shuppan kabushiki gaisha, 1932), Zuzōbu 図像部, 3: 171.

45 Two other images in this variant pose are known: one in Hōryūji reproduced in Mizuno, *Asuka Buddhist Art: Hōryūji*, figure 80, and another in Konshōin, Nagano Prefecture, reproduced in Kuno, "Asuka-butsu no tanjō," figure 10.

46 *Shoji engi shū* 諸寺縁起集, *DNBZ*, 83: 22, and *Shōyoshō* 聖譽鈔, *DNBZ*, 72: 6.

47 *Shōtoku Taishi denshiki* 聖徳太子伝私記, *DNBZ*, 71: 300.

48 Kyoko M. Nakamura, trans., *Miraculous Stories from the Japanese Buddhist Tradition: The Nihon Ryōiki of the Monk Kyōkai* (Cambridge, Mass.: Harvard University Press, 1973), 191–2.

49 For the inscription see *Nara rokudaiji taikan: Hōryūji II*, 23.

50 For an excellent English summary of the temple's history see Kurata Bunsaku, *Hōryūji: Temple of the Exalted Law* (New York: Japan Society, 1982), 20–31. See also *Nara rokudaiji taikan: Hōryūji I*, 7–12.

51 The most obvious example of this revival is the statue of Yakushi in the Golden Hall. It was once thought to date to 607 but is now generally acknowledged to date from around the time of the temple's reconstruction. For a discussion of this issue see Mizuno, *Asuka Buddhist Art: Horyuji*, 30–9.

52 Images were believed to capture the spirit of the person represented and therefore could be used to harm the living. See Aston, trans., *Nihongi*, 2: 110. The first portrait of a layman representing Shōtoku Taishi dates to the eighth century.

53 Emperor Wu of the Liang (r. 502–49) called himself Huang-ti p'u-sa 黄帝菩薩 (Emperor Bodhisattva), and the founder of the Sui dynasty (585–618) called himself a *cakravartin*. Arthur Wright, *Buddhism in Chinese History* (New York: Atheneum, 1968), 51, 67.

54 It is also the basis for the cult of the divine boy, which has permeated Japanese Buddhism to this day. See Hayashi, *Taishi shinkō*, 13–17.

55 Tamura, "Hanka shiyui-zō to Shōtoku Taishi shinkō," 89–95.

56 For an overview of the development of the cult see Joseph Kitagawa, "The Career of Maitreya with Special Reference to Japan," *History of Religions*, 21 (November 1981): 108–25.

57 On the origins and significance of this name see Sylvain Lévi, "Maitreya le Consolateur," in *Etudes d'Orientalisme à la Memoire de Raymonde Linossier* (Paris: Librairie Ernest Leroux, 1932), 355–402.

58 For a fuller discussion see Chapter 6, this volume.

10

Awaiting Maitreya at Kasagi

KAREN L. BROCK

Introduction

A colossal cliff-face image of Maitreya as Buddha was, for centuries, the principal object of devotion at Kasagidera 笠置寺 high atop Mt. Kasagi (Figures 1a and 1b). Located some twenty kilometers northeast of the modern city of Nara, Kasagidera is now accessible either on the Kansai main line from Kyoto or by bus from Nara. In medieval Japan, one traveled to this precipitous mountain peak either by boat down the Katsura 桂 and Kizu 木津 rivers from Kyoto or overland through the mountains from Nara. Remarkable outcroppings of granite dot Mt. Kasagi's slopes, and it was on one huge boulder about 15 by 21 meters in size that the image of Maitreya was engraved (Figure 2). A battle and fire at Kasagidera in 1331 destroyed the temple halls and reportedly obliterated all trace of Maitreya.[1] Today the cliff face is bare; only a shallow depression in the rock remains as evidence of this once impressive standing figure.

Fortunately, a painting in the Yamato Bunkakan, the so-called *Kasagi mandara* 笠置曼荼羅, provides visual evidence for the appearance of the colossus and Kasagidera in the late thirteenth century (Figure 3).[2] Maitreya, draped in red monastic garb, seems about to descend from the dark cliff face. A mandorla surrounds Maitreya's body and the halo that circles his head. Flanking the central image are two arhats in half-scale. The arhat in front offers Maitreya a robe; the second stands behind holding an incense burner. The Buddha's height appears equal to that of the thirteen-story pagoda. A multi-bay hall on stilts stretches along a narrow ledge in front of the image. The only living figures in the painting are a pair of pilgrims approaching the temple from the left and a monk whose head is barely visible beyond the roof of the foreground hall. This monk returns Maitreya's direct gaze.

This representation of Maitreya as a standing Buddha flanked by two

Figure 1a. Mt. Kasagi. Kasagi-chō, Sōraku-gun, Kyoto-fu. Photograph by the author.

Figure 1b. Approach to the Kasagi Maitreya. Photograph by the author.

Figure 2. The Maitreya Stone at Kasagidera. Photograph by the author.

arhats has no known precedent in Japan. The three engraved figures do not form a simple devotional triad with adoring disciples flanking a central Buddha. Rather, the grouping depicts an event taking place at a specific moment in time. The arhat handing the robe up to Maitreya may be Śākyamuni's eldest disciple, Mahākāśyapa. Some scriptural sources of the Maitreya legend recount that, upon his deathbed, Śākyamuni entrusted his robe to Mahākāśyapa that the latter might transmit it to Maitreya after his descent. The second arhat's identity will be examined below.

The carving of the Kasagi Maitreya must have been an important event. The scale of the image, 15 meters in height, and the difficulty of such an undertaking in a precipitous mountain region suggest that substantial patronage was required. Yet no contemporary record of the Kasagi Maitreya exists. The founding legends of the temple appear in *Miraculous Origins of Kasagidera*, a text dated 1482, distressingly late as a historical source.[3] Many of the legends therein can be corroborated, however, by disparate earlier records. An elaborate description of the creation of the Kasagi Maitreya appears in *Tales of*

Figure 3. *Kasagi mandara*. Late thirteenth or early fourteenth century. Ink and colors on silk, 75.5 cm × 54.8 cm. Yamato Bunkakan, Nara. Photograph courtesy of Yamato Bunkakan.

Times Now Past, a thirty-chapter compilation of Buddhist and secular tales thought to date from the early to middle twelfth century.[4] There the carving of the colossus is ascribed to a celestial being who descended in response to a vow by a son of Emperor Tenchi 天智 (r. 668–71). This pious legend has been universally dismissed, and most modern writers on the Kasagi Maitreya agree that the image was carved in the eighth, not the seventh, century.[5]

Although the Kasagi Maitreya has virtually vanished, its significance for Maitreya worship in medieval Japan has not been overlooked. Hiraoka Jōkai 平岡定海 devotes considerable attention to Kasagidera in his lengthy study of Maitreya devotionalism in Japan.[6] Before 1007, when Kasagidera was visited by Fujiwara no Michinaga 藤原道長 (966–1027), the Kasagi Maitreya had achieved fame as a pilgrimage site on the way east to Ise Shrine. During the thirteenth century, under the direction of two prominent Nara monks, Jōkei 貞慶 (1155–1213) of Kōfukuji and Sōshō 宗性 (1202–78) of Tōdaiji, Kasagidera received imperial support and reached its maximum size and complement of halls and residences. It was during repeated visits to Kasagi between 1233 and 1260 that Sōshō wrote an ambitious five-chapter compendium of references to Maitreya in Buddhist literature, the *Digest of the Miraculous Response of Maitreya* (*Miroku nyorai kan'ō shō* 彌勒如來感應抄).[7] The lone monk in the painting of Kasagidera may well be a representation of this prolific medieval scholar or perhaps of his predecessor Jōkei, whom he revered.

But what of the origin of the cliff-face Maitreya at Kasagi? In all of Jōkei's appeals for support for the temple, written between 1196 and 1204, he emphatically asserted the fame of the Kasagi Maitreya, well known from the founding legend, but gave no clue to the origin of the image. This question – the source and original significance of the Kasagi Maitreya in the eighth century – is the focus of this chapter.

Visual Evidence for the Kasagi Maitreya

The original appearance of the Kasagi Maitreya can be deduced from several pictorial sources of varying reliability. The *Kasagi mandara* ought to be our primary evidence, but when the painting was first made available to scholars it occasioned a controversy that lasted more than a decade.[8] The crucial point of contention was the date of the painting: Was it an accurate portrayal of the Kasagi Maitreya before its destruction in 1331, or did it represent a post-1331 reconstruction based on drawings and recollection? The latter view was taken by Adachi Ken in 1939, who argued two main points: Discrepancies between the rendering of the Buddha in the *Kasagi mandara* and earlier drawings of the image showed the painting to be inaccurate, and the gallery in front of the image did not appear to be the Worship Hall known from documentary sources. Nishimura Tei,[9] Yashiro Yukio, and Horiike Shunpō all disagreed with Adachi, and together their arguments present a convincing case that the *Kasagi mandara* accurately represents the temple and its image in approximately the middle to late thirteenth century, that is, during Sōshō's period of activity there.

The controversy over the Worship Hall need not concern us, but the visual evidence cited by Adachi and the others may be examined here. In the *Kasagi mandara* Maitreya stands on a double lotus pedestal. His left hand is raised, with thumb to index finger forming a circle in the gesture of appeasement or, alternatively, discourse (*vitarkamudrā*). His right hand extends palm out in the symbolic gesture of fulfillment (*varadamudrā*).[10] Maitreya's pose is not frontal. He does not gaze directly out from the cliff, but rather is turned slightly toward anyone who approaches him from the left along the narrow ledge of ground. His shoulders and feet indicate a slight shift in posture. His right foot is in profile; his left foot is foreshortened, turned toward the viewer. The two lotus pod bases that support the feet give a convincing representation of three dimensions. Maitreya is a fleshy, heavy-set figure, particularly wide across the hips. Folds of drapery accent his girth, circling around his stomach and his thighs. In the painting, the drawing of Maitreya overlaps the boat-shaped mandorla in two places with his robe and pedestal, confusing the spatial relationship between niche and image. The two arhats are approximately half the scale of Maitreya. That holding the incense burner echoes Maitreya's pose, whereas Mahākāśyapa is shown in profile view and as he raises up the garment hides his face, as if turning from Maitreya's radiance. The painting shows the cliff-face image painted in color and a mid-twelfth-century record states that "once the Kasagi Maitreya was painted its miracles became fewer in number."[11]

Today only the shallow niche remains, but its slight asymmetry confirms that the original image did turn toward approaching pilgrims. Furthermore, the existence of the flanking arhats can be glimpsed in the slight depressions of the rock to either side of Maitreya. The image was drawn on the boulder in engraved lines, rather than carved in relief. Although no trace of these lines survives on the badly abraded surface, another huge boulder at Kasagi retains a clear engraved image of a bodhisattva (Figure 4). The lines that define this magnificent image are less than a centimeter in depth, and the surface of the rock is in far better condition than that for Maitreya. Both boulders face a steep valley, but their differing orientations – Maitreya faces east, whereas the bodhisattva faces south – may account for the differences in their preservation.

Drawings in iconographic compendia of the twelfth and thirteenth centuries provide further depictions of the Kasagi Maitreya. The earliest is *Miroku bosatsu gazō shū* 彌勒菩薩畫像集 (Figure 5), datable to 1101.[12] The differences between this earlier drawing and the *Kasagi mandara* caused Adachi to discredit the accuracy of the latter. He noted that in the drawing the drapery folds swing across the body of Maitreya, denying rather than accenting the legs underneath, and that Maitreya stands on a single lotus flower base rather than two. The drawing differs also in the proportions of the Buddha, now taller and more slender, more than twice the scale of the arhats, and especially in the portrayal of Mahākāśyapa, who frankly gazes on Maitreya without handing him the robe. A halo circles Maitreya's head, but there is no full-body mandorla. That the original image was indeed within such a mandorla can still

Figure 4. Engraved bodhisattva at Kasagidera. Photograph by the author.

be seen at Kasagi. Two slightly later drawings, in *Shoson zuzō* 諸尊圖像 and *Shika shō zuzō* 四家抄圖像, are similar to this 1101 sketch, although the latter shows Maitreya's feet protruding on two giant lotus flowers.[13]

By contrast, the Kasagi Maitreya as seen in the early thirteenth-century *Kakuzen shō* 覺禪抄 appears in its natural setting (Figure 6).[14] He is shown surrounded by the body mandorla and by the massive boulder on which he is carved. In front along the bottom, rectangles suggest the wooden platform also seen in the *Kasagi mandara*. Strangely, however, only Mahākāśyapa is shown here, holding a bowl rather than a robe. Instead of the arhat with incense burner behind Maitreya, a much smaller scale Buddha, whose pose is the reverse of the colossus, appears on a boulder to Maitreya's right.[15] Thus although this drawing seems to be a quick sketch made at the site, there are discrepancies both with the *Kasagi mandara* and with the other drawings.[16] The *Kakuzen shō* sketch, however, does show the clinging drapery style and double lotus pedestal of the *Kasagi mandara*. All of the drawings confirm that

Figure 5. *Miroku bosatsu gazō shū,* detail of Kasagi Maitreya. Circa 1101. Ink on paper. Ninnaji, Kyoto. After *T: Zuzō-hen,* 6:50.

the image depicted the interaction between Maitreya and the arhat facing him.

Further knowledge of the appearance of the Kasagi Maitreya comes from copies in stone. The earliest and most significant is the engraved cliff-face Maitreya at Ōnodera 大野寺, near Murō Village, east of Nara (Figure 7). Engraved within a sunken mandorla-shaped niche, the Ōnodera Maitreya is 13.6 meters in height, slightly shorter than that at Kasagi. Maitreya appears alone, without the flanking arhats. The circumstances behind the Ōnodera image, unlike those concerning the Kasagi Maitreya, are known. Retired Emperor Gotoba 後鳥羽院 (1180–1239), who also donated funds to Kasagi, commissioned the work in 1207, a Kōfukuji priest took charge of the workmen, and the eye-opening ceremony was concluded on the seventh day of the third month of 1209. Gotoba, his empress, and various courtiers attended.[17] The fact that a similarly colossal rock-cut Maitreya required imperial patronage and was three years in the making suggests a like process for the Kasagi Maitreya.

Figure 6. *Kakuzen shō*. Early thirteenth century. Ink on paper. After *T: Zuzō-hen,* 5:38.

The *Kasagi mandara*, the *Kakuzen shō* drawing, and the Ōnodera cliff-face image should be taken together as the best evidence for the appearance of the Kasagi Maitreya. The cliff-face Maitreya flanked by two arhats was done in line engraving like the Ōnodera Maitreya. Maitreya's pose, hand gestures, body type, and drapery style are consistent in all three. One or both arhats are included in all but the thirteenth-century stone copies, suggesting that these copies represented a subtle shift from the iconography, and hence the meaning, of the original. From these observations an analysis of the iconography and source of the original Kasagi Maitreya may now proceed.

The Transmission of the Robe

The visual evidence shows that the Kasagi cliff-face carving represented Maitreya receiving Śākyamuni's robe from Mahākāśyapa. The details of this episode in Maitreya's career can be gleaned from several accounts. In section 44 of *Ekottarā-agama* (from which the East Asian *Sūtra on Maitreya's Descent* was copied),[18] Śākyamuni instructs four of his disciples, Mahākāśyapa,

Figure 7. Ōnodera Maitreya, detail. 1207–9. Engraved cliff face. Height 13.6 m. Outside Murō Village, Uda-gun, Nara Prefecture. Photograph by the author.

Kuṇḍopadhānīya, Piṇḍola, and Rahula, not to enter *nirvāṇa*, but instead to remain in the world until Maitreya appears. "You must wait for my Law to come to its end, then you may enter *nirvāṇa*." Śākyamuni particularly singles out Mahākāśyapa and predicts that he will go to a mountaintop (unnamed in the text) in Magadha, central India, where he will remain until Maitreya ascends the mountain with a host of disciples to find the arhat in his mountain cavern. "At that time Maitreya will extend his right hand and point out Mahākāśyapa, telling all that he was formerly a disciple of Śākyamuni." The crucial point is that Mahākāśyapa's practice of asceticism, particularly meditation, was unsurpassed. Śākyamuni further prophesies that, upon seeing Mahākāśyapa and hearing Maitreya's lectures, all listeners will become arhats themselves, as disciples of Maitreya. Although *Ekottarā-agama* states that Maitreya dons Mahākāśyapa's robe, the details of the transmission from Śākyamuni are left out.

Another description of Maitreya's encounter with Mahākāśyapa appears in *Sūtra on Maitreya Attaining Buddhahood.*[19] Maitreya with his retinue goes to Vulture Peak (Grdhrakūṭa) and climbs up to the top of Mt. Fox-spoor (Lang-chi shan 狼跡山), which rumbles from top to bottom.[20] He then presses both hands to the side of the mountain in a gesture resembling that of a *cakravartin* opening a city gate. The mountain opens to reveal Mahākāśyapa, whom Brahmā anoints with fragrant oil to awaken him from his trance. Bending down on his right knee, Mahākāśyapa hands Maitreya the robe from Śākyamuni that he has preserved, while telling Maitreya that Śākyamuni entrusted the robe to him as the latter was about to enter *nirvāṇa*. After all assembled have paid their respects to Mahākāśyapa, the arhat flies into the air, where he undergoes several transformations before he disintegrates into ashes and enters *nirvāṇa* at last.

These narrative accounts in the two Maitreya Sūtras were investigated first hand by two Chinese pilgrims to India, Fa-hsien 法顯 and Hsüan-tsang 玄奘 (602–64). Fa-hsien set out for India in the year 399 A.D. to seek rules and regulations of the Vinaya. His travels brought him to Cock's-foot Mountain (Kukkutapādagiri, Chi-tsu shan 鷄足山) in the country of Magadha:

> From this place going south three li, we arrive at a mountain called the Cock's-foot. The great Mahākāśyapa is at present within this mountain. He divided the mountain at its base, so as to open a passage (*for himself*). This entrance is now closed up (*impassable*). At a considerable distance from this spot there is a side chasm; it is in this the entire body of Mahākāśyapa is now preserved.[21]

Fa-hsien's record continues with a description of the mountain as a place where healing or an encounter with an arhat might occur. Although he claims to have seen Mahākāśyapa, Fa-hsien makes no mention either of the arhat's wait for Maitreya or of Śākyamuni's robe.

Hsüan-tsang visited Cock's-foot Mountain in 637. Although he did not actually see Mahākāśyapa, his eyewitness account of the terrain and of the legend of Mahākāśyapa is more detailed and knowledgeable than Fa-hsien's:

> To the east of Mahī river we enter a great wild forest, and going 100 li or so, we come to Kukkuṭapādagiri, the Cock's-foot Mountain. It is also called Gurupādāhgiri, the "Mountain of the Venerable Master." The sides of this mountain are high and rugged, the valleys and gorges are impenetrable. Tumultuous torrents rush down its sides, thick forests envelop the valleys, whilst tangled shrubs grow along its cavernous heights. Soaring upwards into the air are three sharp peaks; their tops are surrounded by the vapours of heaven, and their

> shapes lost in the clouds. Behind the hills the venerable Mahā-Kāśyapa dwells wrapped in a condition of Nirvāna.[22]

Hsüan-tsang continues his account with Śākyamuni's instructions to Mahākāśyapa and the transmission of the robe. For twenty years Mahākāśyapa preserved the "true law,"

> . . . and then, in disgust at the impermanence of the world, and desiring to die, he went towards Cock's-foot Mountain. Ascending the north side of the mountain, he proceeded along the winding path, and came to the south-west ridge. Here the crags and precipices prevented him going on. Forcing his way through the tangled brushwood, he struck the rock with his staff and thus opened a way. He then passed on, having divided the rock, and ascended till he was again stopped by the rocks interlacing one another. He again opened a passage through, and came out on the mountain peak on the north-east side. Then having emerged from the defiles, he proceeded to the middle point of the three peaks. There he took the *Kashāya* garment of Buddha and as he stood he expressed an ardent vow. On this the three peaks covered him over; this is the reason why now these three rise up into the air.[23]

The passage ends by paraphrasing the *Sūtra on Maitreya Attaining Buddhahood* and closes with the observation that now nothing is to be observed on the mountain.

The accounts of Fa-hsien and Hsüan-tsang inspired others, who did not actually go to India, to record the story. The Chinese Vinaya patriarch Tao-hsüan 道宣 (596–667) wrote in 664:

> Mahākāśyapa is now sitting inside a cliff west of Vulture Peak. He has entered cessation *samādhi*. When 5,670,000,000 years have passed, Maitreya Buddha will descend. [Mahākāśyapa] will hand him the great robe given by Śākyamuni and then will achieve *nirvāṇa*.[24]

Tao-hsüan identifies the mountain where Mahāyāśyapa dwells as near Vulture Peak, his description agreeing with that of Hsüan-tsang. A contemporary both of Hsüan-tsang and Tao-hsüan, Tao-shih 道世, wrote in his famous miscellany *Fa yüan chu lin* 法苑珠林 (compiled in 668) an account based on Hsüan-tsang's record and states that the latter visited the site accompanied by some three thousand people, who climbed the mountain with him. Elsewhere, Tao-shih also says that it is on Vulture Peak that Mahākāśyapa entered *samādhi*.[25]

In all of these accounts the fascination centers upon Mahākāśyapa encased within the rocky peak waiting for Maitreya. If we eliminate hyperbole, Hsüan-tsang's description of the heavily forested, boulder-strewn peak of Cock's-foot Mountain so resembles the rugged terrain atop Mt. Kasagi that the locale seems to have been chosen specifically with Mt. Cock's-foot in mind.[26] The second arhat seen at Kasagi does not appear in any account of Maitreya's encounter with Mahākāśyapa. Although various identifications have been suggested, he may represent an unnamed member of Maitreya's entourage, included to show proper veneration for Mahākāśyapa's feat.[27] The Maitreya Sūtras and these Chinese texts that elaborate on Mahākāśyapa's vigil were known and copied in Japan during the first half of the eighth century.[28] All were copied out by Sōshō in *Miroku nyorai kan'ō shō* as he sat in front of the Kasagi Maitreya in the mid–thirteenth century.[29] For him, at least, the narrative behind the Kasagi Maitreya was clearly the encounter with Mahākāśyapa.

Source

The founding legend of Kasagidera records that the colossus was carved during Emperor Tenchi's reign (668–71). Yet the characteristic Maitreya of seventh-century Japan was a meditating prince in pensive attitude, well represented by the small gilt bronze Maitreya at Yachūji, datable to 666.[30] No examples of a standing Maitreya as Buddha are known from Emperor Tenchi's era, or the seventh century in general. During the first half of the eighth century, large-scale Buddhist imagery in painting and sculpture consisted primarily of ensembles: a central Buddha flanked by attendant bodhisattvas, disciples, and various guardian figures. Such groupings depicted preaching or "Pure Land" (Jōdo 浄土) scenes, whether of Śākyamuni, Amitābha, Maitreya, or Bhaiṣajyaguru.[31] The wall paintings formerly in the Hōryūji Golden (Main) Hall included representations of all four Buddhas: Maitreya paired with Bhaiṣajyaguru on the north wall, Śākyamuni on the east, and Amitābha on the west. (The worshipper enters the hall from the south, so there is no scene there.)[32] All of the major capital temples, built in the first half of the eighth century, had halls dedicated to such preaching assemblies.[33] The major exception to this plan was the colossal bronze Vairocana at Tōdaiji, inaugurated in 743 by Emperor Shōmu 聖武 (701–56, r. 724–9).[34]

A major reorientation in eighth-century Buddhist art occurred in the 750s and 760s, due partially to the depletion of national energy and resources by the Vairocana project. In 753, the arrival of the eminent Chinese master of Vinaya Chien-chen 鑒真 (Japanese name, Ganjin, 688–763) and more than forty followers altered the direction of Buddhist art and thought within a few decades.[35] The sculptures in the Golden Hall at Tōshōdaiji 唐招提寺, founded in 759 as a center of Vinaya study, are remarkably different from those at other Nara temples. The central seated image of Vairocana (Rushana 盧舎那) is flanked by a standing Sahasrabhuja Avalokiteśvara (Senjū Kannon 千手觀音) and by a standing "Healing" Buddha, Bhaiṣajyaguru (Yakushi 藥師); the three sculptures are equally large in scale.[36] The altar is narrow and as an ensemble the grouping has none of the depth or narrative detail found in ensembles representing preaching scenes. Among the myriad items brought to Japan by Chien-chen in 754 were sculptures of Sahasrabhuja Avalokiteśvara, Maitreya, Bhaiṣajyaguru, and Amitābha, any of which could have served as up-to-date models for the Tōshōdaiji sculptures.

It is the standing image of Bhaiṣajyaguru at Tōshōdaiji that immediately invites comparison with the Kasagi Maitreya (Figure 8). The image is 369.7 centimeters in height and can date no earlier than 796, since a coin minted in that year was found inside the palm of its left hand. The statue's hand gestures are the same as, but exactly opposite to, those of the Kasagi Maitreya. The lowered left hand could not, however, have held the medicine bowl common in representations of the Healing Buddha. The image looks down slightly but exhibits no shift in posture, no sense of movement to either side or toward the viewer. Two other standing Buddha images are now kept in the Treasure House at Tōshōdaiji; both are entirely of wood, less than half the size of the Golden Hall image. These Buddhas are fleshier and more fully rounded in their bodily forms. Thus at Tōshōdaiji there are three standing Buddha images that show a change from the preaching seated Buddha type common in the early eighth-century ensembles to a standing Buddha as devotional image.

These shifts in pose, style, and iconography seen at Tōshōdaiji may thus be directly attributed to fresh impulses from mid-eighth-century China. Furthermore, the Tōshōdaiji images show that the Kasagi Maitreya is indeed of like inspiration. Yet a drawing or painting, rather than a sculpture, must have provided the details of movement and the slightly three-quarter pose of the Kasagi Maitreya and two arhats. Given the narrative content of the representation of the Kasagi Maitreya and two arhats, we might expect that its iconography and style stem ultimately from a narrative rather than strictly devotional prototype.

In addition to the sculptures, Chien-chen also brought paintings depicting the pure lands of Maitreya, Bhaiṣajyaguru, and Amitābha. He offered the Amitābha Pure Land painting to the court in 754, whereas that for Bhaiṣajyaguru was eventually hung in the refectory at Tōshōdaiji. Although the paintings are lost, a huge tattered embroidery of Amitābha in his Western Paradise, the so-called *Taima mandara* 當麻曼荼羅, provides evidence in Japan for the general appearance of those paintings.[37] An elaborate architectural setting with Amitābha at the center is bordered by narrative scenes that include depictions of his descent (*raigo* 來迎). These are the earliest representations of Amitābha's descent in Japan, a subject that did not become a major artistic

Figure 8. Bhaiṣajyaguru. Ca. 796. Gilt, wood-core dry lacquer. Height, 369.7 cm. Tōshōdaiji, Nara. Photograph courtesy of Sakamoto Research Lab.

theme until the late tenth to eleventh centuries. It was the Kasagi Maitreya's similarity to a descending Amitābha that first led to the confusion in identification of the *Kasagi mandara*.[38] The Taimadera Western Paradise embroidery is the only surviving example of such large-scale paradise scenes from eighth-century Japan. Many more are known to have existed.[39]

Evidence from desert cave-chapel sites in northwestern China confirms that similar paradise scenes with flanking narratives illustrated the Maitreya Sūtras. Several late seventh- to tenth-century caves at Tun-huang include Maitreya assemblies painted on either the north or south walls, opposite those for other Buddhas, usually Amitābha.[40] In an early T'ang seventh-century example in cave 329, Maitreya sits with legs pendent in the center of a vast architectural panorama surrounded by a host of attendant deities.[41] In eighth-century examples, the central assembly is augmented with narrative scenes squeezed in around the edges and upper right and left corners of the composition. In the upper left corner of the north wall of cave 445 a meditating arhat is barely visible in the blackened recesses behind a sculpted bodhisattva (Figure 9). Just below to the right, however, we find the standing figure of Maitreya surrounded by two bodhisattvas and one adoring monk (or arhat) pointing up to the meditating arhat. Cave 447 repeats Maitreya and his retinue but not the meditating arhat, showing that there was some range in illustrating the narrative of Maitreya's climb up Mt. Cock's-foot to reveal the meditating Mahākāśyapa.[42]

The moment of transmitting the robe is clearly seen in a narrative detail from a similar paradise scene at the nearby Yü-lin 楡林 cave site. Langdon Warner published photographs of Yü-lin cave 25 (Stein cave 5) in 1938.[43] In the upper left, tall peaks shelter an arhat in a cave (Figure 10). Just below and across a stream the same arhat kneels with robe in hand, facing the standing Maitreya, who extends his right hand forward to receive it. The subject, although not the exact pose, is unmistakably the same as the Kasagi Maitreya – Mahākāśyapa hands Maitreya Śākyamuni's robe. Watching the two figures from behind is a group of bodhisattvas and lay figures.

Yü-lin cave 25 predates graffiti written on the walls of the cave in 901. Given the comparable eighth-century scenes at Tun-huang, its actual date may be several decades, if not a century, earlier. Records of wall painting in Ch'ang-an 長安 temples also attest that Maitreya assemblies graced the walls of several temples in the capital city.[44] The conclusion to be drawn from this revealing Chinese evidence is that the representation of Maitreya receiving the robe from Mahākāśyapa was but one episode in a more comprehensive pictorial narrative depicting Maitreya's descent. The source of the Kasagi Maitreya's pose and iconography thus may have been a painting, embroidery, or drawing of Maitreya preaching, surrounded by a narrative cycle inspired by either of the Chinese Maitreya texts, *Sūtra on Maitreya's Descent* or *Sūtra on Maitreya Attaining Buddhahood.*

The Kasagi Maitreya in the Late Eighth Century

The idea of carving a colossal representation of Maitreya's encounter with Mahākāśyapa on a mountaintop was certainly novel for eighth-century Japan. Mt. Kasagi, with its forbidding outcroppings of granite and steep precipices, seems at first an unlikely place for any major construction. In his

Figure 9. Detail from Maitreya Paradise, cave 445. Eighth Century. Tunhuang. After *Chūgoku sekkutsu,* 3:175. Reprinted with permission of Heibonsha, Tokyo.

discussion of the *Kasagi mandara*, Horiike Shunpō addresses the question of the strategic location of Kasagi vis-à-vis the Nara capital. As can be seen in Figure 11, Mt. Kasagi overlooks the Kizu River, which descends from the Iga River in Iga Province. Tōdaiji lands in that province supplied the capital city with lumber, which was transported downriver, past Mt. Kasagi.[45] *Kasagidera engi* records the legend that Emperor Shōmu ordered Priest Rōben 良辨 (689–773), superintendant of Tōdaiji, to go to Kasagi to see that lumber for the Great Buddha Hall negotiated the rapids safely. In a cave (Figure 12) at Kasagi, Rōben performed secret rites that called forth a thunder deity to split the rocks and a dragon king to clear them away with torrential rains.[46] Horiike cites this legend to suggest that stoneworkers may have been employed near Kasagi to remove any obstructing boulders, and he thus attributes the Kasagi Maitreya to the personal beliefs of those anonymous

Figure 10. Detail from Maitreya Paradise, cave 25. Ninth to tenth centuries. Yü-lin. After Langdon Warner, *Buddhist Wall-paintings: A Study of a Ninth-century Grotto at Wan Fo Hsia* (Cambridge, Mass., 1938), plate 38. Reprinted by permission of Harvard University Press.

stoneworkers, a conclusion that does not, however, account for the visual and iconographical evidence.

Kasagidera engi links the temple to Tōdaiji in another legend, that concerning Rōben's chief assistant, Jitchū 實忠 (active 760–815). The legend says that in 751 Jitchū entered the same cave where Rōben had meditated and passed through in a northerly direction to the Inner Court of Tuṣita Heaven. There he witnessed ceremonies to Ekādasamukha Avalokiteśvara (Jūichimen Kannon 十一面觀音), which he then instituted at Kasagi and later at Tōdaiji.[47] Research on the subject of these rites at Tōdaiji shows that not only is this tale a fabrication, but the ceremonies at Tōdaiji began as late as the 770s.[48] In spite of the difficulty of accepting these two accounts from *Kasagidera engi* as fact, most writers on the Kasagi Maitreya speculate that one or both of the Tōdaiji monks were somehow responsible for the carving of the image. Yet records of Jitchū's

Figure 11. View of Kizu River from Mt. Kasagi. Photograph by the author.

activities do not confirm that he ever visited Kasagidera, although he did personally supervise the collection and transport of lumber for later Tōdaiji projects.[49]

In 767 Rōben and Jitchū commissioned a group of stone carvers to erect an earthen stūpa near Shinyakushiji 新藥師寺, south of Tōdaiji.[50] Fifteen out of an original thirty-six carved stones from this monument survive, making it our best datable evidence for stone carving in the late eighth century in the capital region (Figure 13). The technique of carving in shallow relief, the small scale of the stones (about one meter in height), and the subject matter, single Buddha images, triads, and preaching ensembles, are considerably different from the Kasagi Maitreya. According to an eighth-century record, this stūpa was constructed ostensibly "to offer to the nation."[51]

The decade of the 760s was one of increasing tension between the political and religious establishments. In 763 the former Empress Kōken 孝謙 (718–70) became a nun and two years later reascended the throne assisted by her trusted healer Dōkyō 道鏡 (?–771), who received rapid promotions in the sangha and in the political arena. Famine, political intrigue, and armed

Figure 12. The Senjū Cave on Mt. Kasagi. Photograph by the author.

rebellion broke out during the next few years. Work slowed at Tōdaiji in favor of moves by the empress to garner support for other temples and to build her own establishment, Saidaiji. By 766 Dōkyō had received the unprecedented title of "Dharma-king" (Hō-ō 法王) and was on the brink of being proclaimed emperor. Given the extremely volatile political situation at that time, we may speculate that the Shinyakushiji stūpa was secretly built by Rōben and Jitchū in the hope that the impending disaster could be averted and order restored to the sangha.[52]

The association between Tōdaiji and Kasagidera does not appear only in the legends of *Kasagidera engi*. As told in *Konjaku monogatari shū* the founding legend states:

> After the image of Maitreya appeared at this temple time passed. A man called Priest Rōben came to see it. People say that ceremonies were carried out there from his time on. Later many halls and

Figure 13. Buddha triad no. 7, located on the east side, at the center of the first level of the Zutō earthen stūpa. 747. Carved granite, 111.0 cm × 117.0 cm. Higashiōji-chō, Nara. Photograph by the author.

> residences were built, and it is said that many monks live there, practicing their austerities.[53]

A twelfth-century compilation of Tōdaiji records, *Tōdaiji yōroku*, mentions Kasagidera second in its list of branch temples after Shinyakushiji: "This temple was founded by the thirteenth prince of Emperor Tenchi (see the founding legend)."[54] This statement implies that an early version of *Kasagidera engi* was already known at Tōdaiji. Nowhere else in all of *Tōdaiji yōroku* is Kasagi mentioned. Yet elsewhere there is one tantalizing passage about Rōben: "It is said that Priest Rōben is an incarnation of Maitreya Bodhisattva."[55] Although this seems to be an unusual claim for a figure who spent his life devoted to Avatamsaka (Kegon 華嚴) teachings and the construction of the colossal Vairocana image, perhaps it is a veiled reference to Rōben's involvement in the planning or carving of the Kasagi Maitreya.

It may not be possible to elaborate on the association between Tōdaiji and Kasagidera or to state with certainty that Rōben or Jitchū had the image carved; nonetheless, the iconography, source, medium, and location of the Kasagi Maitreya all point to unusual circumstances behind its creation. The iconography itself suggests that the audience for the scene of Maitreya receiving the robe from Mahākāśyapa might have been the sangha rather than an emperor or lay patrons. Whereas the eighth-century emperors concentrated their energies and resources on grandiose schemes for building and outfitting capital temples, the newly arrived Chien-chen and his followers preached adherence to the Buddhist precepts and self-cultivation at several of those temples. With the obvious deterioration of the sangha and the unorthodox rise to power of Dōkyō, an atmosphere of protest could have manifested in the unofficial carving of Maitreya at Kasagi as well as in the Shinyakushiji stūpa.

Why carve Maitreya, and why depict the particular moment of transmitting the robe? Perhaps the answer lies in a broader trend of attempting to link Japan more closely to India as the source of Buddhism. It was an emigré Indian, Bodhisena (ca. 702–60), who was chosen to lead the dedication ceremonies for the Tōdaiji Vairocana in 752.[56] In the following year, a stone was carved with a representation of the Buddha's footprints based on a design transmitted from India to China and later to Japan (Figure 14).[57] This stone, now housed at Yakushiji, bears inscriptions that refer to records of Śākyamuni's footprints in rocks in India.[58] Kept with the footprint stone in Yakushiji is an eighth-century stele inscribed with a sequence of poems composed in praise of the Buddha's footprints.[59] The poems are remarkably clear about the footprints as a tangible link to past and future.

> As we behold them, let us praise
> the footprints trod in by
> the master
> going on ahead to leave us,
> until we meet directly:
> until we meet face to face. (No. 6)

> Copying onto rock
> and worshipping
> Śākya[muni]'s holy footprints
> I would reverently bequeath them
> to the Buddha yet to come:
> I would humbly offer them up![60] (No. 9)

Drawings of the Buddha's footprints had been brought to Japan as early as the late seventh century, but they seem not to have gained much recognition until the mid–eighth century.[61] This particular stone was carved at the request of a member of the imperial family, Prince Chinu 智努 (693–770), who became an active patron of Chien-chen and Tōshōdaiji. He or his descendants may have given the stone to Tōshōdaiji.[62]

This yearning for connections to Śākyamuni in the past and Maitreya in the future intensified in Japan with the arrival of Chien-chen. In addition to the aforementioned sculptures and paintings, Chien-chen brought with him a number of items of Indian origin: three thousand relics of Śākyamuni, a lapus

Figure 14. Stone with engraving of the Buddha's footprints. 753.69 cm × 108 cm. Yakushiji Nara. Photograph Courtesy Sakamoto Research Lab.

lazuli jar, two pairs of grass sandals, and earth from the Jetavana monastery. The Indian earth was sprinkled on the Tōdaiji ordination platform and Tōshōdaiji itself was founded on the model of the Kukkutarama monastery.[63] Chien-chen also brought Hsüan-tsang's record, and his disciples saw their master's ordeal in coming to Japan as the eastern counterpart to Hsüan-tsang's western journey.[64] For the first proper ordination ceremony in Japan, held in 754 in front of the colossal Tōdaiji Vairocana, Chien-chen's follower Fa-chin 法進 (709–78) wrote:

> All of us are disciples of the Law left behind by Śākyamuni . . . for many ages we will not meet with Maitreya. If we do not desire escape [from the cycle of births and deaths] in this life, I fear we will revert to floating on the waves.[65]

Thus not only was Chien-chen's mission dedicated to establishing proper ordination and study of the rules, he also intended that Japan take its place in the continuum from Śākyamuni to Maitreya.[66] Traveling with Chien-chen to

Japan may have been the Chinese stonecutters with the expertise needed to carve the Kasagi Maitreya.

The circumstances surrounding Chien-chen's death and the creation of his portrait sculpture have prompted a number of scholars to suggest that the statue was a substitute for a "real-body image" (*chen-shen hsiang* 真身像). Chien-chen and his followers surely knew of several famous monks in China whose bodies remained intact upon their deaths.[67] In other words, it was hoped that Chien-chen's body would not decay upon death, but would be preserved intact. If such was his (or more likely his followers') wish, the primary reason would have been to demonstrate to others the sanctity achieved by Chien-chen and the strength of his adherence to the Buddhist precepts. Had his body indeed survived, Chien-chen might have been thought to have entered *samādhi*, in preparation for Maitreya's descent.

During his travels in India, Hsüan-tsang recorded several instances of entranced arhats; one in particular addresses the crucial question of *how* to wait for Maitreya on earth. In the country of Dhānakataka (Andhra), Hsüan-tsang heard the legend of the master Bhāvaviveka, who wondered:

> "In the absence of Maitreya as a Buddha, who is there that can satisfy my doubts?" Then in front of the figure of the Bôdhisattva Kwan-tsz'-tsai [Avalokiteśvara] he recited in order the Hridaya-dhāranī, abstaining from food and drink. After three years Kwan-tsz'-tsai Bôdhisattva appeared to him with a very beautiful body, and addressed the master thus: "What is your purpose?" He said, "May I keep my body till Maitreya comes." Kwan-tsz'-tsai Bôdhisattva said, "Man's life is subject to many accidents. The world is as a bubble or a phantom. You should aim at the highest resolve to be born in the Tuṣita Heaven, and there, even now, to see Him face to face and worship."[68]

In spite of the bodhisattva's advice, the master continued to press his desire. At last the bodhisattva directed him to a mountain cavern where Vajrapāni dwelled. There the master recited *dhāranī* to Vajrapāni, and eventually he entered into the rocks of a mountain cavern, which closed around him. Hsüan-tsang's account of this legend of a learned ascetic reciting *dhāranī* in the mountains so that he might be allowed to wait there for Maitreya's descent provides an obvious model for others to follow. Retreat to the mountains, adherence to the Buddhist precepts, recitation of *dhāranī* are activities that would seem to facilitate the wait.

This legend predates such practices in Japan by a century. In reaction to the deteriorating political and religious climate of the post–Great Buddha era, monks fled the capital and the highly politicized atmosphere of the sangha in great numbers. They built hermitages throughout the mountains, and many of these retreats later became temples whose origins are as mysterious as that of the Kasagi Maitreya.[69] The practice of austerities in the mountains was officially prohibited from 764 to 770, but that ban was lifted in 770. By that time, mountain Buddhism was actively encouraged and a new era of Buddhist practice was underway.[70]

The founders of Tendai and Shingon sects in the early ninth century, Saichō 最澄 (767–822) and Kūkai 空海 (774–832), considered retreat to the mountains essential to their practice of Buddhism. No wonder that both mention waiting for Maitreya in their writings. Saichō moved to Mt. Hiei 比叡山 after his ordination at Tōdaiji and lived there in a grass hermitage. A letter from Saichō to a follower relates:

> Between the one vehicle of the Lotus Sūtra and the one vehicle of the Shingon, which is superior? People who follow the same teacher and have the same sentiments are considered good friends. You and I both made connections with [the Buddha] in this life, and we are both waiting to see Maitreya.[71]

Elsewhere Saichō expresses the wish that he will meet Maitreya soon and vows to uphold the precepts until then.[72]

Kūkai's earliest writings and practice also show the strong expectation that he would meet Maitreya. In his 797 *Indications of the Goals of the Three Teachings* (*Sangō shiki* 三教指歸), Kūkai defends the teachings of Buddhism through the words of a mendicant monk like himself:

> Therefore, the compassionate Buddha, on his last day on earth, instructed Maitreya, the virtuous Mañjuśrī and others, saying that Maitreya would be the Buddha of the future, and that other disciples should assist him and devote themselves to the salvation of sentient beings. Thereupon, the Bodhisattva Mañjuśrī, the great Mahākāśyapa and the others sent a message to all countries declaring that Maitreya would assume the throne of the kingdom of the true teachings. When I heard this message, I made all necessary preparations and started out at once for the Tuṣita Heaven where Maitreya resides. But the path is far from human habitations and is filled with difficulties; there are many crossroads and the way is not well defined.[73]

Before Kūkai wrote this, he too had wandered through the mountains in the footsteps of other ascetics.[74] "According to the meditation sūtras, meditation should be practiced on a flat area deep in the mountains."[75] Kūkai at last settled upon Mt. Kōya 高野山, which he saw as the Matrix Realm (Garbhadhātu).

> [Maitreya] lives in his place of honor in the Matrix Realm and assists Mahāvairocana in his acts of virtue. Residing in the Tuṣita heaven, he

> makes Śākyamuni's teachings flourish. Maitreya has already attained enlightenment but for now he [waits to succeed Śākyamuni] in the eastern palace.[76]

After Kūkai's death, he and Mt. Kōya became inextricably linked, for Mt. Kōya was perceived as the place where Maitreya would descend on earth.[77] Although Kūkai is said to have declared upon his deathbed that he would be reborn in Tuṣita Heaven, that legend owes its popularization to Kūkai's followers. By the tenth century, it was believed that Kūkai had entered *samādhi* (*nyūjō* 入定) and that his body could be found in a cave on the mountain. According to a twelfth-century legend, Abbot Kangen 觀賢 (852–925) visited Mt. Kōya and entered the cave; there he saw that Kūkai's hair had grown a foot, but his clothing had decayed. Kangen reverently shaved Kūkai, dressed him in clean clothing, and restrung the beads of the rosary he held in his hand.[78] The legend of Kūkai in *samādhi* waiting for Maitreya to descend to Mt. Kōya seems to be an assimilation of the legends of Mahākāśyapa's wait on Cock's-foot Mountain and Bhāvaviveka's desire to preserve his body for Maitreya. Thus it was a Japanese monk, rather than the Chinese Chien-chen, who came to symbolize Mahākāśyapa's wait in Japan.

The Kasagi Maitreya, which Kūkai might have known, certainly predates the legend of Kūkai in *samādhi* on Mt. Kōya.[79] Had the capital not been moved to the site of modern-day Kyoto and had the court not shifted its support to Kūkai and Saichō and their newly imported esoteric practices and methods of ordination, the Kasagi Maitreya might not have remained unnoticed. Whereas the precipitous terrain of Mt. Kasagi prevented any sizable temple from being constructed there, Mt. Kōya was an ideal spot for the monastic establishment that Kūkai founded. After the Kūkai legend spread, hundreds of pilgrims climbed Mt. Kōya to worship the cave or be buried near there, so that they would accompany Kūkai when he met Maitreya.[80] The Kasagi Maitreya would become famous in the capital only when the growing conviction that the world had entered the Final Age of the Law, Saddharma-vipralopa (*mappō* 末法), spurred on pilgrimages to sites associated with Maitreya.[81] Even during its most prosperous era, the thirteenth century, the principal audience for the Kasagi Maitreya was the Buddhist clergy, who were concerned about maintaining strict adherence to the precepts and carrying out meditative practices in order to meet Maitreya. For most of its history, however, the Kasagi Maitreya was known only to wandering ascetics who practiced their austerities among the caves and boulders of Mt. Kasagi, much in the manner of the arhats who lived among the mountains surrounding Vulture Peak.[82]

Appendix: "An Account of the Founding of Kasagi Temple by a Son of Emperor Tenchi"

Now it was a long time ago that during the reign of Emperor Tenchi, there was a prince. He was wise of mind, talented, and loved exceedingly the "way of letters." Yet hunting was his passion, and he made it his profession to kill pigs and deer day and night. He always carried his bow and arrow, and together with a cadre of hunters he would spread out through hills and valleys to capture wild animals.

Once he went hunting along the eastern slopes of Kamo Village in the Sagara District of Yamashiro no kuni. The prince urged his horse to follow a deer up the slopes of the mountain. When the deer headed off to the east, he followed in the deer's tracks, but when he drew his bow, the deer suddenly disappeared. "Perhaps he has fallen over the cliff!" he thought, so he threw down his bow and pulled out a rope, but the horse had gone on unaware. The deer had indeed fallen from a high cliff. The horse, in advancing so swiftly, was about to fall after the deer. His four feet pranced about on a small jutting precipice. There was no place for the horse to turn around in and even if the prince dismounted there was nothing but a deep valley below, with no room for his feet. If the horse moved an inch they would plunge downward. Looking below, he saw it was more than a hundred-foot drop. He couldn't even see the bottom, nor did he know what lay east or west. His spirit left him as his heart pounded wildly, and he knew that now he and the horse would surely die together. Then the prince cried out a vow, "If you are here, oh gods of the mountain, save me! If you do I'll carve an image of Maitreya on this cliff!" Then signs appeared allowing the horse to back out slowly to a wider area.

Then the prince dismounted and prostrated himself in tears. So that he might find the place again he placed his grass hat there before turning home. A day or two later he returned, searching for his hat. Descending from the mountain peak he circled down to the base of the cliff. Looking up he couldn't even see the top which seemed hidden in the clouds. The prince grieved, knowing he had not the power to carve a Maitreya image on such a sheer cliff face. Then a celestial being took pity on him, and carved the Buddha for him. Clouds descended to make it dark as night. Even in darkness, he could hear the patter of little stones flying to the earth. In just a short time the clouds dispersed and it became light once again.

Then the prince looked up at the cliff to see that an image of Maitreya had been freshly carved. Looking at it, the prince worshipped it in tears. Then he returned home.

From this time onward the place was called Kasagi Temple. Since he had placed his hat there as a marker (*kasa o shirushi ni oki* 笠をしるしに置き) it ought to be called "the hat rack" (*kasa oki* 笠置き) though that was simplified to Kasagi.

Surely, in these latter days of the world this is a rare kind of Buddha. People should sincerely worship it. Even those who barely move their feet or bow their heads must trust that they will be born in the Inner Court of Tuṣita Paradise, and there plant the seed that will meet with Maitreya Bodhisattva when he appears.

After the image of Maitreya appeared at this temple time passed. A man called Priest Rōben came to see it. People say that ceremonies were carried out there from his time on. Later many halls and residences were built, and it is said that many monks live there, practicing their austerities.

NOTES

1 Known as the Genkō 元弘 incident. Emperor Godaigo (1288–1399) took refuge at Kasagi after his plot against the Kamakura military government was discovered. The battle of Kasagi is recounted in detail in Helen C. McCullough, trans., *Taiheiki* (New York: Columbia University Press, 1959), 66–92. The author climbed Mt. Kasagi in late October 1984.

2 Painted in ink and colors on a panel of silk, 75.5 cm high by 54.8 cm wide. Formerly in the Hara Collection, Yokohama, the painting was misidentified in the nineteenth century as depicting the thirteen-story pagoda on Mt. Tonomine 多武峰 and its main image of Amitābha. When it was designated an "important cultural property" (*jūyō bunkazai* 重要文化財) in 1936, the subject was identified as the Kasagi Maitreya; see Monbushō 文部省, *Nihon kokuhō zenshū* 日本國寶全集 (Tokyo: Nihon kokuhō zenshū kangyōkai, 1938), pt 83, no. 1641. In Japan, the misleading appellation *mandara* (mandala) is given by convention to paintings of temple and shrine precincts. Several articles debating the date of the painting followed the work's recognition (see note 8).

3 *Kasagidera engi* 笠置寺縁記, in *Dainihon Bukkyō zensho* 大日本佛教全書 (Tokyo: Suzuki Research Foundation, 1970–3), 83: 325–35.

4 Yamada Yoshio et al., eds., *Konjaku monogatari shū* 今昔物語集, Nihon koten bungaku taikei, vols. 22–6 (1959–63; rpt. Tokyo: Iwanami shoten, 1971–6), 24: 114–16. A translation of this legend is presented in the Appendix.

5 See notes 8 and 9.

6 Hiraoka Jōkai, "Nihon Miroku jōdo shisō tenkai shi no kenkyū" 日本彌勒浄土思想展開史の研究, in *Tōdaiji Sōshō shōnin no kenkyū narabini shiryō* 東大寺宗性上人の研究並に史料 (Tokyo: Nihon gakujutsu shinkōkai, 1958–60), 3: 417–752. See also Hayami Tasuku 速水侑, *Miroku shinkō – mō hitotsu no Jōdo shinkō* 彌勒信仰 – もう一の浄土信仰 Nihonjin no gyōdō to shisō, no. 12. (1971; rpt. Tokyo: Hyōronsha, 1980); and Tsuruoka Shizuo 鶴岡静夫, "Kodai ni okeru Miroku shinkō" 古代に於ける彌勒信仰, in *Nihon kodai Bukkyōshi no kenkyū* 日本古代仏教史の研究 (Tokyo: Bunkadō, 1962), 293–342. For a summary in English of the work of these Japanese scholars, see Janet Ruth

Durstine Goodwin, "The Worship of Miroku in Japan" (Ph.D. diss., University of California, Berkeley, 1977).

7 Also published by Hiraoka, *Tōdaiji Sōshō*, 3: 201–416.

8 The articles on the *Kasagi mandara* and its relationship to the carved image are the following: Iwa Shūsō 岩周巣, "Kasagidera sekibutsu kozu ni tsuite" 笠置寺石佛古図について, *Shiseki to bijutsu* 8, no. 3 (1937): 8–17; Adachi Ken 足立康, "Kasagidera Mirokuzō to Kasagi mandara" 笠置寺彌勒像と笠置曼荼羅, *Nihon chōkoku shi no kenkyū* 日本彫刻史の研究 (Tokyo: Ryūginsha, 1941); Yashiro Yukio 矢代幸雄, "Tanbishō" 歎美抄, *Yamato bunka* 2 (1951): 27–51; Horiike Shunpō 堀池春峰, "Kasagi mandara shiken" 笠置曼荼羅私見, *Yamato bunka* 8 (1952): 47–53; and "Kasagi to Kasagi mandara ni tsuite no ichi shikiron" 笠置と笠置曼荼羅についての一試論, *Ars Buddhica* 18 (1953): 55–65.

9 Nishimura Tei 西村貞, *Nara no sekibutsu* 奈良の石佛 (Osaka: Zenkoku shobō, 1943), 361–76.

10 E. Dale Saunders, *Mudrā: A Study of Symbolic Gestures in Japanese Buddhist Sculpture* (New York: Pantheon, 1960), 51–75.

11 Adachi, "Kasagidera Mirokuzō," 426, quoting *Honchō seiki*.

12 One scroll, at Ninnaji, Kyoto, reprinted in *T: Zuzō hen*, 6: 50. Another, less reliable copy belongs to the Daitōkyū kinen bunko in Tokyo.

13 *Shoson zuzō* was compiled by Shinkaku 心覺 (1117–80) in the mid–twelfth century. A copy in Tōji is reproduced in *T: Zuzō hen* 3: 710. The early-thirteenth-century *Shika shō zuzō* is reproduced in *T: Zuzō hen*, 3: 837.

14 Compiled by Kakuzen (1143 to after 1213), between 1176 and 1213. *T: Zuzō hen*, 5: 38.

15 This second Buddha may correspond to a boulder labeled "Yakushiseki" in that location at Kasagidera. The same boulder is visible behind the pagoda in the *Kasagi mandara*.

16 Kakuzen appends a note in his *Kakuzen shō* addressing this descrepancy: "It is said that on the right is a monk holding a robe, and on the left a monk worships with an incense burner."

17 Nishimura, *Nara no sekibutsu*, 205–19; and Kuno Takeshi 久野健, *Sekibutsu* 石仏, Book of Books, vol. 36 (Tokyo: Shogakkan, 1975), 112–14. A small-scale copy dated 1274 is carved on a boulder near Gansenji, northeast of Nara. Its inscription relates that the carver, Sueyuki 末行, made the image so that his father would attain rebirth in Tuṣita Heaven. Nishimura, *Nara no sekibutsu*, 359–60; Kuno, *Sekibutsu*, 194.

18 *Tseng-i a-han-ching* 增一阿含經, T 2. 789a, and *Mi-lo hsia-sheng ching* 彌勒下生經, T 14. 422b–c.

19 *Mi-lo ch'eng-fo ching* 彌勒成佛經, T 14. 433bc–434a. Editor's note: In addition to these two scriptural sources, one of the other Chinese Maitreya Sūtras (T 454) reports Maitreya's meeting with Kāśyapa, though there is no mention of the robe in that version. A meeting between Kāśyapa and Maitreya is also mentioned in two other important sources having no exact parallel Chinese translation, the Sanskrit *Maitreyāvadāna* and the Khotanese **Maitreyasamiti*, though again without the robe detail in both cases.

20 Editor's note: The Chinese Lang-chi shan 狼跡山 at T 14. 433b13 apparently reflects a reading of *kukkura* (dog) for *kukkuta* (cock), an easy mistake to make since the sound is quite close in Sanskrit in some Prakrits.

21 Translated by Samuel Beal, *Si-yu-ki: Buddhist Records of the Western World* (London: Kegan Paul, Trench, Trübner, 1906), 1: lxvi–lxvii.

22 Slightly adapted from ibid., 2: 142–4. The original passage is in T101. 919. Sāshō copied this and other passages from Hsüan-tsang's record relevant to Maitreya in chapter 2 of *Miroku nyorai kan'ō shō*, 264–76.

23 Ibid.

24 Tao-hsüan, *Chi shen chou san-pao kan-t'ung lü* 集神州三寶感通録, T 52. 430.

25 T 53. 504a, 511c.

26 *Kasagidera engi* relates, "This mountain is not of our land. A sacred pinnacle from Vulture Peak broke off and came here to become the peak of Maitreya of the Garbha-dhātu (*taizō-kai* 胎藏界)."

27 Both Nishimura, *Nara no sekibutsu*, 368, and Horiike, "Kasagi mandara shiken," 47, say that the second arhat is Rahula without giving a convincing reason for this identification. See the Chinese examples cited below for support for my suggestion that the second arhat is a member of Maitreya's retinue.

28 Ishida Mosaku 石田茂作, *Shakyō yori mitaru Narachō Bukkyō no kenkyū* 写経より見たる奈良朝佛教の研究, Tōyō bunko ronsō, vol. 17 (1930; rpt. Tokyo: Tōyō bunko, 1966).

29 *Miroku nyorai kan'ō shō*, 26*ff*.

30 See Chapter 9, Figure 6.

31 The term "pure land" is commonly found for such preaching scenes in Japanese documents of the period. Writers on the subject for China more commonly use *pien-hsiang* (*hensō* 變相), roughly translated as "transformed configuration" and meaning a visual counterpart to doctrine. See notes 33 and 40.

32 Tanaka Ichimatsu 田中一松, *Hōryūji kondō hekiga* 法隆寺金堂壁畫 (Wall paintings of the Hōryūji monastery) (Kyoto: Benridō, 1952).

33 For a general introduction to eighth-century sculpture see Jirō Sugiyama, *Classic Buddhist Sculpture: The Tempyō Period*, trans. and adapt. Samuel Crowell Morse, Japanese Arts Library no. 11 (Tokyo: Kodansha International Ltd. and Shibundo, 1982). The fourteen volumes of *Nara rokudaiji taikan* 奈良六大寺大觀 (Tokyo: Iwanami shoten, 1968–73) are the best source of illustrations, recent scholarship, and primary sources of the major Nara temples. Kameda Tsutomu 亀田孜 has studied representations of Maitreya Pure Land in "Miroku jōdozō" 彌勒浄土像 and "Nara jidai no Miroku jōdo" 奈良時代の彌勒浄土, both reprinted in *Nihon Bukkyō bijutsu shi josetsu* 日本佛教美術史序説 (Tokyo: Gakugei shorin, 1970).

34 Emperor Shōmu's edict to begin the project is translated in full in Wm. Theodore de Bary, ed., *Sources of Japanese Tradition* (New York: Columbia University Press, 1958), 1: 104. The Chinese precedents for the Great Buddha are discussed in Samuel Crowell Morse's introduction to Sugiyama, *Classic Buddhist Sculpture*, 13–24 and also 78–82, 121–6.

35 The primary source of information on Chien-chen is his biography, *Tō Daiwajō tōsei den* 唐大和上東征傳, dated 779. The best edition is that by Kuranaka

Susumu 藏中進, *Tō Daiwajō tōsei den no kenkyū* 唐大和上東征傳の研究 (Tokyo: Ōbūsha, 1976). Takakusu Junjirō 高楠順次郎 has translated the text in "Le Voyage de Kanshin en Orient (742–54) par Aomi no Mabito Genkai (779)," *Bulletin de l'Ecole Française d'Extrême-Orient* 28 (1928): 1–41, 442–72, and 29 (1929): 47–62. Andō Kōsei 安藤更生 has studied Chien-chen in detail in *Ganjin daiwajō den no kenkyū* 鑒真大和上傳の研究 (Tokyo: Heibonsha, 1960) and *Ganjin wajō* 鑒真和上, Jinbutsu sōshō, no. 146 (Tokyo: Yoshikawa Kōbunkan, 1978).

36 Sugiyama, *Classic Buddhist Sculpture*, plates 99–121.

37 The original is completely reproduced in Bunkazai hogo iinkai 文化財保護委員會, *Kokuhō tsuzure-ori Taima mandara* 國寶綴織當麻曼荼羅 (Kyoto: Benridō, 1963). Numerous thirteenth- and fourteenth-century copies of various sizes preserve the original composition. For more on the history of this and other paradise paintings, see Jōji Okazaki, *Pure Land Buddhist Painting*, trans. and adapt. Elizabeth ten Grotenhuis, Japanese Arts Library no. 4 (Tokyo: Kodansha International Ltd. and Shibundo, 1977).

38 See note 2.

39 See Kameda's articles in note 33.

40 The best publications on the Tun-huang paintings are Tun-huang wen-wu yen-chiu suo, ed., *Chūgoku sekkutsu: Tonkō bakukōkutsu* 中國石窟:敦煌莫高窟, 5 vols. (Tokyo: Heibonsha, 1980–2), vols. 3 and 4 for T'ang caves; and the older Matsumoto Eiichi 松本英一, *Tonkōga no kenkyū* 敦煌画の研究 2 vols. (Tokyo: Tōhō bunka gakuin, 1937), which analyzes Maitreya paradise imagery in detail in vol. 1, pp. 91–109. The author would like to thank Mrs. Lucy Lo, Far Eastern Archives, Princeton University, for her help with Tun-huang material.

41 *Chūgoku sekkutsu*, vol. 3, plate 45.

42 Akiyama Terukazu 秋山光和 has studied the Maitreya narratives and the relationship between the wall paintings and a silk painting in the Stein Collection, British Museum, in "Miroku geshō kyōhen hakubyō funpun (S 259 v) to Tonkō hekiga no seisaku" 彌勒下生経変白描粉本と敦煌壁画の製作, *Monumenta Serindica* (Kyoto: Hōzōkan, 1963), 6: 47–74. The Stein painting, which does not include Mahākāśyapa, is reproduced and discussed in Roderick Whitfield, *The Art of Central Asia* (Tokyo: Kodansha International, 1983), 2: 308–13.

43 Langdon Warner, *Buddhist Wall-paintings: A Study of a Ninth-century Grotto at Wan Fo Hsia* (Cambridge, Mass.: Harvard University Press, 1938).

44 A clear description of such a painting appears in the mid-ninth-century *Ssu-t'a chi* 寺塔記 for the Pao-ying-ssu 寳應寺 of Ch'ang-an: "A hanging painting by Han Kan of Maitreya's final incarnation on earth. Maitreya was shown wearing a purple monk's robe. A Bodhisattva on His right with upturned face, and the two lions, all reached the level of divine inspiration." Translated by Alexander Soper in "A Vacation Glimpse of the T'ang Temples of Ch'ang-an: The Ssu-t'a-chi by Tuan Ch'eng-shih," *Artibus Asiae* 23, no. 1 (1960): 26.

45 Horiike, "Kasagi to Kasagi mandara ni tsuite no ichi shikiron." Mt. Kasagi is also 5 kilometers east of the Kuni capital, in use by Emperor Shōmu from 740 to 743 just before the start of the Great Buddha project.

46 *Kasagidera engi*, 325.

47 Ibid.

48 Horiike, "Kasagi to Kasagi mandara," 624.

49 See *Tōdaiji gonbettō Jitchū nijūkyū kajōji* 東大寺權別當實忠二十九個條事 (Twenty-nine acts of Jitchū) in *Tōdaiji yōroku* 東大寺要録, ed. Tsutsui Eijun 筒井英俊 (Osaka: Zenkoku shobō, 1944), 263–70. On Jitchū and his activities see Sugiyama Jirō, *Classic Buddhist Sculpture*, 160–5.

50 Popularly known as the "Head Stūpa" (*zutō* 頭塔) from the belief that the head of Abbot Genbō 玄昉 (?–746) is buried there, Kuno, *Sekibutsu*, 120–7. As of June 1987, the northeast corner of the stūpa has been excavated. The original shape of the stūpa, a 10-meter-high, three-level earthen pyramid raised upon a 12-meter-thick platform, has been determined, and it is expected that more carved stones may be found in the process of excavation.

51 "Kokka no tame ni tatematsuru" 國家の為に奉る, *Tōdaiji gonbettō Jitchū nijū kyū kajōji*, in *Tōdaiji yōroku*, 267.

52 The effect of Empress Shōtoku (Kōken) and Dōkyō on Nara temple projects, particularly Saidaiji, is discussed by Sugiyama, *Classic Buddhist Sculpture*, 165–75. For more on the political climate of the period, see Yokota Ken'ichi 横田健一, *Dōkyō* 道鏡, Jinbutsu sōshō, no. 18 (Tokyo: Yoshikawa kōbunkan), 1959; and Ross Bender, "The Hachiman Cult and the Dōkyō Incident," *Monumenta Nipponica*, 34, no. 2 (1979): 125–54.

53 See Appendix.

54 *Tōdaiji yōroku*, 247.

55 Ibid., 30.

56 A monk from southern India, Bodhisena arrived in Japan in 736, along with the Chinese Tao-hsüan 道璿 (702–60); they introduced meditational and esoteric practices, primarily at Daianji.

57 The various versions of Buddha's footprint stones in India, China, and Japan have been treated by Tanaka Shigehisa 田中重久, *Nihon ni nokoru Indo-kei bunbutsu no kenkyū* 日本に遣る印度系文物の研究 (Tokyo: Tōkōdō, 1943), 175–236; by Kanai Kasatarō 金井嘉佐太郎, *Bussokuseki no kenykyū* 佛足跡の研究 (Tokyo: Bukkyō shorin chūsan shobō, 1971); and in English by Roy Andrew Miller, '*The Footprints of the Buddha': An Eighth-century Old Japanese Poetic Sequence* (New Haven, Conn.: American Oriental Society, 1959).

58 The Yakushiji footprint stone inscriptions are translated by Douglas E. Mills, "The Buddha's Footprint Stone Poems," *Journal of the American Oriental Society* 80 (1960): 229–42. The inscription says, "According to *Hsi-yü-chuan*," which may refer to a now lost "Record of Western Regions" similar to that written by Hsüan-tsang. The stone is illustrated in *Nara rokudaiji taikan*, vol. 6, *Yakushiji*, 236–40.

59 For the complex history of the stele, the footprint stone, and the question of whether they belong together, see notes 57 and 58.

60 Translated by Miller, '*The Footprint of the Buddha*,' 108, 114. Miller's treatment of the linguistic qualities of the poems is exhaustive, but he does not account for the Maitreya content.

61 Dōshō 道昭 (629–700), who went to China in 653, studied with Hsüan-tsang and

is said to have received a drawing of the footprints directly from him. The inscription on the Yakushiji stone indicates that those prints are copied from Dōshō's version.

62 This is the theory of Tanaka, in *Nihon ni nokoru*, 212–19.

63 The account of the earth appears only in the fourteenth-century *Tōshōdaiji ge*, in *Dainihon Bukkyō zenshū*, 64: 150, along with a discussion of the correctness of the ordination platform according to Indian precedent. The spiritual link to the Kukkutārāma monastery is discussed by Hōan 豊安 (764–840), third abbot of Tōshōdaiji, in *Ganjin wajo san-i-ji* 鑒真和上三遺事 (dated 831), *Dainihon Bukkyō zenshū*, 72: 34.

64 Hence the name and format of Chien-chen's biography, which shows striking parallels to Hsüan-tsang's record.

65 *Tōdaiji jukai hōki* 東大寺授戒方軌, T 74.25.

66 This is nowhere more clear than in another work by Hōan, *Kairitsu denraiki* 戒律傳來記 (dated 830), *Dainihon Bukkyō zenshū*, 64: 146–9, the first chapter of which discusses the rise of Vinaya in India and its transmission to China and Japan. Therein appears a fascinating legend about a monk who went to India to ask what would prove that Chinese monks had obtained proper vows. The monk encountered an arhat who could not answer his inquiry. The arhat went into meditation and thereby went to Tuṣita Heaven to ask Maitreya, who replied that a golden flower would appear in the monk's hand as proof. Maitreya thus appears as guarantor of the transmission of the Law. Hōan may have copied this legend from Tao-shih's *Fa yüan chu lin*, T 53.944c–945a.

67 Among them, Hui-neng 慧能 (638–713), the sixth patriarch of Ch'an, was actually seen by Chien-chen. Kosugi Kazuo 小杉一雄, "Nikushinzō oyobi ihaizō no kenkyū" 肉身像および遺灰像の研究 and "Ganjin wajōzō no nikushinzō setsu to shuhitsu nyūjō setsu" 鑒真和上像の肉身説と朱櫃入定説, in *Chūgoku Bukkyō bijutsu shi no kenkyū* 中国仏教美術史の研究 (Tokyo: Shinjusha, 1980); Andō Kōsei, *Nihon no miira* 日本のミーラ (Tokyo: Mainichi shinbunsha, 1961); and Inoue Tadashi 井上正, "Ganjin wajozō josetsu" 鑒真和上像序説, *Museum* 314 (1977): 17–26.

68 Slightly adapted from Beal, *Si-yu-ki*, 2: 224–5.

69 Murōji is an excellent example. See Tsuji Hidenori 逵日出典, *Murōji shi no kenkyū* 室生寺史の研究, Kodai sangaku jiin no kenkyū, vol. 2 (Tokyo: Gannandō shoten, 1979).

70 For more on mountain Buddhism see Hori Ichirō, "On the concept of *Hijiri* (Holy-man)," *Numen*, 5, fasc. 2 (1958): 128–60.

71 Translated by Goodwin, "Worship of Miroku," 67. See Hiraoka, *Tōdaiji Sōshō shōnin*, 3: 528.

72 Tsuruoka, "Kodai ni okeru Miroku shinkō," 309.

73 Yoshito Hakeda, *Kūkai, Major Works* (New York: Columbia University Press, 1972), 130.

74 Ibid., 15–16.

75 Ibid., 47.

76 Adapted from Goodwin, "Worship of Miroku," 69.

77 A document by a Kūkai follower, dated 845, says that the practice of meditation on Mt. Kōya will bring about the appearance of Maitreya. Hiraoka, *Tōdaiji Sōshō shōnin*, 3: 529.

78 *Konjaku monogatari shū*, ch. 11, 105–7. Partially translated and discussed by Goodwin, "Worship of Miroku," 129–40. A recent study of the *nyūjō* legend is Matsumoto Akira 松本昭, *Kōbō daishi nyūjō setsuwa no kenkyū* 弘法大師入定説話の研究 (Tokyo: Rokkō shuppan, 1982).

79 *Kasagidera engi* relates that Kūkai carried out rites in front of the engraved image of Ākāśagarbha (still extant at Kasagi) during the Kōnin era (810–13).

80 See Goodwin, "Worship of Miroku," 129–40.

81 The most important sites were Mt. Kōya and Mt. Kinpu, deep in the Yoshino area south of Nara.

82 On the mountain Buddhism of Kasagi, see Toyoshima Osamu 豊島修, "Kasagisan no shūgendō" 笠置山の修験道, in *Kinki reizan to shūgendō* 近畿霊山と修験道, ed. Gorai Shigeru 五來重, Sangaku shūkyōshi kenkyū, vol. 11 (Tokyo: Meisho shuppan, 1978).

11

Mt. Fuji as the Realm of Miroku

The Transformation of Maitreya in the Cult of Mt. Fuji in Early Modern Japan

MARTIN COLLCUTT

Introduction: The Life-in-Death of Jikigyō Miroku

On the thirteenth day of the sixth month of 1733, a sixty-two-year-old oil merchant from Edo climbed to the seventh stage of Mt. Fuji, to a place known as Eboshi Rock. There he set up a flimsy portable shrine that he had carried with him, entered it, and began a fast of thirty-one days and nights during which he allowed himself only a cup of melted snow daily. It was to be a mortal fast. On the thirteenth day of the seventh month he died or, as those who heard of his death believed, entered a deathlike state of meditation, *samādhi (nyūjō).*

This ascetic oil dealer was known as Jikigyō Miroku. He was the sixth-generation leader of a popular devotional cult, the sodality of Mt. Fuji, or Fujikō, that had many adherents among countrypeople around the mountain and among the townspeople of Edo. On his final pilgrimage Miroku was accompanied by a disciple, Tanabe Jūroemon, to whom he recounted his spiritual experiences and conveyed his teachings. These were recorded in the *Sanjūichinichi-no-onmaki* (The sacred scroll record of the thiry-one days).[1]

This record describes his final ascent in rather mystical terms:

> At the seventh hour of the thirteenth day of the sixth month of the eighteenth year of the Kyōhō era (1733), together with my companion, I set out from Ishimuro. In my high wooden clogs I began the climb. On my clogs were written the names of the thousand gods and Buddhas. Treading with my clogs, I straddled the twofold rock of the eightfold Buddha of Mt. Fuji. A hope of 45 years is today attained. Entering the inner chamber of the Tuṣita Heaven I will transform all sentient beings.[2]

We see here a cluster of what might be called "Maitreyan imagery." Jikigyō clearly saw himself entering Maitreya's realm either to wait for the coming of Maitreya or to bring about some great spiritual or social transformation through his own fast. At the same time, in the references to the gods, the Shinto *kami,* and to the asceticism of mountain devotion there are also elements that clearly have little to do with traditional Buddhist Maitreya devotion.

Because the word "Miroku" means "Maitreya" in Japanese, because, as the above quotation shows, the elderly oil merchant called Miroku presented himself as entering the antechamber to the Tuṣita Heaven, where he would not merely await the coming of Maitreya for his own salvation, but actively seek to transform the lives of others, and because Miroku was believed by his followers not to have died but to have entered a state of suspended life – like that of Kūkai awaiting Maitreya – Jikigyō Miroku's experience and teaching are generally viewed as instances of Maitreyan devotion in Japan, or at least as expressions of a popular devotion that incorporated Maitreyan elements. At the same time that these Maitreyan features were superimposed upon, and integrated with, deep veins of popular mountain devotion and an ascetic, Yamabushi tradition centering on Mt. Fuji, they mingled with the agrarian aspirations of local farmers and with the everyday morality of Edo townspeople – like Jikigyō Miroku himself – who considered ascetic practices on the mountain to be a natural expression of, and source of energy for, their daily business lives.

This chapter attempts to disentangle some of the intricate strands of popular devotion clustering about Mt. Fuji in order to expose and evaluate Maitreyan elements within the multifaceted beliefs of Jikigyō Miroku and other members of the eighteenth-century Fujikō. First, I shall attempt to define the role of Maitreya within early Fuji devotion and then show how that role changed over time as the canonical Buddhist Maitreya was gradually displaced by a popularized offshoot of Maitreya known as Miroku.

Mt. Fuji as Sacred Mountain

The antiquity and strength of mountain devotion in Japanese religious life are well known.[3] In this volume, for instance, there is a study of the role of Maitreya in the early Kasagi cult that will serve as a useful point of reference for the altered role of Maitreya in later popular Japanese religion.[4] The religious significance of Mt. Fuji has also been thoroughly researched.[5] In this section, therefore, I merely point to some of the major strands of devotion to Mt. Fuji before the eighteenth century that seem to provide the substrate for the beliefs and practices of the Fujikō and the role of Maitreya in the Fuji cult.

We should first of all recognize the powerful emotional impact – an impact that may or may not have religious overtones – that Mt. Fuji has always exerted on the Japanese consciousness. This soaring, perfectly conical, snow-capped, active volcano that is highly visible from the Pacific littoral as well as the eastern provinces of Japan has impressed the Japanese emotionally and spiritually from the very dawn of their civilization. By the time the *Manyōshū,* one of the earliest Japanese literary classics, was compiled in the eighth century Fuji had already been invested with majesty and divinity:

Rising between the lands of Kai
and Suruga,
where the waves draw near,
is Fuji's lofty peak.
It thwarts the very clouds
from their path.
Even the birds
cannot reach its summit
on their wings.
There, the snow drowns the flame
and the flame melts the snow.
I cannot speak of it,
I cannot name it,
this occultly dwelling god![6]

Such emotional and literary reactions to Mt. Fuji proliferated with time – so much so that it is no exaggeration to say that there has not been a time when the Japanese imagination has not been moved by Fuji. The *Taketori monogatari,* for instance, tells the tale of Kaguya-hime, a celestial maiden, whom a cluster of legends associate closely with Mt. Fuji. Nō plays, such as *Fujisan* and *Hagoromo*, incorporate the themes of Kaguya-hime as spirit of the mountain or make Fuji the Mt. Hōrai of Japan, a paradise of immortals. Saigyō (1118–90) was only one of many Heian period poets who saw the smoke from Fuji as a metaphor for the passing fires of love:

Trailing in the wind
the smoke of Fuji
vanishes in the sky;
Whither has it gone
the fire of my love?

Kaze ni nabiku
Fuji no kemuri no
sora ni kiete
yukue mo shiranu
waga omohi kana[7]

The warrior Minamoto Yoritomo wrote of Fuji while on a victory ride to Kyoto and no doubt viewed the mountain as a fitting symbol of his own new-found power and authority. A later Shogun, Ashikaga Yoshinori, had heard so much of the mountain that he went from Kyoto to see it and compose verses in its honor. By the medieval period, Fuji was being depicted in art. One of many fine illustrations is that contained in the scroll painting of the life and teachings of Ippen Shōnin showing Ippen and his ragged band of mendicant followers on pilgrimage below the mountain. Many more instances of this kind could be given, but these few should make the point that before, or alongside, religious and spiritual associations, Mt. Fuji has always had a deep hold on the emotions of the Japanese and on their literary and artistic imaginations.

It is clear from the *Manyōshū* quotation above that Fuji had assumed religious significance in the Japanese consciousness well before the eighth century. More so, even, than that of other sacred mountains, its perfect conical shape soared upward, linking the earthly world with the divine. The plume of smoke constantly rising from its summit suggested vast spiritual energies, and the snow that covered it for most of each year provided a natural symbol of purity and freedom from pollution. From an early period shrines were built on its slopes, the mountain was made the home of a variety of Buddhist and Shinto deities, its peak was associated with several different paradises, and its inner fires with the Buddhist hells. Maitreya came to have a role among this group of deities. But Fuji was never devoted to Maitreya or Maitreya's paradise as exclusively as, for instance, Mt. Kasagi or Kimpusen. Nor was Maitreya present as strongly as in the beliefs associated with the mountain centers of Omine, Kumano, Kazuraki, Kōyasan, or Hieizan.[8]

From the ninth century or earlier the deity most closely associated with Fuji was Asama Daimyōjin. This deity also came to be called Asama Gongen and Sengen Daibosatsu. The word "Asama" has the sense of "fiery mountain." "Sengen" is merely an alternative reading of the two characters of the compound Asama. The early beliefs focusing on Mt. Fuji are sometimes called Asama *shinkō* or Sengen *shinkō*. The object of worship was first the mountain itself, which was believed to be a divinity (*kami*) in its own right – a divine force whose shifting moods could bring plenty, hardship, or disaster to those human beings who lived in its shadow. Then, in shrines, such as the Fuji Hongū Asama Jinja in Ise, that were built on its lower slopes the divinity of the mountain was worshipped as Asama Myōjin, "the Great Divinity of the Fiery Volcano"; as Asama Gongen, "the Manifestation of Asama"; or as Sengen Daibosatsu, "the Great Bodhisattva Sengen (Asama)." All of these titles referred to the Shinto *kami* Kono-hana-saku-ya-hime-no-mikoto, who was at the core of the indigenous cult of Mt. Fuji.[9] The various titles, however, also had Buddhist and syncretic overtones. The word "Gongen" signifies a manifestation of a deity in the form of a human being, often a monk. It is a term that clearly implies the overlay of Shinto with Buddhism and the operation of *honji suijaku* thinking, the assimilation of Shinto *kami* with Buddhas and bodhisattvas. Sengen Daibosatsu is an even clearer attribution of Buddhist authority to the spirit of the mountain. This Shinto–Buddhist amalgam in the early cult of Mt. Fuji was later enriched by Taoist elements when the characters for "Sengen" came to be written with new characters alluding to the immortals, or sages, of Chinese myth.

As Buddhism developed in Japan, Fuji also became associated with powerful Buddhas and their cosmic realms or paradises. One of the earliest and deepest of such associations was with the realm of Dainichi Nyorai, the cosmic Buddha Vairocana. Dainichi is particularly venerated in esoteric Buddhism, being the Buddha who holds the center of two great mandalas representing the potential and dynamic aspects of the universe in esoteric Buddhist thought. The association of Dainichi with Fuji continued through the Middle Ages and is reflected, for instance, in the *Sangoku denki*, a Shingon-inspired collection of legends of India, China, and Japan compiled in the fifteenth century.[10] One of these describes how the Japanese culture hero Prince Shōtoku descended through the crater of the volcano and encountered a coiled dragon who turned into Dainichi Nyorai.[11] In this Dainichi-centered devotion Fuji thus came to be linked with the two great Shingon mandalas and also with Kūkai, the founder of Shingon Buddhism in Japan, and his mountain monastery on Mt. Kōya. The Dainichi of the Taizōkai mandala was seen as the *honji* for Sengen Daibosatsu, whereas the Dainichi of the Kongōkai mandala was viewed as the *honji* of the Daimyōjin of Ashitaka, a neighboring peak.[12]

The summit of Fuji, however, was also believed to give access to other Buddhas and their paradises. From the late Heian period those who felt particular devotion to Amida looked up to Fuji with aspirations for rebirth, seeing its summit as one of the entrances to the Pure Land of the Western Paradise. In the late sixteenth century Kakugyō, the founder of the Fujikō, sang that Fuji is "the Pure Land of Amida Buddha."[13] And if Amida's paradise was above, the Buddhist hells were believed to lie beneath Fuji, entered by a dreaded cave known as the *hitoana,* or "manhole."[14]

Other layers of Buddhist symbolism were added to the beliefs connected with Dainichi and Amida. By the Kamakura period eight subpeaks of Mt. Fuji were being visualized as a lotus with eight petals, or paradises, over each of which sat a Buddha. The eight were Dainichi, Sengen, Amida, Yakushi, Kannon, Jizō, Fudō, and Śākyamuni.[15]

It is significant from our point of view that in all this richness of Shinto, Taoist, and Buddhist association with Mt. Fuji there is little evidence of any strong Maitreyan strand before the sixteenth century. It would be rash, however, to suggest that a current of devotion as strong as that to the future Buddha had been in the Asuka, Nara, Heian, and Kamakura periods in Japan should have been completely absent from the wealth of spiritual possibilities associated with Japan's most sacred mountain.

Indirect evidence for the association of Maitreya with Mt. Fuji in these early centuries is provided by the fact that the summit of Fuji was the site for the burial of sūtras. A cache of sūtras was unearthed from a sūtra mound on Fuji in 1930.[16] Although it is not certain that these sūtras were dedicated to Maitreya, as Christine Guth points out in Chapter 9 the burial of sūtras to be read at the coming of Maitreya was a common practice in Maitreyan devotion in the age of the Latter Days of the Law (*mappō*), which was believed to have beset Japan from the late eleventh century. Thus although Maitreya may not have been a principal focus of worship within the complex of the early Fuji cult, the fact that Fuji was the location of sūtra burying in the medieval period suggests that the future Buddha may have been associated with the volcano, whose summit would then have seemed to many devotees to soar into the Tuṣita Heaven.

The Ascetic's Path to Paradise

Fuji was not only venerated from afar. It was also climbed. The volcano is snow-covered and wind-whipped for most of the year. Its upper slopes are clear of snow for only a few months each summer. Moreover, the surface above the tree line is of rock and volcanic ash. It can be climbed in summer without special climbing equipment, but it is a hard climb, even in the best of weather. Now bands of mountaineers climb it in winter, and tens of thousands of pilgrims and tourists scramble up each summer to peer into its crater and, especially, to view a sunrise from its summit. Before the late nineteenth century, however, most of those who climbed the mountain did so for spiritual reasons: to strengthen themselves spiritually or acquire magical powers through ascetic practices, to worship one or another, or several, of the divinities associated with the mountain, to seek a paradise there, or to draw on, or appease, the volcano's dormant powers.

The first recorded climbers of Fuji are legendary figures. Mention has already been made of Prince Shōtoku's encounter with Dainichi Nyorai in the bowels of the volcano. Another early legendary climber was the magician and founder of Shugendō, or mountain asceticism, En no Osune (Gyōja), who was exiled by the court to eastern Japan in 699 and is reputed to have flown to the summit of Fuji every night.[17]

From the *Fujisan-ki* (Records of Mt. Fuji) by Miyaka no Yoshika in the mid-Heian period, we know that veneration of Mt. Fuji and climbing for religious reasons was practiced and that a number of trails to the summit were known in some detail. These early climbers were probably itinerant priests or *yamabushi* (mountain ascetics), members of an amorphous and still undefined but extensive cult of mountain worship that came to be known as Shugendō.

In its beliefs and practices Shugendō blended worship of mountains as expressions of the native deities with esoteric Buddhist rituals drawn from Shingon and Tendai teaching.[18] As *yamabushi* climbed and practiced austerities in the mountains, they recited Shingon mantras and conducted esoteric rituals.

Among the ancient centers for *yamabushi* activity were the mountain ranges of Omine, Kumano, and Yoshino in the Kii Peninsula, the mountains of Kyushu and Shikoku, and the three great mountains of northeastern Japan, the Dewa Sanzan. Among the *yamabushi* who practiced their austerities on Mt. Yudono in the Dewa Sanzan, for instance, there were several like Shinyōkai Shōnin who are believed to have fasted into a deathlike state (*nyūjō*) with the intention of relieving the common people of famines and natural disasters.[19] Like Kūkai, who was widely believed to have entered *nyūjō* at the Oku-no-in on Mt. Kōya to await the coming of Maitreya, these ascetics are still venerated as "living Buddhas" (*sokushinbutsu*).[20] Pilgrims climbing the Dewa Sanzan still believe that if they encounter one of these Buddhas on the trail they will be offered merciful compassion and the promise of rebirth.

In time, Fuji and the mountains of central Honshu were drawn into this network of sacred mountains and became the haunts of *yamabushi* seeking magical power and spiritual enlightenment. Although the main branches of Shugendō came to be attached to the monasteries of Onjōji and Daigoji near Kyoto, Yamabushi traveled widely. They made use of temples all over Japan and in many places established "support groups" (*kōsha*) among the local villagers. These not only offered prayers and food for the *yamabushi;* they also provided new members and served as centers through which devotion to particular mountains spread among the common people. The outdoor lives and spartan austerities of *yamabushi* also had a profound appeal for medieval warriors. Ashikaga Yoshinori went to view Fuji and composed verses to express his awe. He did not climb it, but both Hōjō Sōun and Takeda Shingen, among the most powerful of Kanto warriors, are said to have climbed Fuji.

From the sixteenth century, due to the activities of the *yamabushi* ascetic Kakugyō, a cult of Mt. Fuji began to take on clearer definition. And with the choice of Edo as the seat of the Tokugawa *bakufu* and its growth into one of the world's most populous cities, interest in the snow-capped volcano that could be seen so dramatically in all its moods from the very center of Edo increased markedly. Many Edoites, even those who did not belong to Fujikō groups, aspired to climb Fuji at least once in their lives. By the mid-Edo period, climbing Fuji was becoming something of a popular boom. The network of trails that exists today had been opened up. Stone huts were built at the entrances to these trails and shrines set up along the ascents. During the Edo period the Yoshida trail was the most popular, with some eight thousand people per year setting out from there by the mid-Edo period. There were several other popular entries to the mountain, however, and as many as thirty thousand people may have climbed in busy years.[21] To climb Fuji, pilgrims dressed in white robes, straw sandals, and broad-brimmed sedge hats. As they climbed, they tinkled bells and chanted incantations at small shrines and sacred rocks on the way to the summit. Scenes of the Fuji pilgrimage drew the attention of the great Edo printmakers like Hokusai.[22] Those who could not express their veneration for the mountain and its deity, Sengen Daibostasu, by actually climbing it could do so by visiting one or other of the great shrines in Edo that had within them a model of Mt. Fuji. Members of the Fujikō provided illustrations or models of Edo's sacred mountain to be worshipped within such shrines as the Komagome Fuji Shrine, the Fukugawa Hachimangû, and the Kanda Jinja. There were at least eight such major centers of Fuji devotion in the city of Edo by the late eighteenth century.[23]

The Development of the Fujikō

During the Edo period, those most active in spreading devotion to Mt. Fuji were either the *yamabushi* and *goshi,* who practiced their austerities on the mountain, or members of the organized Fuji cult, Fujikō. This section and those that follow examine the contribution to Fujikō teaching made by two ascetic leaders of the Fujikō – Kakugyō and Miroku – in an attempt to expose the role of Maitreya within the cult. First, however, it would be helpful to sketch very briefly the history of Fujikō as a movement in Edo and early Meiji period society.

Organized groups (*kō*) with particular devotion to Mt. Fuji began to spring up in Edo from the early seventeenth century as townspeople came into contact with Yamabushi who wandered into the city.[24] The strange garb of these mountain ascetics, their evocation of spiritual and magical prowess, their devotion to Fuji and claims for its protective and saving powers must have exerted a strong fascination on those citizens who came into contact with them. An ascetic like Kakugyō, who was believed to have saved thousands from plague, would quickly have earned a tremendous reputation as a spiritual leader and built up an enthusiastic following.

The focus of devotion of Fujikō members was Sengen Daibosatsu, also known as Asama-sama. Sengen was believed to be the creative force of the universe, source of life, and essence of the sun, moon, and stars. The spiritual cement of Fujikō was the powerful belief in the magical powers of mountain ascetics and in the sharing of those powers by the *kō* members. Ascetics like Kakugyō, who were believed to have been possessed by Sengen Daibosatsu, provided the link between the powers of the mountain and its divinity and the aspirations of ordinary people. Through pilgrimages, prayer rituals, and the distribution of paper talismans with magical characters written on them (*ofusegi*), members believed they would ease childbirth, protect themselves from fire or other disaster, and enjoy health and wealth.[25] The basic aim of Fujikō membership, therefore, was the securing of material benefits in this life (*gensei riyaku*) through prayer ceremonies (*kaji kitō*) and magical practices. However, the *kō* were also guildlike organizations stressing both self-help and mutual cooperation. As such, they advocated a morality of daily life for the commercially minded townspeople of Edo and local villagers. This ethic combined elements of Shinto, Buddhism, Confucianism, Taoism, yin–yang thought, folk belief, magic, and practical experience.[26] In time a transformed Maitreyan belief also appeared within it. This was expressed most clearly by the sixth patriarch of Fujikō, Jikigyō Miroku, and by the articulation of a belief in the imminence of "Miroku's world," a world of eternal peace and bountiful rice harvests.

These groups met to recite prayers, to read the injunctions of their ascetic teachers, and to organize pilgrimages to the mountain or visits to shrines closer to the city. Fuji devotion enjoyed such a boom that people talked of the "808 *kō* of Edo."[27] The actual number may have been closer to 400, but it still represents a vital and enthusiastic popular movement.

Aizawa Seishisai, in his *Shinron* (1825), suggested that there were as many as 70,000 Fuji devotees.[28] Another early nineteenth-century source states that pilgrims from a number of *kō* climbed in groups of 450 or so. The Edo groups had a loose regulating organization of patriarch, junior patriarch, and seven elders. There were twenty-five principal *kō* in different parts of the city, each with a number of branches. In time *kō* were also organized in the surrounding villages.[29] In the mid–Edo period the two most effective leaders of Fujikō were Jikigyō Miroku and Murakami Kosei. From their time the *kō* split into their two major lineages. Miroku's lineage quickly became the dominant one. The Edo *bakufu* did not look with favor on the unorthodox beliefs and magical practices associated with Fujikō. The movement's popularity with Edo citizens was seen as a possible source of civil unrest. From 1742 the *bakufu* issued repeated prohibitions against the Fujikō, but without appreciable success in containing the movement.[30] This kind of organized devotion to Mt. Fuji continued into the Meiji period, when it came to be expressed by such religious offshoots of the Fujikō as Fusō-kyō, Maruyama-kyō, and Jikkō-kyo.[31]

The Life and Teachings of Kakugyō Tōbutsu

Kakugyō was a mountain ascetic, a practitioner of Shugendō. The sources on his life are late and sketchy and combine legend with hagiography. According to one of the earliest of these uncertain records, the *Gotaigyō no maki* (Record of great austerities), allegedly compiled by one of his followers in 1620, Kakugyō was born in 1541 in Nagasaki into a branch of the Fujiwara family. In 1559, at the age of eighteen, he left his home province and moved to Mito in the Kanto, where he became the disciple of a *yamabushi*. Three years later, while he was performing austerities in a village graveyard in northeastern Japan, he had a dream in which En no Gyōja directed him to Mt. Fuji. Kakugyō set out for Fuji and entered the *hitoana*. There he engaged in severe austerities (*aragyō*), one of which was to stand for one thousand days on tiptoe on a six-inch-square board. It was during the performance of austerities of this kind that he is said to have encountered Sengen Daibosatsu and to have become one with the spirit of Fuji.[32]

In 1572 Kakugyō climbed to the summit of Fuji, one of many such climbs. When he was not on the volcano, he wandered from province to province, engaging in austerities. According to a strong Fujikō tradition, Tokugawa Ieyasu visited him in the *hitoana* in 1583. Ieyasu is said to have come twice more, seeking advice on political matters. Not surprisingly, there is no record of this in any *bakufu* documents.[33] In 1620 there was a plague in Edo. Kakugyō and his disciples used their spiritual powers for the relief of the city. They were credited with saving thousands of citizens by conducting prayer rituals. This relief work earned Kakugyō a reputation as a powerful healer and bearer of magical powers, but it also brought him to the attention of the political authorities. He was imprisoned and questioned on suspicion of being a secret Christian. Eventually released, he returned to his cave and died there in 1646 at the age, tradition has it, of 106.

Through his austerities in the *hitoana,* Kakugyō was believed to have become the possessor of magical powers. Other records add details to the list of his austerities and magical accomplishments. They included standing on tiptoe for long periods, climbing (he is said to have climbed Fuji a hundred times), standing naked in the cold or bathing in icy water, fasting, and doing without sleep. Through these practices Kakugyō claimed that the stars and the moon came down to him, that he became one with the mountain and the universe, and that he was initiated into magical characters and phrases by Sengen Daibotsatsu. With these he believed that he gained the power to help people, to heal sickness, and to bring peace to the country. His teachings and charms (*fusegi*) were written on paper slips and given to his followers or to those in trouble.[34]

Although a messianic quality can be detected in Kakugyō's belief that he had been possessed by Sengen Daibosatsu and given the gift of powers of healing and the ability to improve society, in the scattered writings attributed to him, or those purporting to describe his life, there is hardly any direct reference to Maitreya. There is at least one reference to Amida's Pure Land, mentioned above, but even that does not seem to have been a major strand in his thinking or practice. For Kakugyō, Fuji was almost totally identified with Sengen Daibosatsu, or Myōō Sengen, behind whom was Dainichi Nyorai. In

Kakugyō's thought, however, Sengen's attributes are more those of a *kami* than a Buddha.

> We use no other principal image.
> We sincerely serve both hearts of our parents
> and the five grains.
> Morning and evening we worship
> Fuji Sengen Daibosatsu, the sacred heavenly Sun,
> and heavenly Moon.
> We have no other objects of worship.[35]

For Kakugyō, Fuji was the expression of creation and natural harmony, born of a cosmic union and itself a source of life and energy:

> This mountain is born from the union of Heaven and Earth.
> It is the source of *yin* and *yang*.
> It is the very inhalation and exhalation of the Great One,
> of the Sun and the Moon.
> It is the Wondrous Sovereign Sengen (Myōō Sengen).
> It is the root of all.
> Human beings are all born of it.
> It is the *yin* spirit and the *yang* spirit
> of the Three Luminaries:
> the Sun, the Moon, and the Stars.[36]

Kakugyō and later leaders of the Fujikō were not merely ascetics and visionaries. They provided rituals, prayers, and pilgrimage practices for their followers. More than this, they encouraged them to observe a morality in their everyday life, one in which devotion to Mt. Fuji and belief in its magical efficacy were blended with emphasis on the virtues of filiality, hard work, and thrift. Kakugyō, for instance, drew up a set of injunctions that were recited daily by members of the Fujikō. These advocated venerating Sengen Daibosatsu, developing the spirit of ascetic practice (*dōgyōshin*), and abstaining from excessive indulgence in gambling, drinking, and dalliance with women of the pleasure quarters.[37] The virtues stressed in Fujikō were entirely appropriate to the shopkeepers, artisans, clerks, and laborers who comprised the bulk of Fujikō membership and would have contributed to their success and prosperity in the bustling urban community of Edo. They reflect not so much a desire for any radical change in the existing social order as a belief that improvements could be made in everyday life by the cultivation of modest virtues, and that where such virtues were insufficient to deal with personal or social crises the magical powers of Sengen Daibosatsu could be invoked. Apart from his injunctions, much of Kakugyō's teaching was encapsulated in mandala-like diagrams of the mountain that were used devotionally by his followers in the Fujikō.[38] Although these representations of the mountain contain the titles of Sengen Daibosatsu and other deities associated with Fuji, they do not make explicit reference to Maitreya.

The absence of overt references to Maitreya in Kakugyō's writings and in his Fuji mandalas tends to confirm the impression that the Buddhist version of the Buddha Maitreya or bodhisattva Maitreya was not a prominent feature of Fujikō belief in its early stages. Although Kakugyō and his followers invoked the Pure Land of Amida in their chants and visualized the summit of Fuji as the entrance to a pure land,[39] even that pure land was not clearly defined in early Fujikō teaching. As far as Maitreya is concerned, the most that can be detected in Kakugyō's day is a vague eschatology of salvation, without any overt association with Maitreya.

The Incorporation of Maitreya, as Miroku, into Fuji Devotion

As we have seen, Maitreya did not have a prominent place in the Shugendō-centered Fuji cult during the Middle Ages. Nor did Maitreya touch a central chord in Kakugyō's thought or practice. After Kakugyō, however, something that can be described as a form of Maitreyan devotion – or more correctly a transformed and popularized version of Maitreya devotion in which the popular deity Miroku was substituted for Maitreya – became increasingly evident within the Fuji cult. This became noticeable in the notion of the "World of Miroku" hinted at by the sixth-generation Fujikō leader Jikigyō Miroku. This section introduces the world of Miroku and assesses the role Maitreya may have played within it. From our point of view it is particularly important not to assume that, merely because "Miroku" is the Japanese term for "Maitreya," Maitreya neccessarily had a central role in any "world of Miroku." We are here dealing with two different traditions, interrelated in origin but diverging over time. Popular Japanese conceptions of Miroku as a deity of rice and plenty may have had their starting point in notions of the Buddhist Maitreya, but with time they took on a life and iconography of their own. In the process the original Buddhist vision of Maitreya grew increasingly indistinct.

Jikigyō was born in Ise in 1671. As a child he was apprenticed to a merchant in Edo. While still a youth he came under the influence of a leader of one of the Fujikō and became a member. For the remainder of his life, Jikigyō combined his activities as a merchant and family head with fervent Fujikō practices. These involved daily prayers, regular meetings, and annual ascents of the mountain.[40] As a merchant, he was frugal and honest with his customers and built up a thriving business selling oil and other commodities. His reputation for honesty was such that it was said that he would scrape the last drops of oil from the barrel so that his customers should not be cheated. Jikigyō conformed to the ideal of the prudent Edo merchant.

In 1730 Jikigyō's life was transformed. While climbing near the summit of the mountain, he had the first of several intense visions in which he was possessed by Sengen Daibosatsu and became one with the volcano. He believed that Sengen had called on him to spread devotion to Fuji among the townspeople of Edo and then to give up his life in order to usher in a better world. He vowed to devote himself to spreading Sengen's teachings for eight years and then to fast to death on the mountain. A year or so later Jikigyō had another intense encounter with Sengen Daibosatsu in which, because of the famines and disasters of the age, he was urged to advance his death by five years, to 1733.[41]

During his visions Jikigyō received from Sengen Daibosatsu the title Miroku. The most immediate meaning of "Miroku" in spoken Japanese is Maitreya, the future Buddha. Some association with the canonical Buddhist Maitreya was probably present in Jikigyō's thought. Although Jikigyō nowhere describes a specific linkage with Maitreya, it can be inferred from his determination to give his life in order to usher in a better world. However, Jikigyō did not use the characters that are normally used to translate Maitreya into Japanese (彌勒). Instead, he used two characters meaning "body" and "material benefit" (身禄). In doing so, he added new layers of meaning to the concept of Maitreya, layers that were not present in the original Buddhist conception but were rather associated with the figure of Miroku – a bearer of material blessings, especially rice – that had been developing over centuries in popular Japanese religious belief. The character *mi* that he used, for instance, not only bears the meaning of a physical body, but also has connotations of self, person, heart as well as the sense of one's personal history, fortune, and future – as in *mimoto* and *minoue*. It also has the important meaning of status (*mibun*), a strand of thought that was very strong among all status groups in Japanese society in the Edo period. The character *roku* conveys the meanings of a grant of food or income from a superior, such as a samurai's stipend, of material goods, and of happiness.

This combination of aural and visual associations in the word "Miroku" must have come to Jikigyō in a moment of mystical experience. Kakugyō and subsequent Fujikō leaders had a strong interest in mantras and verbal talismans, and there is no doubt that in Jikigyō's case his title was not lightly assumed. The two characters of the name Jikigyō, adopted when he first joined Fujikō, also illustrate the importance attached to appropriate titles. *Gyō* means "practice." In Shugendō this involved praying, chanting, climbing, and performing other austerities and was a character commonly used among Fujikō leaders. *Jiki* means "food." For Jikigyō as for Kakugyō and other Fuji cult leaders "food," particularly rice, had an important meaning.[42]

Thus we can see in Jikigyō's life and thought, as well as in the manner of his death, a blending of ideas. Behind Mt. Fuji and Sengen Daibosatsu were shadows of Dainichi Nyorai and Maitreya. Although the primary focus of the Fuji cult remained the mountain itself and Sengen Daibosatsu, hints of waiting for Maitreya's descent were combined with popular Japanese conceptions of a pure land of plenty. The idea of Maitreya, or Miroku, as a source of food and material happiness was linked with the Edo townspeople's ethic of frugality, hard work, and willing acceptance of one's status in a feudal society.

Jikigyō's views on Maitreya or Miroku are not presented discursively in his writings. Nowhere in the *Sanjūichinichi-no-maki,* for instance, do the characters for the canonical Buddhist Maitreya appear. He provides only scattered clues. In trying to define a Maitreyan component in his thought, we are forced to work from indirect references. When we tease out Jikigyo's ideas about the world of Miroku, salvation, worldly benefits, status, and everyday morality, what do we find?

Returning to Edo after his first encounter with Sengen Daibosatsu, Jikigyō divided his fortune among his relatives and employees and devoted himself to spreading the teachings of Sengen Daibosatsu while working as an oil peddler. In 1731 he erected a sign in front of his home proclaiming the coming of what he called "Miroku's world."[43]

Unfortunately, Jikigyō did not expand on this brief oracle. So it is difficult to know precisely what he had in mind. However, it is worth noting here that, in referring to Miroku's world, Jikigyō used the characters not for Maitreya but rather for his own name Miroku. Whatever this new dispensation was to be, it would not be a purely traditional Buddhist experience of Maitreya's coming. It seems rather to have been envisaged as a world in which a state of mind receptive to Miroku would exist. In *Sanjūichinichi-no-maki* Jikigyō describes this state of mind as follows:

> This teaching of Miroku is not directed at venerating a name. Miroku comes into being when you remove evil and make yourself straight and when this is reflected in the mirror of the heart.[44]

In fasting to death on Mt. Fuji, Jikigyō Miroku saw himself not only becoming one with the mountain and Sengen Daibosatsu, but also "entering the inner chamber of the Tuṣita Heaven and securing salvation for all sentient beings." But in what sense was this Tuṣita Heaven Maitreya's paradise? For Jikigyō, it was most immediately Mt. Fuji itself. This is made clear by another statement in the *Sanjūichinichi-no-maki:*

> In the inner chamber of the . . . Tuṣita Heaven there is a single jewel (*tama*). This true jewel (*magatama*) assumes forms (*katachi*). The venerable Miroku teaches that this is the origin of light in the East.[45]

What we have here is Mt. Fuji, likened vaguely to Mt. Sumeru, as center of the universe and location of the Tuṣita Heaven. Within this Japanese Tuṣita Heaven, however, is not the bodhisattva Maitreya, but a sacred jewel, associated strongly with Japan and the Japanese imperial line, that is the source of light in the East. The venerable Miroku referred to may imply the Buddhist Maitreya, in which case Maitreya would be equated with Sengen Daibosatsu and Mt. Fuji. However, since the characters used are those of Jikigyō's title "Miroku," it is quite possible that Miroku's teaching here means simply Jikigyō's teaching, informed now by his spiritual union with Sengen Daibosatsu. In this case the world of Miroku is only subliminally Maitreyan. It is much more consciously the world of the volcano and its native divinities presided over by Sengen Daibosatsu and realized on earth by Jikigyō and his followers.

Several times in the *Sanjūichinichi-no-maki* Jikigyō refers to Fuji as a bodhisattva (*bosatsu*) or as "a single Buḍdha in one body" (*ichibutsu ittai*).[46] By "bodhisattva" here, he probably meant Sengen Daibosatsu rather than Maitreya. Fuji is equated with Sengen Daibosatsu, and both are equated with Japan. In their unity as a single body, they are the source of the sun, the moon, and the stars.

Although the role that Jikigyō allots to Maitreya in his thought is difficult to define precisely, he describes other characteristics of the world of Miroku quite plainly. Some of these characteristics are unique to the Fuji cult, but many of them obviously derive from the popular belief in Miroku as a source of peace and plenty. For Jikigyō, as for Kakugyō and other Fuji cult members, a plentiful supply of food, especially rice, was the supreme expression of the power of Sengen Daibosatsu, and Fuji, in the earthly world of Miroku. Miroku's world was to be primarily one of peace and material well-being, of bountiful harvests. This kind of thinking developed early in the agrarian society of Japan, but it naturally intensified in years, like those in the middle and late Edo periods, when famine or natural disaster afflicted large areas of the country. The *Sanjūichinichi-no-maki* contains many references to the idea of rice as the cardinal blessing of the mountain. In several places rice, as a staff of life and manifestation of Fuji and Sengen Daibosatsu, the origin of creation and pillar of the world, is described as a bodhisattva (*bosatsu*) or the true bodhisattva (*makoto no bosatsu*). And since human beings consumed rice in order to live, they too were regarded as bodhisattvas: "Human beings daily offer the eighty-eight-fold bodhisattva [rice] to their bodies" (the characters for 88 [八十八] can be reformulated into the single character for rice [米]).[47]

> In origin, heaven and earth, spirits, and all creation are Moon and Sun and Sengen bodhisattva [Sengen Bosatsu]. That is the source of rice, and fire, and water. The light of the true jewel of the bodhisattva

> [rice] which the mother eats is born with the accumulation of ten moons.[48]

Here rice is not only viewed as an expression of Sengen Daibosatsu; it is treated as a life force made active in human life by the very acts of eating and giving birth. From this it should be clear that one of the key features of Jikigyō's vision of the world of Miroku, a feature that he hoped to enhance through his own fasting and death, was that of material plenty, in the form of rice, as an expression of the compassionate workings of Fuji and Sengen Daibosatsu.

How was such material plenty to be brought into the world of Miroku? Jikigyō's own death was clearly intended to hasten that process. But did he visualize some kind of violent social transformation? Or a sudden new dispensation? Or the coming of a Maitreya? Or of some other bodhisattva? Precisely how the world of Miroku was to be ushered in, other than through his own death, is not made explicit. There is, however, no call for a political revolution and no questioning of the Tokugawa political order. Nor is there any apocalyptic vision of violent social or religious reform. Jikigyō seems rather to have emphasized stability and to have believed that the world of Miroku would be brought about by human effort, discipline, and everyday moral values. Its essential elements were already present in human hearts and in the Tokugawa social order. There was little that was mysterious or magical about it. As one Fujikō chant expressed it:

> When you climb Mt. Fuji there is nothing.
> Good and evil both come from our hearts.
> Don't think that Paradise is one thousand
> leagues away.
> If the Way is straight it doesn't take a single step.
> When you look for Paradise it is in yourself.
> When you eat with pleasure the heart is joyful.[49]

Mt. Fuji, Sengen Bosatsu, the world of Miroku or of Maitreya, the pure land, whatever paradise was imminent, it sprang in essence from within the human heart. For Jikigyō the problem was clearly one of maintaining a sincere attitude to human life. Paradise did not sit like a cloud over the summit of Mt. Fuji. The world of Miroku was here and now, rooted in material existence and created out of human work and the enjoyment of everyday life.

Miroku's world accepted the four-part status hierarchy of Tokugawa society but at the same time stressed the importance of the harmony and cooperation of all four parts:

> The [system of] the four status groups: warriors, farmers, artisans and merchants is in harmony with the celebration of heaven and earth. In

> their functions of blending with and assisting each other they provide the basis for the ordering of all things. Of these four groups, from those at the top of society that have rank and status and draw high stipends to those of no rank or status at the bottom of society, all are in origin one.[50]

The virtues that count for most in the world of Miroku are those that serve well in this present world rather than in some future paradise. Beneath the mystical language of the *Sanjūichinich-no-maki,* Jikigyō stressed a secular ideal to be realized through the practice of popularized Confucian virtues of Edo townsperson society. Filial piety was important, both as an expression of gratitude to parents and as a mark of reverence for Mt. Fuji: "To show filial devotion towards one's parents is to show reverence for the Sun, Moon, and Sengen Daibosatsu."[51] Jikigyō also emphasized the virtues of integrity (*shojiki*), kindness (*nasake*), compassion (*jihi*), and frugality (*fusoku*).[52] These, however, were not mere moral abstractions. In Jikigyō's thought they were part of a work ethic that stressed saving and the accumulation of wealth. For him devotion to the diligent pursuit of one's family business was at least as important as devotion to religion: "Before going on pilgrimages to temples and shrines it is important to stress the Way of daily service in the family occupation."[53] Status, family occupation, and wealth were inherited from parents, entrusted to individuals, and passed on to their descendants. By diligent application, the practice of simple virtues, participation in a *kō,* or solidarity group, people could not only transmit this inheritance but increase it.

Several times in the *Sanjūichinichi-no-maki,* Jikigyō uses the term *umaremasu,* meaning "birth and increase." He uses it in the sense of increasing wealth in this life and of being reborn to increased happiness in the next:

> Among the four status groups, samurai, in serving their lords with absolute sincerity clarify the principle of being reborn richer tomorrow than they are today. Farmers, artisans, and merchants in working at their own occupations, when they work diligently and avoid idleness, give birth to greater wealth in themselves tomorrow than today.[54]

In the world of Miroku wealth or poverty was directly proportional to the efforts of individuals and their families. Moreover, those who worked hard in this life could expect rebirth into even greater prosperity. Those who were lazy could expect to be reborn only in reduced circumstances (*umare otoru*). In keeping with this ethic of material accumulation, Jikigyō placed a very positive value on gold and silver. Society as well as the individual benefited from their acquisition and redistribution: "Gold and silver are a boat to carry us across this floating world."[55]

Conclusion

How should we evaluate the role of Maitreya in the Fuji cult in Japan? Perhaps that role can be brought out most sharply by contrast with the centrality of Maitreya in the Kasagi mountain cult described in Chapter 10 of this volume. At Kasagi in the ancient and medieval periods, Maitreya was clearly the focus of devotion. Moreover, the mountain was dedicated to a Maitreya still squarely within the canonical Buddhist tradition. On Fuji, by contrast, Maitreya was present, but as a background figure. The future Buddha was never the most important deity associated with Fuji. That role was played by Dainichi or Sengen Daibosatsu. But Maitreyan beliefs are hinted at in the medieval sūtra-burying practices, in the rituals of Shugendō ascetics, and in the references to the Tuṣita Heaven made by Jikigyō Miroku. However, from the medieval period these already diluted Maitreyan beliefs were further overlaid by popular notions of a quasi-Maitreyan figure known as Miroku. It was Miroku's coming and Miroku's world, rather than Maitreya's, that Edo townspeople anticipated when they heard of the death by fasting of Jikigyō Miroku.

Two factors contributed to the subliminal role of Maitreya in the Fuji cult. In the first place there was no essential reason that Maitreya should have been represented on Mt. Fuji at all. Different mountains had different clusters of patron deities. Kasagi and a few other mountain complexes in Japan were distinguished by the intensity of their devotion to Maitreya. On most Japanese mountains Maitreya was at best a secondary focus of devotion. In the case of Fuji, the early history of the cult makes it clear that the primary focus of devotion was Sengen Daibosatsu and Dainichi Nyorai. Once established, this pattern prevailed through later centuries.

That Maitreya's secondary role in Fuji devotion did not grow over time but was, if anything, diminished or transformed can be linked to a broader transformation of Maitreya belief that was taking place in Japan from the medieval period on. This was the growth of a popular conception of Miroku that may have had its origin in Maitreyan devotion, but gradually grew away from it and eventually transformed it in the popular imagination. Devotees of Maitreya in ancient and medieval Japan, such as those at Kasagi, were hoping for the advent of a bodhisattva in some distant future who would offer the means of spiritual salvation. Believers in Miroku in early modern Japan hoped for the advent of a savior who would provide material relief from famine and hardship here and now. The Fuji cult, Fujikō, as it developed in the Edo period was an example not simply of this phenomenon taking place on Mt. Fuji, but of the general displacement of the influence of the canonical Maitreya that had taken place in the Japanese religious world.

No doubt there were in Japan monks and nuns who still had a particular devotion to Maitreya, temples in which sūtras related to Maitreya were read or ceremonies in his honor still held. But they were few. From the medieval period on, as Miyata Noboru and other scholars have shown, it was Miroku rather than Maitreya who seized the Japanese popular imagination as a source of hope and salvation in a troubled world. This may have been what happened to Maitreya on Mt. Fuji. Not strongly established enough from the ancient period to maintain a clear-cut Buddhist identity, the presence of Maitreya as a subliminal figure within the Fuji cult was still strong enough to induce the kind of transformed Maitreyanism advocated by Jikigyō in heralding his world of Miroku.

NOTES

1 *Sanjūichinichi-no-onmaki* 三十一日の御巻, in Murakami Shigeyoshi 村上重良 and Yasumaru Yoshio 安丸良夫, eds., *Minshū shūkyō no shisō* 民衆宗教の思想, *Nihon shisō taikei* 日本思想大系 (Popular religious thought) (Tokyo: Iwanami, 1971), 67:424–51.

2 Ibid., 426.

3 Japanese mountain devotion has been carefully studied. See, for instance, Hori Ichirō, *Folk Religion in Japan* (University of Chicago Press, 1958); Hori Ichirō, "Mountains and Their Importance for the Idea of the Other World in Japanese Folk Religion," in *Folk Religion in Japan* (University of Chicago Press, 1974), 141–79; H. Byron Earhart, *A Religious Study of the Mt. Hagurō Sect of Shugendō: An Example of Japanese Mountain Religion,* Monumenta Nipponica Monographs (Tokyo: Sophia University, 1970); and Carmen Blacker, *The Catalpa Bow* (London: Allen & Unwin, 1975). Of the recent work in Japanese the most comprehensive is the eighteen-volume *Sangaku shūkyō shi kenkyō sōsho* 山岳宗教史研究叢書 (Collected studies in the history of mountain religion) under the general editorship of Wakamori Tarō 和歌森太郎, Gorai Shigeru 五來重, et al. (Tokyo: Meichō Shuppan, 1977).

4 See Chapter 10.

5 On Fuji devotion see, for instance, Inobe Shigeo 井野邊茂雄, *Fuji no shinkô* 富士の信仰 (Devotion to Mt. Fuji) (Tokyo: Meichō Shuppa, 1983); Endō Hideo 遠藤秀男, "Fuji shinkō no seiritsu to Murayama shugen" 富士信仰の成立と村山修験, in Suzuki Shōei 鈴木昭英 ed., *Fuji, Ontake to chūbu reizan* 富士御嶽と中部霊山, *Sangaku shūkyō shi kenkyū sōsho*, vol. 9

6 *Manyōshū* 萬葉集, 3:319. Translated by Ian Hideo Levy, *The Ten Thousand Leaves* (Princeton, N. J.: Princeton University Press, 1981), 1:179.

7 *Shinkokinshū* 新古今集, 1613. Hisamatsu Sen'ichi 久松潜一 et al., eds., *Shinkokinwakashū* 新古今和歌集 (The new collection of Japanese verse old and new) (Tokyo: Iwanami, 1964) 331.

8 On the role of Maitreya in these various mountain complexes see Miyata Noboru 宮田登, *Miroku shinkō* 彌勒信仰 (Maitreya devotion) (Tokyo: Yūzankaku, 1984); Miyata Noboru, *Miroku shinkō no kenkyū* ミロク信仰の研究 (Studies in Miroku devotion) (Tokyo: Miraisha, 1975); and Hayami Tasuku 速水侑, *Miroku shinkō* 彌勒信仰 (Maitreya devotion) (Tokyo: Hyōronsha, 1971).

9 Endō, 26–30.

10 *Sangoku denki* 三國伝記 (Chronicles of the three countries), in Bussho Kankōkai 仏書刊行會, ed., *Dai Nihon Bukkyō zensho* 大日本仏教全書 (Collected works of Japanese Buddhism) (Tokyo: Bussho Kankôkai, 1912), vol. 148.

11 Ibid., 322–3.

12 *Fujisan no honji* 富士山の本地 (The deities of Mt. Fuji), in Yokoyama Shigeru 横山重 et al., eds., *Muromachi jidai monogatari shū* 室町時代物語集 (Collection of tales from the Muromachi period) (Tokyo: Inoue Shobō, 1962), 2:299.

13 Miyata Noboru, "Fuji shinkō to miroku" 富士信仰とミロワ (Miroku in Fuji devotion), in Sakurai Tokutarō, ed., *Sangaku shūkyō to minkan shinkō no kenkyū* 山岳宗教と民間信仰の研究, Studies in Mountain Religion and Popular Belief, Sangaku Shūkyō shi sōsho (Tokyo: Meichō Shuppan, 1976), 6:290.

14 A number of legends cluster about the *hitoana*. In an *Azuma kagami* 吾妻鏡 (Mirror of the East), entry for 1203, there is a tale of a warrior Shirō Tadatsune who went down into the *hitoana* and encountered Sengen Daibosatsu in the form of a dragon.

15 Inobe Shigeo, "Fuji no shinko" 富士の信仰 (Fuji devotion), in Wakamori Tarō 和歌森太郎 ed., *Sangaku shūkyō no seiritsu to tenkai* 山岳宗教の成立と展開 (The establishment and development of mountain devotion Sangaku shūkyō shi sōsho) (Tokyo: Meichō Shuppan, 1975), 1:129.

16 Miyata, *Miroku shinkō no kenkyū,* 151.

17 Endō "Fuji shinkō," 31. There are many legends about the marvelous exploits of En no Gyōja. See, for instance, that in *Nibon ryōiki* 日本靈異記, book 1, no. 28, translated by Nakamura Kyōkō, *Miraculous Stories from the Japanese Buddhist Tradition: The Nibon Ryōiki of the Monk Kyōkai* (Cambridge, Mass.: Harvard University Press, 1973), 140–2. See also H. Byron Earhart, "Shugendō: The Traditions of En no Gyōja, and Mikkyō Influences," in *Studies of Esoteric Buddhism and Tantrism* (Kôyasan: Kōyasan University Press,1965), 297–317.

18 For a brief history of the development of Shugendō see, for instance, Miyake Hitoshi 宮家準, *Shugendō* 修験道 (Tokyo: Kyōikusha, 1978).

19 The mummified living Buddhas of Mt. Yudono are discussed in Togawa Yasuaki 戸川安章, *Dewa sanzan shugendō no kenkyū* 出羽三山修験道の研究 (Studies in the Shugendō of the three mountains of Dewa) (Tokyo: Kōsei Shuppan, 1973), 68–73.

20 Ibid.

21 Entry for "Fujisan" 富士山, Mt. Fuji, in *Sekai dai hyakka jitten* 世界大百科事典 (World encyclopedia) (Tokyo: Heibonsha, 1967), 273.

22 This is especially evident in Hokusai's "One Hundred Views of Mt. Fuji," for example.

23 Inobe, *Fuji no shinkō,* 341–65.

24 The history of the Fujikō, their organization, and practices is discussed in detail by Inboe, *Fuji no shinkō* chaps. 4 and 5.

25 Ibid., chap. 3; and Yasumaro Yoshio, "Fujikō" 富士講, in Murakami and Yasumaro, eds., *Minshū shūkyō no shisō,* 635–6.

26 Ibid.

27 Inobe, *Fuji no shinkō,* 163.

28 Aizawa Seishisai 會沢正志齋, *Shinron* 新論 (The new theses), in Imai Usaburō et al., eds., *Mitogaku* 水戸學 (The writings of the Mito school, *Nihon shisō taikei,* no. 53) (Tokyo: Iwanami, 1973), 49–159.

29 Inboe, *Fuji no shinkō,* 180.

30 The *bakufu's* attitude toward Fujikō is detailed in ibid., 216–53.

31 Yasumarō Yoshio, "Maruyama Kyō" 丸山教 , in Murakami and Yasumarō, eds., *Minshū shūkyō no shisō,* 649.

32 The *Gotaigyō no maki* 御大行の巻 (Record of great austerities) has been published as *Kakugyō Tōbutsu Kū ki* 角行藤仏㤂記 (The record of the Venerable Kakugyō *Tōbutsu*), in Murakami and Yasumarō, eds., *Minshū shūkyō no shisō,* 452–81. Kakugyō's biography is also dealt with in Inobe, *Fuji no shinkō,* 6–26, and by Iwashina Koichriō 岩科小一郎 , "Sōseiki no fujikō" 創成期の富士講 (The formative phase of Fujikō), in Suzuki ed., *Fuji, Ontake to chūbu reizan,* 58–68. Kakugyō's place in popular religious movements of the Edo period is discussed by Royall Tyler, "The Tokugawa Peace and Popular Religion: Suzuki Shōzan, Kakugyō Tōbutsu, and Jikigyō Miroku," In Peter Nosco, ed., *Confucianism and Tokugawa Culture* (Princeton, N. J.: Princeton University Press, 1984), 101–9.

33 Kakugyō's alleged encounters with Ieyasu are described in some detail in the *Gotaigyō no maki.* During them Kakugyō passed on to the Shogun admonitions from Sengen Daibosatsu. In them Fuji is presented as the "central pillar of the universe" and "source of all creation." Ieyasu, as ruler of the country, is likened to it and urged to rule with justice, humanity, wisdom, filial piety, and frugality. *Kakugyō Tōbutsu Kū ki,* in Murakami and Yasumarō, eds., *Minshū shūkyō no shisō,* 473–6.

34 Ibid., 482.

35 Ibid., 480.

36 Cited by Iwashina, "Sōseiki no fujikō," 65–6.

37 Ibid., 67.

38 See, for instance, the *Kakugyō tōbutsu kūki,* 457, 458, 466, 468, 483.

39 Miyata, "Fuji shinkō to miroku," 290.

40 The core of Jikigyō Miroku's biography is provided by the *Sanjūichinichi-no-onmaki,* in Murakami and Yasumarō, eds., *Minshū shūkyō no shisō,* 424–51. Inobe, *Fuji no shinkō,* 32–50; Iwashina, "Sōseiki no fujikō," 68–75, and Tyler, "The Tokugawa Peace and Popular Religion," 107–9, all provide useful biographical sketches.

41 *Sanjūnichinichi-no-onmaki,* 425.

42 For further discussion of the importance of names, titles, and characters in the thinking of Kakugyō and Miroku see Tyler, "The Tokugawa Peace and Popular Religion," 110–11.
43 Yasumaro Yoshio 安丸良夫, *Nihon no kindaika to minshū shisō* 日本の近代化と民衆思想 (Tokyo: Aoki Shoten, 1974), 97.
44 *Sanjūnichi-no-onmaki,* 444.
45 Ibid., 443.
46 Ibid., 427
47 Ibid., 428
48 Ibid.
49 Cited in Yasumarô, *Nihon no kindaika to minshū shisō,* 103.
50 *Sanjūnichinichi-no-onmaki,* 435.
51 Ibid.
52 Ibid.
53 Ibid., 431.
54 Ibid., 429.
55 Ibid., 438.

12

Maitreya in Modern Japan

HELEN HARDACRE

Introduction

This chapter attempts to uncover the significance of Maitreya in Reiyūkai Kyōdan 靈友會教團. In this Japanese lay Buddhist group, Maitreya is associated neither with expectation of rebirth in the Tuṣita Heaven nor with anticipation of Maitreya's imminent descent. Thus Reiyūkai's Maitreya cannot easily be consigned to either the devotional or the millenarian categories by which Maitreyan phenomena are so often classified in Japanese Buddhological scholarship.[1]

This group's interest in Maitreya is not, however, confined to its blurring of interpretative categories. The group has compiled its own *Maitreya Sūtra* and also practices pilgrimage to a mountain it has named Mirokusan 彌勒山, "Maitreya Mountain." A study of the scripture and the pilgrimage reveals a relation between text and context that identifies the place of Maitreya in the world view of the group. From this examination it is clear that we cannot assume that possession or even ritual use of a text about Maitreya automatically guarantees that the people concerned actually appropriate its ideas and imagery into their thought and behavior.

Reiyūkai's *Maitreya Sūtra*

Reiyūkai is a Japanese Buddhist lay group that was founded between 1919 and 1925 in Tokyo by Kubo Kakutarō 久保角太郎 (1882–1944) and his sister-in-law Kotani Kimi 小谷喜美 (1901–71).[2] As of 1984, it had roughly 3 million members, including branches in seventeen foreign countries. Deriving from the Nichiren 日蓮 tradition, Reiyūkai created lay persons' rites of ancestor worship through daily recitation of the *Blue Sūtra*, its abridgement of the *Lotus Sūtra*. Personal salvation is believed to follow upon the salvation of ancestors through these lay rites, without priestly mediation. The group is dedicated to vitalizing (members would say "reviving") traditional Japanese family-centered values, such as respect for and obedience to elders (filial piety), gratitude to elders and benefactors (*on* 恩), and performance of duty (*giri* 義理). Women form an active part of the membership and take pride in preaching these values to youth, an activity they regard as a legitimate extension of the mother role to society at large and to other people's offspring.

Reiyūkai utilizes a scripture called the *Maitreya Sūtra (Miroku kyō* 彌勒經*)*. It was compiled for the group by one of the greatest Buddhologists of the twentieth century, Watanabe Shōkō 渡邊照宏 (1907–77).[3] Watanabe was engaged in research on Maitreya while Kubo Tsugunari 久保繼成, third and present president of Reiyūkai, was reading Sanskrit under Watanabe's direction, during the 1950s. In his research on Maitreya, Watanabe hoped to improve the classic *Miroku Jōdo ron* 彌勒浄土論, a study of Maitreyan texts by Matsumoto Bunzaburō 松本文三郎.[4]

Around 1955, the foundress Kotani Kimi began formulating plans for a youth-training facility to be called Mirokusan. She commissioned Watanabe to compile a scripture dedicated to Maitreya to be used by Mirokusan pilgrims. She began meeting with Watanabe in 1960, and shortly thereafter he began contributing articles on Maitreya to Reiyūkai's monthly newspaper, *Reiyūkaihō* 靈友會報.[5]

Watanabe left no records of the considerations guiding his compilation of Reiyūkai's *Maitreya Sūtra*, but the scripture's contents suggest that he intended to include all the major textual motifs relating to Maitreya and, in addition, original translations of texts unknown to his predecessor Matsumoto. The result was first published in May 1964 and has been in use in Reiyūkai since that time.

Table 1 correlates each section of Reiyūkai's scripture with its source, and thereafter each section is discussed in detail.

The *Maitreya Sūtra* is written in semiclassical Japanese and is composed of fifty-eight leaves. As Table 1 indicates, it is not a canonical work but a compilation of canonical and semiscriptural excerpts. A summary of its components follows.

Section 1: "Miroku jōbutsu kyō"

This brief section, occupying only a single leaf, exhorts all to listen to the Dharma as it shall be revealed in succeeding sections.

Section 2: "Kengukyō Maki dai jūni habari hon dai go-jū"

Occupying leaves 2 to 8, this section relates that, when a son bearing

Table 1. *Sources of Reiyūkai's* Maitreya Sūtra

Reiyūkai's *Maitreya Sūtra* by section	Canonical source
1. "Miroku jōbutsu kyō" 彌勒成仏經	1. *Mi-lê-ch'eng fo-ching,* T 456, p. 428
2. "Kengukyō maki dai jūni" habari hon dai go-jū 賢愚經巻第十二波婆梨品弟五十	2. *Dama muka nidana sūtra;* Chinese translation in *Dai Nippon kōtei daizōkyō,* 9, sei 4.
3. "Shō miroku hosshu kyō" 聖彌勒發趣經	3. "Ḥphag-pa byams pa ḥjug-pa shes-bya-ba theg pa chen-poḥi-mdo," *Tōhoku Catalog,* no. 865
4. "Kan miroku bosatsu jōshō" tosotsuten kyō 觀彌勒菩薩上生兜率天經	4. "Kuan-mi-lu-p'u-sa-shang-shêng-tou-shuai-to-t'en-ching," T 452, pp. 418–20
5. "Miroku geshō kyō" 彌勒下生經	5. "Mi-lê-hsia-shêng-ch'êng-fo-ching," T 14, no. 453, pp. 421–3
6. Miroku tōrai kyō" 彌勒當來經	6. *Anagata-vamsa;* see *Journal of the Pali Text Society* (1886): 4–53

the thirty-two marks of the superior being was born to a king, a sage prophesied an extraordinary career and bestowed the name Maitreya upon him. Maitreya grew up in the company of fifteen companions, hearing the Dharma expounded by the sage. Resolving to attain Buddhahood, Maitreya took the tonsure. His companions became arhats, and Maitreya received a robe from Śākyamuni.

Section 3: "Shō miroku hosshu kyō"

Translated from Tibetan by Watanabe Shōkō, this work explains why Maitreya has that name.[6] It occupies leaves 9 to 19. In the era of the Buddha Ratnacattra, there lived a bodhisattva named Firm Resolve. He vowed to attain supreme, perfect enlightenment through the following practice. He would take no food until he had ordained one thousand people in the five precepts. He persevered for 84,000 years and proselytized 100,000 people. Then for 42,000 years he praised the Three Treasures and the Mahāyāna, after which he led numerous beings to supreme, perfect enlightenment for another 84,000 years, and after that, for a further 21,000 years, he taught countless beings how to meditate. Gods and heavenly beings proclaimed that in recognition of Firm Resolve's unsurpassed compassion, he should henceforth be called Bodhisattva Maitreya.

Section 4: "Kan miroku bosatsu jōshō tosotsuten kyō"

This section, leaves 20 to 42, is chiefly dedicated to a description of the Tuṣita Heaven. It begins with a prophecy by Śākyamuni that Maitreya will be reborn there in twelve years.

Maitreya tirelessly preaches Dharma in the Tuṣita Heaven, and all who aspire to become his disciples should visualize the wonders of the Tuṣita Heaven, observe the precepts, and aspire to be reborn there. Those who praise Maitreya, call upon his name, and accumulate merit will achieve this rebirth. Those devotees will accompany Maitreya when he descends to the earth in 56 trillion years, and at that time they will meet myriad Buddhas and in their presence experience the aspiration to attain Buddhahood.

Section 5: "Miroku geshō kyō"

This section, leaves 43 to 54, describes the material conditions during Maitreya's reign. Human beings will live to the age of 84,000 years. In the center of the earth will be a marvelous palace of seven jewels, surrounded by lakes and ponds filled with lotuses of every conceivable color. In the palace will dwell a *cakravartin* king, and to him the birth of Maitreya will be predicted.

When Maitreya is born, he will be blessed with great height, strength, and wisdom. Recognizing the suffering of the world, he will sit in meditation beneath the Dragon Flower Tree and become the Buddha Maitreya. Nagas and heavenly beings will cause a shower of flowers and incense to honor him. Maitreya will conduct three Dragon Flower Assemblies, and countless persons will attain arhatship through hearing him preach.

Section 6: "Miroku tōrai kyō"

Occupying leaves 55 to 58, this section relates the characteristics of those who will meet Maitreya. Those who disrupt the harmony of the Sangha, like Devadatta, or slander the Buddha's disciples will not see Maitreya. But those who give alms, keep the precepts, plant *bodhi* trees, build bridges and roads, and dig wells will meet Maitreya, as will those who honor their parents and present flowers, lamps, and food to the Buddha.

Since the *Maitreya Sūtra* is such a remarkable compendium of Maitreya lore, we might suppose that Reiyūkai is an active cult of Maitreya, but in fact it is not. Despite its great store of Maitreya imagery, Reiyūkai puts little of it to use, actualizes only a fraction. The significance of Maitreya in this lay Buddhist group can be assessed only by a combination of analysis of the written text and analysis of Reiyūkai's use of the text. For Reiyūkai the text is not primarily a document but a scripture used orally, in ritual, in a very particular setting. The context of the scripture's use is essential to an understanding of its meaning, and we turn to a consideration of that context next.

The Mirokusan Pilgrimage

Reiyūkai members associate their *Maitreya Sūtra* mainly with the Mirokusan pilgrimage, a three-day set of rituals and exercises. It is primarily in this context that Maitreyan imagery and ideas are integrated with the practice of ancestor worship and related ethical concepts that constitute the core of the group's world view.

Mirokusan is located on a mountain on the Izu 伊豆 Peninsula, the nearest city being Atami 熱海. In the 1930s (the precise date is unknown), the founders of Reiyūkai made a vow at the Ise 伊勢 Shrine to establish a *kaidan* 戒壇, or ordination platform, and Mirokusan represents the fulfillment of that vow.

The ordination platform has a special significance in Japanese Buddhism. Japan's first *kaidan* was established in 755 at Tōdaiji 東大寺, representing the six Nara sects, and in 759 a second was built by Ganjin (鑑真 Chien-chen) at Tōshōdaiji 唐招提寺. In the first instance, the building of a *kaidan* on Japanese soil made it possible to carry out formal ordination of monks and nuns in Japan without sending ordinands to China or Korea. Later establishments of *kaidan* at Hieizan 比叡山 by Saichō, at Kōyasan 高野山 by Kūkai 空海, and at Minobusan 身延山 for the Nichiren school signified the independence of the Tendai 天台, Shingon 真言, and Nichiren schools and an end to the necessity of having monks ordained by other schools.

Nichiren established a model for Kotani and Kubo. According to legend, Nichiren made a vow at Ise to establish a *kaidan,* and this vow was fulfilled in the completion of Minobusan. Following his example, the founders of Reiyūkai traveled to Ise and vowed to the gods of heaven and earth before the locked gates of the Inner Shrine to establish an ordination platform. Completed in 1964, Mirokusan redeemed the founders' vow.

Yet is there not a fundamental contradiction in the idea of a lay group establishing a place to ordain clergy? Whereas former Buddhist schools erected *kaidan* to express their independence from those schools in which they originated, Mirokusan constitutes a statement of Reiyūkai's independence from the clergy as a whole. The pilgrim does not go there to be ordained.

Instead, he goes for *shugyō* (修行, spiritual training), to make a vow, and, making vows, is spoken of as a bodhisattva.

Mirokusan is also a mountain utopia, an ancient idea in Japan. In virtually all varieties of Japanese religion, the mountain symbolically represents the other world, the abode of deities, spirits, and ancestors, the meeting place of heaven and earth. The mountain has a special connection with the cult of Maitreya in Japan, which is seen in the phenomenon of *kyōzuka* 經塚, mounds housing sūtra reliquaries built on mountains to await the coming of Maitreya. Also closely relating the cult of mountains to Maitreyan symbolism is the belief that Kūkai remains in *samādhi* on Kōyasan until Maitreya appears. At Reiyūkai's Mirokusan the symbolic associations of sacred mountains focus and heighten the experience of traditional values created there and support the impression of the sacrality of those values.

The Mirokusan pilgrimage is in the tradition of retreats on mountains for *shugyō*. There are both secular and religious varieties, or perhaps one should say that sponsors may be religious bodies or secular organizations seeking to imbue their employees with religious or semireligious values. The strategies employed by the two have much in common.

The Mirokusan complex includes a dormitory, a cafeteria, lounges, a large worship hall, a pagoda housing a statue of Maitreya, and Kotani's tomb. From a survey of the membership in 1977, I found that 78 percent of respondents had participated more than ten times in the pilgrimage, and another 20 percent had participated between one and ten times.[7] Separate pilgrimages are held for those above or below the age of thirty, though the activities are not radically different.

The journey to Mirokusan is preceded by important preliminaries. It is usual for pilgrims to go in large groups, as I did in 1976, with a group of 540 members from Osaka. The pilgrimage officially begins with recitation of Reiyūkai's abridgement of the *Lotus Sūtra*, the *Blue Sūtra*, at a branch meeting hall, which is the point of departure. About Mirokusan itself it is explained only that through the pilgrimage it is possible to change karma and "open destiny" (*unmei o akeru* 運命を開ける). Unlike other pilgrimages in Japan, the route of march – overnight chartered bus is the usual mode of conveyance – is closely regulated to prevent the use of alcohol and unsupervised contact between the sexes. Prayers are said the entire time the bus is in motion as a prayer card is passed from seat to seat.

A definite break with the secular world is made as the pilgrims' bus enters the precincts of Mirokusan. The ascent of the mountain is an entry into sacred space, marked by the donning of a special sash and recitation in unison by everyone present of the *daimoku* 是目, "Namu myōhō renge kyō" 南無妙法蓮華經, the phrase hailing the *Lotus Sūtra*, here used as a mantra to strengthen the pilgrim and create the proper attitude of seriousness and dedication. Only a short interlude during which pilgrims are allowed to store their belongings in the dormitory and to become acquainted with pilgrims who have come from other parts of Japan interrupts this prolonged initial period of restraint and control.

The main ritual business of the first day is recitation of the *Maitreya Sūtra,* which takes about an hour and a half. The pilgrim is called to worship by closed-circuit television in the dormitory rooms, whence he or she departs for the worship hall. A leader at the front of the hall conducts the recitation, for which pilgrims again don sashes, and the audience follows along by reading sūtra booklets distributed to all. I encountered no one who knew the sūtra from memory. At no time is there any explanation or discussion of the sūtra or the figure of Maitreya.

After an uncomprehending recitation that leaves all quite weary, especially after an overnight bus trip on which sleep remains a vain hope, pilgrims are allowed to relax. Dinner, like all meals, is vegetarian, and in the evening pilgrims can participate in folk singing, watch a movie on the life of the founder Kotani, or talk informally with group leaders or such personalities as *sumō* wrestlers who are Reiyūkai members.

Cycles of Control and Release

The rhythm of the Mirokusan pilgrimage is one of prolonged, controlled, regimented activity followed by periods of release and relaxation. Pilgrims are heavily supervised and their movements tightly circumscribed during the periods of *shugyō,* and after enduring these sessions, they are rewarded with opportunities for free expression of an emotional nature. Over the three days tension builds in cycles of *shugyō* and release, culminating in a final, cathartic session during which vows are taken. The first such cycle begins with recitation of the *Blue Sūtra* before departure for Mirokusan and concludes with the period of relaxation on the evening of the first day (see Table 2).

The final activity of the release portion of the first cycle, on the evening of the first day at Mirokusan, is a discussion session held in small groups in the sleeping rooms. Here, for the first time, pilgrims are allowed to express their reactions to the events of the pilgrimage. Small circles of five or six are formed, and a leader is assigned to guide discussion of themes established in advance and circulated in pamphlets that all pilgrims receive. The themes are as follows: "In what situation do you most admire your parents?" "What does the Inner Trip [Reiyūkai's English-language slogan for itself] mean to you?" "What do you do to promote this religion at work or school?" and "How do you feel when reciting the sūtra?" The leaders had evidently been instructed to concentrate on the last of these.

The technique of leadership adopted at this first small face-to-face

Table 2. *Cycles of control and release at the Mirokusan pilgrimage*

Cycle		Regime	Time
1	Control:	Recitation of *Blue Sūtra*	Predeparture
		Bus trip	Day 1
		Ascent of Mirokusan	
		Recitation of *Maitreya Sūtra*	
	Release:	Dinner	
		Informal discussion	
		Relaxing activities	
		Discussion of reactions to sūtra	
2	Control:	Recitation of *Blue Sūtra*	Day 2
		Scolding	
		Worship at Kotani's tomb	
		Training in shouting "Hai!"	
	Release:	Vow session	
		Practice for third-day vow session	
3	Control:	Recitation of *Blue Sūtra*	Day 3
		Small-group discussions	
	Release:	Final vow session	
		Worship at Maitreya pagoda	

gathering is meant to establish rapport. First leaders elicit the inevitably negative reaction to sūtra recitation, admitting that they felt the same at first. Then they defuse this negative reaction with a promise that endurance will be rewarded.

Contemporary young Japanese are seldom accustomed to sitting on the heels, the ordinary posture for recitation, for an hour at a stretch and find it as painful as a Westerner does. Novices also report that recitation of the sūtra does not give them an understanding of its meaning, and hence they must proceed blindly, which is a punishing, boring experience. Novices are generally intimidated by the sight of a large number of people reciting scripture in earnest and are likely to feel that their allegiance to the rest of society (which they as well as Western sociologists are likely to perceive as secular in character) is somehow placed in doubt by participation. Thus after some initial hesitation, novices generally admit that they dislike sūtra recitation and are relieved to hear that their feelings are shared not only by fellow novices but, in the past, by leaders as well.

Discovery of this shared feeling is the key to the rapport leaders hope to create. They must then take the floor and put before the group the idea, in the form of their own, personal experience, that sūtra recitation has made them stronger individuals, that it has something to offer the novice as a reward for enduring a painful, uncomprehending experience.

This strategy works only when leaders are as numerous as or more numerous than novices, when they can create a mood of enthusiasm for sūtra recitation without becoming too specific. Rapport is threatened when inquiries about the meaning of the sūtra are allowed to become an object of shared attention. Although leaders have been trained to create an impression of shared emotions and a sense of group membership, they generally cannot answer such questions as "What is the meaning and purpose of sūtra recitation?" "What are the main points of the *Lotus Sūtra,* and why is it important in life?"

In the 1930s an event occurred that sounded the death knell for doctrinal study in Reiyūkai. At that time two branch leaders of the organization, Naganuma Myōko 長沼妙佼 (1899–1957) and Niwano Nikkyō 庭野日敬 (b. 1906) began holding study groups on the *Lotus Sūtra,* and they attracted many members in this way. Kotani Kimi, however, saw in their efforts a specious logic chopping, subverting believers' simple devotion to the sūtra. For her, an analytic approach to the sūtra was not only misguided but dangerous. She recited the sūtra as *shugyō*, as a means to train and discipline and to imbue a faithful believer with the powers proclaimed in the sūtra. She publicly castigated Niwano and Naganuma, who left Reiyūkai with all the members in their charge and in 1938 founded Risshōkōseikai 立正佼成會. Since this incident there has been no serious attempt at doctrinal instruction in Reiyūkai.

On the second day the second cycle of control and release begins at 5:30 am, when the closed-circuit television comes on and broadcasts such American rock and roll hits as "Let's Get It All Together!" to awaken the pilgrim and provide a somewhat incongruous musical background for recitation of the *Blue Sūtra.*

A new form of *shugyō* is introduced on the second day. Room leaders, peers of the novices, join older leaders in scolding the novices. The subject of scolding may be quite trivial; it may concern, for example, lining up slippers outside the sleeping rooms in a straight line, folding the bedding neatly, or sweeping the room. Even in a faultless room some error will be seized upon as an occasion to lecture novices. Novices must show more effort, be more grateful and humble, more serious, more fervent in the worship hall.

Zeal in the worship hall is an object of special attention, and after making speeches reprimanding us for lacking the proper spirit in shouting "Hai!" in group meetings, leaders drilled us in shouting "Hai!" louder and louder, raising our fists clenching rosaries. This is the proper posture to demonstrate impassioned sincerity. It is particularly important that pilgrims meld themselves into a single group, participating willingly in the scheduled activities, suppressing their inclinations to do otherwise.

Scolding, obedience to leaders, and conformity to the schedule are to be endured, not questioned. The desired reaction of the young pilgrim is repentance for poor performance and resolve to strive for greater conformity to the organization's expectation. Implied is the idea that youth should obey their elders (a well-known ideological corollary of ancestor worship wherever it is found) and an unexplicated reference to the value placed on the practice of repentance.

Repentance is an important practice in the new religions generally. Reiyūkai's third president, Kubo Tsugunari, has discussed it at length in what may be taken as his answer to the doctrinal vacuum in Reiyūkai, a book titled *Zaikeshugi Bukkyō no susume* 在家主義仏教のすすめ (An encouragement to lay Buddhism).[8] In that work and based on the "Meditation on Samantabhadra" chapter of the *Lotus Sūtra,* Kubo explains repentance as the direct realization of one's error or staining of the heart-mind.[9] Repentance is believed to destroy karmic hindrances, to create merit, and to constitute the first step in the practice of the bodhisattva.[10]

Also on the second day, pilgrims walk to Kotani's tomb, located in the rear of the worship hall, and chant the *daimoku* for about ten minutes. Although the placement of the tomb is clearly patterned after that of Kūkai on Kōyazan, no explanation is provided. Pilgrims are told only that this is the founder's grave (*haka* 墓).

The second cycle of *shugyō* and release is completed on the evening of the second day, when meetings for members of each of Reiyūkai's branches are held. The Eighth Branch, whose members I accompanied, made up the largest portion of those in attendance at this pilgrimage. In the meeting we were charged to demonstrate the strength of the branch by verbal volume in the final session on the third day. By way of practice, we were drilled again in shouting "Hai!" louder and louder.

The third and final cycle of *shugyō* and release took place on the third day, when our *shugyō* consisted of sūtra recitation and group discussions for the purpose of making an announcement (*happyō* 發表) or vow (*chikai* 誓) before the altar in the worship hall. All through the session, there had been shorter vow sessions as part of the release from *shugyō,* and all were leading up to the final, most emotional session.

The vow sessions are the necessary accompaniment within the framework of the pilgrimage as a whole to the more tightly controlled exercises such as sūtra recitation. Carried out on the second and third days, the vow sessions are held for the purpose of instructing the novice on approved values and channeling them through the organization of Reiyūkai. They are presided over by a master of ceremonies, who calls upon those present to come forward in the worship hall. At that point, rosary in hand, everyone jumps up on the benches and screams, "Hai!" hoping to be recognized. Upon recognition, a person goes to the microphone in front of the main altar and makes a vow. The content of the vow generally includes repentance for past wrongs and a promise to reform. More often than not, the vow is delivered with a great display of emotion, and crying is not uncommon for either sex. The pilgrims repent for not having been sufficiently filial, for not having been grateful enough to their ancestors. They promise to reform by putting Reiyūkai's teachings into practice in their lives.

In the pilgrimage's overall rhythm of control and release, sūtra recitation is the core of controlled *shugyō,* and the vow sessions are the center of the release portion. In the control section, Maitreya lore is partially and imperfectly transmitted, as are the ideas appearing in the *Blue Sūtra,* recited twice, whereas the *Maitreya Sūtra* is recited only once. However, this transmission is not reinforced by explication or discussion, and leaders discourage analysis of either text. In the vow sessions leaders provide a model of behavior they hope the novice will emulate and in doing so experience repentance, indebtedness, and gratitude.

Pilgrims are taught by leaders' examples to unloose in vow sessions a flood of emotion accumulated during periods of close supervision. Control is exerted by enforcing conformity to a rigid schedule, by forcing pilgrims to submit to unaccustomed activities like sūtra recitation, and by forcing them to endure prolonged admonishment about essentially inconsequential matters. The natural desire to escape from these forms of control is shaped by leaders' behavior in the vow sessions. They rush to the microphone and deliver "vows" consisting of repentance to parents, ancestors, and senior colleagues in Reiyūkai. Leaders strongly urge novices to deliver vows also, and the vows of compliant novices follow leaders' examples in form and content. Immediately and inevitably following repentance comes an equally fervent expression of gratitude to and renewed dependence on the same figures and a promise to persevere in order to repay the debt.

Repentance, gratitude, and dependence are slightly separated moments of the same cathartic experience. This combination of emotions is what Reiyūkai wants its pilgrims to experience.

Seeing leaders express these emotions, the novice is taught the acceptable terms in which to express his or her own relief at being loosed from the control of *shugyō*. Even skeptics who voice distaste for crowd behavior are caught up in the roar of "Hai!" leaping up and down on the benches to be called upon to speak, crying profusely at the microphone to the thunderous applause of the crowd.

Kubo Tsugunari has written that a direct experience of repentance, dependence, and gratitude is the essence of human existence.[11] Sūtra recitation is understood in Reiyūkai as proof of true repentance. The object of repentance should include one's ancestors as well as living people, because one's own behavior affects them. The link between ancestor and descendant is one of shared karma, some of which is inherited. Ancestors cannot attain Buddhahood without descendants' ritual care in the form of sūtra recitation, and so long as they do not attain Buddhahood, they may cause harm to their descendants. Thus descendant and ancestor affect each other, and the channel for these effects is their karmic connection, which persists eternally. Sūtra recitation not only demonstrates the descendant's repentance but also constitutes a prayer for the ancestors' attainment of Buddhahood, because the merit of recitation is transferred to ancestors by the reciter.

Praying for the ancestors' Buddhahood is equivalent, Kubo writes, to making a vow to improve oneself.[12] This identification rests on the reciprocal workings of karma between ancestor and descendant just explained. To engage in sūtra recitation and other forms of *shugyō* is a form of self-improvement in Reiyūkai and is furthermore spoken of as the *shugyō* of the bodhisattva. The master of ceremonies at Mirokusan calls the pilgrims "young bodhisattvas," using this term for both men and women, and signs urging all members to "become bodhisattvas" (*Zenkaiin wa bosatsu ni narō!* 全会員は菩薩になろう) are everywhere in evidence.

In a vague, nondoctrinal sense, then, Mirokusan vows are bodhisattva vows, and the Mirokusan pilgrimage is conceived of as the setting in which to take the bodhisattva vow. Reiyūkai expresses the hope that all humanity will become bodhisattvas.

The figure of Maitreya presides over these vows by virtue of their being made in a worship hall dedicated to him, on a mountain named after him, but other than this, his involvement is minimal. The situation is pregnant with implication (will these young bodhisattvas achieve Buddhahood under Maitreya's reign?), but none of the possibilities are spelled out. The pilgrims may draw their own conclusions, but discussion is not encouraged. The *Maitreya Sūtra* is not brought to bear on the lessons of the vow sessions at all. At most, Maitreya presides over the pilgrimage as a whole, imparting his blessings to the completed work.

The lack of explication may account for the fact that most Reiyūkai members do not make strong distinctions between Maitreya and Śākyamuni. Reiyūkai has a shorter pilgrimage to its headquarters, called Shakaden 釈迦殿 (where Śākyamuni is enshrined), with the same alternation of rigid control and emotional release in vow sessions. Leaders channel raw emotion toward an experience of the sacrality of conservative, family-centered values in exactly the same way as at Mirokusan. Pilgrims have similarly vague conceptions of both figures.

Almost as an afterthought, pilgrims file by the pagoda housing a statue of Maitreya on the way to their buses after the final vow session. The exercise is completed with a bow. There is no explanation of this brief act of worship. If it is raining, worship at the pagoda is canceled.

Pilgrims' experience at Mirokusan and Shakaden is not without parallel in secular society. The Mirokusan pilgrimage shares much with secular programs for spiritual training. At secluded retreats, frequently in the mountains, employees of banks, corporations, and family businesses are lectured on filial piety and their debt to their parents, often with heavy emphasis on the mother's sacrifice, including graphic accounts of the pain of childbirth. Participants are frequently called upon to beg their parents' forgiveness. The hope is that they will realize that, just as they can never repay their mother for what she has endured for their sakes, they can never fully repay the debt they owe their employers, acting *in loco parentis.*[13]

In combination with lecture sessions, participants are given group tasks, often tests of physical endurance, and only after proving their perseverance are they allowed release in cathartic displays of emotion. The message imparted is similar to that in Reiyūkai: "The meaning of being adult . . . is to realize one's connectedness to others and to learn how to maintain these links."[14] Both secular and religious *shugyō* aim to heighten the feelings of gratitude and dependence by playing on dependency feelings, especially of the mother–child relationship, and then extending and harnessing these to the context of work, marriage, or membership in a religious organization. Reiyūkai treats parents and ancestors as equivalent in terms of the debt pilgrims owe them, but what has any of this to do with Maitreya?

Text and Rite in the Formation of Conceptions of Maitreya

At Mirokusan, Maitreya presides over the experience of repentance, gratitude, and dependence and over the mountain utopia as a whole. By extension, he will preside over a perfected world in which all have become bodhisattvas, but this has little relation to the scripture that bears his name. There Maitreya ascends and descends, and his name is justified, none of which is really brought home to Mirokusan pilgrims. Standing apart from the experience of repentance, gratitude, and indebtedness, Maitreya remains peripheral to most pilgrims, as does Śākyamuni in the Shakaden pilgrimage.

The appropriation of Maitreya seen in Reiyūkai is, however, quite congruent with Japanese usage generally. Japanese examples of the expectation that Maitreya will take an active role in any dramatic reconstruction of the world are few, as illustrated in other chapters in this volume.

Japanese religions, and the new religions in particular, adopt the perspective of meliorism, the doctrine that society and the world are to be improved by collective moral improvement. From this point of view, nothing but human effort can be counted upon to effect substantive betterment. It is naïve to expect supernatural aid. According to this view, Maitreya may preside over a perfected world, but he has no role in perfecting it. Seen in the light of the history of Japanese religions, Reiyūkai's Mirokusan pilgrimage represents not a radical break with the past but a continuing effort to apply knowledge of Maitreya to collective improvement. Betterment of the whole, members would point out, is exactly what a bodhisattva should strive for.

NOTES

1 Beginning with the work of Matsumoto Bunzaburō (see below), it has become common to distinguish between texts emphasizing a devotee's ascent to and those emphasizing Maitreya's descent from the Tuṣita Heaven. Ascent and descent come to be associated with "devotional" and "millenarian" tendencies, respectively, and analysis of Maitreyan phenomena in general becomes an exercise in classifying a particular manifestation into one of the two categories. For a concise bibliography on this scholarship, see Miyata Noboru, "Miroku shinkō no kenkyū seika to kadai" 弥勒信仰の研究成果と課題 in *Miroku shinkō,* ed. Miyata Noboru, Minshū shūkyōshi yosho, 13 vols. (Tokyo: Yūzankaku, 1984), 8:301–22.

2 Except where otherwise indicated, discussion of Reiyūkai, its *Maitreya Sūtra,* and the Mirokusan pilgrimage is based on my fieldwork from 1976 to 1980 and from 1983 to 1984 and on my *Lay Buddhism in Contemporary Japan: Reiyūkai Kyōdan* (Princeton, N. J.: Princeton University Press, 1984).

3 After graduating from the Tokyo Imperial University's Department of Indian Philosophy, Watanabe studied Sanskrit and other languages in Germany. Upon returning to Japan, he took a university post, but ill health forced him to resign. For the rest of his life, he continued his research in affiliation with Tōyō University 東洋大學, at the Buddhist Studies Institute at Narita, and at the Tōyō Bunkō 東洋文庫.

4 Information gained in discussion with Watanabe's third son Shōkei.

5 Watanabe's contributions to the *Reiyukaihō* spanned the period from August 1969 through January 1975, nos. 138–91.

6 Watanabe did not publish a full translation of this work elsewhere, but a paraphrase for the laity was included in vol. 3 of his *Watanabe chosakushu* 渡邊著作集, 8 vols. (Tokyo: Chikuma shobō, 1982), chap. 4.

7 This survey is described in detail and its results presented in my *Lay Buddhism,* Appendix.

8 Kubo Tsugunari, *Zaikeshugi bukkyō no susume* (Tokyo: Inna torippu sha, 1978).

9 Ibid., 178.

10 In *Lay Buddhism,* 132–3 I have traced the scriptural roots of this conception of the idea of repentance in Buddhist thought.

11 Kubo, *Zaikeshugi bukkyō,* 223.

12 Ibid., 241.

13 Two excellent studies of secular *shugyō* are Dorinne K. Kondo, "Work, Family, and the Self: A Cultural Analysis of Japanese Family Enterprise" (Ph. D. diss. Harvard University, 1982), and Thomas Rohlen, "Spiritual Training in a Japanese Bank," *American Anthropologist* 75 (1973).

14 Kondo, "Work, Family, and the Self," 61.

Epilogue

A Prospectus for the Study of Maitreya

ALAN SPONBERG

Introduction

The historical development of the Maitreya legend is but one of many topics in the study of Buddhism and the cultures of Asia; yet it remains a topic of perennial fascination. Maitreya has continually attracted both the veneration of Buddhist practitioners and the attention of scholars of Buddhism. For those within the tradition, Maitreya has held a place of honor and reverence comparable to that of Śākyamuni himself: His ongoing presence within this world system has maintained the immediacy of Gautama's teaching, and the certainty of his future Buddhahood ensures both the continuity and the legitimacy of the Dharma. Seen from the perspective of scholars and others looking at Buddhism from the outside, the Maitreya legend has taken on still further significance as the Buddhist expression of a number of classical themes in the study of religion. In his guise as Buddhist messiah, in particular, Maitreya has provided for many Westerners a bridge to what otherwise has seemed to some an alien, world-denying, atheistic religion.

It is easy, however, to misrepresent the importance of Maitreya in Buddhism – easier still to misunderstand the nature and significance of the actual role he has played within the tradition. Maitreya has only rarely been the most prominent devotional figure in any Buddhist culture. In fact, he is more often overshadowed by other cult figures, by the cult of Śākyamuni in Theravāda cultures, or by that of one of the many bodhisattvas and Buddhas popular in Mahāyāna Buddhism. In considering Maitreya in the context of the history of religions, moreover, there is the additional danger of misinterpreting Maitreya's place in Buddhism precisely because of the apparent parallels with other traditions. Some Western scholars have undoubtedly been too quick, in their quest for the universal structures of all human religious experience, to map the Maitreya myth in Buddhism onto categories prominent in Semitic religions – too quick to assume that, as a "messianic figure," Maitreya must share the same prominence and the same character as others in that archetypal role.

In spite of these potential distortions, or indeed because of them, a careful examination of Maitreya's place within the tradition is clearly a desideratum at this point in our study of Buddhist cultural history. The Maitreya legend is, after all, one of the relatively few elements of the Buddhist tradition that has had some place in every historical and cultural variation of the tradition. Moreover, it is an element of the Buddhist tradition that has proved to be an unusually rich source for later developments. By necessity, any study of Maitreya must be as multifaceted as the figure himself. What then, we might ask, is the core of this Maitreya myth, what was the theme on which such a rich profusion of variations could be built? Below I shall argue that the core is best understood not as a single, monolithic theme, but rather as a complex of interrelated themes. First, however, I shall summarize some features of Maitreya that have emerged in this volume. With an idea of some of the characteristics that distinguish Maitreya within the Buddhist pantheon, we will be in a better position to take up the question of core themes.

Maitreya: Some Characteristic Features

Perhaps the most striking characteristic of Maitreya, in contrast to other mythic figures of the Buddhist tradition, is his multivalence, the fact that his characterization allows such rich variation. Maitreya's potential for mythic elaboration is far greater than that of Śākyamuni, the latter being a figure far more bound by his historicity. Although Maitreya is depicted as a future Buddha, the next for this world system, the exact nature of his role as the next Buddha was left sufficiently open in the core tradition to provide fertile ground for elaboration. To be sure, there are many other cases of thematic and iconographic development and variation within Buddhism. With Avalokiteśvara, for example, we have a prominent case of radical transformation in a Buddhist cult figure, but one that differs, I would argue, from the type of development we see with Maitreya. In the case of Avalokiteśvara's metamorphosis into Kuan-yin, the transformation appears to be less an inherent function of the original characterization and more a specific response to a particular cultural situation. In contrast, the open-ended multivalence of Maitreya, should be seen, I think, as an integral aspect of his basic character.

One might argue that this open-ended lack of definition is simply the result of the lack of prominence given the future-Buddha theme in early South Asian Buddhism, that it in fact reflects Maitreya's relative insignificance in the canonical sources. Certainly he does become a more prominent figure in later texts like the *Mahāvastu* and the *Anāgatavaṃsa*. But there is another possible explanation we should not overlook. Perhaps the nature of his role is simply different from what we would expect of a messianic figure. Perhaps the lack of development was quite intentional, part of the very characterization of the role, so to speak. Maitreya's place as the future Buddha seems now to have been established quite early in Buddhist history. That the details of his future role were initially left so richly ambiguous may argue as well for the significance of Maitreya's place as for his obscurity or unimportance. In the early canonical sources the prophetic and eschatological potential of the future-Buddha theme was not explored in great revelatory detail – that much is certain. Perhaps the failure to specify in greater detail the dimensions of Maitreya's future role reflects a concern not to overdetermine the figure playing this role in the case of Buddhism.

It is just with regard to this point, in fact, that we can see one of many places where we might be misled if we measure Maitreya's place in Buddhism against the expectations of a more explicitly messianic tradition like Christianity. We should note, in other words, that the value of the "messianic theme" within Buddhism may stem from its very lack of specificity, from its openness to development and elaboration by the later tradition. If we assume that Maitreya is significant only to the extent to which he fulfills our own expectations of the messianic role, we are indeed likely to minimize his place in early Buddhism and certain to overlook the actual nature of the role he did play. Looking at the history of the Maitreya theme within Buddhism, it seems now quite clear that his appeal in the later tradition was in large part a function of the open-ended possibilities inherent in the core theme.

If Maitreya's inherent multivalence is one general characteristic, certainly another is his humanity, both the degree to which he is endowed with ordinary human characteristics and the fact that he is so accessible to human understanding and contact as well as emulation. Though the mythic figure Maitreya does not appear to be based on any historical individual, one does find in the very early literature depictions of an ordinary disciple named Maitreya, one well within the normal range of human characteristics. Even if these stories represent a motif originally distinct from and independent of the theme of Maitreya the future Buddha, they were assimilated into that core legend very early and seem to have become an important feature. In his study of Maitreya in South Asia P. S. Jaini (Chapter 3) draws attention to the numerous accounts, mostly in Mahāyāna sources, that depict Maitreya's shortcomings and failings as a bodhisattva in training. In the *Lotus Sūtra*, for example, even though the notion of Maitreya's future buddhahood is taken for granted, we nonetheless find Maitreya the disciple depicted in all too familiar human terms. Mañjuśrī recounts there that in an earlier life Maitreya was a disciple named Yaśaskāma, or Seeker of Fame, one who "was slothful, covetous, greedy for gain and clever," one who was also "excessively desirous of glory, but very fickle."[1]

The contrast here with accounts of Gautama's bodhisattva career should not be overlooked. Why were Maitreya's shortcomings as a bodhisattva given such prominence? They help explain why Maitreya takes longer than Gautama to achieve buddhahood, but they raise the additional exegetical problem of explaining why he eventually surpasses Gautama to become a Buddha presiding over the world at a much more desirable point in the cycle of evolution and devolution. This negative characterization serves, in part at least, to underscore Maitreya's humanness, and I think we can discern in that humanness part of the reason that Maitreya was seen as such a suitable representative of Buddhist aspiration for the contemporary age.

Whether in sixth-century China or in Southeast Asia today, Maitreya came to be seen as a recognizably human figure, one who demonstrates the potential of the Buddhist path even more immediately than the long-past example of Gautama. Moreover, Maitreya is of this world even now, dwelling in a realm that is much closer to us than is obvious to the Western observer with a rather different concept of what a heaven is. Tuṣita Heaven, Maitreya's abode until he is born once again among humans as a Buddha, is no remote, transcendent paradise. It is very much a part of this world system, one of a series of connected levels of existence, and not even the highest of those levels at that. In Buddhist cosmography these realms are so interconnected, in fact, that the skilled meditator moves easily among them in the exercise of yogic techniques. Much of the attractiveness of Maitreya as a cult figure stems from the fact that he is accessible to the aspirant, through meditative trance and through rebirth – even now, long before his awaited advent as the next Buddha. Even more than Śākyamuni, Maitreya has been seen, in this sense, as a Buddha for the present, for those of this world and for those in even the most desperate of times.[2]

Finally, we should recognize a perhaps less obvious characteristic of Maitreya that has emerged over the course of his development within the tradition: his ability to function as a mediating agent. It is Maitreya who ensures the link between the Dharma of the past and the Dharma of the future, Maitreya who confirms the renewal of the perpetual cycle of regeneration. Moreover, he does so through his presence in Tuṣita Heaven as a bodhisattva at just that time, so distant from the days of Śākyamuni, when decline is overwhelmingly evident, thus connecting our present plight with both past and future. This mediating aspect of his nature must be a central one, for it recurs in many forms throughout the development of the myth.

There are a number of disparate instances in which the role of mediation appears to be operative, especially in those cases involving the gradual assimilation and attempted reconciliation of several contending forces within Buddhist mythology. Though still quite polarized in the earliest sources of the Maitreya legend, the dichotomy between the *cakravartin* ideal and the Tathāgata ideal eventually finds its resolution in several later Maitreya traditions, for example. The dichotomy also between the aspiration for a better world and the aspiration for release from this world finds effective resolution in various developments of the Maitreya myth. Finally, in more recent Japanese developments, we even find Maitreya playing a mediating role in the relationship between men and women.

Theme and Variation: A Fugue in the Manner of Bach

These characteristics of Maitreya – his multivalence, his humanity, his immediacy, and his mediating agency – are particularly important, because they were the characteristics that enabled Maitreya to take on such a variety of guises in various Buddhist cultures throughout history. But if the historical development of the Maitreya theme is so rich in transformation and variation, is there any point in attempting to comprehend that development as a whole? Or would such an attempt involve the unnecessary hypostatization of an ideal "Maitreya" that does not really exist, one that never existed? Would it perhaps be more appropriate simply to speak of a number of historically distinct "Maitreyas," each with only the most tenuous circumstantial relation to the others? I think not, even though such a ploy might well seem to simplify our task. The continuities that emerge in this volume show that we must attempt to understand Maitreya both diachronically and cross-culturally, that it is impossible to understand fully any particular instance of the myth, no matter how historically remote, without recognizing the way in which that instance still represents a variation on a common core of themes. The degree of elaboration, as well as the historical and cultural range over which the various Maitreyas are distributed, makes this a difficult task, to be sure. The developments of the theme will, by their nature, obscure the continuities. It is difficult even to envision the complexity of the process of development involved in a case like this, especially when we are working on only one particular variation.

I am reminded of the intricacy of a complex fugue, a musical form that is simple at its core but subject to great elaboration and nuance in its extension. In this case, what we have is similar to a multiple fugue, one of the triple and quadruple fugues Bach wrote near the end of his life. In these compositions several distinct, though related themes are introduced in the beginning and then subjected to increasingly elaborate variation. The range of possible variations is vast, yet some aspect of the original themes is always retained, even if not immediately obvious. In such a multiple fugue, moreover, one or another of the original themes will be dominant in a given variation. The others remain present, but latent, later to reemerge, often with even richer potential for variation and development than before, since each subsequent variation draws on all that has gone before, on an ever richer exposition and development of the opening themes and their interrelationship.

For our purposes I want to draw attention especially to the continuity that links the opening themes and their subsequent variations in such a fugue. Note in particular what is required, given the complexity of that link, if one is to understand the composition as a whole. With Bach's late fugues we can, to be sure, derive a great deal of pleasure from listening to any one of the variations on its own: Some of them might even stand quite well as independent pieces. Yet our pleasure and our appreciation of the fugue as a whole are greatly enhanced when, on repeated listening, we are gradually able to discern the underlying themes running through the composition, themes that are repeatedly modified and altered but always in a way that links them back to the opening statement. Surely it is only with that degree of comprehension that we begin truly to understand the fugue.

To appreciate fully the place of Maitreya within the history of Buddhist culture, we must learn to listen to history in a similar way. The ideal approach to material as complex as this is one that thoroughly explores the distinctiveness of each variation while still seeking to discern the underlying thematic continuities. It is only by recognizing the original themes and determining how they have been transformed that we can begin to discern the historical and cultural individuality of the variation. Even in instances in which the Maitreya of the early scriptural sources has become almost unrecognizable through thematic evolution and cultural accretion, those changes themselves can be understood only in light of the broader tradition. We must continually move in both directions at once. We can study the Maitreya myth only in some particular expression, but to establish the characteristic uniqueness and value of that given expression, we must simultaneously seek to understand the way in which it presents a variation of the core themes made available by the tradition. Once we have recognized which themes were elaborated – and which were not – in a given historical setting, we can begin to ask *why* this particular permutation developed when it did. That, in turn, will tell us more about the distinctiveness of the instance at hand. In that sense, the kind of understanding we need requires attention both to the culturally specific context of the expression under study *and* to the thematic core available for variation in that case.

Maitreya: Three Approaches for Further Research

With the fugue analogy in mind, I would like to present a prospectus for future studies of Maitreya-related themes. The range of scholarship presented in this volume is far from exhaustive, but it is sufficient to illustrate a number of possibilities for further research, possibilities that can be usefully grouped under three interrelated headings: (1) research on the core tradition, on the sources of the Maitreya myth; (2) research on specific historical instances of the development and appropriation of that core tradition; and (3) more general and comparative work examining the place of the Maitreya material in the broader study of the history of religions. Each of these represents a necessary sphere of inquiry, and it is natural that individual scholars will, because of their individual training and interests, tend toward one or the other. Nevertheless, as this volume demonstrates, none of these three can be pursued effectively in isolation from the other two. It is necessary that we focus our individual efforts in the most effective way possible, but it is also imperative that any work on a topic as complex as the Maitreya myth be undertaken in the light of research being done on other aspects and other dimensions of the same topic.

The value of a project defined in terms of any one of these three areas is likely to be a direct function of the extent to which it can address its findings to those working in the other two. This was one of the broader goals of the conference on which this volume is based, one for which we brought together individuals working from several different disciplinary backgrounds on Maitreya-related subjects in different cultural and historical contexts. The high degree of stimulation and enthusiasm generated during the course of the conference confirmed the conviction that we do have a great deal to say to one another, in spite of differences in both interest and approach. Let us look more closely at each of these three areas of research.

Sources of the Tradition

The first area involves research on the sources of the Maitreya legend – study of the components of the story and how they came to be assembled in the earliest accounts. This field involves two related activities: work on individual sources and, at a second level, efforts to identify the common features that link the sources and enable us to group them into families or developmental lines. Much of the work to be done here is textual in nature, though very important contributions are yet to be made from those working on archaeological and art historical evidence as well, especially if that work can be integrated into the broader framework of Maitreya studies. As valuable as these latter sources may prove to be, however, it is surprising how much work remains to be done even on the early textual sources, a lacuna that continues to undermine seriously work being done in the latter two areas I shall discuss below. Some early sources, the *Maitreya-vyākaraṇa* and the *Cakkavattisīhanāda sutta,* for example, have been translated, but other, perhaps even more important sources like the *Maitreyāvadāna* have not.[3] Several accounts have surveyed the textual history of the early Maitreya literature, but these will need continual revision as we gain a better understanding of Maitreya's role in the early tradition.[4]

In addition to literary, historical, and philological research on texts, work in this area should include efforts to identify the basic components of the myth, both themes and motifs. By "motifs" I mean the explicitly articulated narrative constituents of the accounts, and by "themes," the more basic – and often only implicitly expressed – issues the myth seeks to address. Important themes include continuity and legitimacy, regeneration and renewal, messianism and millennialism, the tension between liberation in this world and salvation somewhere beyond, and the tension between worldly and spiritual power and authority. The Maitreya myth has been associated with all of these themes, and we need to determine more accurately the extent to which and the way in which they are appropriate interpretative categories. We need to know which themes were central in the early formulation of the myth. One way to accomplish this is to chart more carefully the constituent narrative motifs present in various accounts in order to determine which were most frequently employed to articulate which theme. Important motifs include the relationship between Maitreya and Śaṅkha, the role of Kaśyāpa and his robe, Maitreya as Ajita, the three assemblies, and a number of other details, such as the sacrificial post, that may not be thematically so important but that provide valuable reference points for determining the relationship between different lines of development. Sylvain Lévi provided an excellent example of this type of study in his exhaustive investigation of the Maitreya-as-Ajita motif, for example, although the centrality he sought to give that one motif will no doubt have to be revised in light of a more careful consideration of the other motifs.[5]

Developments of the Tradition

The second general area of Maitreya studies involves research on culturally specific instances of the tradition. The distinction between sources and developments is, to be sure, a fluid one; for as the fugue analogy suggests, sources of any given variation include not only the original thematic statement but all the previous variations. What was a new development in Central Asia becomes for China a source, and so on down the line, historically and geographically. There is no need to draw a sharp line between which material falls within the first category and which in the second. There is an important distinction to be made here nonetheless, one that can best be seen at the practical level of how we approach the material and what questions we ask of it. In examining the sources of the Maitreya myth, as discussed in the preceding section, we are attempting to identify the core themes and motifs that provide the building blocks employed to construct the distinctive variations we find in the later, more culturally specific variations. In this second type of research, our concern is to determine what was made of those core themes in a given historical and cultural context, how they were elaborated, which were emphasized, which were left latent, and why. Although an awareness of the continuities remains important in this second approach, we must be especially concerned here with the cultural context of the expression of the Maitreya myth presently under study, with what is distinctive and peculiar about this specific instantiation of the Maitreya theme.

The purpose of studies falling under this heading should be twofold. First they should strive to present as rich an account of a given instance as possible, the ideal being the thick description of good ethnography. As that first goal is realized, there should be an effort to integrate that new data into the broader context, drawing on and modifying the results of those working in the first area discussed above. With some sense of the core themes available at a given point in the historical development of Maitreya, along with a thick description of that development, we can begin to consider how certain themes are emphasized or altered under the influence of different circumstances. And as we accumulate a wider range of such studies, our ability to discern both themes and variations will increase as well, for each of these two types of research will inform and supplement the other.

Maitreya in the History of Religions

The third important area of Maitreya studies is, again, one that cannot be severed from the other two; indeed, it can be built only upon the foundation they provide. There has been much discussion regarding method in the broader, comparative study of religions. My own view is that history of religions is certainly a valid disciplinary approach, though it is one I have found most fruitful when it emphasizes the distinctiveness of the various traditions rather than assumes some underlying structure to which all the variations of human experience and expression can be reduced. The presence of analogous elements in different traditions is unquestionable. The study of those parallels, however, is likely to lead to true cross-cultural understanding only when they are examined with special attention to difference, to the dissimilarities inevitably present. The study of Maitreya in the context of the history of religions provides an excellent case in point. Here we have an aspect of Buddhism that resonates significantly with some of the most cherished themes of the Judeo-Christian tradition. We can learn a great deal, for example, from a consideration of "Buddhist messianism" – but only if we are willing to allow our own culturally generated concept of messianism to be significantly transformed and expanded. To the extent that we merely map

Maitreya onto the Judeo-Christian concept of a messiah, however, we have failed in two ways: by truncating the prospect of any rich interpretation of Buddhism and, more insidiously, by further entrenching the cultural parochialism of our own views in asserting their universality.

Let us look at this problem more closely in the context of Maitreya studies. There are two different, though related pitfalls we must avoid when making cross-cultural generalizations regarding the place of Maitreya in the broader history of religions. First, we must be careful not to characterize the Maitreya tradition on the basis of too narrow a sample. Second, we must not assume that the conceptual categories applicable to Western religious traditions will be equally applicable to the Maitreya data, at least not until those categories are subjected to careful and conscious redefinition.

The first problem is most likely to arise if our view of Maitreya is too restricted historically, and especially if it has emerged primarily from the later, more culturally specific and more highly elaborated expressions of the myth. The studies presented in this volume show that important continuities are maintained even in the most evolved and assimilated expressions of Maitreya, but they also show that Maitreya is an extremely malleable symbol, one that lends itself readily to incorporation into historically new and culturally indigenous themes – hence the importance of both of the first two areas of study: We can begin to generalize only after we have a clear idea of the core themes and how they were appropriated in different circumstances. We can always limit our generalizations about the nature of Maitreya to what we find in one specific cultural-historical expression, of course, but then we must make it clear that we are speaking of Maitreya in a given instance, that we are speaking of one particular "Maitreya," and not about Maitreya throughout the tradition.

Even with a sufficiently broad perspective on the history of the Maitreya myth, there is still the second pitfall that must be avoided in making second-level generalizations. Any attempt at cross-cultural understanding is necessarily an activity of interpretation. We cannot understand an alien culture without appeal to ideas and categories that are artifacts of our own culture. The problem here stems not from the necessity of using concepts generated by our own culture, however, but from using those concepts without sufficient recognition of their culture-bound character – often with the latent assumption that their apparent categorical status entails some degree of universality. Certainly there is much experience that our culture shares with any other human culture, no matter how distanced both culturally and historically. I do not mean to raise the specter of cultural relativism in any radical or solipsistic sense. But many of our interpretative categories are culturally relative in a more limited sense, and with regard to that fact we must indeed take care. In mapping Buddhist experience onto our Western concepts, onto those categories employed in the Western study of the history of religions, we must be especially attentive to those instances in which the Buddhist data *do not* match our categories.

With respect to this problem, the study of the development of the Maitreya myth is again an especially interesting case in point. The information that we have on Maitreya lends itself readily to interpretation in terms of several prominent and familiar categories: It is frequently cited in cross-cultural discussions of eschatology, of apocalyptic social movements, of millenarianism generally, and of messianism. These terms can provide a useful framework for exploring the Maitreya tradition, as demonstrated by their occurrence in the chapters of this book, even though the authers sometimes disagreed on which categories are the most applicable in this case. If we are to employ these categories most fruitfully, however, we must be very careful to specify not just the ways in which they apply to the Maitreya data, but also to the ways in which they do not – at least not as they are conventionally understood. If, for example, there is a sense in which it is appropriate to characterize the Maitreya myth as millenarian, as the golden era preceding his advent does suggest, we must make clear that in the core tradition Maitreya differs significantly from other, more familiar millennial figures. His role is clearly postmillennial in the core tradition. It is one that marks the high point of the evolution rather than its inauguration. Only in that light can we begin to assess the actual significance of those instances in both Southeast and East Asia where we do find apocalyptic, premillennial, revolutionary social movements that have appropriated certain elements or themes of the Maitreya myth.

There is a similar case when messianism is used as an interpretive category. Again, there is no question that Maitreya should be included in any discussion of messianism in world religions. But the point of doing so must be to expand and to modify our concept of messianism, not simply to plug Buddhism into it. In this case, we need to point out, for example, that in most instances of the tradition Maitreya's role is more that of a teacher or a guide than that of a savior who intervenes on one's behalf. Distinctive and significant, moreover, is the fact that he *does not* come as a judge who singles out the righteous nor as the leader of an army to smite the wicked. The dominant theme in the messianic aspect of Maitreya's role lies in the fact that he is a precursor and a harbinger, his rebirth validates human aspiration for Buddhahood, even after the death of Śākyamuni, thus affirming the continuity and legitimacy of the Dharma. Seeing his exemplary role in this light allows us all the better to note the distinctiveness of Maitreya appearing as one who hears confessions, a theme that seems to have been introduced in Central Asia.

If there is thus a sense in which one might fruitfully characterize the Maitreya myth as millenarian and even messianic, the category of eschatology poses more difficult problems and involves the greatest potential for misunderstanding. It is also here that we can most clearly see the need to consider the latent assumptions often built into our own culturally specific concepts. In a Judeo-Christian context these three categories have become inextricably intertwined: To be millenarian and messianic is by definition, according to the mainstream of that tradition, to be eschatological. Indeed, the latter term is often used to refer by metonymy to the composite Christian doctrine of the Second Coming as a whole, one that tends to include strong apocalyptic elements as well. But this is a usage specific to that tradition, and understood in this way, the term is far too inclusive to be applied usefully to Buddhism.[6]

Even if we attempt to employ the term in a more restricted sense, there are still problems. In its most literal sense, "eschatology" refers to any teaching of an eschaton, any teaching of the end and culmination of history. Viewed in that light, the Maitreya myth seems distinctive to me precisely for its *lack* of eschatological content, a fact all the more significant if we do acknowledge some element of millenarian messianism. In the core tradition, Maitreya is the next Buddha, not the *final* Buddha, a point that has far too often been obscured in contemporary scholarship. He is one of a series of Buddhas, occurring in lists that include reference to later Buddhas as well. The millennium in Buddhism does not mark the end of time, nor does it inaugurate the ultimate fulfillment of history. It acknowledges rather the social and material prosperity associated with the recurrent realization of the Dharma in the world, a process that continues through time, occurring again and again, through an ongoing cycle of evolution and decline. The specific role of Maitreya in that depiction is to link past with future and to validate the transhistorical validity of the Dharma, not to bring it to an end. To lose sight of this fundamentally different conception of history and of the place of humankind in history is to miss a crucial characteristic of the Buddhist view of human existence.

These, then, are the three areas of study or approaches that I hope will shape future studies of Maitreya. Although I have related these observations specifically to the study of Maitreya-related topics, much of the broader value of the conference for me lay in the fact that many of the problems we discussed were problems of interpretation that go beyond the study of Maitreya, hermeneutical problems that must arise in any historical study of a cultural tradition so rich in both theme and variation. With that in mind, I hope that this volume will be of value to more than those few scholars working specifically on Maitreya. There are many other figures of Buddhist mythology that warrant scholarly attention, even if few have had as varied and as persistent an impact on so many different Buddhist cultures as Maitreya, the future Buddha.

NOTES

1 Translated from the Sanskrit and discussed further by P. S. Jaini in Chapter 3, this volume.

2 Jan Nattier made the important observation that we must not overlook the possibility that the human shortcomings ascribed to Maitreya in the *Lotus Sūtra* may in fact reflect a genuine deprecation, one instigated perhaps by those whose own cultic practices were in danger of being overshadowed by a growing interest in the Maitreya cult. My concern here, however, is with what is made of this characterization once it becomes part of the tradition. Whatever may have been the original motivation for the characterization of Maitreya as deficient or limited in some way, it is a motif that recurs in many Mahāyāna works, as Jaini demonstrates in Chapter 3. Once accepted into the tradition, it was a motif that had to be taken at face value by Buddhists who accepted those texts.

3 The *Maitreya-vyākaraṇa* has been translated into French by Sylvain Lévi and the *Cakkavattisīhanāda* by T. W. Rhys Davids, and the *Anāgatavaṃsa* is soon to appear in a translation by Ria Kloppenborg and D. Meegaskumbura. (For bibliographic details on these and other translations and editions of Maitreya scriptures, consult the list of primary sources appended to Chapter 3.) Nagatomi Masatoshi presented an English translation of the *Vyākaraṇa* at the conference, but unfortunately it was not available for publication.

4 Works that provide a survey of the various Maitreya scriptures include Matsumoto Bunzaburo's 松本文三郎 *Miroku jōdo ron* 彌勒浄土論 (Tokyo: Heigo shuppansha, 1911), Noel Peri's review of Matsumoto's study in *Bulletin de l'Ecole Française d'Extrême-Orient,* 11 (1911): 439–58; Ernst Leuman's *Maitreya-samiti, das Zukunftsideal der Buddhisten* (Strasbourg: Trübner, 1919), Sylvain Lévi's "Maitreya le Consolateur," in *Etudes d'Orientalisme publiées par le Musée Guimet à la mémoire de Raymond Linossier* (Paris, 1932), vol. 2; and Etienne Lamotte's "Le Messie Maitreya," in *Historie du Bouddhisme Indien* (Louvain: Institut Orientaliste, 1958), 775–88. All of these are now at least somewhat out of date. Lévi is the most exhaustive, though Lamotte, who summarizes the previous accounts, is more balanced, lacking Lévi's insistence on deriving Maitreya directly from Mithra.

5 Lévi, "Maitreya le Consolateur."

6 In contrast to the theological traditions, recent historical scholarship on Jewish and Christian messianism has become more critical in qualifying the use of these terms. Jan Nattier discusses these conceptual developments and their significance to the study of Maitreya in Chapter 2, especially notes 41 to 46.

Index